Worlds of Labour in Latin America

Work in Global and Historical Perspective

Edited by
Andreas Eckert, Sidney Chalhoub, Mahua Sarkar, Dmitri van den Bersselaar, Christian G. De Vito

Work in Global and Historical Perspective is an interdisciplinary series that welcomes scholarship on work/labour that engages a historical perspective in and from any part of the world. The series advocates a definition of work/labour that is broad, and especially encourages contributions that explore interconnections across political and geographic frontiers, time frames, disciplinary boundaries, as well as conceptual divisions among various forms of commodified work, and between work and 'non-work'.

Volume 13

Worlds of Labour in Latin America

Edited by
Paola Revilla Orías, Paulo Cruz Terra,
and Christian G. De Vito

DE GRUYTER
OLDENBOURG

ISBN 978-3-11-135822-2
e-ISBN (PDF) 978-3-11-075930-3
e-ISBN (EPUB) 978-3-11-075938-9
ISSN 2509-8861

Library of Congress Control Number: 2021947262

Bibliographic information published by the Deutsche Nationalbibliothek
The Deutsche Nationalbibliothek lists this publication in the Deutsche Nationalbibliografie; detailed bibliographic data are available on the Internet at http://dnb.dnb.de.

This volume is text- and page-identical with the hardback published in 2022.
Cover image: Satori Gigie (Wilfredo Limachi Mamani), El Algodonero. La Paz, Bolivia, October 2016 Printing and binding: CPI books GmbH, Leck

www.degruyter.com

In memory of María Ullivarri.

Table of Contents

Paola Revilla Orías, Paulo Cruz Terra and Christian G. De Vito

Worlds of Labour in Latin America: An introduction

The essays that make up this volume demonstrate the significant reflections on the world of labour and workers that have taken place across Latin America in recent years. Those reflections have occupied a place in the work of many research projects coming out of Latin America that deal with a wide variety of problems at different times, in different places and on different analytical scales. This dynamic has captured the attention of scholars, studying past and present realities of labour, from other continents, especially Europe, and has fostered an exchange of ideas that has contributed significantly to comparative views of certain phenomena. At this level, the agenda appears busy and full of promise.

The exchange was not limited to emails between academics residing in distant locations. A face-to-face encounter was possible in Bolivia in 2017, which was a driving force. That year, the historian Rossana Barragán had the idea of holding the first "International Labour and Workers Congress for Latin America and the Caribbean" in the city of La Paz. It took place from 2nd to 8th May thanks to excellent management by its organising committee and the support of various institutions: the International Institute of Social History (IISG) in Amsterdam, the *Centro de Investigaciones de la Vicepresidencia de Bolivia* (CIS), re:work in Berlin, the Friedrich Ebert Foundation (FES), the Bolivian National Museum of Ethnography and Folklore (MUSEF), the Department of History at the Universidad Mayor de San Andrés (UMSA), the *Ministerio de Planificación* in La Paz, the International Organisation for Migration (IOM) and the International Labour Organisation (ILO). Through their representatives, all of them acted as a conduit to enable and promote rapprochement and dialogue between dozens of academics from 17 different countries. The scope of this meeting gave birth to the *Red Latinoamericana Trabajo y Trabajadores* (REDLATT) which currently coordinates an electronic magazine, REVLATT, and which had another meeting from 2nd to 4th October 2019, this time in Lima, Peru, as part of the 3rd Congress of the American Association of Social History (ALIHS). That same year, a selection of 30 works from the first meeting were published in Spanish in the volume: *Trabajo y Trabajadores en América Latina, siglos XVI–XXI* compiled by Barragán with the support of the CIS.

A previous and very inspiring experience for historians of the world of labour, took place in Brazil in 2001, where *Mundos do Trabalho* was born, from the network of historians within the *Associação Nacional de História (ANPUH).*

https://doi.org/10.1515/9783110759303-001

This working group organised different events and a journal, and published a special issue of the *International Review of Social History* in December 2017. These activities all positioned Brazilian labour history not only as an important field of specialisation and reflection for the history of the American Continent, but also as an example of the renewed significance of labour history in the Global South, alongside histories of India and South Africa.[1] REDLATT's intention went a little further, seeking to cover the entire Latin American region.

This volume, *Worlds of Labour in Latin America*, published with the support of re:work, is a selection of 10 essays among those that were presented at the 2017 Congress and later published in the volume in Spanish mentioned above. It aims to reach a wide audience of English-speaking readers and includes contributions from authors from Argentina, Bolivia, Brazil, Mexico, Peru and Spain, who, from a historical and sociological perspective, analyse a series of problems relating to labour relations. The chapters weave together different periods of Latin American colonial and republican history from the viceroyalties of New Spain (now Mexico) and Peru and the Royal *Audiencia de Charcas* (now Bolivia), to Argentina, Uruguay, Chile and Brazil.

The contents of this book reflect the development of Latin American labour history across broad geographical, chronological and thematic perspectives, which seek to review and revisit key concepts at different levels. The works are closely linked to the most recent trends of Global Labour History and in turn, these chapters enrich them. A number of major themes emerge from a careful reading of the essays.

For example, it is essential to go beyond the dichotomy of free and unfree labour. The authors analyse the combinations and coexistence of multiple labour relationships in the workplace as a *continuum* of coercion.[2] Norberto Ferreras concentrates on non-economic coercion, analysing the role of the ILO as a supranational organisation, in structuring free and unfree labour relations in the first half of the 20th century. For the 19th and 20th centuries, María Luisa Soux points out the need to study coexisting of forms of labour in depth rather than assuming that each regime of land ownership and management implied a specific and clearly defined type of labour relationship. In turn, Paula Zagalsky and Isabel Povea's contribution underlines the coexistence of various systems for recruiting labour, and how those regimes changed over time, in the silver mines of Potosí, in the Audiencia de Charcas, and Guanajuato, in the viceroyalty of New Spain,

1 See Fontes et al., eds. 2017..

2 Which connects with the long-standing debate synthesised by Brass and van der Linden, eds. 1997.

between the 16th and 18th centuries. They also provide very insightful interpretations of the factors (economic, cultural and political) that facilitated a diversity of labour relations. Rossana Barragán connects with this proposal in her study of the labour regimes in Potosí in the 18th century. She describes how workers were often simultaneously *mitayos*, *mingas* and *k'ajchas*, and how that was key for the labour regime, as well as for the strategies adopted by the workers. Cristiana Schettini and Diego Galeano show how an individual was able to use multiple identities and cross many borders, literally and metaphorically, to navigate the worlds (legal and illegal) of labour in South America, and how this led them to engage in all sorts of activities and labour relationships. On this point, they connect with Barragán's discussion of the multiple working identities that a single individual might adopt. Prevalent throughout these works is the desire to understand how different actors construct and deconstruct, define and redefine their labour relations. This goes hand in hand with a revision of the meanings of associated concepts such as freedom and coercion in certain historical contexts. The relevance of this topic in reflections on Latin America complements and contributes to the development of research carried out in other regions of the world.

Another over-arching theme in these essays is that of the ambiguity that is implicit in paid contractual labour in the scenarios studied. Zagalsky and Povea, Soux and Francisco Quiroz all review the wide variety of situations that resulted in labour relations mediated by a contract and a remuneration, and reflect on the extent and nature of coercion that could exist in those circumstances. Zagalsky and Povea specifically look at the system of working for *raya y partido* in the mines, where in addition to a remuneration (*jornal*), the labourer received a percentage of production as an incentive; and also, the existence of "debt peonage" in the mines of Guanajuato. At the same time, they recognise the importance of less coercive forms in the context of paid work. Quiroz shows how the hundreds of contracts that he analyses conceal a wide range of working conditions as different as those of the "*jornaleros*" (day labourers) and the young apprentices, "*muchachos*". He also draws our attention to the complexity of payment systems, be that in kind, in money, or in services. In the case of enslaved peoples, for example, what they earned legally belonged to their master, but sometimes they were also given part of those earnings, through which they were able to accumulate some money of their own. He also maintains that the daily wages of *mitayos* and slaves served as the basis for defining the wages of formally free urban workers.

Soux looks at contracts transferring land ownership that also transferred the customs linked to different forms of service and servitude, in dealings between the landowners or employers, and the tenants or labourers (*yanaconas*, *colonos*), on the farms and smallholdings of Charcas. Norberto Ferreras identifies debt bondage and *yanaconazgo* as ambiguous contractual forms. His study of the *truck system* in Argentina and Brazil, allows him to develop an understanding of "payment in kind" and "debt peonage." Laura Caruso and Andrés Stagnaro recount how the workers worked to pay their debts and not the other way around. Debt was created to force the worker to work. Julián-Vejar complements these views with an archaeology of the creation of precarious labour and precarious societies under neoliberal policies in Chile. Some authors are also driven to review terms such as "working class," which, beyond being automatically and thoughtlessly associated with salaried work, must be understood in the context of the multiplicity of labour relationships that characterised the societies they study. Victoria Basualdo warns against trying to unify the broad range of activities and lines of action undertaken by workers and unions, and the various logics that underlie them.

It is no less important to recognise in these chapters, in particular those of Julián-Vejar, Basualdo, Renán Vega and Luz Ángela Núñez, the balance between a rigorous academic approach and an explicit awareness of the political implications of the historical narrative in the present. Although it is more evident in the essays that deal with more recent contexts, the implications of the chapters looking at past centuries are not insignificant, particularly where they address issues that persist and have serious implications for the present-day populations of the societies studied. An awareness of these implications, and of the asymmetric power relations that prevail in the formal and informal worlds of labour they are studying, along with a sense of responsibility and commitment, characterises the work of these Latin American historians.[3]

Another relevant aspect that the authors are not indifferent to, is the role played by ethnicity in the workers' experience. Zagalsky and Povea analyse the composition of the workforce focusing on the role of tribute in the hiring of an indigenous workforce. Barragán shows how indigenous people were categorised as "lazy" in order to legitimise the *mita*, and how discourses to delegitimise it used the opposite argument, making a comparison with the situation of the miners of New Spain, a workforce made up of both indigenous and non-indigenous workers. Quiroz's essay foregrounds the study of categories in the caste system, and their role in coercive labour in the context of urban

3 In some cases, that leads them to distance themselves from proposals such as those of *global history*, which they perceive as less concerned with the Latin American reality. This has been observed before by Paulo Fontes, Alexandre Fortes and David Mayer. See their text, "Brasilian Labor history in Global Context: Some Introductory Notes" (Fontes et al, 2017). Far from being a limiting factor, this reflects the important multilateral dialogue that has yet to take place.

Lima. It reveals the legal and social considerations that underpinned the formation of Spanish guilds and how their members sought to prevent people of other origins from becoming master craftsmen. Soux reveals the centrality of the issue of ethnicity assimilated as *indigeneidad* in the legislation following independence in Bolivia in the context of legal and practical issues of land tenure. In addition, he analyses the persistence of servitude and of certain relationships of dependence in labour practices involving the participation of the indigenous population up until the 20th century. A clear example is the arguments about the "civility of the Indian" that sought to prevent the abolition of *pongueaje* in 1940. As Basualdo comments, in Latin America the structure of the labour market is highly segmented, racialised, and has an undeniable colonial legacy of patriarchal structures, which as Julián-Vejar points out, largely explains the fragility of life and the social fabric in these contexts.

When it comes to gender and sexuality issues, Zagalsky and Povea mention the role of women in the mines. Renán Vega and Luz Ángela Núñez analyse the reality of single women in the first half of the 20th century, associated with prostitution, as well as the constitution of exclusive all-male enclaves for working men by transnational companies even when managers were allowed live with their families. The authors refer to a "brutalised sexuality," a result of the naturalisation of affective and corporeal commerce. Schettini and Galeano propose that labour historians learn from the history of gender that "makes visible" and transforms some of the activities that were considered feminine at the beginning of the 20th century. They tell of people who claimed a female social identity at the crossroads of multiple borders, not only of gender but also sexual identity, and the paid and unpaid activities that allowed them to survive between legality and illegality.

The way in which the authors deal with the subject of places of coercion is particularly suggestive. Zagalsky and Povea make it especially clear why some labour regimes, forms of labour coercion and their combinations, were "deployed" – as Jairus Banaji would say – in complex trajectories and in certain contexts in colonial Spanish America.[4] The specific focus on places of coercion, makes these essays particularly advantageous for considering those interactions, especially in Quiroz's contribution in his analysis of the artisan workshops of Lima. Schettini and Galeano highlight the importance of focussing on connected sites and on the mobility of the actors. Barragán goes a little further when she refers to the same individual coexisting in several "labour situations" in Potosí in the 18th century. When addressing the creation and maintenance of

4 Banaji, 2010: 113–116.

the enclave of a transnational company in Colombia in the 1920s and 1940s, Vega and Nuñez highlight policies for recruitment, socio-spatial segmentation, and environmental impact, among others. They also refer to the fact that some workers occupied land and used it for subsistence work, which they read as a strategy of resistance to proletarianisation. More than any other academic discipline, Latin American labour history has emphasised the importance of focusing the lens of analysis on the interactions between workers rather than on abstract labour relations. In fact, in his case study, Julián-Véjar reveals how the individuation of the discourse on the heroism of the 33 miners overshadowed the archaeology of the event itself, to the detriment of the workers themselves.

An analysis of the role played by norms and regulations, and by the delegated authorities of the Crown and the State also emerges in the essays in this volume. Zagalsky and Povea mark clear differences between the situations in the viceroyalties of New Spain and in Peru, specifically the jurisdiction of the Real *Audiencia de Charcas*, where, as they point out, there was less intervention in the economy and in the regulation of the labour market, as well as in the relations between employers and workers. This had a notorious effect on the political relationship between the economic elites and the Crown authorities, and on their management of mechanisms for the coercion of labour. Barragán highlights the dialectic between the colonial state and the economic elites in relation to the role of the *k'ajchas,* and she mentions the broader debate on the *mita* in the late 18th and early 19th centuries, in which various members of the elites adopted conflicting positions. In addition, she refers to the concept of the "public good" as it was used to legitimise the coercion of the workforce. Quiroz gives an account of a state that supported the formation of guilds of Spanish craftsmen to defend their privileges in colonial Lima. They would also have intervened in defence of pay for indigenous workers, which met with more than a little resistance from employers, although it was established in the contracts. He also tells how the State sought to regulate the mobility of enslaved people within the context of urban Lima. However, that mobility took place in any case, albeit illegally, because employers and slave owners benefited from it.

Basualdo considers the theme of the State to be central in its relationship with the economic elites and studies its role in processes of repression in the 20th-century South-American dictatorships. Schettini and Galeano demonstrate the kind of control exercised by the states of Argentina, Brazil and Uruguay over the mobility of the workers through many means, including expulsions, deportations, and forms of identification. Soux dwells on the role of the law and the failure to implement it, as well as how the discourse on work and the freedom of labour was put to political use in 19th-century Bolivia. Julián-Véjar in turn refers to the narrative processes that intervened in the construction and symbolic appropriation of the imagery of the miner as a hero, through which they ended up being stigmatised by society. A "precarious society," which, for the author, takes shape as a result of deregulation and the commodification of public goods, among other characteristics of the relationship between the State and neoliberalism.

Caruso and Stagnaro's essay focuses on the interactions between Latin American national states and supranational organisations such as the International Labour Organisation (ILO), on issues of labour. Ferrera complements this reading and highlights how the governments of Argentina and Brazil reacted differently to the inspections, campaigns and debates resulting from discussions within the League of Nations and the ILO. Vega and Núñez, for their part, see the enclaves of transnational companies as "states within the State," operating through concessions that gave the companies sovereignty over territories in which the State maintained a police and military presence.

Directly linked to what has been said, it is worth noting the efforts of the authors to introduce comparative and transnational approaches. Quiroz presents a comparative analysis over time between the contracts drawn up in the city of Lima in the 16th and 18th centuries. The reading of two distant and distinct realities, Guanajuato in the 18th century and Potosí in the 16th and 17th centuries, is more of a "dialogue" than a comparison, according to Zagalsky and Povea in their analysis of both mining centres at key moments of their mining production. Schettini and Galeano reveal a transnational approach by introducing us to the trips of the Princess of Bourbon who transited between Brazil, Argentina and Uruguay. Regarding the essays that address the role of the ILO, Ferreras compares the reactions of Argentina and Brazil to the policies and discourses of this supranational organisation, and Caruso and Stagnaro assess a broader Latin American perspective on studies of its history and role. It should be noted that this research is driven by the initiatives of transnational organisations, specifically the "ILO-Latin America Interdisciplinary Network." Likewise, the network organised for the study of the dictatorships of the second half of the 20th century, which includes academics from Brazil, Argentina, Chile, Paraguay and Uruguay, provided the impetus for Basualdo's essay.

Clearly, the coexistence of various coercive labour regimes forces a rethink of the linear view of historical change, and raises questions about orthodox approaches that assume political, economic, and cultural changes would necessarily lead to free and salaried labour. To delve deeper into this aspect, it is necessary, on the one hand, to understand the ways in which the actors built labour relations of different kinds, which move the discontinuity of certain forms of work, and redefine them within a broader social framework. Soux's essay demonstrates the importance of overcoming the traditional or colonial divide in the post-independence setting of Bolivia. She reveals continuities and discontinuities in the analysis of the transformations undergone by the State, by labour systems such as *pongueaje* in the first half of the 20th century, and by the workers themselves, specifically the shift from *yanaconas* to *colonos* and tenants.

An important challenge addressed in these essays is the questioning of the concept of "modernity." Ferreras highlights the discursive construction, at the level of the ILO, of certain forms labour relations that allowed Argentina and Brazil to be seen as 'modern' countries that subscribed to classic liberal ideas of "freedom." This often hid their denial of pending issues, where it was convenient to relegate them to a colonial past. On the other hand, it is necessary to consider whether academics themselves have generated discourses centred around the idea of modernity, and the ways in which they do that. In this volume the authors take different perspectives. Quiroz confirms multiplicity but tends to see it in a context that is governed by certain universal standards of change towards "modernity" when he states, for example, that although, even in the 18th century, there were wages, these were not "modern wage relationships." Soux also frames her arguments within an abstract standard of modernity. Thus, in the process of identifying forms that often refer to extinct institutions, but not to their cultures of exploitation, she mentions in her conclusions that the "principles of the old regime" still remained in force. In previous sections she assumes that "non-salaried labour relations" are by definition a sign of pre-capitalist working conditions. On the other hand, other authors highlight the compatibility of capitalism with extra-economic coercion in all areas.

At the same time, Soux deconstructs the discourse of modernity and linear approaches to historical change, showing the political use of concepts and themes in relation to what she describes as the "feudal character of the *haciendas*," in the debate on agrarian reform in Bolivia in 1953, which was similar to debates occurring in other regions such as Italy in the 1950s. More recently, key concepts in this debate such as "feudal" and "semi-feudal" have been critically explored by historians in India.[5] Ferreras problematises the issue of "proletarianisation" after the abolition of slavery, and analyses the limitations imposed on workers among other coercive labour mechanisms implemented. The author is well aware of the need to avoid teleological analyses of changes in labour relations and invites us to understand the concepts of dependence and freedom as two poles under a constant tension "that is not resolved at a given moment," in the sense that there is no clear break between them, no moment of no return. This argument draws from Tom Brass's proposal on "deproletarianisa-

5 See Brass, 2011.

tion."[6] In the same way, he explicitly connects his reflection with Marcel van der Linden in his critique of the concept of "modern and contemporary slavery."[7]

Based on these notes, some critical considerations can be made for a possible future research agenda. The essays in this volume are set in Latin America and the authors' gaze does not transcend those regional, or even at times, national spaces. A transnational approach could increase the sensitivity of the research, broadening the space studied, to integrate similar problems in other regions of the Globe. Because, to what extent can national history be separated from transnational history, when both draw on diverse local traditions of exploitation that are maintained because they are profitable? The fact that the starting point for this investigation has been different contexts in Latin America, and that the editorial initiative itself set that course, does not mean that greater effort cannot be made, in the future, to connect with other realities. That would allow us to better explore the complex history of empires, population migrations, and other common themes. In fact, in some cases, it is the authors themselves who indicate this route to us. Ferreras declares his desire to "advance in a regional and global direction," although his study here focuses on only two nation states, Argentina and Brazil. Caruso and Stagnaro emphasise the need for a broader view, of a global – although not globalising – perspective. In doing so, they emphasise an important detail: the need not to settle for a reading within frameworks centred on discourses of nationalism. Indeed, a worldwide trend in academia is to take the nation-states that emerged in the 19th century as the spatial units of research, inescapable reference points that end up framing the perspective. This also happens with certain regionalisms or localisms that may well cast more shadow than they shed light on local processes. Comparative studies would be enriched by going beyond these traditional units of analysis; not by ignoring them, but by surpassing them, and not overestimating the role they play in day-to-day labour relations. A renewed look at connected local realities and experiences would illuminate multiple linkages, networks, actors, and processes. Undoubtedly, more is gained than is lost by opening up the geographical focus, in terms of understanding the complexity inherent in a different dimension and at different scales. In this sense, the dissemination of this material also constitutes an invitation to further explorations that take a new look at the trans-regional connections, developed over the centuries, that characterise a history shared with the rest of the world.

---

6 *Ibid.*
7 Linden, 2013.

References

Banaji, Jairus. 2010. *Theory as History. Essays on Modes of Production and Exploitation.* Historical Materialism Book Series, vol. 25. Leiden/Boston: Brill.

Brass, Tom, and Marcel van der Linden, eds. 1997. *Free and Unfree Labour: The Debate Continues.* New York: Lang.

Brass, Tom. 2013. *Labour Regime Change in the Twenty-First Century: Unfreedom, Capitalism and Primitive Accumulation.* Studies in Critical Social Sciences. Leiden/Boston: Brill, 2011.

Fontes, Paulo, Alexandre Fortes, and David Mayer, eds. 2017. "Brazilian Labor History: New Perspectives in Global Context. International Review of Social History." *International Review of Social History* 62 (December). Special Issue S25: 1–22, URL: http://www.cambridge.org/core/journals/international-review-of-social-history/issue/40A7178FF8991AD35477C728581A76AA.

Linden, Marcel van der, 2013. *Trabalhadores do Mundo. Ensaios para uma História Global do trabalho.* Campinas: Unicamp.

Paula C. Zagalsky, Isabel M. Povea Moreno

A diverse world: A panoramic view of colonial mine labourers based on case studies from the viceroyalties of New Spain and Peru

Abstract: This study presents a panoramic view of the world of mining work during the Spanish American colonial period. It is based on the analysis of two paradigmatic cases of large-scale silver production at the height of their respective histories: the Cerro Rico de Potosí, during the 16th and 17th centuries in Peru, and the district of Guanajuato in New Spain, during the 18th century. As we are considering such different periods of time, a dialogue, rather than a direct comparison, is proposed to allow us to investigate the diversity of forms which developed in mining work in Spanish colonial America. This means looking at the forms of labour that, emerged and often coexisted within the framework of the same mining region. From a broader perspective, the study aims to underline points of similarity and difference between the two contexts. At the same time, it investigates specific forms of mining labour, looking deeper into their historical significance, and offering an interpretation articulated through the categories of 'free' and 'unfree' labour. The aim is to dismantle a series of long-standing assumptions, such as the prevalence of forced labour in Potosí, and of free and wage-earning labour in New Spain.

Keywords: world of labour; silver mining; viceroyalty of New Spain; viceroyalty of Peru

---

Note: We would particularly like to thank Felipe Castro Gutiérrez for his comments on a preliminary version of this article, presented to the Congress that gave rise to this book, although ultimate responsibility for the content of this version lies with the authors. Finally, let us point out that some fragments of this Chapter, centred on the Villa Imperial de Potosí, were previously published by Zagalsky (2014b).

Doctor in History at the Universidad de Buenos Aires (UBA). *Consejo Nacional de Investigaciones Científicas y Técnicas* (CONICET) and the UBA. Contact: pzagalsky@gmail.com / Doctor in History at the *Universidad de Granada. Centro de Investigaciones y Estudios Superiores en Antropología Social* (CIESAS), Mexico City. Contact: isabelpovea@gmail.com.

https://doi.org/10.1515/9783110759303-002

Introduction

The process of European conquest and domination of the American continent was marked by the search for, and extraction of, precious metals, especially silver and gold. Between 1550 and 1800, the dominions of Portugal and Spain in America contributed to the development of the global economy with more than 80 percent of the silver and more than 70 percent of the gold produced worldwide (Cross, 1983: 403).[1] The figures presented in Cross' classic text are more than eloquent in terms of the role played by American silver production in the global context. They also enable us to observe the contribution made by the larger colonies in Iberian America.

Table 1: Percentage of Ibero-American silver and gold in world production, 1500 – 1800

	Silver			Gold		
	1600s	*1700s*	*1800s*	*1600s*	*1700s*	*1800s*
Viceroyalty of Peru	57.1 %	61.0 %	32.5 %	35.7 %	60.1 %	36.0 %
Brazil					1.7 %	44.1 %
Viceroyalty of New Spain	11.4 %	23.4 %	57.0 %	3.4 %	4.3 %	4.8 %
Percentage of world production	68.5 %	84.4 %	89.5 %	39.1 %	66.1 %	84.9 %

Source: Cross 1983: 403.

Within the dominions of Portugal and Spain, different mining centres stood out, varying in importance throughout the colonial period. In the case of Brazil, colonial silver production played a negligible role compared to gold. It became the Latin American region with the highest levels of gold production, especially during the 18th century. In the territory of New Spain, we have the cases of Zacatecas, Guanajuato, Real del Monte and San Luis Potosí. All were outstanding centres of silver production active since the 16th century, but for the most part excelling in the 18th century.[2]

1 The information in this section comes from a set of key texts, which allow us to situate and weigh up the cases analysed in the broader Latin American colonial, Spanish imperial, and global economic contexts: Cross, 1983; Garner, 1988; Bakewell, 1990; TePaske, 2010; Hausberger and Ibarra, 2014.

2 The mines of San Pedro, in the jurisdiction of San Luis Potosí, also had very significant gold production, making them unique in New Spain. After smelting, the silver there came out mixed with gold (Serrano, 2008: 40).

In the territory of the viceroyalty of Peru, silver extraction was also highly significant, with the Cerro Rico de Potosí being the main mining centre during the 16th and 17th centuries. Located in the current territory of the Plurinational State of Bolivia, during its heyday (c.1575–1630), its royal treasury registered 90 percent of all Peruvian silver production.[3] Starting in the 1630s and throughout the following century, several other important silver mining centres stood out in the Peruvian context (Oruro, Carangas, San Antonio del Nuevo Mundo, Hualgayoc, Cerro de Pasco, Chachapoyas, Cailloma, Huantajaya, among others). However, they never reached the production levels of Potosí or those of the mines of New Spain (TePaske, 2010: 141–212).

If we consider the Ibero-American colonial period in its entirety, more silver than gold was produced overall, with the viceroyalty of New Spain being the largest producer in America. However, it should be noted that there were two boom cycles: the first between 1570 and 1630, led by the viceroyalty of Peru, and the second between 1770 and 1800, dominated by the mines of New Spain. Potosí, one of our case studies, emerged not only as the largest silver producer in Peru, but also in all of Latin America, during the 16th and 17th centuries, leading the first boom cycle. During the second half of the 18th century, the figures for silver production in the Peruvian viceroyalty would reach their maximum peak, although that was without the leading role of Potosí, which did not even reach half of the production it had seen during the late 16th century boom. Despite this increase, by the end of the 18th century, the volume of Peruvian production had been far surpassed by that of New Spain. Throughout the 18th century, the value of New Spain's silver production increased, registering spectacular growth between the 1770s and 1810s. At that time, Guanajuato was the largest silver producer in both New Spain and the world, with annual production worth more than five million *pesos* (Brading, 2012: 349). Looking at data from Humboldt, Pierre Vilar (1974: 415) points out that Guanajuato in the 18th century was even more productive than Potosí in the 16th.

Classic works have already been written on the colonial silver production of Potosí and Guanajuato, the largest silver producers of each viceroyalty. These constitute essential reference works, both for our case studies, and for the histo-

3 It should be noted that during the period of the Potosí boom, silver production from some nearby mines was counted as coming from Potosí as it was registered at the same royal treasury. It is commonly admitted that it is impossible to estimate exactly how much of this silver was not from Potosí itself. The best-known case is that of Oruro, but other small mining centres can be included, for example: Aullagas, Berenguela, Salinas de Garcimendoza, Sicasica and, perhaps Chocaya around the 1630s (Gavira Márquez, 2010: 215–244 and personal communication with Raquel Gil Montero).

ry of Latin American mining in general.[4] The available literature reveals a number of recurring issues and questions: debates around estimates of total production; the relationship between pre-Hispanic and colonial mining; the different stages and types of organisation of mining production; regulations, practices, and debates on the organisation of the workforce; and, especially in the case of New Spain, analysis of the mining elite. In addition, there are a few useful comparative analyses focused particularly on the quantification of silver production (Klein, 1991: 154–217; Bakewell, 1991: 58–72; Brading and Cross, 1972: 545–579; Garner, 1988: 898–935).

This study presents a panoramic view of the world of mining during the Spanish American colonial period. To that end, two paradigmatic cases have been selected, focussing on centres of large-scale silver production: the Cerro Rico de Potosí, during the 16th and 17th centuries, in the viceroyalty of Peru, and Guanajuato in New Spain, during the 18th century. As has been pointed out above, these two mining centres were, albeit at different times, the largest silver producers in the world. An analysis of labour in these two settings, looking at their respective boom periods and relating them to each other, offers us the opportunity to observe a set of variables present in scenarios of peak production, visualizing the systems of labour, and forms of payment that emerged in those conditions. The broad perspective offered by this analysis allows us to bring new ideas and questions to the discussion, that may ultimately provide nuance to some commonly held positions.

Bearing in mind that these case studies correspond to very different periods and contexts, rather than a comparison, we propose a dialogue that allows us to investigate the enormous diversity of forms of labour that emerged in the world of mining in Spanish America. This means that we must examine different forms of labour that often coexisted within the framework of a single mining region. On the one hand, in addressing the world of labour and its diversity, we will refer to the miners themselves, their ethnicities, gender, origins, and financial status; the types of labour carried out; the existence of salaries and wages, and the payments actually made; the forms of coercion that affected labourers; connections

---

4 The available literature relating to mining in Potosí is so extensive that it is impossible to cite in its entirety, however we highlight some of the exemplary works here: Cobb, 1977; Sánchez Albornoz, 1978; Assadourian, 1979; Assadourian, 1982; Saignes, 1984 and 1985; Cole, 1985; Bakewell, 1989; Arduz Eguía, 1985; Tandeter, 1992; González Casasnovas, 2000; *Robins*, 2011; Brown, 2012. In relation to Guanajuato, there is an extensive bibliography, within which we highlight some works that have left their mark: Brading, 2012; Castro, 2002; Villalba Bustamante, 2013; Blanco, Parra and Ruiz Medrano, 2011; Caño Ortigosa, 2006: 187–209; Pérez Luque and Tovar Rangel, 2006; Caño Ortigosa, and Lacueva Muñoz, 2009: 605–624.

between the 'free' and 'unfree' labour systems, and the possibilities for shifting from one to another. In this way we delve deeper into some of the specific forms of labour adopted in the mines, in order to investigate their historical significance and articulate them into an interpretation based on the categories of "free" and "unfree" labour.

From a broader perspective, this essay aims to underline points of similarity and difference between the two contexts. There is a widespread assumption that mining in Potosí was dominated by forced labour, while in New Spain forced labour is thought to have been almost non-existent compared to the predominance of free, salaried labour relationships. We hope, through this dialogue, to dismantle those generalisations. In order to convey the complexity of colonial mining, the two large mining centres are also analysed within their respective viceregal contexts, and in relation to other silver mining centres in the region.

The Villa Imperial de Potosí and its "Cerro Rico"

Like other mining centres in Peru and New Spain, Potosí relied predominantly on an indigenous workforce.[5] Afro-descendants (enslaved people and freedmen and women) constituted a very small fraction of the workforce in silver mining (unlike gold mining), and always worked on the surface, never underground.[6] *Mestizos* and Spaniards were a minority, playing their role as mine owners, leaseholders, stewards and officials in charge of supervision and justice in the mines.[7] With regard to indigenous labour, a number of systems were used during

5 The societies analysed in this chapter and the documents they produced describe people as *indio* (Indio), *negro* (black), *mulato* (mulatto), *pardo* (mixed indigenous / European and African descent), *mestizo* (mixed indigenous / European descent), *español* (Spaniard) or *esclavo* (enslaved people, not always a synonym for race, but in general assumed to be black and afro-descendant). When we quote or describe how someone was classified during the colonial period, we may employ these literal classifications. In some parts of the chapter, we use critical and contemporary terminology, such as *indigenous people* or *Afro-descendant people* (that included among other historical categories the mulato and pardo populations, and other free African people and their descendants who were classified under the caste system).

6 Among the tasks linked to mining, they worked in the smelters or refineries, as artisans (carpenters, tool makers), and in a few cases, they served mine owners as stewards and managers.

7 There are indications dating from the 18th century that suggest that the mining world was more varied than is usually assumed, like the composition of the *k'ajchas:* in addition to indigenous people, they included mulattoes, *mestizos* and even Spaniards (Tandeter, 1981; Abercrombie, 1996; Barragán Romano, 2015). It would be pertinent in future case studies of Potosí to revisit the question of the composition of the workforce from a long-term perspective, considering the issue up until the 16th century.

the colonial period to organise it, sometimes coexisting and of varying importance: the *indios de encomienda (groups of indigenous labourers granted by the Crown to a conquistador);* enslaved indigenous people (especially in the early colonial decades, the so-called *piezas*); *mitayos* (indigenous people working under the forced recruitment system known as the *mita*); and the "free" wage labourers, known as *mingas* (Bakewell, 1990).[8]

At the very beginning of colonial exploitation of the Cerro Rico de Potosí (1545), the organisation of production and the means of production were both under indigenous control. This is known as the *Huayra* period, and it lasted some thirty years. During that time, the processing of the ore extracted from the depths of the mines (which was of very high grade) was done in *huayrachinas* (clay smelting furnaces). These were set up on the slopes of the hill, and were fed by firewood and wind.[9] From the late 1540s, under the tribute system, the *encomenderos* of the Charcas region (and others from even further afield), sent contingents of tributaries to labour in Potosí for different periods of time and to perform a variety of tasks. A growing population of *yanaconas* settled there during the Huayra period, controlling a good part of both the means of production and the different stages of the mining process.[10] The *yanacona* min-

8 The "free" condition of salaried workers is placed in quotation marks to differentiate it from the contemporary characteristics of free labour. As will be seen, the biggest difference between the free (*minga*) and the forced (*mita*) labourers lay in the higher wages paid to the former and, in some cases, the type of labour they did inside the mines and silver refining plants, but we tend to think that the specific working conditions did not differ so much in other central aspects (length of the working day, weekly stay in the mines, etc).

9 A series of remarkable studies about *huayrachinas* and pre-Hispanic foundry technology can be found in Cruz and Vacher, 2008.

10 The *yanaconas* had a pre-Hispanic origin: the *yanas* were indigenous people who split from the *ayllu* and ethnic groups and broke their ties of kinship, they served as personal servants to the State, the Inca elite and local political authorities, and they were a very heterogeneous group in terms of occupation, origin and social status (Murra, 1989). The Spaniards used this labour, first associating it with the category of slaves, and finally assimilating it to that of maids or servants. There were the King's *yanacona*, but a great majority passed into the hands of individuals who were set up as their patrons. The category of colonial *yanacona* also had a fiscal character: initially excluded from the payment of taxes, from 1566 they were obliged to pay a tribute that was significantly less than that of the rest of the population. They did not participate in shift work, nor were they forced into the Potosí *mita*, all compelling reasons to explain the growth of the category in colonial times. It was, therefore, an ambiguous category: although in theory the conditions were close to being unfree labour, in colonial practice, for an incalculable percentage, it became more of a fiscal category, and undoubtedly blurred indigenous ethnicities (Escobari de Querejazu, 2001; Escobari de Querejazu, 2011; Gil Montero, Oliveto and Longhi, 2015).

ers from Potosí extracted the pure silver for their masters, but they enjoyed the right to exploit the spoils as remuneration for their labour (Matienzo, 1967 [1567]: 25).[11] In the 1560s, in addition to the private contingents of tributaries and *yanaconas*, the Crown forced the Lupaca people of Chucuito (natives from the southwestern shore of Lake Titicaca and included as part of a royal *encomienda*), to send five hundred tributaries a year to perform mining tasks in Potosí (Barnadas, 1973: 261–284; Assadourian, 1979: 237–249; Bakewell, 1989: 65–70).

By the 1570s, a new system of forced labour recruitment had been consolidated: the colonial *mita* system. During the previous decade, in addition to the antecedents mentioned above, a series of factors combined to create this system. For the Crown, besieged by debt, obtaining precious metals became a real priority; however, by that time the quality of the ore extracted at Potosí was falling. Meanwhile, the power struggle with the *encomenderos* and debates about the perpetuity of the *encomienda*, tipped the balance against the *encomenderos* and in favour of royal power which manifested in the viceroyalty in the form of a network of fragmented, regional and local political powers.

In this context, during the 1570s, Viceroy Francisco de Toledo (1569–1581) established a series of measures with which he aimed to achieve several urgent objectives. Firstly, to increase Peru's silver production, which was beginning to decline due to the exhaustion of the highest-grade ores. To achieve this, he introduced the method of extracting silver using an amalgam of silver ore and mercury,[12] he initiated the *mita* labour system in Potosí, and he ordered the construction of a system of artificial lagoons whose waters fed the mills and silver refining plants where the ore was processed (Bakewell, 1989; Cole, 1985). Additionally, he also sought stricter control (financial, social, religious, spatial and political) of the indigenous population. This was implemented with varying degrees of success, through the process of resettlement of the indigenous population known as "*reducir los indios a pueblos.*" This policy of concentrating the indigenous population into townships, based on the European model, disrupted

---

11 The spoils were the discarded material that accumulated in heaps or piles at the entrances to the tunnels. They would go back to recheck or *repallar* the discarded piles in search of silver. Llanos, 1983 [1609]: 40–41.

12 During the period under study, the mercury used in Potosí came from the Peruvian mines of Huancavelica. Toledo also determined the monopoly of the Crown in the production of that mercury, whose extraction relied largely on the sending of forced labour from provinces near the royal mine (Lohmann Villena, 1949; Cobb, 1977; Contreras, 1982; Robins, 2011; Brown, 2012; Povea Moreno, 2014).

the old pattern of dispersed settlements.[13] Another of Viceroy Toledo's measures was the almost total monetisation of the tribute system, setting a *per capita* rate for adult men (18 to 50 years old) but with responsibility for payment falling to the indigenous authorities in the basic fiscal colonial jurisdictions (*repartimientos de indios*). Income from this monetary tribute was increasingly controlled by the royal treasury. At the same time the system favoured increased indigenous participation in mercantile relations (offering their produce on the market, and being employed for money, in relations that were both free and coercive).

The onset of the so-called quicksilver era also led to the almost total concentration of the social means of production in Spanish hands, an exceptional expansion of the scale of production, and an increased demand for labour. This is when the forced labour recruitment system, the *mita*, was consolidated.[14] The *mita* coexisted in Potosí with other less coercive and more voluntary forms of salaried work, such as that of the *mingas* and the *yanaconas*. According to some estimates, by the early 17th century, even during the greatest boom, the proportion of voluntary to compulsory wage labour was 70 to 30 (Assadourian, 1979: 257). Nevertheless, although the forced *mita* system may have been a quantitatively smaller contingent of the workforce than the voluntary one, we must emphasise that it played a decisive role in the provision of labour for mining. On the one hand, the annual contingents of *mitayos* were theoretically divided into three groups. Each of these thirds were required to work for one week and then permitted to "rest" for the following two. However, the design of the system ensured such low average wages for the *mitayos*, that it forced them to be hired during the weeks in which they were not theoretically obliged to work. Thus, the system guaranteed a permanent 'free' workforce for the mining sector (Assadourian, 1979: 257). On the other hand, although Potosí repelled a part of the population who sought to flee their *mita* obligations in the mines, it was also a pole of attraction for many portions of the indigenous population (*mingas* and *yanaconas*) who came individually or with the consent of their native authorities, in search of mineral and commercial wealth.

---

13 There is a very extensive and rich bibliography dealing with the Toledo reduction process. We limit ourselves to citing some pioneering works and other more recent literature: Gade, 1991: 69–90; Malaga Medina, 1993: 263–316; Saignes, 1991: 91–135; Jurado, 2004: 123–137; Zagalsky, 2009: 57–90; Mumford, 2012; Zuloaga Rada, 2012; Saito and Rosas Lauro, 2017.

14 As we shall see, other similar systems of forced recruitment of mining labour functioned in New Spain and Peru, each with their own specificities, but the *mita* system of Potosí was the largest and most extensive (Bakewell, 1989).

The *mita* system, established by Viceroy Toledo in 1573, contained certain links with previous labour systems (including the Inca system),[15] but it was new, because it was official and under the administration of Crown officers and indigenous authorities (*mita* captains). It also standardised previously disparate elements, such as the size of the contingent of labourers, the length of their stay in Potosí, as well as wages, and certain working conditions in the mines and silver refining plants.

The characteristics of the *mita* labour system have been widely studied. Here they are only summarised, however we do note some modifications that occurred in practice during the boom period (Bakewell, 1989; Cole, 1987; Zagalsky 2014a, 2014b). The Potosí *mita* involved the forced temporary migration, theoretically for a period of one year, of indigenous tributaries (men between 18 and 50 years old) from sixteen *corregimientos* (provinces) in the region between the south of Cuzco and the south of present-day Bolivia. The routes of this forced migration reached–in some cases–more than 1,000 kilometres in distance and up to 20 days on the road. Among the provinces forced to take part in the *mita*, most of the indigenous residents of the warm lowlands were exempted, as it was assumed death and illness could result from the abrupt passage to the cold and dry climate of the highlands of Potosí, located more than 4000 meters above sea level.

From 1573, successive viceroys issued general *repartimientos* (assignments) of the *mita*, these were lists of the indigenous people bound to the system, and the colonial beneficiaries. The first *mita* divisions in 1573 and 1575, established annual quotas of approximately 9,500 and 11,000 *mitayos*. From 1578 until the 1680s, the annual *mita* contingent was around 14,000 indigenous tributaries. This annual contingent (the *mita gruesa*) was a percentage of the tributaries in the macro-region bound to the system, with a total population of approximately 91,000 tributaries at the time of Viceroy Toledo's government. The *repartimientos* (districts) of the Charcas region had to send the 17 percent of their tributes to the *mita* each year, those of La Paz 16 percent, those of Cuzco 15 percent and those of Canas and Canches 13 percent. These percentages meant that, in theory, each indigenous tributary repeated his turn at the *mita* every six or seven years. Each tributary belonged to a *repartimiento*, a division of indigenous people or district (in 1610 there were 127 *repartimientos* obliged to participate in the *mita* system). Let us remember that each *repartimiento* might comprise a single ethnic group,

15 Among the works that trace continuity between this forced colonial system and labour practices and certain ritual practices and values associated with mining in the Inca state, one cannot fail to mention Wachtel, 1980: 21–57; Bakewell, 1989; Bouysse-Cassagne, 2005: 443–462; Platt, Bouysse-Cassagne and Harris, 2006.

but in some cases, they brought together several groups or fragments of groups. The *mita* system at Potosí involved an enormous diversity of indigenous ethnicities. The men forced into the *mita* habitually migrated to Potosí along with their wives, children and many of their possessions.

The *mita* allocations for mining production in the viceroyalty of Peru were limited to the mercury mines of Huancavelica and the silver mines of Potosí, with the mines at Porco having a much lower flow, as silver yields were only efficient in the earlier period and were already declining by 1580. Other important mining centres, such as Oruro, Aullagas, San Antonio del Nuevo Mundo, did not receive *mitayos*. This should not, however, lead to the idea that salaried labour there was completely "voluntary" nor that labourers were totally 'free' (Gil Montero, 2011: 297–318; Gil Montero, 2015).

In 1575 a system was established that divided the total annual quota (*mita gruesa*) into thirds. Each third (*mita ordinaria*) had to complete a week-long shift in the mines or silver refining plants, followed by two weeks theoretically at rest. Cole (1985) argues that by the early 17th century, due to a decline in the available workforce, the *mita* contingent was no longer divided into thirds but instead into two. Some testimonies from the boom time (from 1610 and 1612), even question the existence of two shifts, maintaining that the *mita* contingent laboured constantly without 'breaks', or weeks for voluntary employment. In addition, they indicate that by then the *mitayos* remained in Potosí for more than a year (Zagalsky, 2014b: 70–71).

Viceroy Toledo established specific ordinances for *mita* labour in the mines. Let us emphasise that free labour has not received as much attention from historians as the *mita*, perhaps because it was largely unregulated, and therefore less well documented. The weekly shift of the ordinary *mita* theoretically ran from Monday to Saturday, with Sunday being a day off. On Mondays the indigenous captains presented the ordinary *mita* and distributed the labourers among the beneficiaries of the *mita repartimiento*. The specific task of assigning labour was the joint responsibility of the captains and overseers, with the final say going to the town magistrate. Work began Tuesday morning and continued until Saturday night. The working day ran from sunrise to sunset, although in practice the indigenous people worked day and night, in companies (generally of two but sometimes reaching five workers). Each company occupied a single section inside the mine (*suyo o llancana*) and alternated their labour: while one hewed the other rested, and they also shared the heavy picks. The testimony of an *visitador* of the Cerro Rico in 1610 warns about workers' autonomy in the mines, pointing out that the pick men (*barreteros*), and even the less specialised loaders, worked alone or with little control from the indigenous overseers (*pongos*) or work captains (Zagalsky, 2014b: 74–76).

The daily wages Viceroy Toledo set for the *mitayo* varied, depending on the type of work: the *barreteros* who worked in the mines received 3.5 *reales*, those who worked in the silver refining plant (*repasiris*) received 2.75 *reales*, those who transported the ore outside the mines (*apiris*) and from the mines to the silver refining plants (*chacaneadores*) each received 3 *reales* (Capoche, 1959 [1585]: 145; Zavala, 1978: 103, 118–122). Towards the beginning of the 17th century, *mita* wages amounted to 4, 3, and 3.5 *reales*, for the barreteros, repasiris, apiris and chacaneadores respectively. The weekly salary of a *mita barretero* amounted to 3 *pesos* in 1612, while a *minga barretero* received 10 *pesos*. In Oruro in 1612 there were about 6,000 indigenous miners who charged 10 *pesos* a week, just like the *mingas* of Potosí (Zagalsky, 2014b: 75–77).[16]

On the real value of the *mita* wages, sources from the early 17th century estimate the individual cost of the trip to Potosí and the annual residence there at 100 *pesos*, while the annual salary of a *mitayo* (17 weeks of 6 days) was around 45 *pesos* (Bakewell, 1989: 112; 1990). In addition to their wage income, the mitayos could rely on the collective economic resources controlled by the *ayllus* (indigenous communities), which effectively "subsidised" colonial mining production (Assadourian, 1979: 257–268) by either collaborating with the reproduction of workers and their families while they were working for the *mita*, or through guaranteeing commutative payments to avoid *mita* shifts. It is equally important to consider the contributions of women working in the urban markets of Potosí (Mangan 2005; Numhauser, 2005).

On the other hand, various items were discounted from the *mita* wages: the 'grain tax' (*imposición de granos*) of half a *real* per day went to pay the salaries of the *alcalde mayor de minas*, the Protector General, the *visitadores* and the *mita* captains. Furthermore, each *mitayo* had to contribute half a *peso ensayado* for the Hospital, although most of the hospitalised patients were not indigenous people, despite the serious impact mining had on their health (Platt, Bouysse-Cassagne and Harris, 2006: 832). It is estimated that the payment of tributes took around 90 percent of the wage income of the *mitayos* (Assadourian 1979). If we add the family expenses of the *mitayo* residing in Potosí (food, clothing and housing, among others), it is easy to understand why a *mitayo* would need to seek "free" salaried employment during his periods of 'rest' (Bakewell, 1989).

In theory, productivity quotas were prohibited by different ordinances (issued by successive viceroys, Francisco de Toledo, the Marqués de Cañete and

16 General Archive of the Indies, Seville – hereafter AGI Charcas 135, 1612; AGI Charcas 20, R. 8, N.97.

Luis de Velasco). Mining was a job where productivity was marked not only by the number of hours worked but also by the conditions and the state of the mine itself. However, in practice, notwithstanding legislation prohibiting the imposition of quotas, the *caciques* denounced the fact that weekly payments were made subject to the amount of metal "that has been worked and removed in piles and tasks" and not to the number of days and nights worked. As a way of imposing productivity quotas on the labourers, the mine owners and entrepreneurs were not only prone to whip, mistreat or even kill indigenous people in order to discipline the rest, they also calculated the pecuniary penalties imposed by the courts for these practices as another production cost (Zagalsky, 2014b: 77).

A fundamental question for understanding the dynamics of the labour system and the combination of *mita* and free labour is the commutation of the *mita*. The replacement of *mitayos* with *mingas* (voluntary salaried labourers) became frequent practice just a few years after the system was first established in Potosí (Zagalsky, 2014a). The literature tends to state that the voluntary workers developed specialised mining skills (*barreteros*), while the *mitayos* received lower wages and performed the simplest tasks for example, as *apiris* (loaders) and as *repasiris* in the silver refining plants (Assadourian, 1979: 252–257 and Tandeter, 1992). This assumption must be qualified. On the one hand, the *mitayo* and the *minga* were, in many cases, the same person who, at different times or in different weeks, worked in one role or the other. On the other hand, there is evidence that many *mitayos* were responsible for specialised tasks, and they did not always pay money to commute their *mita* obligations (either because they could not or because they did not want to). Another issue that remains unresolved is the transmission of specialised mining knowledge, whether among *mitayos* or *mingas* or between the two groups. This particular combination of forms of work, where some of the same individuals made up both groups, is one of the peculiarities of the experience of indigenous miners in the southern Andes. We find ourselves in a world of predominantly indigenous workers, holding particular knowledge and specialisations, and made up of multiple ethnic identities. They were forced, by a system driven from above, to coexist, both in the urban environment and in the depths of the mines.

A few years after the mining *mita* was established in the 1570s, the *azogueros* (the owners of mines and silver refining plants) adopted a lamentation about the bankruptcy of the *mita* system as their *leitmotif.* Nevertheless, the legal regulations governing the *mita* (*repartimientos* and ordinances) did not undergo any substantial modifications during the first forty years.

The mining district of Guanajuato

In the viceroyalty of New Spain, the colonisers, moved by their need for precious metals, made various incursions into the territory in search of silver and gold deposits. Numerous mines were discovered between 1531 and 1558, and extraction began at Pachuca, Real del Monte, Zacatecas, Tlalpujahua, and others (Mentz, 2010: 117). The veins at Guanajuato were also discovered in that period. The protagonists of the first find were a group of muleteers who, in 1548, were heading out to the recently discovered Zacatecas mines. According to Lucio Marmolejo, while they were resting at a place near the Cerro del Cubilete, they noticed that the stones contained silver: "[S]urprised by that eventuality, they dug a little in the ground where the stones lay, and found that a vein passed through there, promising the most plentiful products, to which they will dedicate themselves in their work" (1883: 144). In the following years, new and rich veins were discovered in the region, such as the prosperous Rayas mine, named after the man who discovered it, Juan de Raya. These discoveries attracted a large population and made it necessary to build roads to link the mining region with supply lines and with Mexico City.

Control of the territory, and the mining deposits of the region, pushed the Spaniards into a war against the natives, the Teochichimecas, which was framed by the project of colonisation of the north-central region (Jiménez, 2006: 109–114; Blanco, Parra and Ruiz Medrano, 2011: 52). This war, which lasted for years, enabled the enslavement of the Chichimecas, in a region where labour was not abundant and was increasingly in demand for the agricultural estates and livestock ranches, as well as for the mining companies. For the 'pacification' of the region, they re-founded the missions and forced settlement of indigenous population from the centre of the viceroyalty, such as the Tlaxcaltecas and the Otomi, so that they would set an example of sedentary ways of life for the Chichimecas. In 1598, a truce was agreed with the Teochichimecas, in what would later become San Luis de La Paz (Blanco, Parra and Ruiz Medrano, 2011: 61).

The development of mining in the region was accompanied by a great demand for workers. The labour system, and the situation of labourers in Guanajuato, underwent many changes over the three centuries of Spanish domination. While the owners of the mines were able to employ enslaved indigenous people in the beginning, they were soon in short supply. Faced with the growing demand for labour, the mine owners asked the authorities to be assigned indigenous workers from the *repartimiento* (that is, assignments of forced indigenous labour). Viceroy Martín Enríquez established the mining *repartimiento* (assignment) for the Guanajuato mines in 1579. On paper, it affected 487 indigenous people from the Bajío of Michoacán (most of them Purépecha), but in practice the groups that reached the mining district were of smaller proportions (Castro, 2002: 231). In New Spain, according to the legislation, the percentage of forced labourers should not exceed 4 percent of the male population. This is in notable contrast to the Peruvian case.[17] At the beginning of the 17th century, there were 132 workers from the *repartimiento* who came weekly to Guanajuato and in 1628, that number increased to 150 (Castro, 2002: 234). Indigenous people were taken to Guanajuato by the distributing judge (*juez repartidor*), together with an indigenous official called a *papite*; the latter handed them over to the *alcalde mayor del real de minas*, and once their service was over, he took them back.[18] Each forced labourer went to the mines for one week every six or seven months and was paid one *real* per day, except on Sunday, which was the day of rest (Gavira, 2015: 85; Castro, 2002: 236 and 243). During the 17th century, there were complaints from some of the communities affected by the labour *repartimiento* destined for Guanajuato. In them it was pointed out that the indigenous people were forced to work on dangerous drainage jobs (Castro, 2002: 230). Some towns complained that they were being obliged to send batches of workers not only to the mining industry in Guanajuato, but also to other mines, such as Inguarán (Gavira, 2015: 82–83). The distance they had to travel from their communities of origin to the mines of Guanajuato was also a source of complaint in some towns in Michoacán located more than sixty leagues away, although the legislation established a limit for forced labour of ten leagues between the towns of the *repartimiento* and the mines.[19]

---

17 Recopilación de Leyes de Indias, Libro VI, Título XII, Ley XXII.

18 According to Felipe Castro, this name possibly comes from the Purépecha *pahpeti* which means "the one who carries or transports people" (Castro, 2002: 238).

19 *Recopilación de Leyes de Indias*, Ley III, Título XII, Libro VI. "That the Indians be paid for the time they work, including the return journey, going from ten leagues." The league was a measure that expressed the distance that a person could travel during an hour, fluctuating enormously, depending on whether it was on foot or not, and according to the geographical characteristics of the terrain (varying between 4 and 5.57 kilometres). In the case of New Spain, researchers have tended to calculate that one league was equivalent to 4.19 kilometres, although a review of the documentation has revealed indications that during the three centuries of colonial rule the value of the league was variable. See, for the Peruvian case, Hemming, 1982; for the variability of the league in New Spain, see Garza Martínez, 2012. Taking a standard measurement of 4.19 kilometres, we verified that the distances indicated in the legislation and practice in the case of New Spain (about 41.9 and 251.4 kilometres respectively) were much lower than the maximum distances mentioned in the Peruvian case of Potosí (in some cases involving distances greater than 500 kilometres).

With the passage of time, the significance of the *repartimiento* mine labourers decreased in Guanajuato, just as it did in rest of the viceroyalty. Several causes could be behind this decrease: 1) The effective reduction of the population in the territories subject to the *repartimiento*, as a result of deaths, escape to regions exempted from the service, or workers settling permanently in the mining districts[20]; 2) the stagnation of mining production; and 3) the congregation of the indigenous population around the mining settlement of Guanajuato, which also provided labour for mining activities.

Along with the forced labour force, we must therefore look at free labour, which ended up taking precedence in the mines of this district. This was a workforce fed, in differing proportions, by people from the indigenous, free Afro-descendant, *mestizo* and Spanish communities. It is possible that the decrease in the indigenous population explains why salaried labour spread throughout the territory of New Spain as a resource for providing of a workforce. The owners of the mines and silver refining plants had to implement different strategies to attract workers. They made use of retention mechanisms such as the well-known debt peonage, but they also reached arrangements that amounted to an improvement in working conditions. For example, we have the *partido*, also known as the *pepena*, which consisted of a percentage of ore that the worker could take for himself once he had completed his *tequio* (the quota that a worker was required to extract in a day).[21] The partido gave labourers greater purchasing power and encouraged them to continue working once their working day was over. In the words of Enrique Florescano (1996: 118), the work done to obtain the *partido* or *pepena* "was an extra job, paid not in money, but with a share of production."

This payment system began as a custom, the result of a voluntary concession from the mine owners (Gamboa, 1761: 461). It must be borne in mind that the lack of currency, especially when extraction work in the mines first began, made it necessary to seek other forms of remuneration, such as payment in kind. For this reason, on many occasions, as Flores Clair explains, the *partido* was implemented because it was the only payment that the owner could offer (1986: 51). On the other hand, payment of the *partido* was essentially limited to the *barreteros*, owing to the vital need for this type of worker specializing in ore extraction.[22]

---

20 Felipe Castro documents some cases of the inhabitants of indigenous communities that had to provide personal mining services fleeing to regions exempt from such obligations (2002: 243–244).

21 The word *tequio* is Nahuatl; *tequiot* means labour (Moreno, 1976: 466).

22 Although it was principally the *barreteros* who received the *partido*, it should be noted that, in some cases, other workers also participated in this payment in kind. Thus, for example, in the

The shortage of these skilled workers added to their value in the eyes of the mine owners. Participation in the profits of the mine acted as an incentive for the workers, although the *partido* system varied from one mining centre to another. In Guanajuato, once the *tequio* was completed, for which the worker was paid 4 *reales* in the 18th century, he then kept half of what he extracted during the rest of the day (Brading, 2012: 202–203). In the second half of the 18th century, some mines tried to reduce or abandon payment in kind. These attempts were prompted, on the one hand, by the increase in the productivity of the mines, which enabled some mine owners to pay their labourers a monetary wage and completely abandon payment in kind; and on the other, due to the advantageous position that the mine owners found themselves in against the workers, following the repression of the riots at Guanajuato in 1767, led by the labourers. The Rayas mine was one of the first to abandon the *partido*, later it also ceased in the Valenciana mine in exchange for increasing the salary of the *barreteros*, which reached 10 *reales* a day by 1803 (Brading, 2012: 204).

Tax exemptions for indigenous and *mulato* workers who laboured in the mining and metallurgical industries in Guanajuato, and across New Spain, was another mechanism designed to attract and retain labour in mining. Title V, books VI and VII of the *Recopilación de las Leyes de Indias* established that indigenous people, freed Afro-descendants had to pay tribute, however,

> the [indigenous people] who go to the mines, because they extract a lot of silver, and because most earn between four and five *pesos* a month, will easily be able to pay at least two *pesos* a year, [...]. We command it be ordered that they be taxed with moderation, so that no one forsakes the mines, and that they be well instructed in doctrine, and treated as is convenient for their salvation and well-being.[23]

Despite the fact that the legislation established a tax status for indigenous, African free people and Afro-descendant labourers, in the royal mines of New Spain, the practice of tax exemption was very common. Indeed, it was so deeply rooted that attempts by the Crown to collect tribute from the mining labourers provoked discontent and protests, which led to local or regional pardons being issued that relieved those workers of the obligation (Povea Moreno, 2016: 54). In the mining district of Guanajuato, an attempt to collect tax from the indigenous people who

---

case of Real del Monte, the *ademadores* (workers in charge of propping and strengthening the tunnels with wood) also had access to a share of the production. In addition, the *barreteros* separated some ore from his share for the workers who were linked to him, such as his labourers, blacksmiths, doctors and *malacateros* (in charge of the extraction machinery) (Navarrete, 2007: 100–101; Ladd, 1992: 80).

23 Recopilación de Leyes de Indias, Libro VI, Título V, Ley IX.

worked in the mines took place in 1729, causing great agitation among those affected. In Santa Ana, unrest prevented the collection of the tax, and later, in Marfil the workers took up arms to demand tax exemption.[24] While the resistance lasted, work in those mines was paralysed, which must have created pressure to find a solution to the problem. Finally, in 1731, a Royal Provision was issued that granted tax exemption to the mine and silver refinery owners of that district.[25] This was maintained until new fiscal measures were introduced by the Inspector General, José de Gálvez.

Re-establishing the collection of taxes from the miners of Guanajuato was one of the punitive measures implemented after the popular revolts that occurred in the city in 1767 (Castro, 1996: 191 and 206). Both the city council and the mining authority of Guanajuato requested that Viceroy Carlos Francisco de Croix, the marques of Croix, allow tax exemption for mining labourers, claiming that it was too difficult to create a register of the population employed in mining in Guanajuato (Povea Moreno, 2016: 58; Villalba, 2013: 40 – 42). The response to this request was a refusal that caused great discomfort among both miners and mine owners. The latter, concerned about the possible impact on the supply of labour that would result from the collection taxes, reached an agreement with the authorities through which they would pay a fixed sum of 8,127 *pesos* per year, to cover the tax obligations of all mining labourers in the jurisdiction of Guanajuato (Povea Moreno, 2016: 58).[26]

During the 18th century, the labour system, the payment of salaries, and the number of labourers were not uniform across all the mines in the Guanajuato district. Variations resulted from factors such as the extraction conditions underground, or how much capital the mine owners had (Villalba, 2013: 50). This is illustrated in a report from 1773 on the state of mining in the region, produced by officials of the Royal Treasury (*Caja Real*) of Guanajuato.[27] In it, a range of possibilities are identified: some mines were worked for '*raya y partido*' that is, a system consisting of a salary plus the incentive of a share of production;

---

24 Archivo Histórico del Palacio de Minería (hereafter AHPM), 1783, box 13, doc. 15, f. 3rd. Brading mentions a revolt of mining workers in Guanajuato against the collection of taxes in 1732 (2012: 368).

25 AHPM, 1783, box 13, docs. 6, 13 and 15. Archivo Histórico de la Universidad de Guanajuato (AHUG), P.C.L. 1732 Book 36, ff.77v–81r.

26 Other mining centres also contributed fixed amounts as a tribute, without the need for tax registration. It may be that these amounts were the result of agreements between local authorities and the different mining councils (Povea Moreno, 2016: 58 – 59).

27 Archivo General de la Nación, México (from now on AGNM), Minería, vol. 11, f. 1 – 47. From a transcript of the same in López Miramontes and Urrutia, 1980: 13 – 39.

others were worked only for the partido; yet other mines were worked by *buscones*, who worked in exchange for metal ore; others worked for short periods through *amparos (special permission)*, etc. At the same time, free labour appeared alongside coerced labour in some mines. In this regard, it should be noted that, in the second half of the 18th century, there was an increase in the *repartimientos* for mining in New Spain, which included the miners of Guanajuato. Many workers departed from the mining centre as a result of the partido being abandoned or reduced (as mentioned above). This, combined with the boom in Guanajuato mining, created a fierce demand for labour, prompting new requests for repartimientos of indigenous people to mitigate the shortage of labourers and reduce costs (Castro, 2002: 247). In 1779, the Guanajuato mining council requested batches of four or five hundred indigenous labourers; however, it is not clear whether this request received a positive response from the Crown.[28] Probably, the numbers of indigenous people coming to this mining centre from Michoacán, remained at the traditional figure of around one hundred and fifty. Their daily wage was also kept at one and a half reales, to which employers had to add a daily food ration and one *peso* for the return journey.[29] In practice, these additions to the wage were not always paid; for example, it was not unusual for mine owners to fail to comply with the requirement to pay for time spent travelling to the mining centre and back to the communities (Povea Moreno, 2015: 10).

We do not know the exact and total number of workers employed in the Guanajuato mines in the second half of the 18th century. Documentation relating to the riots of 1766 and 1767 provides some figures, but the vested interest the authorities had in exaggerating the numbers of rebelling workers should not be forgotten. Thus, in 1766 the authorities spoke of a total of 40,000 miners, of whom between four and six thousand would have been involved in the uprising (Villalba, 2013: 48). On the other hand, although there is no adjusted data giving the total number of workers, we do have information that gives insights into the disparity in numbers between some mines and others. While the large mining and refining estates came to employ vast numbers of labourers, many mines employed only four or five. For example, if we look at the figures given by Humboldt at the beginning of the 19th century, in the La Valenciana mine, one of the most prominent in the district, 1,800 workers were employed underground and 1,300 in surface mining activities (Villalba, 2013: 49). This is in stark contrast to the re-

28 Felipe Castro mentions that the mine owners abandoned their demand to increase the numbers of forced labourers in each group (*tanda*) and settled for the traditional repartimiento (2002: 255). However, M. Concepción Gavira Marquez affirms that there are reasons to believe that the requested increase did take place (2015: 88).

29 AGN Minería, Vol. 148, f. 236r.

ality of many other smaller mines. For example, take the case of the San Bartolo mine, part of the Real de La Fragua, which was worked around 1773, by just one or two *buscones* (López Miramontes and Urrutia, 1980: 23).

Historical and historiographic similarities and differences: Interpretive outline and open questions

Having set the scene for labour in the two mining regions that are the focus of this work, it is now up to us to create a dialogue between those two realities. We seek, on the one hand, to point out the commonalities and differences that are discernible between the two; and, on the other, to determine the reasons and rationale that would explain them. This panoramic view helps us appreciate issues in the world of mining that transverse the two spaces, albeit subject to particular conditions and characteristics specific to the time and place. It is an initial interpretive approach, offering answers that are by no means considered conclusive, but rather, suggest some future lines of research.

In both spaces, forms of free labour coexisted with other more coercive ones. It is true that Potosí is associated with the image of forced labourers working shifts in its mines, while mining in Guanajuato, and New Spain in general, has been linked to free, wage labour. Let us highlight here, therefore, the presence of free labourers in the mines of Potosí, a presence that may have increased over time but was there from the very beginning of the *mita* system, and about which much still remains to be said. We should also highlight the existence in the mines of Guanajuato of the *repartimiento*, even though it never reached the level of importance it had in Potosí. At the same time, attention must be paid to the fact that both in Guanajuato and in Potosí, the realities of the labour force were not immutable. Both mining regions saw changes: the Potosí *mita* underwent transformations over the more than two centuries of its existence, and in Guanajuato the forced recruitment of workers diminished with the passage of time, until their numbers increased again at the height of the mining boom.

One of the most notable differences between one region and the other is that, in the Peruvian case of Potosí, mining labourer and indigenous person were considered almost synonymous, whereas in New Spain that was not the case. In Peruvian mining, the labour force came mainly from the *ayllus*, and this remained the case throughout the entire period of Spanish domination.[30] The ethnicity of workers in the mining centres of New Spain was far more diverse. In Guanajuato indigenous and *mestizo* people, Spaniards, *mulatos* and enslaved and free African people made up the labour force, albeit in different proportions. In the Potosí, by contrast, indigenous labourers dominated mining, with only the occasional presence of Spaniards and enslaved African people working as administrators or stewards.

What reasons are usually given to explain these differences? The most common explanation given for the role of non-indigenous sectors in mining in New Spain is the geographical locations of the mining centres. They were located far from the dense nuclei of indigenous settlements, in areas with small populations. This contrasts with the close proximity of indigenous labour to the Potosí mining region. However, Guanajuato itself, and other mining districts such as Real del Monte, were in fact located in densely populated areas (unlike Zacatecas and San Luis Potosí). On the other hand, although the Potosí region (part of the Audiencia de Charcas in the viceroyalty of Peru) was inhabited by indigenous communities, it was probably not the most densely populated area (compared to the area located further north, near Lake Titicaca). Additionally, it should not be forgotten that the *mita* system itself involved the forced and permanent mobilisation of the population of settlements in areas far from Potosí, in some cases more than 1,000 kilometres away.

Explaining the differences becomes even more complex when we take into account the different periods of time in which the productive boom of each mining region took place. The heyday of Potosí occurred during the first century of Spanish domination, when indigenous populations were first experiencing the colonial condition, and the implementation of new rules. They negotiated "pacts," which largely took the form of obligations to provide a labour force. There was a great need for indigenous labour and this was provided, to a large extent, by setting up tributary forms of labour that involved varying degrees of coercion (Gil Montero and Zagalsky, 2016).

We should also point out that there must have been consensual forms that contributed to maintaining the forced labour system, for example, links to the earlier practices and beliefs that tied labour, particularly around metals and mines, to spaces, beings and values venerated since pre-Hispanic times. These

30 Documentary evidence from the 18th century complicates the panorama usually associated with Potosí, as, in addition to indigenous people, it suggests there would also have been *mulatto*, *mestizo* and even Spanish labourers (Barragán, 2015). It would be interesting if future studies of the Potosí case were to consider question of the ethnic composition of the workforce, from a long-term perspective.

customs endured in various ways during at least the first colonial century (Bouysse-Cassagne, 1998 and 2005; Platt, Bouysse-Cassagne and Harris, 2006; Zagalsky, 2014). We would also propose a hypothesis, which requires further research: a possible additional element may have contributed to the consensual process that helped sustain a forced labour system of the dimensions and durability of the Potosí *mita*. That was the practice of *k'ajcheo* (indigenous ore extraction mines at weekends). This was highly visible and widely denounced in the 18th century (Tandeter, 1992; Abercrombie, 1996; Barragán, 2015), however, it could perhaps have a longer history, traceable back to the 16th century itself.

In the case of Guanajuato, labour requirements were low during the first hundred and fifty years, and the indigenous population present in the area around the mine was sufficient to meet the demand. As we explained above, wages, along with a variety of different working arrangements, were the most common means of attracting the population to mining work. As they did not have a *repartimiento* of the proportions and scope of that of Potosí, during the peak of the productive boom, in the second half of the 18th century, with the resulting increased demand for labour, the owners of the mines and silver refineries had to apply different strategies to attract and retain workers. Fundamentally, they appealed to mechanisms that mixed the coercive with the consensual: for example, debt peonage and working arrangements like the *partido*.

Advantageous working conditions in the mines of the Guanajuato attracted the indigenous population, but also non-indigenous people: formerly enslaved free African people, *mestizos*, *mulatos* and Spaniards. The presence of the latter in the labour force, according to Margarita Villalba's estimation, experienced an increase from the 1780s, as a result of stimuli, created by the authorities at that time, for Spanish people involved in various trades, including those linked to mining such as *barrenadores*, *piqueadores* and administrators (2013: 54). This progressive increase in the numbers of Spanish labourers was also favoured by the mobility of the mining labourers between regions (Villalba Bustamante, 2013: 54–55).

Another difference between the two contexts is related to the financial category ascribed to the labourers. In the case of New Spain, although the legislation determined that indigenous people and freed Afro-descendants, between the ages of 18 and 50 years old, had to pay tax, in the mining districts of New Spain, tax exemption for mining labourers was a deep-rooted custom. Various laws and provisions at different times and in different local areas, relieved mining labourers of their tax obligations. Workers in the Guanajuato mining district were also favoured by these tax exemptions, which were threatened by the new fiscal measures at the end of the 18th century, just as happened in other mining centres of the viceroyalty.

Meanwhile, in Potosí, the indigenous population that worked in mining (whether *mitayos* or free labourers) continued to pay tax throughout the colonial period, that is, during the boom and also during the periods of decline.[31] Perhaps the reasons for such a difference must be sought in the lack of large-scale coercive methods in the mines of New Spain, and the resulting difficulties in mobilising and retaining the necessary labour force. In this way, the tax exemptions for labourers should be seen as a labour acquisition strategy on the part of mining entrepreneurs, combined with the concession by the Crown of their right to receive this income. The continuation of tax exemption in the long term could also be a result of fears of a possible workers' uprisings in response to any attempt to reinstate the tax burden (Pérez Rosales, 2003: 200). Such fears were by no means unfounded, if one considers the events that occurred in a district of the province of Guanajuato in 1729 to 1731, already mentioned above. This apprehension among mine owners must have also been behind the agreement reached between the Guanajuato mining council (*diputación*) and the authorities, by which the council agreed to pay a fixed amount in tax on behalf of the mining labourers.

In terms of working conditions, we see a wide variety of situations that range from free, salaried work to unfree labour (similar to slavery), and forms of forced labour or labour with coercive elements (however these were not entirely comparable to slave labour). Between these three points on the continuum, specific conditions could vary from one extreme to another, even in the case of the working conditions affecting a single individual worker at different times. Consider, for example, the case of voluntary, salaried labourers, who were, in theory located at the "free" extreme of the spectrum, yet coercive mechanisms were frequently deployed against them. Labour under the *mita* system was not actually considered unfree labour, since in theory it involved the payment of a salary, and the forced element of the work was only for a limited period of time. It was a system established as part of the obligations of indigenous subjects of the Crown, alongside with the payment of taxes. In practice, it had numerous coercive aspects: it involved forced migration, sometimes from hundreds of kilometres away, and it was not always paid with a salary. Compliance with the theoretical time limits on *mita* labour (one week in every three for a year, in cycles that were repeated every seven years) was not always maintained either. In practice, the *mita* also offered options which brought the condition closer to somewhat freer forms of

31 On the importance of tribute as a constitutive element of rights and obligations between the Crown and its indigenous subjects in the Andean area, see Platt, 2016; Gil Montero and Zagalsky, 2016.

labour: the option of being employed as salaried *mingas* during 'idle' weeks for notably higher wages; the system of commuting *mita* obligations with cash payments; and the possibility of escape.[32]

On the other hand, the *repartimiento* in New Spain, which in the case of Guanajuato experienced an intensification during the boom of the second half of the 18th century, was part of an equally coercive system, linked to that of the Andean colonial *mita*. It should be noted that the mine owners of New Spain always yearned for the introduction of a *mita* system, with its greater scope in terms of numbers of forced labourers and time spent in service in the mining centres. In the mid-18th century, increased mining production turned this desire into strong pressure for an increase in the number of forced indigenous labourers being sent to the mines, and an increase in the time they had to serve. There is documentary evidence that, in Real del Monte, in 1771, they managed to extend the period of time forced labourers had to remain in service, from one week to five (Castro, 2002: 246–247). In the case of Guanajuato, we are not aware of an extension of this type, but there is evidence of the increased presence of forced labour.

Although the proportions are much smaller, the Guanajuato *repartimiento* presented characteristics similar to those of the *mita* in Potosí. For example, it involved forced migration from a wide radius, exceeding in practice the distances established on paper. As noted above, the laws set a maximum distance of ten leagues between the indigenous communities affected by the *repartimiento* and the mining centres where they were sent to work, but some of the villages compelled to send groups of workers, were more than 60 leagues away (Povea Moreno, 2015: 9–10). Likewise, the *repartimiento* in New Spain developed practices very similar to those registered in Andean mining; for example, the custom of substituting compulsory assignments of workers for cash payments, a practice that has been documented in the case of the Guanajuato *repartimiento* (Castro Gutiérrez, 2002: 252–253; Mentz, 1999: 299).

Finally, in relation to the political aspect, it is worth reflecting on the different ways in which the colonial state intervened in the organisation of mining labour. Of course, these differences were due in part to how the colonial state responded to the specifics of each context. However, it may also be the case that differences in state policy created different situations in each colonial space. In the case of Potosí, in the viceroyalty of Peru, they did not rely on poor Spaniards

---

32 Many of those who paid money to avoid their week of *mita*, also ended up being employed during that time as *mingas*. Hence commutation could act as a push towards freer forms of labour. As for the escapes, in some cases, they also opened the possibility of more "free" forms of work, for example: working as *mingas*, in Potosí or in other mining centres.

or mestizos as labourers, instead relying on indigenous labour (it should be noted that there is evidence that these other actors were present as labourers in other smaller-scale mining centres, however, they were always a minority.) In Peru there was very direct state intervention, in, for example, the organisation of the *mita* labour system; the intervention of the *corregidores* in the dispatch of the *mita* contingents (together with the *mita* captains); the intervention of the *corregidor* of Potosí and other officials (visitadores and the *alcalde mayor)* in the specific processes of the *mita* (i.e., the assignments of labourers among the different owners and leaseholders of the mines and refining plants).

In the case of New Spain, and Guanajuato in particular, the regulation of forced labour was much less detailed and specific, guided by the general norms contained in the *Recopilación de las Leyes de Indias.* Free labour, which dominated in New Spain, was subject to far less state regulation, and each mining centre adopted the "rules" that it considered most appropriate. In Guanajuato, free labour prevailed, but during the second half of the 18th century, with the boom and attempts to lower the cost of labour, they began to request labourers from the *repartimiento* for the mines. These requests were met with the provision of indigenous forced labour from Michoacán. There were numerous complaints from these communities requesting that they be exempted from this coercive labour. The *enganchadores* and others associated with the process of rounding up labourers were not civil servants but private employees of the refinery and mine owners. It can be noted that, in Real del Monte, in the second half of the 18th century, the *repartimientos* were also mobilised by private individuals know as *recogedores.* Understanding the intensification of the *repartimiento* in mining in New Spain at that stage of the 18th century leads us to consider the role and capacity of the large businessmen or mining investors to intervene in the decisions of the viceregal authorities (Povea Moreno, 2015: 6).

Of course, the great miners (Pedro Romero de Terreros, José de la Borda, Antonio de Obregón or the Fagoaga) were men close to the organs of power and decision-making. Consider also the gifts and loans they made to the Crown, hoping to obtain privileges and honours in return (Couturier, 2003: 155). By way of example, during the Anglo-Spanish War (1779–1783), Antonio de Obregón, Count of Valenciana, the main shareholder of the most productive mine in Guanajuato, donated 25,000 *pesos* to the Crown (Valle Pavón, 2016: 74).

When we weigh up the similarities and differences between the two cases, we envision the Andes as a world where the Crown intervened more directly: it was a space further from the Iberian Peninsula, more politically unstable, where perhaps the presence of the State was more necessary to maintain the reproduction of the colonial order. Meanwhile, New Spain presents greater diversity in terms of types of labour force and systems, and less intervention from the Crown to codify and control that labour, at least prior to the Bourbon reforms. Thus, political variables, together with the other factors considered here, had their bearing on the configuration of the complex world of labour in Latin American colonial mining.

Sources

Archivo General de Indias (AGI): AGI Charcas 135, "*Memoria de la mita*," 1612. AGI Charcas 20, R.8, N.97.

Archivo General de la Nación de México (AGNM): AGNM Minería, vol. 11.

Archivo General de la Nación de México (AGNM): AGNM Minería, vol. 148.

Archivo Histórico del Palacio de Minería (Mexico) (AHPM): AHPM 1783, caja 13, documentos, 6, 13 and 15.

Archivo Histórico de la Universidad de Guanajuato (AHUG): AHUG P.C.L. 1732 Libro 36.

References

Abercrombie, Thomas. 1996. "Q'aqchas and La Plebe in rebellion: Carnival vs. Lent in 18th century Potosi." *Journal of Latin American Anthropology* 2 (1): 62–111.

Arduz Eguía, Gastón. 1985. *Ensayos sobre la mistoria de la Minería Altoperuana*. Madrid: Editorial Paraninfo.

Assadourian, Carlos Sempat. 1979. "La producción de la mercancía dinero en la formación del mercado interno colonial." In *Ensayos Sobre el Desarrollo Económico de México y América Latina (1500–1975)*, edited by Enrique Florescano. Mexico: Fondo de Cultura Económica.

Assadourian, Carlos Sempat. 1982. *El sistema de la economía colonial. Mercado Interno, Regiones y Espacio económico*. Lima: Instituto de Estudios Peruanos.

Bakewell, Peter J. 1991. "Los determinantes de la producción minera en Charcas y en Nueva España durante el siglo XVII." In *El sistema colonial en la América Española*, edited by Heraclio Bonilla. Barcelona: Editorial Crítica.

Bakewell, Peter J. 1990. "La Minería en la Hispanoamérica Colonial." In *Historia de América Latina. 3. América Latina Colonial: Economía*, edited by L. Bethell. Barcelona: Editorial Crítica.

Bakewell, Peter J. 1989. *Mineros de la montaña roja. El trabajo de los indios en Potosí 1545–650*. Madrid: Alianza Editorial.

Barnadas, Joseph. 1973. *Charcas. Orígenes Históricos de una Sociedad Colonial*. La Paz: CIPCA.

Barragán, Rossana. "¿Ladrones, pequeños empresarios o trabajadores independientes? K'ajchas, trapiches y plata en el cerro de Potosí en el siglo XVIII." *Nuevo Mundo Mundos Nuevos* (March). https://doi.org/10.4000/nuevomundo.67938. Accessed 16 October 2017.

Blanco, Mónica, Alma Parra and Ethelia Ruiz Medrano. 2011. *Breve historia de Guanajuato.* Mexico: FCE-Colmex.
Bouysse-Cassagne, Thérèse. 1998. "Le palanquin d'argent de l'Inca petite enquête d'ethno-histoire à propos d'un objet absent". Techniques et Culture 29: 69 – 112.
Bouysse-Cassagne, Thérèse. 2005. "Las minas del centro-sur andino, los cultos prehispánicos los cultos cristianos." *Bulletin de l'Institut Français d'Etudes andines* 34 (3): 443 – 462.
Brading, David A. 2012. *Mineros y comerciantes en el México borbónico (1763 – 1810).* Mexico: FCE.
Brading, David A. and Harry E. Cross. 1972. "Colonial silver mining: Mexico and Peru." *The Hispanic American Historical Review* 52 (4): 545 – 579.
Brown, Kendall. W. 2012. *The History of Mining in Latin America: From the Colonial Era to The Present.* Alburquerque: University of New Mexico Press.
Caño Ortigosa, José Luis, and Jaime J. Lacueva Muñoz. 2009. "Guanajuato: plata y azogue en una villa minera (1665 – 1733)." In *Orbis Incognitvs. Avisos y legajos del Nuevo Mundo*, edited by Fernando Navarro Antolín, 605 – 624. Huelva: Universidad de Huelva.
Caño Ortigosa, José Luis. 2006. "Mineros en el cabildo de Guanajuato:1660 – 1741." *Anuario de Estudios Americanos* 631: 187 – 209.
Capoche, Luis. 1959 [1585]. *Relación General de la Villa Imperial de Potosí*, edited by L. Hanke. Madrid: Ediciones Atlas.
Castro, Felipe. 1996. *Nueva ley y nuevo rey. Reformas borbónicas y rebelión popular en Nueva España.* Zamora: El Colegio de Michoacán, UNAM-Instituto de Investigaciones Históricas.
Castro, Felipe. 2002. "La resistencia indígena al repartimiento minero en Guanajuato y la introducción de la mita en Nueva España." *CLAHR:Colonial Latin American Historical Review* 11 (3): 229 – 258.
Cobb, Gwendolyn Ballantine. 1977. *Potosí y Huancavelica: Bases Económicas, 1545 – 1640.* La Paz: Banco Minero de Bolivia.
Cole, Jeffrey A. 1985. *The Potosí mita, 1573 – 1700: Compulsory Indian Labor in the Andes.* Stanford: Stanford University Press.
Contreras, Carlos. 1982. *La ciudad del mercurio, Huancavelica, 1570 – 1700.* Lima: Instituto de Estudios Peruanos.
Couturier, Edith B. 2003. *The Silver King. The Remarkable Life of the Count of Regla in Colonial Mexico.* Albuquerque: University of New Mexico Press.
Cross, Harry E. 1983. "South American Bullion Production and Export, 1550 – 1750." In *Precious Metals in the Later Medieval and Early Modern Worlds*, edited by J. F. Richards. Durham, NC: Carolina Academic Press.
Cruz, Pablo and Jean Vacher, eds. 2008. *Mina y metalurgia en los Andes del Sur. Desde la época prehispánica hasta el siglo XVIII.* Sucre: IRD-IFEA.
Escobari de Querejazu, Laura. 2011. "Mano de obra especializada en los mercados coloniales de Charcas. Bolivia, siglos XVI – XVII." *Nuevo Mundo Mundos Nuevos.* https://doi.org/10.4000/nuevomundo.60530. Accessed 16 October 2017.
Escobari de Querejazu, Laura. 2001. *Caciques, yanaconas y extravagantes. La sociedad colonial en Charcas s. XVI – XVIII.* La Paz: Plural-Embajada de España en Bolivia.
Flores Clair, Eduardo. 1986. "Minas y mineros: pago en especie y conflictos, 1790 – 1880." *Historias* 13: 51 – 67.

Florescano, Enrique. 1996. "La formación de los trabajadores en la época colonial, 1521–1750." In *La clase obrera en la Historia de México. Tomo I: De la colonia al imperio*, edited by Enrique Florescano, and Pablo González Casanova. Mexico: Siglo Veintiuno, UNAM-Instituto de Investigaciones Sociales.

Gade, Daniel. 1991 "Reflexiones sobre el asentamiento andino de la épica toledana hasta el presente." In *Reproducción y transformación de las sociedades andinas, siglos XVI–XX.* Vol I., edited by Segundo Moreno Y. and Frank Salomon. Quito: Ediciones ABYA-YALA.

Gamboa, Francisco Xavier de. 1761. *Comentarios a las Ordenanzas de Minas.* Madrid: Oficina de J. Ibarra, calle de las Urosas.

Garner, Richard L. 1988. "Long-term Silver Mining trends in Spanish America: A Comparative Analysis of Peru and Mexico." *The American Historical Review* 9 (4): 898–935.

Garza Martínez, Valentina. 2012. "Medidas y caminos en la época colonial: expediciones, visitas y viajes al norte de la Nueva España (siglos XVI–XVIII)." *Fronteras de la Historia* 17 (2): 191–219.

Gavira Márquez, María Concepción. 2010. "Política minera y conflictos entre Potosí y Oruro a principios del siglo XVII." *Anuario de Estudios Bolivianos, Archivísticos y Bibliográficos* 16: 215–244.

Gavira Márquez, María Concepción. 2015. "*Entiendan que desobedecen:* estrategias de resistencia de la población indígena michoacana ante la coacción para el trabajo en las minas." In *Los otros rebeldes novohispanos: imaginarios, discursos y cultura política de la subversión y la Resistencia*, edited by Carlos Rubén Ruiz Medrano. San Luis Potosí: El Colegio de San Luis.

Gil Montero, Raquel. 2011. "Free and unfree labour in the colonial Andes in the sixteenth and seventeenth centuries." *International Review of Social History* 56 (S19): 297–318.

Gil Montero, Raquel and Paula C. Zagalsky. 2016. "Colonial Organization of Mine Labour in Charcas (Present-Day Bolivia) and Its Consequences (Sixteenth to the Seventeenth Centuries)." *International Review of Social History* 61 (24): 71–92.

Gil Montero, Raquel, Lía Guillermina Oliveto and Fernando Longhi. 2015. "Mano de obra y fiscalidad a fin del siglo XVII: dispersión y variabilidad de la categoría yanacona en el sur andino." *Boletín del Instituto de Historia Argentina y Americana Dr. Emilio Ravignani* 43: 59–93.

González Casasnovas, Ignacio. 2000. *Las Dudas de la Corona: La Política de Repartimientos Para la Minería de Potosí (1680–1732).* Madrid: Consejo Superior de Investigaciones Científicas.

Hausberger, Bernd and Ibarra, Antonio, eds. 2014. *Oro y plata en los inicios de la economía global: de las minas a la moneda.* Mexico: El Colegio de México.

Hemming, John. 1982 [1972]. *La Conquista de los Incas.* Mexico: Fondo de Cultura Económica.

Jiménez, Alfred. 2006. *El gran norte de México. Una frontera imperial en la Nueva España (1540–1820).* Madrid: Editorial Tébar, S.L.

Jurado, María Carolina. 2004. "Las reducciones toledanas a pueblos de indios: aproximación a un conflicto. El repartimiento de Macha (Charcas), siglo XVI." *Cahiers des Amériques Latines* 47 (3): 123–137.

Klein, Herbert S. 1991. "Las economías de Nueva España y Perú, 1680–1809: La visión a partir de las cajas reales." In *El sistema colonial en la América Española*, edited by Heraclio Bonilla. Barcelona: Editorial Crítica.

Ladd, Doris M. 1980. *Génesis y desarrollo de una huelga. Las luchas de los mineros mexicanos de la plata en Real del Monte, 1766–1775.* Mexico: Alianza Editorial.
Lohmann Villena, Guillermo. 1999 [1949]. *Las minas de Huancavelica en los siglos XVI y XVII.* Lima: PUCP.
López Miramontes, Álvaro and Cristina Urrutia. 1980. *Las minas de Nueva España en 1774.* Mexico: Instituto Nacional de Antropología e Historia.
Llanos, García de. 1983 [1609]. *Diccionario y maneras de hablar que se usan en las minas y sus labores en los ingenios y beneficios de los metales.* La Paz: IFEA-MUSEF.
Málaga Medina, Alejandro. 1993. "Las reducciones toledanas en el Perú." In *Pueblos de Indios. Otro urbanismo en la región andina*, edited by Ramón Gutiérrez. Quito: Ediciones Abya-Yala.
Mangan, Jane. 2005. *Trading Roles. Gender, Ethnicity, and the Urban Economy in Colonial Potosí.* Durham: Duke University Press.
Marmolejo, Luci. 1883. *Efemérides Guanajuatenses, o datos para formar la historia de la Ciudad de Guanajuato*, edited by Tomo I. Guanajuato. Imprenta del Colegio de Artes y Oficios, a cargo de Francisco Rodríguez.
Matienzo, Juan de. 1967 [1567]. *Gobierno del Perú.* Edited by Guillermo Lohmann Villena. París, Lima: IFEA.
Mentz, Brígida von. 1999. *Trabajo, sujeción y libertad en el centro de la Nueva España. Esclavos, aprendices, campesinos y operarios manufactureros, siglos XVI a XVIII.* Mexico: Centro de Investigaciones y Estudios Superiores en Antropología Social.
Mentz, Brígida von. 2010. "La plata y la conformación de la economía novohispana." In *Historia económica general de México. De la Colonia a nuestros días*, edited by Sandra Kuntz. Mexico: Colmex.
Moreno, Roberto. 1976. "Salario, tequio y partido en las Ordenanzas para la minería novohispana del siglo XVIII." In *IV Congreso del Instituto Internacional de Historia del Derecho Indiano.* 465–484. Mexico: UNAM.
Mumford, Jeremy. 2012. *Vertical Empire. The General Resettlement of Indians in the Colonial Andes.* Durham and London: Duke University Press.
Murra, John V. 1989. *La organización económica del Estado inca.* Mexico: Siglo XXI.
Navarrete, David. 2007. *Propietarios y trabajadores en el distrito minero de Pachuca, 1750–1810.* Mexico: Servicio Geológico Mexicano.
Numhauser, Paulina. 2005. *Mujeres Indias y Señoras de la Coca. Potosí y Cuzco en el siglo XVI.* Madrid: Cátedra.
Pérez Luque, Rosa Alicia and Rafael Tovar Rangel. 2006. *La contabilidad de la caja real de Guanajuato. Una aproximación a su historia económica (1665–1816).* Guanajuato: Universidad de Guanajuato. Centro de Investigaciones Humanísticas.
Pérez Rosales, Laura. 2003. *Familia, poder, riqueza y subversión: los Fagoaga novohispanos 1730–1830.* Mexico: Universidad Iberoamericana, Real Sociedad Bascongada de los Amigos del País.
Platt, Tristan, Thérèse Bouysse-Cassagne, and Olivia Harris. 2006. *Qaraqara-Charka. Mallku, Inka y Rey en la Provincia de Charcas (Siglos XV–XVII). Historia Antropológica de una Confederación Aymara.* La Paz: Instituto Francés de Estudios Andinos, Plural Editores, University of St. Andrews, University of London, Inter American Foundation, Fundación Cultural del Banco Central de Bolivia, La Paz.

Platt, Tristan. 2016 (1982). *Estado boliviano y ayllu andino: Tierra y tributo en el Norte de Potosí*. Centro de Estudios Sociales, La Paz, Bolivia

Povea Moreno, Isabel M. 2016. "La oposición al cobro del tributo en los reales de minas de Nueva España en la segunda mitad del siglo XVIII." In *Economía, sociedad y cultura en la historia de la minería latinoamericana*, edited by José Alfredo Uribe Salas, et al. Mexico: Universidad Michoacana de San Nicolás de Hidalgo, INAH, Fundación Vueltabajo

Povea Moreno, Isabel M. 2014. *Minería y reformismo borbónico en el Perú. Estado, empresa y trabajadores en Huancavelica, 1784–1814*. Lima: Instituto de Estudios Peruanos/Banco Central de Reserva del Perú.

Povea Moreno, Isabel M. 2015. "Coacción y disensión. Protestas frente a los repartimientos mineros en Perú y Nueva España, siglo XVIII." *Estudios de Historia Novohispana* 53: 1–17.

Recopilación. 1681. *Recopilación de Leyes de los Reynos de las Indias: mandadas imprimir, y publicar por la magestad católica del rey don Carlos II, nuestro señor: va dividida en quatro tomos, con el índice general, y al principio de cada tomo el índice especial de los títulos, que contiene*. Madrid: Iulian de Paredes.

Robins, Nicholas. 2011. *Mercury, Mining and Empire: The Human and Ecological Cost of Colonial Silver Mining in the Andes*. Bloomington: Indiana University Press.

Saignes, Thierry. 1984. "Las etnias de Charcas frente al sistema colonial (siglo XVII)." *Jahrbuch für Geschichte von Staat, Wirtschaft und Gesellschaft Lateinamerikas* 21: 27–75.

Saignes, Thierry. 1985. "Notes on the Regional Contribution of the mita in Potosí in the Early Seventeenth Century." *Bulletin of Latin American Research* 4 (1): 65–76.

Saignes, Thierry. 1991. "Lobos y ovejas. Formación y desarrollo de los pueblos y comunidades en el sur andino (Siglos XVI–XX)." In *Reproducción y transformación de las sociedades andinas*, edited by Segundo Moreno Yáñez and Frank Salomon. Quito: Ediciones ABYA-YALA: MLAL, Movimiento Laicos para América Latina.

Saito, Akira and Claudia Rosas Lauro, eds. 2017. *La concentración forzada de las poblaciones indígenas en el Virreinato del Perú*. Lima: PUCP.

Sánchez Albornoz, Nicolás. 1978. *Indios y Tributos en el Alto Perú*. Lima: Instituto de Estudios Peruanos.

Serrano, Sergio. 2008. "*...¡hay oro y no nos avisan a los amigos!...* Contrabando y evasión fiscal en el Cerro de San Pedro Potosí durante la primera mitad del siglo XVII." *Revista de El Colegio de San Luis, Vetas* 10 (29): 36–62.

Tandeter, Enrique. 1981. "La producción como actividad popular: ladrones de minas en Potosí." *Nova Americana* 4: 43–65.

Tandeter, Enrique. 1992. *Coacción y Mercado: la Minería de la Plata en el Potosí Colonial, 1692–1826*. Buenos Aires: Sudamericana.

TePaske, John J. 2010. *A New World of Gold and Silver*, edited by Kendall Brown. Leiden: Brill.

Valle Pavón, Guillermina del. 2016. *Donativos, préstamos y privilegios. Los mercaderes y mineros de la ciudad de México durante la guerra anglo-española de 1779–1783*. Ciudad de México: Instituto de Investigaciones Dr. José María Luis Mora.

Vilar, Pierre. 1974. *Oro y moneda en la historia (1450–1920)*. Barcelona: Ariel, S. A.

Villalba, Margarita. 2013. "El trabajo en las minas de Guanajuato durante la segunda mitad del siglo XVIII." *Estudios de Historia Novohispana* 48: 35–83.

Wachtel, Nathan. 1980. "Los mitimas del valle de Cochabamba: la política de colonización de Wayna Capac." *Historia Boliviana* I 1: 21–5.

Zagalsky, Paula C. 2014a. "La mita de Potosí: una imposición colonial invariable en un contexto de múltiples trasformaciones (siglos XVI–XVII; Charcas, Virreinato del Perú)." *Chungará* 46 (3): 375–395.

Zagalsky, Paula C. 2014b. "Trabajadores indígenas mineros en el Cerro Rico de Potosí: tras los rastros de sus prácticas laborales (siglos XVI y XVII)." *Mundos do Trabalho* 6 (12). https://doi.org/10.4000/rhj.1122. Accessed 16 October 2017.

Zagalsky, Paula C. 2009. "El concepto de "comunidad" en su dimensión espacial. Una historización de su semántica en el contexto colonial andino (siglos XVI–XVII)." *Revista Andina* 48: 57–90.

Zavala, Silvio A. 1978. *El servicio personal de los indios en el Perú (extractos del siglo XVI)*. Vol 1. Mexico: El Colegio de México.

Zuloaga Rada, Marina. 2012. *La conquista negociada: guarangas, autoridades locales e imperio en Huaylas, Perú*. Lima, IEP-IFEA.

Rossana Barragán R.

Forced labour as a "public good"? Voices and actions in Potosí (17th to 18th centuries)

Abstract: The main question in this essay is how to reconcile the more empowered, free, and autonomous world of the *k'ajchas* with the personal service of *mita* first established in the name of the "public good," yet described in the late 17th century by some among the colonial authorities as a "horror," and by others in the late eighteenth century as "temporary slavery." This chapter seeks to contribute to current thinking about what workers did to confront the *mita* and mining labour more generally. My approach is both to listen to what we have called the "voices from above" and to examine "actions from below," as these were interwoven and interlinked. My central argument is that the *mita* system was both delegitimised by being called into question at the highest levels of colonial power and undermined by the *mita* workers themselves–the *mitayos*. The *mitayos* not only evaded the *mita* but also sought to make the most of the economic opportunities they saw in mining by working as salaried *mingas* (hired labourers) and even as *k'ajchas*, or independent miners. It is important therefore to consider different working situations, rather than different types of labourers. In all the cases, the creation of more autonomous spaces enabled labourers to generate their own economic resources. This perspective allows us to add to the analysis of open rebellions, deployment of their eveyday weapons (James Scott), and pacts of reciprocity (Tristan Platt), the importance of self-economic involvement of *mitayos*, *k'ajchas*, and *trapicheros* as a modality to break its total dependency in search for more creative degrees of autonomy.

Keywords: Potosí; personal service; *mita*; mining; free labour, unfree labour, and independent labour; indigenous agency

Introduction

"His name ... is Agustín Quespi, his fatherland is this Villa ..." This is how the popular hero Quespi was introduced by the chronicler, Bartolomé Arzans de Orsúa y Vela, in his history of the Villa Imperial de Potosí. Quespi totted a couple of pistols, along with his tools, and was accompanied by four *apiris (labourers*

Senior Researcher at the International Institute of Social History (IISG), Amsterdam. Contact: rba@iisg.nl

https://doi.org/10.1515/9783110759303-003

employed to carry ore). Having no mine of his own, he scavenged from "deserted" mines, taking the ore and leaving no trace or damage. Quespi inspired fear among indigenous people and Spaniards alike; he flogged the mountain rangers and even resisted the *alcalde mayor de minas* (the local mines magistrate) who in response to complaints from the *azogueros* (the principal owners of the mines and refining mills),[1] had issued a warrant for his arrest. But he was not to be caught, for it was said that he had made a pact with the devil. He had friends too, because he paid his *quintos* (a tax of one-fifth) to His Majesty and was liberal with his divine worship. His wealth, and the esteem in which many Spaniards and priests held him, kept him safe for a time, but in the end, ruin came to Agustín Quespi, the *k'ajchas*'s captain,[2] after he was accused of demolishing structures in the mines, murder, and flogging Spaniards while resisting justice, as well as generally being a ringleader of bandits.

This old story shows the strength and power of a character like Quespi, and the historical research realized corroborates the image of *k'ajchas* like him. The *k'ajchas* who went to the hill at weekends were described as "ore thieves." They were linked to the owners of the *trapiches*, rudimentary mills used to crush the ores,[3] and both groups became more empowered in the mid-18th century. In fact, there were approximately 500 of them – men and women – and they had accumulated a wealth of practical experience and technical knowledge (Barragán, 2014 and 2017). They constituted an important contingent of workers and silver smelters, for they produced between thirty and fifty per cent of the silver in Potosí.[4] The activity of the *k'ajchas* and *trapicheros* was by no means incidental nor marginal in Potosí in the 18th century. In fact, it was central to it, making up another facet of the mining at Potosí and its workers.

How then should we understand and reconcile the world of the *k'ajchas* and *trapicheros* with that of forced labour and coercion in the Potosí *mita?* The *mita*

1 The name comes from *azogue* or mercury, used to produce silver by amalgamation.

2 See Vela, 201. The term appears in several different ways. The word *K'ajcha* was Quechua and alluded to the sound of the slingshot used to scare off anyone who came too close to them inside the mines (Anonymous, *Descripción histórica de Potosí*, 1759: 256). Gunnar Mendoza, in 1965, suggested that in Quechua it means "spirited, daring, frightening," relating the meaning to the clandestine work they did during the night (Hanke and Mendoza, 1965, T. II: 477). However, he also considered its meaning in Aymara, related to thunder or lightening (Mendoza, 1983: xli).

3 A *trapiche* was a place where ore was ground using large rocks. It resembled the antique Indian and Inca practice of grinding ore, which the Spanish called *quimbalate*. It involved the use of "a half-moon shaped" boulder to crush the ore placed beneath it.

4 The proportion of the total ore extracted attributable to the *k'ajchas* might have been around 15 to 35 percent, but a recent source suggests that between 1751 and 1774 it was nearer 50 percent. AGI Charcas 692, Cuerpo 13.

was considered a "horror" by Matías Lagunez, the *Oidor* (judge) of the Audiencias of Quito and Lima at the end of the seventeenth century. Lagunez went so far as to advocate its abolition, while Victorián de Villaba, Prosecutor of the Audiencia of Charcas at the end of the 18th century, described it as "temporary slavery." So, what kind of work and activity were the *k'ajchas* and *trapicheros* involved in, and what was their position with regard to the *mitayos?*

The interest here is in workers' agency. The history of miners in the 20th century is one of fierce, unionised struggle, but when we think of the colonial era the predominant image remains that of passive subjects, labourers who suffered the consequences of the mining *mita.*[5] That is at least in part the result of a convergence of three factors, the first of which is that the *mita* has always been seen from the critical but compassionate viewpoint of the colonial authorities. Secondly, the authorities debated and questioned the *mita* for a number of reasons, one of which was their opposition to the mining sector more generally, as it was considered to be the privileged beneficiary of a continuous flow of labourers. Thirdly, the *mita* existed for more than two and a half centuries, and there are less sources on how the *mitayos* themselves confronted the *mita.*[6]

This chapter will analyse those interwoven and interlinked factors – the "voices" from above and the "actions" from below – to explore what labourers did to resist the *mita* and to ameliorate their insertion in the mining work.[7] The central argument is that the *mita* was indeed called into question at the highest echelons of colonial power, which I believe delegitimised it, but it was also undermined by the *mitayos* themselves. I suggest that the decrease in numbers of *mita* labourers should be understood as desertion from a poorly paid job, as re-

5 It is essential to remember that mining work in Bolivia is, to this day, among the most demanding jobs, and that it takes place in very dangerous conditions.

6 The question is why the *mita* does not appear much more visibly in the archives when we have hundreds and thousands of files on land distribution, or on the legitimacy, or not, of the *caciques*. It does not always feature as a central demand in the uprisings and rebellions of the 18th century. However, in the case of Tupac Amaru there was an explicit demand articulated against the *mita*. In a letter he wrote in 1777, he referred to travel, the distance, the change of climate, and also the "business" of "selling" of indigenous people. He pointed out that they were treated like slaves. He also asked that the Province of Canas y Canchis should not be obliged to send *mita* to Potosí. He spoke of painful goodbyes and of a population in decline (see Lewin, 1967: 320–323). Platt, Bouysse, and Harris noted that the protests of the Charka and Qaraqara *caciques* against mining work were few, and limited to asking that the number of *mitayos* not be increased (Platt, et al., 2006: 368). The case of the "new" *mita* in 1795 did, however, lead to widespread protests.

7 In this chapter we provide more general perspectives, without including all the details of every aspect that we address in the book we are working on.

flected in absenteeism and migration but also in the cash payments made to relieve individuals of the obligation to go to Potosí at all. Then again, if they did go, payment for exemption from the *mita* meant that they could obtain different employment in better conditions for higher wages, and perhaps even more importantly would benefit from greater autonomy and resources. *Mita* workers thus developed strategies to find work that offered better conditions.

The *mita* therefore cannot be understood without considering the wider dynamics of the world of mining labour in Potosí. From this perspective it is important to remember that many of the *mingas* (hired labourers) could also be *mitayos*, a fact that some scholars have mentioned, albeit tangentially rather than as the central theme that I proposed in 2014. Furthermore, different workers converged in the economic activity of the *k'ajchas* and the *trapiches*. Although historical literature has dealt with the *k'ajchas* (see the historiographical review in Barragán, 2014), their relationship with the *trapiches* has not always been addressed. Similarly, the implications of the fact that between them they produced so much of Potosí's silver have yet to be considered.

Finally, no proper consideration has yet been given to how these characteristics indicate a particular situation in the Potosí mines whereby the status of "*mita*," "*minga*," or "*k'ajcha*" might constitute temporary activities and categories of labour for the same individual – to which we might add their principal activities as peasants and shepherds. We should therefore consider the possibility of different working situations in some cases, rather than different types of workers, and the interconnections between them. Recognition of that is vital to any analysis of workers' agency and responsive strategies. Nevertheless, the economic circuit began with an obligation of "personal service" in the *mita*, nominally set up in the name of the "public good" of the Crown, although that very question was vigorously debated–from above as much as from below.

In the name of the "public good": Personal service, "free, voluntary, and obligatory" forced labour

Although it is not possible to go into detail about the system of personal services established during the first few years of colonisation, it is necessary to present a brief summary recalling some of the key points and highlighting the relevant colonial authors and officials. A review of early sources shows that unpaid labour was regarded as personal service, a privilege granted to colonists as part of the *encomienda* in the early days of colonisation. After the debates involving Bartolomé de las Casas and the legislation that followed,[8] indigenous peoples were considered *free vassals*, which meant that they could not be made slaves, although they were obliged to work. The fact that they were compelled to do so in the name of the "public good" invoked the Spanish belief in the idleness and laziness of the *indios*, and in many cases their servile nature.

The same view was held by Juan de Matienzo, a judge of the Audiencia of Charcas. In his book Gobierno de Perú[9] he wrote that the natives were "hostile to labouring," and that it was necessary to force them to work.[10] The Viceroy of Peru, Francisco de Toledo, expressed a similar opinion, stating that if one waited for their "willingness to work," there would be no labour force available, although he also recognised that the Spanish colonists were wont to ask for a *repartimiento* or the assignation of indigenous workers for absolutely any job. Both for that reason and because of the chaotic "distribution" of labour and the paltry wages it paid, at the end of his term in office Toledo reported that he had dealt with those particular aspects of the situation regarding the employment of natives.[11] He ordered that only the Viceroy could assign indigenous labourers, and issued a series of *repartimiento* ordinances for the mines, *tambos* (roadside lodges), and for "the service of the cities."[12] In effect, a large part of the indigenous population was thereby rendered subject to various *mitas* under the *repartimiento* system, those *mitayos* being precisely defined by Matienzo as "*repartimiento* Indians who served in companies that they call *mitas*" (Matienzo, 1567–1910: 25).

It is clear therefore that "*mitayo*" was not exclusively synonymous with "worker" in the Potosí mines. Furthermore – and however contradictory this

---

8 Personal service was widely debated, giving rise to the New Laws of 1542 to 1543 that sought to abolish the *encomiendas*, the application of which had even led to civil wars. These laws declared the indigenous people to be vassals, prohibiting them from being enslaved. "And because our main attempt will and has always been the preservation and increase of the Indians, and that they may be instructed and taught in the ways of our holy Catholic faith, and well treated, as free people and our vassals"; "[H]aving as we have the natives of our aforementioned Indies, Islands and Land Masses of the Ocean-Sea as our free vassals"; "No Indian may be made a slave". For a brief synthesis of this period in Charcas, see Bridikhina and Arze, 2016.

9 He posited in 1567 that they were "pusillanimous and shy," which comes "from them naturally, that they abound with cold sullen fury." Their humour or temperament explained their peculiar and particular context. Melancholy, or black bile, was dry and cold, and made reference to the earth, which was related to autumn, evening, and old age. Matienzo, 1567–1910: 14.

10 *Ibid.* 16–19.

11 "Memorial que D. Francisco de Toledo dio al Rey nuestro Señor del estado en que dejó las cosas del Perú en el Virrey y Capitán General trece años que comenzaron en 1569". In: Relación de los Virreyes y Audiencias que han gobernado el Perú. Lima, 1867: 21.

12 Ordinances "De los Mesones y ventas." *Ibid.*

might appear to us today – according to Viceroy Toledo himself, at the end of the 16th century personal service was understood to be a labour obligation "without pay" (in Zavala, 1978: I: 99), as opposed to "voluntary" but "obligatory" labour done and paid "for the common and public good." That is why Toledo's new labour regulations and provisions emphasised wages and salaries.[13]

Legislation relating to personal service was passed during the early decades of the seventeenth century. The Royal Decree of 1601 sought to protect indigenous peoples' freedom as vassals "without a hint of slavery or other subjugation and servitude," although at the same time it regulated their labour. That decree established a very obvious state of tension between free will, compulsion, and the use of force.[14] "The public good," in the sense of paid labour "for the republic," began to be used to justify coercion, although there was recognition too of an organic division of labour.[15] In the mid-17th century the great jurist Juan de Solórzano Pereira defined personal service as the service required, by the *encomenderos*, of the indigenous people, against their will, for any purpose (labour, domestic service, work in the mines, etc.) (see Solórzano, 1703: 27). In his *Política Indiana* of 1647, Solórzano proposed that kings and princes should be afforded coercive power over their vassals "as long as they understood it to be in the interests of the universal good" (*ibid.:* 49). In support, alongside the sacred scriptures, Solórzano cited Matienzo and several other authors to underline the obligations that exist in times of war, and also the necessary interdependence of the different tasks carried out by different members of the republic, comparing them to the biological functions of the human body (*ibid.* 47 et seq.).

---

13 The King requested of Toledo in 1575 that "the said Indians not be led against their will, but as free men [...]." (emphasis added, in Zavala 1978 I: 99). Matienzo had already stated that it was not taking away their freedom to compel them to work for pay (Zavala, I: 56).

14 Several documents recognised that the mines could not be serviced without the Indians, and that meant "forcing or compelling them to labour and earn and not be idle." The "concert" (agreement or contract) should be voluntary, but without ceasing to be obligatory (Zavala, 1978 I: 4.). There were frequent references to the "*repartimiento* (or distribution) of Indians."

15 "*Tratado que contiene tres pareceres que ha compuesto el padre Fray Miguel de Agia, de San Francisco*" (Turin, 1603–1604). Agia drew a distinction between unpaid personal service for the *encomendero*, a perpetual servitude that was without public interest, and the tributes and the *repartimiento* or distribution of Indian labour done in the service of the Republic, with public freedom, for pay (with payment), and without violence, in a condition of natural and Christian freedom (in Zavala, 1979 II: 18. "It takes away their idleness without depriving them of their freedom"). He also said that it was necessary that "there be feet that walk, and hands that work, and heads that govern, and that some command and others serve and obey"; "All are members of the mystical body of this Indian republic" (*ibid.:* 20).

It was in this context that labouring in the mines of Potosí was imposed, as described by Viceroy Toledo at the end of the sixteenth century.[16] The Potosí mining *mita* recruited labourers from 16 provinces and required the annual mobilisation to Potosí of around 12,000 men between 18 and 50 years of age, working weekly shifts in groups of 4,000. Because they were required to work one week on and two weeks off for a whole year in Potosí, they took their families with them, so that every year approximately 40,000 people travelled to Potosí.

The burden such huge annual migrations placed on the indigenous communities led to great changes. By the end of the 17th century those migrations were the subject of serious challenges from above, and we analyse these first, because they shed light on the actions taken by the *mitayos* themselves in challenging the *mita* from below.

The strategies of the *mitayos* and mining workers: Desertion, cash payments, and the emergence of the *k'ajchas* and *trapiches*

Research shows that the number of *mita* workers declined significantly from 1630 to 1640 and that silver production in Potosí decreased simultaneously in line with the continuing fall in the size of the indigenous *mita* population, as can be seen from the following graph:

16 For an overview of the late 16th century, see Bakewell, 1989; Zagalsky, 2014; Bridikhina, 2015.

Potosí silver production and number of *mitayos*, 1545 – 1817

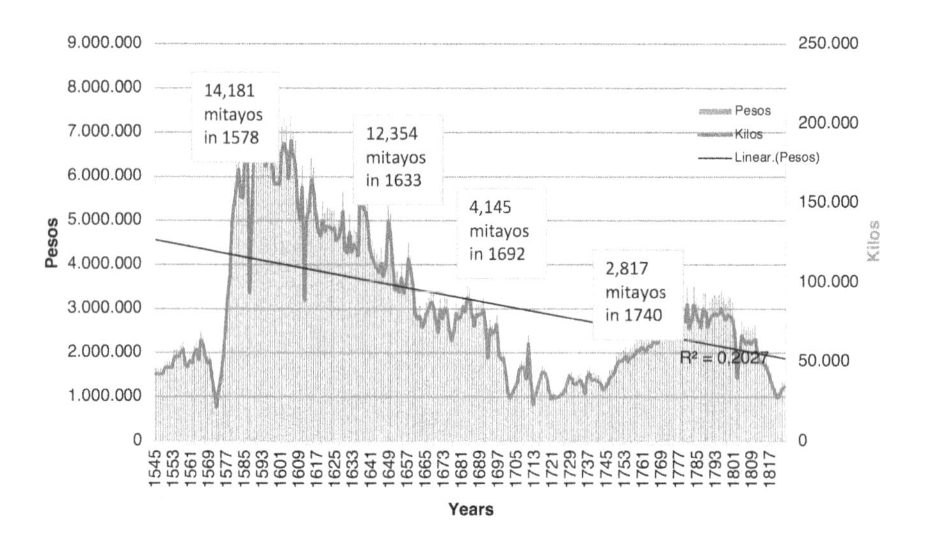

Figure 1: Richard Garner, www.insidemydesk.com, graph by author.

The decline in the number of *mitayos* observed in the graph conceals the system of cash payments. Thus, from 1606 – 1608 at least twenty to 25 percent and perhaps up to 50 percent of the *mita* was paid off in cash rather than labour (Cole, 1985: 37 – 38; Zagalsky, 2014: 385). Mine owners came to speak of *indios* in terms of money (Bakewell, 1989: 123 – 124, 197; Cole, 1985: 57)[17] and it is important to emphasise that the sums paid were quite considerable. The sum delivered by just two towns in the Pacajes province totalled 16,408 *pesos* and the province as a whole brought in 50,000 *pesos* around 1660 to 1665 (Cole, 1985: 37). The amount of money extracted from the *mitayos* overall could reach as much as 587,000 *pesos*, that is double the tax income generated by silver mining in Potosí for the Crown (around 300,000 *pesos* according to a report by Cruz, cf. Cole, 1985: 92). So, how did the communities obtain such sums?

17 There is a distinction between *mita* payments and "pocket Indians" (*indios de faltriquera*), although the two phenomena were linked. In principle the sum paid by those who did not go to the *mita* was to be used to employ others as hired workers or *mingas*. However, when such payments went directly into the pockets of the mine owners, they were referred to as "*indios de faltriquera*." That was considered a form of blatant extortion and corruption, because the money was not used for production.

A number of different individual and collective strategies have been explored in the literature. Common ones included temporary work, selling one's labour on the *haciendas* (large estates) or in cities, and the sale of produce whether from privately or commonly owned land (the so-called community wealth, or *bienes de comunidad*). Another way for them to obtain cash was by appointing *indios colquehaque* (literally "silver Indians"), in the communities (Sánchez Albornoz, 1978: 103). The *colquehaque* paid significant sums that freed them from their own obligations as well as those of other members of their communities. Other income could be obtained through leasing community lands and above all through active participation in all the business and trade conducted by the members of the communities, using their livestock.

Another important way to earn money was to work for higher salaries as *minga* labourers in the mines, including Potosí. There was therefore an articulation between the two statuses and types of labour, because the *mitayos* might be *mingas* in their idle or rest weeks. Indeed, certain sources suggest a very early date for this practice. Cole pointed out that by 1603 as many as 600 *minga* labourers might in fact be resting *mitayos* (see Cole, 1985: 30). Meanwhile a little-used source from 1692 reveals that Viceroy Toledo might even have intentionally built such opportunity into the *mita* system when he designed it. The Prosecutor of the Audiencia of Lima explained that Toledo ordered the *mitayos* to "rest for two [weeks] like this because they had this relief, and so that in the weeks of rest they could *mingar* (that is, rent themselves out) and apply themselves to the extraction of metals, or work their smelters, foundries, and other enterprises that are more convenient than the daily wage of the mita" (emphasis mine; AGI Charcas 272f. 11v. – 12; see also Cole, 1985: 32 and 43). The Prosecutor also explained that La Palata had proposed a reduction in the number of weeks of rest,[18] which provoked vociferous complaint from the Indians due both to the "short rest" and the fact that they "would not be able to *mingar*" and thereby earn 7 *pesos* instead of only 29 *reales*.[19] The ability to labour as a *minga* to escape the condition of *mitayo* must therefore be considered another powerful explanation for the decrease in the number of *mita* labourers.

Thus, data supports a point made by Smith (2004)–that escape from the *mita* did not mean escape from mining nor from the city of Potosí, because the mining centre was also highly attractive in other ways, offering alternative

18 This was because he wanted fewer Indians leaving the communities for continuous work. From 2,829 that he distributed, he saw an increase in the total to only 5,658, because by having only one week off it was only necessary to double the number (AGI Charcas 272 12v–f.13).
19 AGI Charcas 272f. f. 48.

economic opportunities.[20] The constant absenteeism of the *mitayos* must therefore be considered as a form of desertion, although it hides a multitude of different strategies. Absenteeism, geographical mobility, and desertion constitute some of the best-known expressions of individual and collective strategies of resistance used by workers in different parts of the world. They were also a way of negotiating better conditions and escaping, for some temporarily, for others permanently. Walking or running away, "voting with your feet," has always been one of the most important acts in many societies dominated by non-free labour (see, for example, van Rossum and Kamp, 2016). The peculiarity in Potosí was that one of the objectives of absenteeism was to be able to afford to pay to be exempt from the *mita* system and so to be able to take advantage of the better opportunities on offer in the very same mines.

The decrease in the number of *mitayos* in Potosí, together with the decrease in production, led the *azogueros* (owners of the mines and refineries) to demand a series of measures in their favour. By 1645 they had presented a document entitled "*Pretensiones de la Villa Imperial de Potosí*" which proposed a reactivation plan consisting of a reduction in taxation by the Crown (from the quinto or twenty per cent to a tithe or ten per cent), measures to facilitate the supply of mercury, and a new census of the indigenous population (Cole, 1985: 52–53; González Casasnovas, 2000: 93). The census was to serve as the basis for a reorganisation of the *mitayos* to be sent to Potosí. This was the context for the census of the indigenous population carried out by Viceroy Duque de La Palata in 1689, which showed a significant decrease and altered the distribution of the indigenous population compared to figures for 1570 to 1575. In order to return to, or at least approach, the figures of the early *mita* of the late sixteenth century, the Spanish Crown now found it necessary to include the *forasteros* (indigenous migrants), who had appeared in the provinces subject to the *mita*, and to extend the *mita* to a number of formerly exempt provinces.

La Palata's reforms gave rise both to general opposition and serious analysis, which led to a great debate among the colonial authorities about the *mita*. To analyse La Palata's proposed policy, in 1691 the new Viceroy Monclova summoned a council. The council comprised judges from the Audiencia *de Lima*, the Protector of Indians, the former *corregidor* (governor) of Potosí, and a representative of the mine owners. One of those involved, the Prosecutor Matías Lagunez, left an impressive and voluminous plea calling for the complete abolition of the *mita*. Indeed, it is Lagunez's three main points that have been taken up by historians.

---

20 Gil Montero reached the same conclusion in her recent research on the Visita de La Palata, where she observed that most of the indigenous people from a community were living in Potosí.

First, said Lagunez, there were two *mitas*, the legally sanctioned one, and the one that operated in practice, a position also advocated by González Casasnovas (*ibid.:* 274 and 29). Secondly, Lagunez pointed out that the *mitayos*' labour in the mines subsidised the rest of mining through the low wages paid to them (*ibid.:* 303 and 311), a perspective also supported by Tandeter, who stated that the mining centre in Potosí could not have survived under free-market conditions. The third element of Lagunez's plea was that the "horror of the *mita*" resulted in great mortality, which had brought with it a decline in the indigenous population in the provinces subjected to this labour regime.

Matías Lagunez sought to counter another view that existed at the time, which was that population decline should not be blamed on migration (from the provinces subject to the *mita*, to provinces free of it), but should be attributed directly to the mortality created by labouring in the *mita* itself. He claimed that 58,075 Indians had been "consumed" or "annihilated," amounting to two-thirds of the population counted by Viceroy Toledo in the final few decades of the sixteenth century.[21] Lagunez used this claim to support his attempt to persuade the Crown to abolish the *mita*. The role of *mita* labour in population decline is a topic yet to be fully addressed even in today's historical and demographic literature. Whatever the truth, the older contributions of Sánchez Albornoz, Sempat Assadourian, and Thierry Saignes show that significant migrations occurred as part of the indigenous peoples' strategies for escaping the *mita*, as they took refuge in other towns and communities as *forasteros*, or on the *haciendas*, as *yanaconas* or, ultimately, in the cities (Saignes, 1985: 8).

For the time being, however, it is essential to recognise that Lagunez's interpretation formed part of an important conflict at the time. The matter is complex, but we can say that the Christian viewpoint, pious and humanitarian as it might seem, conceals confrontation and struggle among different economic interests over the greater or lesser control they would have over the workforce.[22] For many sectors in the viceroyalty of Peru the assignment of *mitayos* from sixteen large provinces to benefit just a few silver miners was a policy of absolute priv-

---

21 Toledo had counted 91,498 native tribute Indians. The La Palata inspection, one century later, would find no more than 33,423. AGI Charcas 272. 1261 fs. See particularly f. 99–200. We are conducting an analysis of this document.

22 The more eminent religious authorities considered that altering the geography of the structures and (implicit) agreements seeking greater migration to the mines could mean, as González Casasnovas has shown, endangering agricultural production or that large estates would be left without workers, putting the Catholic Church's own income at risk (income which came in the form of tithes, 2000: 256 and 277). Cole, 1985: 125.

ilege and amounted to a subsidy for the mines, and therefore worked to the detriment of other regions and sectors.

The discussions stimulated during the last decades of the seventeenth century were a result of the three strategies adopted to either confront or evade the *mita*. Let us recall them briefly. First, there were the cash payments made by communities and individual *mitayos* to avoid the *mita* and to pay others to take their place. To pay to be exempted from *mitayo* service required continuous forays into the marketplace (the *trajines*[23] – everyday trade brought by the llama caravans – is fundamental here, cf. Glave, 1989 and Medinaceli, 2010). Secondly, there was the tactic of contriving to not be registered and counted as an absent labourer. Such absentees continually lowered the labour quotas sent to Potosí. Thirdly, there was the option to migrate to provinces free from the *mita*. All three processes are considered in the literature as consequences of the *mita* and as illustrating its impact. At the same time, they should be recognised as the indigenous population's main actions, interventions, and active responses to the *mita*. In the matter of labouring in the *mita* of Potosí, I have already pointed out that both absenteeism and migration were forms of resistance through desertion. It is clear therefore that although the *mita* continued, it was greatly diminished as a consequence of the actions of the *mitayos* and the debates and decisions of the authorities. As a result, labour dynamics became much more articulated and ultimately more complex.

During the 18th century other actors emerged, or became more visible, such as the *k'ajchas*, *trapiches*, and *trapicheros*. Their world expresses the creation of an economic system that paralleled that of the principal mines and refineries, with the same processing chain, from the extraction of ore from the hill to smelting and finally obtaining silver for sale.

Extraction was the responsibility of the *k'ajchas*, who entered the hill on the weekends. Although the practice might have existed earlier, the *k'ajchas* gained greater power during the mid-1700s.[24] Thus, on Thursday, 4 February 1751, in the middle of Carnival, the Caccha Cruz festival was celebrated, sponsored by *the trapicheros*, when the Cross was conveyed from the *k'ajchas* chapel to one of the indigenous parishes of the Villa to celebrate mass there.[25] The 1751 festival, which was surely already established, took place against a background of bubbling tension between the *k'ajchas* and the authorities, some of whom sought to

---

23 The word comes from the Vulgar Latin *Traginare* or *tragino* meaning to drag things, to pull, to trail.

24 AGI Charcas 481, AGI Charcas 435; ABNB ALP Minas 25/13 and ABNB ALP 28/1.

25 According to Arzáns, the Chapel of the Cacchas already existed in 1725, as did the celebration of the Holy Cross (Vela, III: 201).

eradicate the *k'ajchas* and demolish their *trapiches*. The *alcalde de minas* said that when he had climbed the hill "they wanted to kill him... because those cacchas they had risen up... to kill all who opposed them." He also recalled the death of a guard and regretted that when they went to capture four *k'ajchas*, their companions "in a swelling crowd, knocked over the Royal Justice, and took away their prisoners [...]." The authorities, "with the zeal and experience and knowledge of more than twenty years," managed to arrest one of the main captains, Patapata,[26] in June 1752. The prisoner was finally executed by order of the *corregidor* (governor), Ventura de Santelices, because he considered the prisoner to be the captain of the *k'ajchas* and, also in 1752, Mayor Urquizu reported that he had arrested "Vicente Santiesteban, known by the name the Equeqho, one of the principal Cagchas."[27] "Ekeko" is, to this day, the god of abundance, and the nickname given to Vicente might therefore have been a reference to the characteristics of that god. Ekeko is a man who carries all his tools, and everything else he needs to keep body and soul together. He represents the aspiration that none of life's necessities should be lacking. Vicente, the mining Ekeko, undoubtedly went loaded down with all the tools needed to work in the mine, as miners generally did when they climbed the hill. The name might have been similarly connected with the wealth and abundance associated with Agustín Quespi in Arzans' story, itself attributed to Vicente Santiesteban, alias el Ekeko.

The *k'ajchas* took their ore to the so-called *trapiches*. A *trapiche* consisted of an installation in which there was a crusher, with a stone "fly-wheel" that moved over a base stone to grind the ore. An inspection in 1761 to 1762 described the existence of 220 *trapiches*, of which 58 were in the hands of the Spanish and 160 (73 percent) owned by the indigenous populations of the ten curates or indigenous parishes of the city (La Ranchería), where *mitayos* also arrived. *Mestizos* and *mulattos* also owned a few of the *trapiches*.

Documents exist which indicate that the "*yndios trapicheros*" were "employed" as *k'ajchas*, *pongos* (who worked inside the mines), *palliris* (the workers who selected the material), and *barreteros* (the hewers who worked the rock face).[28]. The new governor of Potosí also pointed out that the *curacas* and captains of the *mita*, as well as *mitayos*, *pongos*, and *apiris* (carriers), were also *k'ajchas*. He claimed that they numbered up to 4,000, a figure similar to that for the *mitayos*, with 235 *trapiches*, which would have been built by "curacas and their

---

26 ABNB ALP Minas 25 13, f. 420–421v.

27 ABNB ALP Minas 25 13, f. 402, 18 July 1752; see also Tandeter, 1992: 140–142.

28 AGI Charcas 481, No. 19.

captains responsible for the delivery of the *mita*." Although testimony might exaggerate the mixing that occurred between different types of labourers and different working conditions, it is essential to underline that the people who ran the *trapiches* were related to or might even be, in some cases, the same people who worked extracting ore as *k'ajchas*. Where indigenous authorities, such as the *curacas* of the parishes, were actively involved in the *trapiches*, then both the local population and the *mitayos*, who came to those parishes, were involved in running that particular circuit of production. In order to obtain silver, they had to learn to coexist with the *azogueros*, who benefited from the obligatory labour of the *mitayos*. Taking on the positions of *k'ajcha* and *trapichero* therefore constituted a strategy for taking part in and affecting the economic activity of mining, and undoubtedly a way to seek greater autonomy and profit.

Another important detail from the 1761 to 1762 inspection of the *trapiches* is that we see that a number of women owned mills alongside the male owners. Moreover, certain names, like Bartholomé Canchi, Blas Condori, and María Sissa, are clearly indigenous, although other names recorded included Juan Morales, Joseph Montoya, and Luisa Guevara. Such patronymics do not mean, however, that we are dealing primarily with a non-indigenous population. While some of the *trapichero* names suggest they belonged to *mestizos* or Spaniards, other documentation reveals that they were in fact indigenous individuals. For example, in 1777 one Blaz de Subieta made a request on behalf of his wife, Antonia Ybarra, for a *trapiche* that she had inherited from her first husband, Don Melchor Gutiérrez. Looking at that document, we realised that these were not only indigenous people but specifically that they were indigenous *mitayos* from the Orurillo ayllu, and that Blaz de Subieta was a *zambo*, meaning of mixed African and indigenous ancestry.[29]

The silver obtained in these *trapiches* was sold to the Bank[30] or to other *rescatiris (or buyers)*. The Bank's accounts for 1762 refer to more than 500 *k'ajchas* and *trapicheros*, including women, who sold, in more than 1,500 transactions, a total of almost 200,000 *pesos* worth of silver, representing sixteen per cent of the silver sold by the *azogueros* in that year. Most of the *trapicheros* carried

29 AHP, Cabildo Intendencia, CGI, 288 70 1777.

30 The Banco de San Carlos, under the full control of the Crown, was established in 1779, although there was already a "Bank" that bought the silver from 1752 onwards (Banco de Rescates, 1752–1754). For a history of banks of this type, see Luz María Real Cédula de Incorporación de el Banco de Potosí a la Real Hacienda y ordenanzas para su régimen y gobierno Mendez, 1992; Guillermo Mira, 1997. For its constitution, see AGI Buenos Aires 440. Royal Certificate of Incorporation of the Bank of Potosí into the Royal Treasury and ordinances for its regime and government (Madrid, 1795).

out only a single transaction (327 people or 63 percent), so we assume they were mainly labourers, perhaps *mitayos*, who very occasionally managed to increase their wages or generate additional income. At the other extreme were those who sold greater quantities of silver for large amounts of money. The world of the *trapicheros* therefore contained great internal variety (Barragán, 2014; 2017).[31]

An interesting point for emphasis is that the emergence of the *k'ajchas / trapiche* group effectively created a quasi-parallel economic circuit alongside that of the guild of *azogueros*, which gave rise to intense debate and conflict among the authorities. While a number of *azoguero* businessmen and local authorities proposed radical policies intended to destroy the *trapiches* and advocated prohibition of the practice of the *k'ajchas*, others among their superiors, including such authorities as the governors, the chiefs of the Royal Treasury, the Viceroy, and the Indian Council (Consejo de Indios), took a firm but tolerant stance, because they reaped the benefits of buying the silver (Barragán, 2014). The *trapiches* were never destroyed, partly because the silver they generated "increased the royal tithes" and helped fill the Crown's coffers, but also because of the very large number of people involved.

I proposed in another work (2017) that instead of considering *k'ajchas* work as a "popular weekend activity" as Tandeter suggests, we should see it more in terms of a "popular economy." Popular in the sense of being an activity that was not controlled by the traditional mine owners and refiners, but also because of its magnitude, the large number and diversity of people who took part (which included *mitayos*, *mulattos*, *mestizos*, and poor Spaniards), and the sums they obtained. It was popular too because it was the result of a balance of power. Nevertheless, we should take care not to exaggerate this "popular" feature, for it is clear that while the *k'ajchas* and *trapiches* were unified in opposition to the *azogueros* supported by the Spanish Crown, behind the appearance of unity we find a highly heterogeneous and unequal group. The situation in which *mitayos* could become *k'ajchas* and work in the *trapiches*, which were fed by other workers too, contrasts markedly with the speech given by Victorián de Villaba, who was the *Fiscal* (prosecutor) and Protector of Indians. De Villaba used his speech to challenge the *mita*, thereby prompting a great debate at the end of the 18th century.

---

31 AHP Banco de San Carlos BSC 313, Libro donde se sientan los marcos que se traen al rescate de los trapicheros de esta rivera, 1761–1764. For the *azogueros*, AHP BSC-360 Libro donde se sientan los marcos de plata que los señores Azogueros de esta Villa traen a rescatar a este Banco y mercadería que corre a cargo del Maestre de Campo, 1759–1762.

Villaba's Indian slaves and the great debate

Victorián de Villaba's *Discurso en contra de la Mita* of 1793[32] must be understood in the local context of an increase in the number of *mitayos*, but also in the global context of the political economy of the time (Genovesi, Filangieri, and the Neapolitans[33]). His writing was deeply challenging because he characterised the *mita* as "temporary slavery for the Indians."[34] Although it was not the first time that the *mita* had been so described, his allegation had great effect both at the time and many decades later, as we will see.

Villaba explained that because "the voices of vested interest had prevailed, suffocating those of humanity," he sought to create "doubt" about what was held to be true;[35] and he did it. He managed to shake up existing policies, giving rise to a heated debate. The documents published by Ricardo Levene in 1946 are just some examples of an important and voluminous body of writing produced between 1793 and 1801.[36]

The significance of the debate was that it placed money or the "blood of the body politic" at the centre of waves of discussion, each of which was more expansive and intense than the last, involving officials from different authorities and cities, from the Court, the *azogueros*, and the religious and indigenous authorities. Equally important was that Villaba's discourse led to a series of inquiries into the *mita* in different regions and communities. Finally, he questioned the similarity of the Indian vassals to the vassals of the Iberian Peninsula,

32 This "*Discurso*" was published by Levene, 1946. Villaba was also the author of *Apuntes para una Reforma de España sin trastorno del gobierno monárquico ni la religión* (1797). Villaba was born in Aragon and died in Charcas in 1802. In 1783 he requested a place in the Audiencia of Buenos Aires and in 1789 was appointed Prosecutor of the Audiencia de Charcas, where he arrived in 1791 after having spent a year in Buenos Aires (Buechler, 1989, T. I: 223–224). It was fundamentally Ricardo Levene (1946) who brought him out of oblivion, and for him he was a forerunner of emancipation. More recent works about Villaba include Portillo (2007) and Morelli (2006 and 2010).

33 Villaba was Professor of Law at the University of Huesca and translated fragments of the voluminous work of Filangieri (Ciencia de la Legislación, 1780, 5 vols), and the book *Lecciones de Comercio by Genovesi.* For more about the Neapolitans, see Morelli and Portillo, 2007.

34 Claiming they were slaves was deeply challenging since, in the 16th century, Vitoria had already defended the rationality of the Indians, attacking the theory that they could be slaves (Brading, 1993: 108), while Las Casas developed the argument that all men, even barbarians, had the right to property, self-government, and freedom (*ibid.*: 114).

35 Villaba, "*Discurso*" in Levene, 1946: XXX.

36 Francisco de Paula Sanz's response to Villaba's text runs to more than 150 pages. AGI Charcas 697. *Contextacion al discurso sobre la mita de Potosi escrito en La Plata a 9 de Marzo de 1795.*

which broadened the discussion beyond the labour of the *mitayos* in the mines. What was being called into doubt was the very right to force a part of the population to work, which recalled the famous disputes of the late 16th and 17th centuries.

The initial debate took place between Villaba in his capacity as Prosecutor of Charcas and Protector of Indians, and Francisco de Paula Sanz, who was Governor Intendant of Potosí and was supported by his advisor Pedro Vicente Cañete[37] and the guild of *azogueros*. Two of the most important aspects articulated and debated were first, the importance of silver as the "nerves of the State and the blood of the body politic," and whether the exploitation involved was in fact justified in the name of the public good, which had been the argument constantly advanced ever since the institution of the *mita*. The second important question was whether the allegedly indolent nature of the indigenous people constituted sufficient reason to force them to work.

For Villaba, money did not make a nation's happiness and Potosí itself was an example of how "in mining countries, one sees only the opulence of the few, alongside the misery of infinite numbers of people." He stated, on the one hand, that money itself did not amount to wealth, but was in fact nothing more than an item of universal merchandise; on the other hand, he said that the mines were not public.[38] Paula Sanz argued, however, that Villaba was mistaken in defining as public only the "immediate" products of the "Nation or the Sovereign."[39] In Paula Sanz's view there were certain domains that the King could not transfer to his vassals, and thereby award himself the right to royalties from them; such domains were destined for the public good, as was the case with mines throughout Europe.[40] Nevertheless, the sovereign certainly had the right to a

---

37 The Prosecutor was the defender of the interests of the Royal Treasury and he was also in charge of the defence and protection of the Indians because, according to the jurist Juan de Solórzano Pereira, the "dejected and miserable" causes of the Indians belonged to the King. Cf. Carolina Jurado, 2004: 21. Pedro Vicente Cañete was born in Asunción (Paraguay) and studied in Santiago de Chile. He was Advisor and War Auditor to Viceroy Pedro de Cevallos in Buenos Aires. In 1793 he was appointed Adviser to the Intendency of Potosí. In 1787 he wrote the *Guía histórica, geográfica, física, política civil y legal del Gobierno e Intendencia de la Provincia de Potosí, and later the Código Carolino de Ordenanzas Reales de las Minas de Potosí y demás provincias del Río de la Plata.* In 1803 he was transferred to La Plata, where he was Adviser to the President of the Audiencia. See Gunnar Mendoza, 2005.

38 "Discurso". In: Levene, 1946: XXXII – XXXIII.

39 AGN Colonia Gobierno 14 8 8. Cuaderno No. 1. *Sobre la Mita de Potosí.* Contiene la representación del Gremio de Azogueros de aquella villa con varios documentos. 1795, f. 27v.

40 *Ibid.* f.29 – 30.

share of the produce in the form of the *quinto* (a 20 percent tax on production).[41] Paula Sanz also considered that "in these colonies" there was no other branch of industry as important as mining, and that the *mita* was necessary for "the good of the State".[42]

Another of Villaba's fundamental arguments concerned the need for forced labour in the name of the indolence attributed to the indigenous peoples.[43] Introducing the comparison with Spain, Villaba considered that "laziness" was not an argument to "enslave them in the mines," and that there was no possible justification for "the slavery of men" and even less when humanity was sacrificed to vested interests.[44] Moreover, Villaba saw the ascribed indolence itself as the result of despotism. Finally, he argued that the Indians did not want to work because they were labouring "for another (or others) and not for themselves."

For Paula Sanz on the other hand, the labour of the *mita* already existed at the time of the Incas. He pointed out that Toledo did nothing more than remake the measures of the Inca Guayna Capac. Paula Sanz claimed that there had been "a contract" with the *caciques*, and that forced service had simply been resurrected, but "changed into a voluntary rather than a mandatory contract" under conditions that were not only much more humane but furthermore paid.[45] Paula Sanz stated categorically that it could not be considered slavery. However, he also referred to the laziness and rusticity of the natives, as well as their refusal to work, as justification for making it obligatory. He said that if there were such beings as "industrious Indian volunteers", he would be the first to oppose the *mita*.[46]

As a result of the discussion and debate, a series of inquiries was carried out. Villaba requested reports on the damage caused by the *mita*, from the Protector of Indians in the city of Potosí,[47] the priests of the Chaqui doctrines in the area of Porco and those of the Moscarí doctrine in the area of Chayanta, both in the municipality of Potosí, and from the Intendency of Cochabamba and Puno. One of the first reports was that of Francisco de Viedma, Governor of Cochabamba.[48] He described the journey of "these wretches" with their women – some of

41 *Ibid.* f.37v.
42 *Ibid.* f.177.
43 Villaba, 1793. In: Levene, 1946: XXXI.
44 *Ibid.*: XXXVI – XXXVIII.
45 AGN Colonia Gobierno 14 8 8. Cuaderno No. 1. f. 84 – 85.
46 *Ibid.* f. 177.
47 ABNB. ALP Minas 129/7.
48 ABNB. ALP Minas 129/8.

them pregnant – and children, their abominable accommodation in Potosí, and the jobs they were given. As Matías Lagunez had done a century before, de Viedma emphasised the distribution of fixed quotas that could not humanly be delivered, so that people had to resort to paying others to assist. Thus, for two weeks of labour individuals received only six days' wages – or even less if there was some problem.[49] De Viedma also referred to the situation in Santiago del Paso, in Cochabamba, which had only 34 inhabitants, of whom each year 17 had to be sent to the *mita*. He compared the *mita* to a war that would decimate an army and which would lead to "the extermination of humanity."[50] Viedma's conclusions were important: he argued that "His Majesty" probably lost more in tribute than he gained in the tax on precious metals, as the profits from silver went to the complete "private benefit of the *azogueros*."[51] Here Intendant Viedma was balancing what the indigenous population could provide in tributes, which he considered could amount to an income greater than that received by the Crown treasury in tax from silver. He pondered, in other words, whether the royal coffers ought to give preference to agriculture, which would be based on indigenous communities and private farms, or to mining.

Francisco de Paula Sanz made the counter argument. I would like to highlight here, the enormous difficulty businessmen and authorities had in controlling the workforce. Paula Sanz clearly demonstrates the mine owners' limited control and saw it as justification for coercion. He states that there was not a single production site that was not constantly "crying out" for labour, and that not even cash and "high" wages paid in advance could attract the indigenous people to work.[52] The authorities had also requested a series of inquiries from which a picture emerged of the *mita* in total "chaos and disorder": in fact the *mita* of Porco was considered "ungovernable" because they were unable to meet their quotas, and those who did go to the *mita* deserted at night, even taking the tools with them. More importantly, the authorities reported that the *mitayos* had a tendency to buy themselves out of their obligation, an ancient custom that already existed in the seventeenth century and was quite the norm in the communities of Paria, which were considered to be very well-off (or well situated). The reports mentioned too that the communities of Chayanta had left the *ingenios* without workers, and that the workers from the Province of Cochabamba had fled. Finally, the Sicasica communities, along with the *enteradores* and *cu-*

49 *Ibid.* f. 2 and 49.
50 *Ibid.*
51 *Ibid.* 52–5.
52 *Ibid.* f. 54v.–56.

racas charged with enforcing the mita, dedicated themselves to commerce in the city of Potosí and its surroundings, and once they had finished, they returned to their towns and paid most of the "personal service of their people" in cash.[53]

In the context of this debate, in March 1795 Marcelino Lupa, *cacique* of Moscarí, announced an indigenous rebellion against the so-called new *mita*, which naturally complicated the situation further (Buechler, 1989, T. I: 248 y 250; 259 – 263). Paula Sanz insisted on "the falsehood of the rumours that had spread of the rebellion" and blamed the archbishop, clergy, and, above all, Prosecutor Villaba for the writings, debates, and movements opposing good government and the laws of the kingdom (*ibid.:* 252). Paula Sanz investigated the conduct of the priests, concluding that the number of Indians who served in the churches each year was more than 1,000, which exceeded even the number of those who served in Potosí. The supreme colonial authority in Potosí proceeded to appoint new *mestizo caciques* and began to regulate the conduct of the clergy. Soon after, in May 1795, Paula Sanz was denounced and accused of having violated ecclesiastical jurisdiction. Paula Sanz retorted that sending the regular *mita* contingents had been compromised because word had spread that "the *mita* had been completely abolished."[54]

Various corporations of Potosí then issued the *Representación Apologética de la muy noble Imperial Villa de Potosí*, uniting against Prosecutor Villaba because

> he previously published a pamphlet in which he openly confronted it, describing it as tyrannical, without any respect for the laws that authorise it, or the slightest consideration for the magistrates [...] much less for the impressions that [...] to the detriment of the public and the treasury, would forcibly cause, in our contributing provinces, a situation so decided by the freedom of the Indians, as so entirely contrary to the supposed despotism attributed to the mine owners.[55]

They blamed Villaba for his reliance on the priests, while they, the political elite of Potosí, opposed the "theocratic government" of the clergy who enjoyed "personal services", and the "scandalous contributions demanded by the priests."[56] They claimed that this was the reason for their opposition to the *mita,* and that such fierce complaints had never been heard before "against the alleged tyranny

53 ABNB ALP Minas 129/5.

54 The Royal Decree of 3 August 1796 suspended the new *mita*. Buechler, 1989, T. I: 265 – 267 y 273.

55 ABNB Minas 1796 129/13 F. 2/10v.

56 ABNB Minas 1796 129/13f.10 128; 16 134 y 16v–134v.

of the *azogueros*."[57] They also accused the Audiencia of meddling in "government" affairs, the exclusive domain of the Governor of Potosí,[58] and openly accused the Prosecutor of acting as the representative for the indigenous tyrants and oppressors.

In the *azoguero's Representación Apologética*, we once again find important indications of the actions of the indigenous population. We learn that a "gang" of more than 500 people assaulted the subdelegate of one of the Potosí provinces, forcing him to dismiss one of the indigenous chiefs named by Paula Sanz and accused of the "alleged sale of *mitayos*." The highest provincial authority, the subdelegate, was thus forced to accept the will of the indigenous authorities.[59] Finally, the *azogueros* complained, alluding to Villaba and his collaborators, that "powerful men" were listened to and obeyed by the natives, causing the ruin of sovereignty and royal jurisdiction, which they said should be considered a true crime of state, of *lèse-majesté*, and against the country.[60] The delegitimisation of the *mita* was therefore enormous.

The Potosí authorities accused the *caciques* of allying themselves with Villaba, who was leading them to insurrection by calling the colonial ministers and authorities' tyrants, the *mita* inhumane and barbarous, and the mine owners of Potosí "greedy and insatiable for the sweat and blood of the Indian."[61]

The debate in which Villaba was involved was thus a discussion about forced labour, coercion, and the right to demand that indigenous people be forced to work. Villaba's arguments show continuities but also radical upheavals. Among the latter, it should be noted that once "indolence" was considered to be the result, rather than the cause, of the obligation to labour, the perception of the

57 See ABNB Minas 1796 129/13 f. 3/121. "Validating the barbarism, the rusticity, and the ignorance of the Indians, the seditious ideas that the *mita* service was unjust and tyrannical in its entirety was revived with yet more heat, as proclaimed in word and writing by their Protector" (*ibid.*: f. 4v – 122v).

58 ABNB Minas 1796 129/13 f.6v–124v. On the priests and the *mita* see also ABNB, ALP Minas 129/6.

59 "[A]nd this good magistrate avoided [...] the risk to his life and that the cancer spread to the other *repartimientos*" (ABNB Minas 1796 129/13 4v – 122v / 5 – 123).

60 ABNB Minas 1796 129/13 f. 137 – 19.

61 "They could not have used more effective means to promote it than to argue that the service of the *mita* is inhuman and barbarous, to characterise the ministers who support it as insensitive tyrants: the miners of Potosí as greedy and insatiable for the sweat and blood of the Indian, at whose cost they gather their wealth; the Subdelegate a despot who removes the disaffected *caciques* from his service and replaces them with adherents to his ideas of increasing the *mita*; not even the Governor of the Province is pardoned, as they dare to represent the Viceroy as one from whom no justice can be expected in favour of the Indian against a tribute collector who collaborated in sending the *mita* [...]" (Villaba. In: Levene: 1946: LXVIII).

Indian was completely inverted. Henceforth then, the *mita* could be viewed as unjust and oppressive, and the indigenous people as its victims. Comparing the Indians' situation with that of vassals in Spain was also fundamental, because it allowed Villaba to affirm the "uniformity" and equality of men ("all men are the same in general") as well as to explain some of the actions of indigenous peoples as resulting from "the natural mistrust of the oppressed."[62] It is also possible that in the course of the debate itself, Villaba voiced, at least at certain moments, a much more radical discourse:

> Wretched and miserable Indians [...] you are indolent, brutalised, drunk, thieves, still without religion, still superstitious, and you are not counted when it comes to the Silver that is disseminated by the State! Fortunate azogueros then [...]. You are Knights, you are illustrious, you are human, you reap the benefits, you are disinterested and all the good of the State is attributed to your efforts![63]

Although nothing written by Villaba after 1797 appears to have survived, his arguments were soon reused in various local files and other writings.

Conclusions

The *mita* established at the end of the sixteenth century remained in existence for more than two and a half centuries, and, as Zagalsky pointed out, it remained largely unaltered for much of that time. However, as Cole suggested, it also experienced changes and metamorphoses. González Casasnovas remarked that there were significant differences between the *mita* as it was intended and how it was practised (following Matías Lagunez in the 17th century), but it should be noted that the differences were the result of a correlation of forces. What I am keen to highlight here is the fact that those changes should be attributed not only to the discussions and debates of the colonial authorities, but also to the actions of the *mitayo* workers and their communities.

We have seen that the *mitayo* contingent very quickly diminished in number owing to population decline but also because of the strategies deployed by those affected. However, the colonial authorities delegitimised it as well. All those involved in the *mita* seem to have sought higher wages and more autonomy and independence, giving rise to diverse and potentially interrelated working situations. It is therefore important not think in terms of groups of *mitayos* or coerced

62 Villaba, Contraréplica, in: Levene, 1946: XLIV.
63 *Ibid.* LI.

and forced labourers, as completely distinct from free labourers, *mingas*, or *k'ajchas* and *trapiches*, who were independent or self-employed. One needs to remember too that a large number of the *mitayos* were also peasants, growing crops or keeping livestock in the communities subject to the *mita*, and that they would move from one type of labour to another. Nevertheless, the starting point remains the *mita*. The case of mining in Potosí allows us to think about how different labour relationships were articulated, and the consequences for those relationships (De Vito, 2017). There are interesting connections because we are not dealing with separate free and unfree labour forces, but rather a continuum, as has been emphasised in the literature (van der Linden and Rodríguez, 2014; Brass *et al.*, 1997). Here, at least in part, there were cases in which the same labourers moved through different types of work.

Nevertheless, escaping the *mita* required large amounts of money and was an enormous drain on economic resources. The strategy of paying to escape *mita* obligations required continuous and systematic ventures into the marketplace, so that nowadays it is necessary to rethink the crucial importance of the *trajines* and indigenous participation in the markets (Harris, Larson, and Tandeter, 1987; Glave, 1989). In addition to the resistance which James Scott describes as the deployment of infra-political everyday weapons, we should consider too the existence of the agreements and pacts of reciprocity of rights and obligations discussed by Tristan Platt, and the open rebellions analysed by various authors. Nor should we forget that *mitayos*, *k'ajchas*, and *trapicheros* all participated systematically in the new economy.

The understanding of the *mita* must take into account the remarkable variety of strategies, described above, that were used to confront it. It is also unquestionable that, from the perspective of the colonial authorities, there were individuals who became more critical towards the end of the colonial period, as the *mita* became both a symbol and a paradigm of oppression. In 1802 one of the most radical characters in Buenos Aires, Mariano Moreno, presented his dissertation in Charcas on the labour of the *mitayos*, asking to what extent they should still be used to support mines that were unable to cover their expenses.[64] Only a few years later, in 1809 in the midst of the formation of the first autonomous gov-

---

64 Moreno, 1802–1943: 33. He studied law at the University of Chuquisaca, where he was from 1799 to 1805. He was Secretary of the First Junta of the Government of Buenos Aires. He translated Rousseau's *Social Contract* in 1802, and wrote *La Representación de los Hacendados* in 1809, and the *Plan de Operaciones* and the *Buenos Aires Gazette* in 1810. Moreno and Villaba were linked through Matías Terrazas, a friend of both, in whose library the former was able to read Raynal, Bossuet, and Filangieri (Portillo, 2007: 446). Moreno had also read Viscardo and his *Carta a los Americanos* as a student in Charcas (Brading, 1993: 594).

ernments in defence of the King and in the midst of another open confrontation between the *Audiencia* of Charcas and Potosí, there circulated the famous and anonymous *Diálogo entre el Inca Atahuallpa* and Fernando VII.[65] In it, the *mita* constitutes one of the strongest arguments for questioning and delegitimizing the power of the Spanish King, whom the pamphlet called a tyrant and usurper. The author was clearly returning to the theme addressed seven years earlier in 1802 by Mariano Moreno in his dissertation at the Carolina Academy[66] and 15 years earlier in Villaba's Discurso about the *mita.*[67] That image of the "chains of slavery" would remain even after independence, in Bolivia's own national anthem.

Sources

Archivo y Biblioteca Nacionales de Bolivia (ABNB)

ABNB ALP Minas 25/13. 1752. Competencia de jurisdicción suscitada entre don Ventura de Santelices y Venero, corregidor de Potosí y don Cristóbal de Urquizu, alcalde ordinario de Primer Voto de dicha Villa, respecto al conocimiento de la causa contra los ladrones vulgarmente llamados K'ajchas. Fs. 106.

ABNB ALP Minas 28/1.1751–1753. *Expediente seguido por don Gerónimo Gómez Trigoso y don José Roque de Arismendi, sobre la culpa que les imputó el Corregidor de Potosí en el destrozo y derribamiento de los estribos, puentes y pilares de las vetas de plata, San Miguel y San José, en la labor de Alkjo-barreno, cerro de dicha Villa, cuando esos desperfectos fueron causados por ladrones denominados K'ajchas.* Fs. 457.

ABNB ALP Minas 129/5. 1794–1795. Expediente instruido por don Francisco de Paula Sanz, gobernador intendente de Potosí, sobre los defectos con que hoy corre la mita del Cerro y la Ribera de dicha Villa en los distintos partidos que la contribuyen. Fs. 6

ABNB ALP Minas 129/6. 1795. Reflexiones sobre las diligencias obradas en la Intendencia de Potosí, acerca de la conducta de los curas de Chayanta con motivo del aumento de mita decretado endicho partido, y auto en su razón proveído con remisión a los subdelegados de los partidos de dicha Intendencia para que se publique en forma de bando.

ABNB ALP Minas 129/7. 1795. Informe dirigido por don Juan José de la Rúa, protector de naturales en Potosí, al doctor don Victorián de Villava, fiscal de la Audiencia, sobre los

---

65 The authorship of the *Diálogo* is disputed.

66 Thibauld, 1997.

67 "*Discurso...*", 1793. in Levene, 1946: XXX. One of the viceroys, Count Alba, maintained in the 17th century that the "stones of Potosí and their minerals are bathed in the blood of Indians and that if the money that is extracted from them were squeezed out, more blood would flow than silver," 1946 Appendix XLI.

abusos introducidos en el servicio de los indios mitayos del Cerro y la Ribera de dicha Villa. Fs. 4.

ABNB ALP Minas 129/8. 1795. *Informes que a instancia del doctor don Victorián de Villava, fiscal de la Audiencia de la Plata, expidieron don Francisco de Viedma, gobernador intendente de Cochabamba, el Marqués de Casa Hermosa, gobernador intendente de Puno, el doctor Felipe Antonio Martínez de Iriarte, cura propio de la doctrina de Chaqui, partido de Porco, y vicario pedáneo de Potosí; y el doctor don José de Osa y Palacios, cura propio que fue de la doctrina de Moscari, partido de Chayanta, sobre los perjuicios que a los pueblos de indios de dicha circunscripción se siguen de la mita de Potosí.* Fs. 13.

ABNB ALP Minas 129/13. 1796. Representación apologética de la muy noble Imperial Villa de Potosí, sus tribunales, oficinas y gremios, al excelentísimo señor Virrey del Perú, sobre los acontecimientos de la provincia de Chayanta con motivo de la nueva mita consignada a los caballeros don Juan Bautista Jáuregui y don Luis Orueta, en que incidentemente se trata de las injurias inferidas al señor gobernador intendente, don Francisco de Paula Sanz y demás magistrados y ministros encargados de proveerla en los repartimientos de la misma provincia. Fs. 20.

Archivo Histórico de Potosi

BSC *313 Libro donde se sientan los marcos que se traen al rescate de los trapicheros de esta rivera, 1761–1764.*

BSC 325 *Libro donde se asientan los marcos que se rescatan de los trapicheros de esta Villa y minerales de las provincias de afuera, 1754–1755.*

BSC-360 *Libro donde se asientan los marcos de plata que los señores Azogueros de esta Villa traen a rescatar a este Banco y mercadería que corre a cargo del Maestre de Campo, 1759–1762.*

AHP, *Cabildo Intendencia*, CGI, 288 70 1777.

Archivo General de la Nación, Buenos Aires

AGN Colonia Gobierno 14 8 8. Cuaderno No. 1. *Sobre la Mita de Potosí. Contiene la representación del Gremio de Azogueros de aquella villa con varios documentos. Año de 1795.*

Archivo General de Indias, Sevilla

AGI Charcas 272. *Expediente sobre la mita de Potosí. Año 1692.* 1261 fs.

AGI Charcas 435. Documentos sobre los capchas, 1751–1752.

AGI Charcas 481 No. 19, 1763–1769. Various documents relating to the capchas.

AGI Charcas 700 *Testimonio de la Visita de Cerro Yngenios y Trapiches del Cerro Rico y Ribera de la Imperial Villa de Potosi con expresión de los nombres de las Minas, sus varas, rumbos y frontes. 1789.* 22 de febrero de 1790.
AGI Buenos Aires 440. *Real Cédula de Incorporación del Banco de Potosí a la Real Hacienda y ordenanzas para su régimen y gobierno.* Madrid, 1795.
AGI Charcas 697. Contextacion al discurso sobre la mita de Potosi escrito en La Plata a 9 de marzo de 1795.

References

Abercrombie, Thomas. 1996. "Q'aqchas and La Plebe in rebellion: Carnival vs. Lent in 18-century Potosi." *Journal of Latin American Anthropology* 1 (2): 62–111.
Arzans de Ursúa and Bartolomé Vela. 2012–1965. *Historia de la Villa Imperial de Potosí.* Edited by Lewis Hanke and Gunnar Mendoza. 3 vols. Brown University Press, Providence. Edición Facsimilar de Plural Editores, Casa Nacional de Moneda y Fundación Cultural del Banco Central de Bolivia.
Assadourian, Carlos Sempat. 1982. *El sistema de la economía colonial. Mercado interno, regiones y espacio económico.* Lima: Instituto de Estudios Peruanos.
Bakewell, Peter. 2006 (1989). *Mineros de la Montaña Roja: el trabajo de los indios en Potosí,* 1545–1650. Madrid: Editorial Alianza.
Barragán, Rossana. 2013. 'Indios Esclavos': en torno a la mita minera y los servicios personales, 1790–1812." In *Les révolutions des empires atlantiques. Une perspective transnationale*, edited by Clément Thibaud, Federica Morelli, Alejandro Gomez, and Gabriel Entin. Paris: Pérseides.
Barragán, Rossana. 2014. "K'ajchas, trapiches y plata en el cerro de Potosí en el período colonial." *Anuario de Estudios Bolivianos* 20: 273–320.
Barragán, Rossana. 2017. "Working Silver for the World: Mining Labor and Popular Economy in Colonial Potosi." *Hispanic American Historical Review* 97: 193–222.
Brading, David A. 1993 (1991). *Orbe andino. De la monarquía católica a la república criolla,* 1492–1867, 2nd ed. Mexico: Fondo de Cultura Económica.
Brass, Tom and Marcel van der Linden, eds. 1997. *Free and Unfree Labour: The Debate continues.* Bern: Peter Lang.
Bridkhina, Eugenia, ed. 2015. *Bolivia. Su Historia. Volumen II. La experiencia colonial en Charcas, siglos XVI–XVII.* La Paz: Coordinadora de Historia.
Buechler, Rose Marie. 1989. *Gobierno, Minería y Sociedad. Potosí y el "Renacimiento" Borbónico, 1776–1810.* 2 vols. La Paz: Biblioteca Minera.
Cañete y Domínguez, Pedro Vicente. 1952. *Guía histórica, geográfica, física, política, civil, y legal del gobierno e intendencia de la provincia de Potosí 1787.* Potosí: Editorial Potosí.
Cole, Jeffrey. 1985. *The Potosí Mita, 1573–1700: Compulsory Indian Labor in the Andes.* Stanford: Stanford University Press.
De Vito, Christian G. 2017. "Precarious Pasts. Labour flexibility and labour precariousness as conceptual tools for the historical study of the interactions among labour relations." In *On the Road to Global Labour History*, edited by Karl Heinz Roth. Leiden and Boston: Brill.

Gil Montero, Raquel. 2013. "Migración y tributación en los Andes. Chichas y Lípez a fines del siglo XVII." *Anuario de Estudios Americanos* 70 (1): 39–65.
Glave, Luis Miguel. 1989. *Trajinantes, caminos indígenas en la sociedad colonial, siglos XVI–XVII.* Lima: Instituto de Apoyo Agrario.
González Casasnovas, Ignacio. 2000. *Las dudas de la Corona. La política de repartimientos para la minería de Potosí.* Madrid: CSIC.
Harris, Olivia, Larson Brooke and Enrique Tandeter. 1989. *La participación indígena en los mercados surandinos. Estrategias y Reproducción social, siglos XVI a XX.* Cochabamba: CERES.
Levene, Ricardo. 1946. Vida y Escritos de Victorian de Villava. Buenos Aires: Pruser, S.A.
Lewin, Boleslao. 1967. *La rebelión de Túpac Amaru y los orígenes de la Independencia en Hispanoamérica.* Buenos Aires: Sociedad Editora Latino Americana.
Linden, Marcel van der. 2011. *Workers of the World.* Leiden: Brill.
Linden, Marcel Van Der. 2011b. "Introduction." *Humanitarian Intervention and Changing Labor Relations. The long-term consequences of the Abolition of the Slave Trade.* Leiden: Brill.
Linden, Marcel van der. 2016. "Mass exits: Who, Why, How?" In *Desertion in the Early Modern World. A comparative History,* edited by Van Rossum and Kamp. London-New York: Bloomsbury.
Linden, Marcel van der, and Rodriguez Garcia Magaly. 2016. *On Coerced Labor. Work and Compulsion after Chattel Slavery.* Leiden-Boston: Brill.
Lucassen, Jan. 1997. "Free and Unfree Labour before the 20th Century. A brief overview." In *Free and Unfree Labour: The Debate continues,* edited by Tom Brass and Marcel van der Linden. Berne: Peter Lang.
Matienzo, Juan de. 1567. *Gobierno del Perú.* Lima: IFEA.
Matienzo, Juan de. 1910. [1567]. *Gobierno del Perú.* Buenos Aires: Cia. Sud-Americana.
Méndez Luz María. 1992. "Los bancos de rescate en Hispanoamérica (1747–1832). El proceso histórico y sus fundamentos ideológicos. Estudio comparado para México, Perú y Chile." In *Minería colonial Latinoamericana: Primera Reunión de Historiadores de la Minería Latinoamericana,* edited by D. Ávila, I. Herrera, and R. Ortiz, 87–119. México: INAH.
Medinacelli, Ximena. 2010. *Sariri. Los llameros y la construcción de la sociedad colonial.* Lima: IFEA.
Mendoza Loza, Gunnar. 2005. "El Doctor Don Pedro Vicente Cañete y su Historia física y política de Potosí." *Obras Completas.* Vol. II. Sucre: Fundación Cultural del Banco Central de Bolivia, Archivo y Biblioteca Nacionales de Bolivia.
Mira, Guillermo. 1997. "El Real Banco de San Carlos y la minería altoperuano colonial, 1779–1825." In *La savia del Imperio,* edited by J. Sánchez, G. Mira, and R. Dobado. Salamanca: Universidad de Salamanca.
Morelli, Federica. 2006. "Tras las huellas perdidas de Filangieri: nuevas perspectivas sobre la cultura política constitucional en el Atlántico hispánico." *Historia Contemporánea* 33: 431–461.
Morelli, Federica. 2010. "De la «ciencia del comercio» a la «ciencia de la legislación»: la ruta napolitana a la reforma de la monarquía (siglo XVIII)." In *Las monarquías española y francesa (siglos XVI–XVIII). ¿Dos modelos políticos?,* edited by Anne Dubet and José Javier Ruiz Ibañez. Madrid: Casa de Velázquez.

Moreno, Mariano. 1802–1943. "Disertación Jurídica sobre el servicio personal de los indios." In *Escritos I*, edited by R. Levene. de Buenos Aires: Ediciones Estrada.

Platt, Tristan. 1982. *Estado boliviano y ayllu andino. Tierra y Tributo en el norte de Potosí.* Lima: IEP.

Platt, Tristan, Therese Bouysse-Cassagne and Olivia Harris. 2006. *Qaraqara-Charka: Mallku, Inka y Rey en la Provincia de Charcas (Siglos XV–XVII): Historia antropológica de una confederación Aymara.* La Paz: Plural.

Portillo Valdés, José M. 2007. "Victorian de Villava, fiscal de Charcas: Reforma de España y nueva moral imperial." *Anuario de Estudios Bolivianos, Archivísticos y Bibliográficos* 13. Sucre: Archivo y Bibliotecas Nacionales de Bolivia.

Recopilacion de Leyes. 1741. *Recopilación de Leyes de los Reynos de las Indias.* Tomo Segundo. Quarta Impresión. Madrid MDCCXXXXI. Madrid.

Saignes, Thierry. 1984. "Las etnias de Charcas frente al Sistema colonial (siglo XVII). Ausentismo y fugas en el debate sobre la mano de obra indígena." *Jahrbuch* 21: 27–76.

Saignes, Thierry. 1985. "Caciques, Tribute and Migration in the Southern Andes Indian Society and the 17th Century Colonial Order (Audiencia de Charcas)." London: University of London, Institute of Latin American Studies. Occasional Papers.

Sánchez Albornoz, Nicolás. 1978. *Indios y tributos en el Alto Perú.* Lima: IEP.

Scott, James. 2000 [1990]. *Los dominados y el arte de la resistencia.* Mexico: Ed. Era.

Serulnikov, Sergio. 2006. *Conflictos sociales e insurrección en el mundo colonial andino. El norte de Potosí en el siglo XVIII.* Buenos Aires: Fondo de Cultura Económica.

Serulnikov, Sergio. 2007. "La imaginación política andina en el siglo XVIII." In *Cultura política en los Andes (1750–1950)*, edited by Aljovin de Losada and Nils Jacobsen. Lima: IFEA.

Smith, Matthew. 2004. "Coercion and Choice in the Potosi Mita." *Past Imperfect* 10: 21–44.

Solórzano y Pereyra, Juan De. 1703. *Política Indiana compuesta por Don Juan Solórzano y Pereira.* Amberes: Henrico y Cornelio Vendussen.

Stanziani, Alessandro. 2016. "Runaways: A Global History." In *Deserion in the Early Modern World. A Comparative History*, edited by MatthiasVan Rossum and Jeannette Kamp. London-New York: Bloomsbury.

Tandeter, Enrique. 1981a. "Forced and Free Labour in Late Colonial Potosi." *Past and Present* 93 (1): 98–136.

Tandeter, Enrique. 1981b. "La producción como actividad popular: ladrones de minas en Potosí." *Nova Americana* 4: 43–65.

Tandeter, Enrique. 1992. *Coacción y Mercado. La minería de la plata en el Potosí colonial 1692–1826.* Cusco: Centro de Estudios regionales andinos "Bartolomé de las Casas."

Toledo, Francisco. 1986. *Disposiciones Gubernativas para el Virreinato del Perú*, 1569–1574. Sevilla: Escuela de Estudios Hispanoamericanos CSIC.

Van Rossum, Matthias, and Jeannette Kamp, eds. 2016. *Desertion in the Early Modern World. A Comparative History.* London-New York: Bloomsbury.

Zagalsky, Paula. 2014. "La mita de Potosí: una imposición colonial invariable en un contexto de múltiples transformaciones (Siglos XVI–XVII; Charcas, Virreinato del Perú)." *Chungara* 46 (3): 375–395.

Zavala, Silvio. 1978. *El servicio personal de los indios en el Perú* (extractos del siglo XVI). Tomo I. Mexico: El Colegio de México.

Zavala, Silvio. 1979. *El servicio personal de los indios en el Perú* (extractos del siglo XVII). Volume II. México: El Colegio de México.

Francisco Quiroz

Learning together: Indians, free blacks and slaves in Lima's colonial workshops

Abstract: This study looks at working dynamics in the artisan and manufacturing workshops of the city of Lima from the 16th to the 18th centuries, based on ethnic, cultural and economic criteria, through an analysis of the employment contracts that exist in the archives. That analysis shows that indigenous people, *mestizos*, enslaved people, freed Afro-descendants and Spaniards all worked together in the artisan and manufacturing workshops of the city but that working conditions differed, depending on their caste and the patronage they enjoyed. Slave owners and relatives obtained better conditions for their pupils than the colonial and municipal authorities obtained for their wards. The study analyses a large number of cases from the 16th and 18th centuries. We see that as the colonial period progressed, work in Lima was governed less and less by norms relating to a worker's caste, although that does not mean there was a free labour market in the modern sense.

Keywords: world of labour; colonial Lima; craftsmen; apprenticeships; free and slave labour.

Introduction

Lima is a purpose-built city, created as the administrative centre for a rich, extensive and mostly mountainous territory. As the capital city, it was the residence of the colonial bureaucracy and the "notables" of the viceroyalty, as well as being one of the main commercial centres of the New World. Thus, from the beginning, it was a city of significant economic and demographic dimensions. While it did not become an industrial city, it did develop a wide range of artisan and manufacturing activities (Quiroz, 2008).

Lima was one of the most heavily populated cities in the New World, after Potosí, Mexico and Rio de Janeiro. It was, therefore, a very attractive market. However, Lima lacked two essential conditions to become a centre of production: local raw materials and firewood. Indeed, industrial activities had to be developed with raw materials imported from other areas of the country and even

Doctor in History at the Universidad Nacional Mayor de San Marcos, Lima. Contact: fquirozc@unmsm.edu.pe

https://doi.org/10.1515/9783110759303-004

from abroad. In addition, the rapid deforestation of the coast left the city without fuel. Nevertheless, the presence of figures with significant economic and political influence, who played an important role in the commercial networks of the viceroyalty, allowed the city to become a centre of industrial production. Although never promoted by the Crown, Lima's workshops were able to supply its own urban market and that of the viceroyalty, and even export to other parts of Spanish America. Nevertheless, we must consider the fact that, as a colony, the country was subject to restrictions and even protective prohibitions on overseas trade. For example, the central coastal region did not produce vegetable fibres (such as cotton, flax and hemp) which could have formed the basis for a vast textile industry. Furthermore, despite its significant population, which meant it had its own work force, the city still had to complement its labour needs through internal and external migration and, above all, through the control of its working population.

This essay is divided into two parts. The first provides brief but substantial information about the city itself. It then seeks to establish the specific incidence of the guild order as an institutional framework that sought to control industrial production and the population engaged in that production, a central activity in the framework of modern colonialism. The second part analyses working conditions in the city, taking into consideration the ethnic and cultural diversity of the workers. The main question in the first part is, to what extent did the guilds actually restrict productive activity? The second part seeks to establish how working conditions differed according to caste, within the free, servile and slave populations.

Working Lima

Lima became a city of considerable proportions because of the political and administrative functions that were assigned to it in the context of European colonisation. By the 16th century it already had more than fourteen thousand inhabitants. Fifteen years later, that had risen to 25,000. By the end of the 18th century, the population reached 52,000 and on the eve of independence it was 64,000.

It is not possible to go into details of the demographic breakdown of that population here, but it is important to note that Lima was never strictly speaking a Spanish city. Its population was far from homogeneous, and the so-called *castes* made up a considerable portion of its inhabitants. From the available figures, it can be seen that, throughout the colonial period, the ethnic and cultural composition of Lima was largely stable: as a city it was 40 percent Spanish,

40 percent black, 10 percent *mestizo*, and 8 percent indigenous (Cook, 1968 and 1985; Pérez Cantó, 1985).

Although originally "designed" to be the seat of government and the residence of the social elites, the reality was quite different. The city housed large contingents of enslaved peoples who serviced those elites, and it received free people of different castes who came in search of work. In the city, indigenous people found refuge from their colonial obligations (*mitas*, tributes, and personal service), while free *mestizos* and Afro-descendants were attracted by the availability of temporary jobs in industry, services, and small business. Non-elite Spaniards complemented the picture, dedicating themselves to commerce and small-scale industrial production.

The latter are the master craftsmen and manufacturers who found the city to be a favourable space where they could obtain their part of the colonial wealth through their productive activity. This was never well-received by the colonial regime, but it was tolerated and sometimes even encouraged by private interests. The market was favourable for producers of durable consumer goods (clothing, footwear, tools, furniture, candles, jewellery, etc.) and processed foods (butter, flour, pastry, meats and derivatives, tobacco, and sweets).

However, competitors quickly emerged in these areas. Indigenous people, *mestizos*, freed Afro-descendants and enslaved people all learned the trades that the Spanish producers had considered their exclusive domain. The presence of producers of different castes in Lima provoked adverse reactions on the part of the Spanish population, who saw these workers appearing in numbers that exceeded their own work-force requirements. As such, they began to constitute a serious threat to their activities. To a large extent, it can be said that the most pressing motivation for the organisation of their trades into guilds was the need to counteract the competition of craftsmen from other castes, and to establish effective control over their activity (Quiroz, 1995).

As the old apprentices and workers gained experience and autonomy, new contingents of immigrants set up as independent producers. Numerous enslaved people were trained in workshops on the orders of their own masters, who sought to obtain greater benefits from their servants. Circumstances were such that (especially from the late-sixteenth century onwards) it was very onerous to maintain a large contingent of unproductive domestic serfs. Freed Afro-descendant and *mestizo* peoples, added to the pool of labourers who had received specialist training.

Approximately half of the population of African origin was free or *horra* (liberated). Their presence in large numbers, in trade and production, worried the authorities and slave owners, who would have preferred them to be servants in private homes. Attempts to create special towns for the freed slaves failed, as did attempts to tax them for payments or tributes (such as were applied to the indigenous people), or to force them to serve the Spaniards for a salary or wage.

The same is true of enslaved people. The prohibitions on slaves going out to earn were repeated, and penalties increased as this system of semi-freedom grew increasingly widespread. The pretexts were redundant (an increase in thefts, dances, weddings, baptisms and inappropriate customs, offences against indigenous people in their gardens and urban markets, etc.). However, the conflicting interests of producers, owners, and the authorities combined to make independent activity of enslaved and free Afro-descendants a possibility. While some authorities were interested in social control and some artisans did not want slaves meddling in their work, other members of the authorities had slaves "earning" wages for them; and some producers needed labour because they did not benefit from the labour of the *mitayos*. There were merchants who brought cattle to be slaughtered in the city, seeking to profit from the skins by giving them to the thrashers and tanners of different castes; homeowners who rented spaces for workshops and housing to independent producers, etc. It is therefore no wonder that the ordinances were a dead letter.

The presence of indigenous workers was likewise, simultaneously promoted and decried. It was criticised by those who wanted the indigenous people for labour in the mines, on the large estates (*haciendas)*, or in textile manufacturing (*obrajes*) in the highlands, or by those who wanted them to stay in their towns receiving Christian doctrine and paying their taxes. On the other hand, it was supported by the owners who saw the *mingas* (free labourers) as a cheaper alternative to slave labour (which was expensive by its very nature). Like the Afro-descendants, the indigenous workers also became increasingly independent in productive work, but their fate was a little different.

Indigenous producers knew how to take advantage of the possibilities that came from belonging to the "republic of Indians," using institutions such as guilds and fraternities to that end. In this way, they managed to secure exemption from the taxes and other obligations their Spanish and caste colleagues paid. Soon indigenous producers were free even from other guild responsibilities (exams and inspections).

Some of the *mitayos* who came to Lima for a period of personal service, settled there, adding to the local population. This made indigenous people an important source of available labour for the city's employers. They were much more important than demographic data suggests. They are recorded as being 8 percent of the population, however, the majority of them were inhabitants of working age. From 1566 on, attempts were made to move the indigenous population to the town of Cercado, but they resisted this, and actually lived and worked alone, or for someone else, in houses and workshops all over the city (Vergara, 2005; Cárdenas Ayaipona, 2014).

The needs of non-*encomendero* employers[1] for labour in Lima were increasing, to the point where, towards the end of the 16th century, the indigenous population had become a bone of contention between different social sectors, including the church and the local administration who needed labour for their public works.

Day labourers (*jornaleros*) had made up the workforce for non-*encomendero* employers ever since the city was founded. The colonial administration established a pay scale for the indigenous population that, although very meagre (one silver *tomín* and a quart of corn per day), provoked complaint from Spanish employers who were unwilling to spend money paying indigenous people for the work they did. In 1576, Viceroy Francisco de Toledo regulated Indian wages, setting them at one and a half *tomíns* plus food.[2] When expressed in *reales*, the new official remuneration amounted to 108 *reales* per year, two Indian dresses (cotton), food and treatment of illnesses for *yanakona* and day labourers in the cities and countryside of the central Peruvian coast. In other words, a little more than a *cuartillo* per day (a quarter of a *real* which was an eighth of a *peso corriente*). One might expect that employers would avoid paying these rates, and in fact, in 1676, the provision was re-enacted because it was not being complied with. Nevertheless, the wage rate does serve as a reference, setting pay rates for most of the country's population during the colonial period. Subsequently, in 1591, Viceroy Hurtado de Mendoza freed any *mitayo* who had resided in the town of Cercado for more than five years from their obligations to the *mita*, clearing the way for their use as a workforce for local employers who were not beneficiaries of that coercive regime.[3]

It is in this context that guilds begin to appear in Lima. The guilds emerged following restrictive criteria both on the part of the municipal and colonial authorities, and on the part of the Spanish master craftsmen, who considered themselves entitled to control their trades. In fact, for two or three decades, Spanish master craftsmen had not been concerned with creating guilds for their trades. That changed in the 1550s as the competition they faced from black "colleagues" became increasingly significant. In 1551, the swordsmiths prevented Afro-descendant people from working independently, and this was only the beginning

1 Non-*encomendero* employers are those employers who did not benefit from the colonial *encomendero* system of forced indigenous labour.

2 Archivo Histórico Municipal de Lima (AHML). Libros de cédulas y provisiones de Lima. (legajo 6 ff. 466–468); Libros de cabildos de Lima iii: 577, 491, 592, 595, 672; viii: 275–276, 587.

3 Biblioteca Nacional del Perú. Virreinato. Indios. Trabajo. 1591 A53 f.1.

of a long list of actions by the master swordsmiths to increasingly close access to their trade. In the following decade the masters appointed an *alcalde* for their activity or industry, a further step towards establishing a formal guild. The third step came later, in 1605, with the proclamation of special ordinances for the new guild.

The swordsmiths were followed by blacksmiths in 1552, when they prohibited blacks and Berbers from running their own or their masters' forges. In 1557, the Spanish tailors prohibited blacks from cutting cloth themselves, until they obtained ordinances of their guild in 1636. The *zapateros* (shoemakers) tried to exclude slaves in 1562, and so did the handrail makers and hatters, carpenters and silversmiths. In reality, the primary motive for 'forming a guild' was competition from enslaved and free Afro-descendants. This situation was repeated at the end of the 18th century, when the new economic conditions created by the Bourbon reforms began to harm artisans and merchants. Again, the producers revived their guilds to avoid competition, and again that was based on ethnic criteria.

However, at this later juncture, it was primarily new trades forming guilds: the candle makers in 1785; the chocolatiers in 1787; and the *shoemakers* in 1792. This was not a trend limited to Spanish traders. In the 1800s, it was both Spanish and indigenous button-makers who excluded from their profession the "reprobate castes of chinos, *zambos* and *mulatos*, whose society has always been considered harmful" (Quiroz, 1995: 63).

Officially, the Spanish guilds also incorporated representatives of the non-indigenous castes. They had to include them in their regulations and hierarchical organisation. However, the Afro-descendants who became master craftsmen did not generally mix with the Spanish. Their status was subordinate, and they were only exceptionally considered to be masters in the workshops or full guild members.

The case of indigenous people is especially interesting. Indigenous producers created their own guilds and *cofradías* (fraternities), independent of the Spanish guilds (Fernández Villanova, 2017). In 1634, indigenous and Afro-descendant masons were protected by the city council against the Spanish guild that wanted to encompass them. But the most active trades were those of tailors, shoemakers, and hatters. At the end of the 17th century the indigenous tailors managed to separate themselves from the Spanish guild; in 1721 the hatters did the same; along with the saddle makers, mat weavers, and button makers in 1735.

Great attention was devoted by the Spanish and indigenous guilds to social control. The initial master craftsmen, and those who, over time, came to consider themselves entitled to restrict the exercise of their trades, created guilds in the image and likeness of similar institutions in Spain. However, the colonial guilds of Lima differ, in their functions and dynamics, from those of the peninsular. Rather than a structured corporate entity, the colonial guilds were very simple in their composition, functions, and hierarchies. Very quickly, the so-called senior masters replaced all the guild authorities. That is to say, specific characters appointed by the council and, above all, by the colonial government, became the only leaders of the guilds, and their functions were basically restricted to controlling all those who practised a trade or group of trades, regardless of whether or not they were guild members or qualified masters (Quiroz, 1995) This is also reflected in the workforce. European guild regulations were only partially valid in colonial Lima, and that had an important impact on the shaping of labour relations in the city.

The castes at work

This study analyses 855 labour contracts from the 16th century, and 2,635 contracts from the 18th century found in the *Protocolos Notariales,* at the *Archivo General de la Nación Peru* and the *Biblioteca Nacional.* The extensive available data has enabled me to establish similarities and differences in labour relations. The emphasis is on the working conditions for apprentices and journeymen of different ethnic origins in the context of the development of trades, in order to determine the similarities (common patterns) and differences (particular trends) in the treatment given to labourers according to their social and ethnic-cultural background.

Other factors also influenced working conditions. One of them was the patronage that labourers enjoyed at the time of closing a contract. This refers to whether they were volunteering their labour themselves or if someone else (a master, relative, guardian, colonial or city offical, etc.) was acting as their protector or forcing them to work for an employer. Other factors relate to the employer and the productive unit. In other words, the "nature" of the employer (caste, race), and the dimensions of the workshop, influenced the configuration of hiring patterns and, in general, of working conditions in colonial Lima. A third factor is the trades themselves. Some trades were more demanding than others in terms of formal training and the "quality" of the labourers they hired. Goldsmiths, silversmiths, and crafts working with precious metals were, as a rule, more zealous than other trades.

The data shows interesting trends over time. The almost 900 cases from the 16th century are very representative of Lima at that time (a city of fewer than 20,000 people). However, the 2,635 cases from the 18th century are clearly only a very small sample from a city that bordered on 60,000 inhabitants. This is explained by increasingly informal labour relations and the weakening of the requirements of the guilds in terms of formal learning in order to exercise a trade.

The 16th century sample includes contracts for both journeymen and apprentices. Some 467 masters hired 157 journeymen and 698 apprentices from 1550 to 1600. The majority were Spanish (almost half of the journeymen and a third of the apprentices), followed by indigenous workers (respectively, 29 percent and 44 percent). Enslaved people were a considerably smaller group in both categories.

Table 1: Lima, 16th century. Journeymen and apprentice contracts by caste

	Journeymen	%	Apprentices	%	Totals	%
Spanish	74	47.13	224	32.09	298	34.85
Indigenous	46	29.3	309	44.27	355	41.52
Black	4	2.55	23	3.29	27	3.16
Mestizo	8	5.1	48	6.88	56	6.55
Mulato	3	1.91	37	5.3	40	4.68
Enslaved	22	14.01	57	8.17	79	9.24
Totals	157		698		855	

Source: Compiled by the author, based on the Protocolos Notariales. Archivo General de la Nación. Siglo XVI.

In terms of activity, it is clear that most journeymen and apprenticeships in the 16th century were focused on clothing, with 31 percent of journeymen and 39 percent of apprentices working for tailors. That is strengthened when we add the silk workers and hatters (14 percent in both cases). Seen over time, the contracts were made mainly in the decades after 1570, which concentrated 93 percent of all contracts for journeymen and 83 percent of apprenticeships (half of all of these were in the 1590s).

In the 18th century, things changed. To start with, contracts for skilled workers (journeymen) almost disappeared. In the entire century only four journeymen are hired (three Spaniards and one slave), whereas contracts for apprenticeships total 2,631. The master craftsmen, moreover, are not so numerous. There are only 1,325, which means almost two contracts per master on average, and 94 percent of the masters are Spanish.

Table 2: Lima, 16th century. Contracts by trade.

Trade	Journeymen	%	Apprentices	%	Totals	%
Tailors and hosiers	50	31.85	272	38.97	322	37.66
Silk workers and hatters	22	14.01	96	13.75	118	13.8
Embroiderers	3	1.91	9	1.29	12	1.4
Cord makers	0	0	1	0.14	1	0.12
Dyers	0	0	6	0.86	6	0.7
Tanners	5	3.18	6	0.86	11	1.29
Shoemakers	18	11.46	128	18.34	146	17.08
Saddle makers	2	1.27	17	2.44	19	2.22
Swordsmiths and gilders	4	2.55	12	1.72	16	1.87
Blacksmiths and locksmiths	4	2.55	18	2.58	22	2.57
Gold-rod makers and gold beaters	1	0.64	3	0.43	4	0.47
Silversmiths	9	5.74	29	4.15	38	4.44
Wax candle makers and confectioners	7	4.46	7	1	14	1.64
Potters	3	1.91	3	0.43	6	0.7
Cake bakers and millers	5	3.18	3	0.43	8	0.94
Masons	3	1.91	27	3.87	30	3.51
Carpenters	21	13.38	61	8.74	82	9.59
Totals	157		698		855	

Source: Compiled by the author, based on the Protocolos Notariales. Archivo General de la Nación. Siglo XVI.

Table 3: Lima, 18th century. Contracts for journeymen and apprentices by caste

	Journeymen	%	Apprentices	%	Totals	%
Spanish	3	75	1,362	51.73	1,365	51.77
Indigenous	0	0	724	27.52	724	27.48
Black	0	0	126	4.86	128	4.86
Mestizo	0	0	150	5.63	148	5.62
Mulatto	0	0	47	1.79	47	1.78
Zambo	0	0	63	2.43	64	2.43
Quadroons	0	0	52	1.94	51	1.93
Quinterons	0	0	4	0.15	4	0.15
Enslaved	1	25	103	3.95	104	3.98
Totals	4		2,631		2,635	

Source: Complied by the author, based on the Protocolos Notariales. Archivo General de la Nación. Siglo XVIII.

Table 4: Lima, 18th century. Contracts by trade

Trade	Journeymen	%	Apprentices	%	Totals
Tailors	0	0	509	19.35	509
Embroiderers	0	0	10	0.38	10
Hatters	0	0	111	4.22	111
Handrail makers	0	0	175	6.65	175
Button makers	0	0	364	13.83	364
Dyers	0	0	14	0.53	14
Shoemakers	1	25	420	15.96	421
Tanners	0	0	14	0.53	14
Saddle makers	0	0	87	3.31	87
Carpenters	0	0	167	6.35	167
Carriage makers	0	0	55	2.09	55
Joiners	0	0	49	1.86	49
Coopers	0	0	16	0.61	16
Masons	0	0	19	0.72	19
Potters	1	25	26	0.99	27
Blacksmiths	0	0	125	4.75	125
Tinsmiths	0	0	13	0.49	13
Silversmiths	0	0	379	14.41	379
Gold-rod makers	0	0	35	1.33	35
Gilders	0	0	13	0.49	13
Watchmakers	0	0	9	0.34	9
Petate makers Petateros	0	0	4	0.15	4
Bakers	0	0	2	0.08	2
Comb makers	0	0	1	0.04	1
Firework makers	0	0	2	0.08	2
String makers	0	0	1	0.04	1
Cigar makers	0	0	1	0.04	1
Cake bakers	0	0	1	0.04	1
Chocolatiers	2	50	1	0.04	3
Wax candle makers	0	0	2	0.08	2
Printers	0	0	6	0.22	6
Totals	4		2,631		2,635

Source: Compiled by the author, based on the Protocolos Notariales. Archivo General de la Nación. Siglo XVIII.

Again, tailors, hosiers, hatters and silk workers make up the biggest groups, with 44 percent of the apprenticeship contracts. These are followed by shoemakers (16 percent) and silversmiths (14 percent). The rest of the trades make up very small proportions, some having only a single contract in the entire century.

Working together

Artisan and manufacturing workshops received labourers of all different castes and backgrounds. No pattern of discrimination emerges in this regard. It is true that there were some trades that were identified with a particular caste, but others are inclusive. Among the "closed" trades, the goldsmiths and silversmiths stand out. All the master gold and silver smiths were Spanish and they hired only Spanish workers or enslaved people put to work by their Spanish masters. The Spanish handrail-makers also appealed to the "quality" of their trade in order to prevent others from entering it. One exception, however, was the black master handrail maker Juan Gómez Morato, who in 1704 to 1706 hires four blacks and two Spaniards. On the other hand, indigenous people also had their exclusivities, with button and silk workers becoming trades dominated by indigenous masters over time.

These latter cases are illustrative, as silk makers and button makers were the trades that made the most contracts in the 18th century. The Indian Melchor Lucano hired 34 apprentices between 1737 and 1789 and, of them, 24 were indigenous people, nine were Spanish and one was *mestizo*. The Indian Ventura Temoche had 18 apprentices between 1748 and 1799, of whom fifteen were indigenous and three were *mestizo*. The Indian José Bruno Romero hired sixteen: thirteen indigenous, two Spanish and one *mestizo*. The Indian Roque Ramos hired thirteen: eleven were indigenous and two were Spanish. The Indian Pascual Ramírez hired thirteen: seven indigenous, five Spanish and one *mestizo*. The Indian Marcelo Lucano hired eleven: nine indigenous and two Spanish. The Indian Sancho Cosanchilon hired eleven: seven indigenous and four Spanish. Finally, the Indian Antonio Alvarado hired 11, 10 indigenous and one Spanish.

In other trades the contracts also varied in terms of the caste of the assistants, but few cases registered large groups. The Spanish blacksmith Cosme Damián de Valdez hired eleven apprentices between 1707 and 1723: nine Spanish, one black, and one *mestizo*. Another Spanish blacksmith Juan de la Calle hired eight apprentices: three Spanish, three blacks (one of them a slave), one free *zambo* and one *mestizo*. The Spanish blacksmith Juan José del Pino hired six apprentices: three Spanish, two *mestizo* and one indigenous.

In the case of the carpenters, the Spaniard, Manuel Sánchez Blanco, hired ten apprentices, including five Spanish and five blacks (two of them enslaved). The Spanish carriage maker Alejo de Espinoza had nine assistants: four Spanish, two blacks (one of them a enslaved), one "quadroon" (described as having one quarter "dirty" blood),[4] one *mulato* and one *mestizo*, and his colleague (also Spanish) Esteban Fernández Baizán had nine: seven Spanish, one *zambo* and one black. Perhaps it is appropriate to highlight that Baizán was one of the largest carriage makers in Lima in the second half of the 18th century and, therefore, must have had many more assistants including skilled journeymen and labourers in his workshop all working at the same time.

Working together brought both camaraderie and discord among the workers. The artisan and manufacturing workshops were managed in a patriarchal manner. The workers had to obey the owner in a hierarchical relationship that could lead to arrogance and even physical and psychological abuse towards the assistants. It does not seem an exaggeration to say that the relationship between the employer and his assistants was violent, despite the fact that mistreatment within the workshops and inside the houses was not easily reported.[5]

Domestic violence manifested itself in daily aggressions which, precisely because they were so widespread, were considered normal. This can be inferred from the recommendations made in the contracts, such as that masters should treat their pupils with love and without excessive punishment[6]. The tutors themselves might approve of correction when it was 'paternal'. If the bakeries were private prisons, the workshops often served as correctional facilities. The workshop was an establishment that fulfilled the function of education and instruction, but also of correcting the deviant behaviours of boys through work. Tutors and the authorities regularly forced young people and adolescents into workshop placements as a corrective measure for having run away or for living a "disorderly life" (vagrancy, drinking, etc.). José Arrieta at the age of 13 had to be placed with the tailor José Román in 1785 for having fled to Chile. The 12-year-old mestizo Juan de Berrocal had already been imprisoned for depravity, when the *alcalde del crimen* at the Royal Court placed him to learn a trade as a shoemaker in 1709. The Indian apprentice José Dolores was imprisoned in the royal gaol in Lima for disorderly behaviour and, because he had no protector or trade or income with which to subsist, in 1789 the sub-delegate of the Cercado

---

4 *Quadroon* is one of the so-called "castes." Purity was measured by the blood of the four grandparents: in this case, three of them were white and one was Indian (*mestizo quadroon*) or black (*mulatto quadroon*).

5 Some examples from the end of the colonial period in the Archivo General de la Nación (AGN hereafter) Cabildo Causas Criminales 1773 leg. 5 c. [4] fs.1–13; 1811 leg. 120 c. 1463; 1785 leg. 57 c. 665; 1786 leg. 58 c. 683; 1777 leg. 39 c. 461.

6 Some examples of this paternal treatment in the AGN Protocols (Prot. hereafter) Libro (L hereafter) 44: 935v; Prot. L. 42: 693; Prot. L. 44: 1155v. Physical abuse was a reason to cancel a contract (cf. AGN Prot. L. 533: 135; Prot. L. 42: 570v; Prot. L. 632: 362v).

placed him to learn the trade of button maker. The penalty given to Bartolomé Churruca for theft in 1788 was to remain as an apprentice with a shoemaker with the warning that if he escaped, he would be sent to the Callao prison. The Indian Juan Antonio Enríquez was 14 years old and was in debt to the master Mariano Corona, for which he had been imprisoned, when in 1802 his tutor placed him to learn a trade with another master shoemaker. José Hermenegildo Palomino had to be forcibly taken back to the workshop of carriage maker Domingo Huerta, in 1792, so that he could complete his training after almost two years of interruption.[7]

Relationships between workers could be harsh. Fallings out over work must have been frequent even though this is not reflected in the sources. A fist fight between two shoemakers in 1730 was described by witnesses (all colleagues) as something natural: "[I]t was just one of those quarrels between friends that happen every day."[8]

Remuneration

Payment varied depending on working conditions and caste. In this section, I separate the journeymen working in small artisan workshops from free day labourers in the city's larger manufacturing workshops. A distinction is also drawn between the 16th and 18th centuries.

One of the most important factors was the patronage or support that the contracted parties had at the time of making the deal. The pay and conditions offered depended on the influence held by the person or institution that accompanied the labourer. The following table shows the "godfathers" of the 16th century. For the most part, journeymen came alone to reach a contract with the owners of the workshops. This is an important piece of information as it applies to both the Spanish and the indigenous labour.

In the case of apprentices, the information is to be found in the table below. A significant part of the apprentices are accompanied by their parents or other relatives, although there is still a strikingly high proportion of apprentices, mostly Spanish and indigenous, who went alone, without a "patron."

7 AGN Prot. L. 65: 416; Prot. L. 648: 503; Prot. L. 180: 597v y 830v; Prot. L. 565: 716v; Prot. L. 167: 435v).

8 Archivo General de la Nación. Cabildo Penal 1730 leg. 11 c. [8] f.4; Archivo General de la Nación. Cabildo Penal Provincias 1805 leg. 16 paquete [4].

Table 5: Lima 16th century. Patronage enjoyed by journeymen at the time of making a contract

	Spanish	Indian	Black	*Mestizo*	*Mulato*	Enslaved
Fathers	1	1	0	0	0	0
Mothers	0	0	0	0	0	0
Relatives	1	1	0	0	0	0
Owners (men)	0	0	0	0	0	20
Owners (women)	0	0	0	0	0	2
Institutions	0	0	0	0	0	0
Authorities	1	1	0	0	0	0
No information available	71	43	4	8	3	0
Totals	74	46	4	8	3	22

Source: Compiled by the author, based on the Protocolos Notariales. Archivo General de la Nación. Siglo XVI.

Table 6: Lima 16th century. Patronage of apprentices at the time of the contract

	Spanish	Indigenous	Black	*Mestizo*	*Mulato*	Enslaved
Fathers	31	4	4	3	5	0
Mothers	20	2	6	4	5	0
Relatives	27	6	4	12	3	0
Owners (men)	0	0	0	0	0	33
Owners (women)	0	0	0	0	0	24
Institutions	0	0	0	0	0	0
Authorities	7	33	6	15	12	0
No information available	139	264	3	14	12	0
Totals	224	309	23	48	37	57

Source: Compiled by the author, based on the Protocolos Notariales. Archivo General de la Nación. Siglo XVI.

Lima's artisans had a complex system of remuneration. It could be in services, in goods, in money or in various combinations of these three elements. The greater proportion of one or another depended on the worker's status as a skilled journeyman or apprentice, on their previous experience in the trade, on their ethnic-cultural background (whether they were white, Indian, *ladino*, *mestizo*, black or *mulato*), on their legal status (whether they were free or a enslaved, *encomienda* tributes, or minors), on the 'patronage' that they enjoyed and, finally, on when the contract was made.

Remuneration for the work of artisan apprentices included ten items that would class as services and goods: training, housing, medical attention, good treatment, education and Christian doctrine; as well as food, work clothes, party clothes and tools. That of the peons or skilled labourers might include money in cash or goods.

The apprentices resided in the homes of their masters and were therefore on duty all day (and every day), in most cases also performing various domestic tasks (cleaning, carrying water, running errands to the plaza or market, to the grocery store or tavern, etc). The master had a duty to cure their illnesses as part of the payment (usually limited to eight days illness) and to treat them well (give them *buena vida*, as it was called then), teach them good manners and *buena policia* (customs), and to teach the precepts of the Christian religion (especially, but not exclusively to indigenous people). Only twice have I found that in the 16th century the literacy of the ward was added to other forms of remuneration. In the 18th century, this obligation was also sporadic, but others were added, such as teaching reading and writing, counting, singing and playing musical instruments.[9]

Regarding payment in kind, food takes first place, followed by clothes. It was stipulated that the clothing should be "appropriate to the assistant's person." "Corresponding to him, that he feel no harm", "give him the customary clothes," "what is ordinarily given to an apprentice slave is clean clothes every week," are all formulas that can be found in the contracts. It wasn't strictly speaking a question of special work clothes. The house and workshop were often still the same place, and house clothes and work clothes were easily confused. The clothing consisted of shirts, stockings, breeches of ordinary fabric, jacket, coat, and a doublet with sleeves. Differences of caste are seen in the fabric used to make the garments. Spaniards and mestizo had ordinary cloth or seconds-quality Castille cloth, canvas shirts and cotton stockings; the indigenous people wore ordinary or coarse wool cloth; while quadroons, *zambos* and blacks wore Quito cloth. A slave was entitled to the locally-made cloth (from Cusco, Huamanga or Quito). Sometimes, clothes in the first year were made of poor-quality cloth and in the second year (or at the end) of cloth from Quito. Footwear was replaced more frequently as it wore out faster than clothing. It was changed every month or when required as a result of normal use.

Very few placements established payment only in money. Some examples serve to illustrate this practice which cannot be shown in tables and graphs due to the differing values of money in the 16th century. For the first three years of the contract made in 1578, between the carpenter, Juan Cano and his apprentice, Diego Hernández, the master paid 40 nine-real pesos for his pupil to

9 AGN Sección Notarial L. 732f.205; L. 868f.1088.

dress himself.[10] Likewise, from 1598, the silversmith De la Hoz gave Juan de Escobar 50 *nine-real pesos* to clothe himself during the first year, 100 *nine-real pesos* the second and 60 *nine-real pesos* during the remaining six months;[11] and in 1593 the mason Pedro Falcón paid Gaspar Núñez 100 *nine-real pesos* per year for his clothing plus 20 *nine-real pesos* "for whatever he wanted."[12] The Indian apprentice, Sebastián Yauraman was to receive 28 nine-*real pesos* in 1593 on finishing his apprenticeship, apart from the 12 *nine-real pesos* that his master tailor, Juan Cabezas was to give him each year.[13] The 20 *pesos corrientes* that the Indian journeyman Andrés received at the end of his four-year contract with the blacksmith Francisco de Oviedo, were to acquire the tools of his trade.[14]

Money was also paid when the person who actually received the payment was someone else, whether the labourer was a free man or a slave. On numerous occasions it was relatives or guardians who received the "salaries" of the journeymen and apprentices. In 1573, for example, the master potter, Hernán González paid the daily wage of his "worker" Diego Pérez to the father, with the clarification that if Diego wanted, he could himself receive just 40 *pesos corrientes*, and not in money but in clothes.[15]

When it came to enslaved people, the owner received the daily wage directly from the master craftsman. In such cases the labourer was only fed and housed. Especially from the end of the 16th century on, enslaved people were handed over to masters in order to take advantage of the wages they generated and not have them unproductive at home. To that end they were first put to learn a trade (mainly masonry, carpentry and other construction trades), as Emilio Harth-Terré, James Lockhart and Frederick Bowser demonstrated in their studies (Harth-Terré/Marquez, 1960: 11–16; Lockhart, 1982; Bowser, 1977). Sometimes the apprenticeship was delivered for free.

In 1598 the Lima official Luis Rodríguez de la Serna placed two of his slaves as skilled wood turners, Cristóbal was placed with the carpenter Diego Felipe for a year and a half to make him "a well finished craftsman" so that he could later apply the trade and "earn what a good craftsman usually earns." He placed the mulatto Miguel with the turner Hernando Caballero for two years. In both cases,

10 AGN Prot. L. 28 f.193.
11 AGN Prot. L. 60 f.728.
12 AGN Prot. L. 53 f.159.
13 AGN Prot. L. 53 f.299.
14 AGN Prot. L. 150 f.1v.
15 AGN Prot. L. 71 f.169.

at the end of the terms, if they had not learned the trade, Serna was to receive their wages as if they were already craftsmen: one *eight-real peso* per day.[16]

Other examples refer to hatters in 1598 and 1599. The slave Simón was placed with the master hatter Esteban Narváez for five months. If he did not learn, Narváez had to give his mistress four hats a day until Simón had mastered the trade.[17] Likewise, Juan de la Riaza gave his colleague Diego Fuentes a black named Jacinto for seven months to complete his instruction. Fuentes would keep the product of Jacinto's work, but if at the end of that time he did not emerge "a craftsman in the eyes of other craftsmen," he would pay Riaza six refined hats a day until he did.[18]

Something similar occurred with the free apprentices, especially if they were Spanish. In 1590 the tailor Francisco de Riberos told his apprentice Alonso García that

> [i]f, due to my fault and negligence I did not teach you the trade, I will keep you in my house and I will pay you for each day that it will take you to finish learning the above-mentioned trade that a craftsman would ordinarily acquire in the time specified.[19]

From the ninth decade of the 16th century, it was established that the labour of the indigenous workers was to be remunerated at 12 *nine-real pesos* and two outfits per year. This provision is observed in 164 contracts, while in 59 the remuneration did not reach that amount and in 83 it exceeded it. The latter is due to the fact that they were journeymen or apprentices with some prior qualification.

In the 16th century and part of the 17th century, it was the exception rather than the rule for skilled workers to be remunerated only in money. References to money could be used to measure the amount of goods and/or services effectively payable or to measure the level of indebtedness between the employer and the worker. The relationship remained precapitalist, despite the mention of money in the contracts.

The components of the remuneration received by a journeyman depended on his caste, occupation, the time the contract was drawn up, and his legal status. We can see the difference when the masters were Spanish, if we look at tailors, silk makers, shoemakers and silversmiths, since these four trades offer representative samples.

16 AGN Prot. L. 5 fs.682 and 943.
17 AGN Prot. L. 14 f.1963.
18 AGN Prot. L. 57 f.823.
19 AGN Prot. L. 66 fs.159v, 295 and 462.

Spanish journeymen:

There were 26 contracts for Spanish tailors, the majority for a period of one year. With the exception of one, they all consigned payment in money, varying between 50 *eight-real pesos* and 350 *nine-real pesos* in addition to housing, food and daily clothing (except in five cases). There are five contracts for silk makers registered with salaries between 200 and 608 *nine-real pesos*, plus housing, food and clothing (except in the last case). One of the contracts included the work of the journeyman's wife in domestic service. There were six shoemakers, including a *chapinero* (manufacturer of cork sandals for popular consumption). Here, in the three cases where wages were mentioned, they were relatively lower: one of 6 *reales* per day and the other two of 80 and 100 *nine-real pesos* per year. There were also six silversmiths and the payment ranged from 200 *pesos corrientes* in 1561 to the lowest of 30 *nine-real pesos* in 1599.

Indigenous journeymen:

Comparing the same four trades, it can be seen that there were 14 indigenous people working for Spanish master tailors. Payment was very irregular. Some, such as Juan, who already had knowledge of doublet making, was paid nothing more than in housing, food, healthcare and two outfits in 1571, while the highest nominal "salary" was received by Miguel Alonso in 1583: 160 *nine-real pesos* a year but without any other type of payment. On the other hand, in 1595 Alonso received 12 *nine-real pesos* a month in addition to housing, food, healthcare, Christian doctrine and two sets of clothes. In the case of the silk makers, the 11 Indian journeymen received remuneration consisting of goods and services plus variable amounts of money, between *8 nine-real pesos* and 156 *nine-real pesos* per year. There were only five shoemakers, and they received almost no payment in kind or services and very low allowances in money. Of three Indian journeymen settled with Spanish silversmiths, two were paid 12 and 14 *nine-real pesos* a month in 1585 and 1586, and the third received only 20 *nine-real pesos* a year plus housing, food and health care.

***Mestizo* journeymen:**

Payment in money was common to all four *mestizo* journeymen working with Spanish master tailors. The amounts ranged from 100 *pesos corrientes* in 1557 to 110 *nine-real pesos* in 1582. The three *mestizo* shoemakers received 80, 100 and 130 *nine-real pesos* in addition to food and, in the latter case, also clothing at the end of the contract. There are no registered *mestizo* journeymen working with silk makers or silversmiths.

Mulato journeymen:

I only found a single *mulato* contracted to work with a Spanish tailor. It is from 1593, and he was paid 20 *nine-real pesos* a year plus one outfit and food.

Enslaved journeymen:

Only two slaves are listed as being contracted to work with master tailors. One in 1542 for 200 *pesos* of good gold and another in 1578 for 68 *pesos corrientes*. Likewise, there were two slaves contracted to silk makers in 1598: the framer Damián and the *enfurtidor* Pedro (a felter, who prepared the wool used as raw material for hats). One received eight *reales* and the other six *reales* per working day. I have found only one slave shoemaker. His name was Antón and in 1593 he received nothing more than accommodation, food and good treatment in payment. His master probably received wages that are not listed in the written contract or, failing that, the master's intention was simply that his slave should finish learning the trade.

If originally the main purpose of urban slavery in Lima was for the enslaved people to serve on hand, the masters quickly saw that it was better to use them under the regime that in ancient Rome was called *peculium*. That gave the enslaved the possibility to own their own goods, including the enjoyment of a part of the fruits of their labour, under certain conditions. This generated a system of semi-freedom in exchange for a payment that the slave had to make periodically to the master, called a *jornal*, as it referred to a daily payment, rather than a salary.

To incentivise increased productivity, some masters gave additional (or apparently additional) pay to their dependents. There is an example in 1592, when the silk maker Diego Méndez gave his apprentice 2 *reales* every Sunday in addition to housing, food and clothing. This additional payment would later come to be known as "tobacco" or "brandy" money.

To this same end, in 1598 the aforementioned silversmith de la Hoz allowed his journeyman Escobar to work "overtime":

> Of all the works and work done at night, what he will earn from them, I will split in half, and one part will be for the aforementioned Diego de la Hoz because the house and tools are his and the other half will be for the aforementioned Juan de Escobar for the extraordinary work that he has to do at night.[20]

20 AGN Prot. L. 60 f.728.

Likewise, that same year, Cristóbal de Ocaño, gave two slaves to his colleague Alonso Jaramillo: Damián the framer and Pedro the felter, also already mentioned above. Damián had to frame ten common hats daily, while Pedro had to felt eight. For each additional hat they made they would be rewarded with a *real*.[21]

Age was a determining factor in terms of the treatment given to an apprentice or journeyman. The masters justified the absence of money in the payment of their pupils if they were very young, as a carpenter did in 1599:

> [A]nd because he is a boy of ten or twelve years old, will not be given more than only what is necessary to eat and dress and shoe him and everything necessary to cure him of his illnesses and endow him with the Christian doctrine and teach him good habits and upbringing.[22]

Meagre pay was also justified on grounds of age. To the Indian from Surco (an indigenous town close to the city), Felipe García, his master tailor gave only 10 *nine-real pesos* and, justified this discrimination, stating that it was because he was only ten or eleven years old. The Indian, Diego, was also to receive 10 *nine-real pesos* from his master, the tailor Pedro de Arrones, "because he was small and not profitable in the first years."[23] Officially they ought to have received 12 *nine-real pesos.*

The situation was different for those who did have time in the trade even if they had not 'graduated' as journeymen. Their preferential treatment can be perceived by comparing their skills with those of others, as has been shown on several occasions. Thus, in 1595, the Chachapoyan Indian Domingo Viquin received 50 *nine-real pesos* as a tailor's apprentice because he already had notions of the trade. There are other examples of this in the documentation that could be presented.[24]

How did the masters, about whom we have some information, treat their apprentices or the journeymen in their employ? We can only speak to a few cases here. In those cases, it appears the treatment corresponded to the treatment they themselves received. When, in 1577, the potter Salvador Sánchez was a 'worker' for Rodrigo Hernández, he received a wage of 4 *reales*. Six years later, Sánchez,

21 AGN Prot. L. 115 f.1427.
22 AGN Prot. L. 61 f. 210v.
23 AGN Prot. L. 61 fs.34 and 237v.
24 AGN Prot. L. 144 f. 196.

now a master potter, gave his apprentice Bartolomé López 100 *nine-real pesos* a year, that is, 4 *reales* a day for 225 working days in a year.[25]

Juan Cano learned the trade of carpenter with Francisco Jaura between 1561 and 1564. The first two years he earned 25 *pesos corrientes* and in the final year, 50 "*pesos Corrientes.*" By 1571 he was a master, and he contracted the free *mulato* Diego, in 1577, and Juan Canas and Diego Hernández (both Spanish), in 1579, the first two for six years, and the third for four years. To each one he gave a set of tools, as he himself had received years ago from his teacher. Diego, who was his domestic servant, was paid only 12 *nine-real pesos* from the second year and for the last three years at the rate of 20 *nine-real pesos*. He would only pay Canas in services and clothing and to Diego Hernández would give health care and 40 *nine-real pesos* as well as clothing at the end of the contract.[26] Finally, despite the letter of the contracts, it is difficult to imagine in colonial times, a situation in which workshop owners paid their assistants on time, and exactly what they were due for the time they had worked, or for all the tasks they were carrying out.

Remuneration in the 18th century

Labour contracts in the eighteenth century differ from those of the sixteenth. In fact, only those deals that required a certain formality were registered in the notarial protocols. Of the 2,635 contracts, 1,810 (or 68 percent) were agreements made under the initiative and/or auspices of relatives or authorities. The largest group was women (widowed mothers, aunts, sisters, grandmothers), other relatives, guardians and slave owners, so it is likely that it was only a matter of covering a formality in cases in which some security was required for pupils who, due to various circumstances, were left abandoned by their father and were in need of some guidance in life. This was stated, for example, by the administrator of the foundling house when in 1774 he settled José Bueno with the joiner Pedro Nolasco Rosas: "[B]ecause he is young, it is necessary to give him a trade so that when he is older, he has something to entertain and sustain himself, to ensure the problems that result from idleness do not happen to him." Likewise, the uncle of Spanish Manuel Sangusan stressed "the advantages for the republic

25 AGN Prot. L. 72f. 987 and Prot. L. 74f. 417.

26 AGN Prot. L. 123f. 1540; Prot. L 128f. 654v; L. Prot. 8f. 65v and Prot. L. 28f. 193.

in which the individuals that compose it have the corresponding destinies and trades" when he settled him with a silversmith in 1799.[27]

The rest (32 percent) resulted from the initiative of the workers themselves, or at least, there is no indication to the contrary. As examples, in 1777, the 16-year-old *zambo* Marcelino Zevallos from Piura, settled by his own will with a tailor, because he was helpless and without a coat on his back. In 1779, the 12-year-old boy José Segundo Gutiérrez settled alone with the master tailor José Rodríguez because he found himself "aimless and without destiny and wishing to have a trade by which to subsist".

Table 7: Lima, 18th century, Apprentices Patronage at the time of the contract.

	Spanish	Indian	Black	*Mestizo*	*Mulattos*	*Zambo*	Slave	Totals
Fathers	238	29	23	9	0	8	0	311
Mothers	363	7	61	11	15	24	0	501
Relatives	293	48	19	21	7	11	0	415
Owners (men)	0	0	0	0	0	0	39	39
Owners (women)	0	0	0	0	0	0	61	61
Institutions	12	0	1	2	1	0	3	19
Authorities	65	338	3	29	6	10	0	457
Not specified	391	302	19	78	18	10	0	828
Totals	1,362	724	126	150	47	63	103	2,631

Source: Complied by the author, based on the Protocolos Notariales. Archivo General de la Nación. Siglo IIX.

Although there are a large number of written contracts, most agreements at the time were informal (spoken). The choice of informal contracts suggests that this modality was not as insecure as it might seem at first impression. The personal prestige of the grantor was a considerable part of his "fixed capital" since one's word, and personal trust was central in a face-to-face society such as Lima in colonial times.

Work contracts for journeymen were generally informal because adults could directly contact those in charge of the workshops to get a job. They were informal, moreover (and this is very important already in the 18th century) because the work was not stable. Market fluctuations prevented the use of contracts that forced both parties to continue a working relationship in conditions of economic insecurity; rather, the employment was established without long- or

27 AGN Sección Notarial L. 93 f.33v; L. 44 f. 767.

medium-term conditions. Deals were made almost daily and stability was provided by the frequency with which a journeyman worked with a master and the trust that was generated between them. Hiring was free, to the extent that relationships could be free in a society where servitude and slavery prevailed.

The dealings of one of the city's greatest tanners with his apprentice may be illustrative. Matías del Solar took the free black Marcos de Argandeña on as an apprentice in 1717, and he had to be in the workshop at six in the morning every working day for two years. In the first year he would only feed him and put two *reales* in his hand at weekends, while in the second year he would pay him for half of all the tasks he worked on. In another case from 1710, Juan Esteban and Francisco de Escobar only had to be fed in the workshop of the handrail maker Felipe de Alcócer.[28] The recruitment of artisan labour continued to take place based on non-economic methods such as debts or fidelity commitments generated during the apprenticeship. At the end of the apprenticeship, it was customary for a finished apprentice to stay on in his master's workshop.

However, compared to previous centuries, it is possible to establish some differences regarding relationships within the workshop, such as the prohibition on performing domestic tasks, the lower incidence of specifications as to the quality of the clothes, in accordance with the "quality" of the people, and the corresponding dress that was given in part payment, as well as the inclusion of greater detail about the hours to be worked. This was stipulated in practically all contracts "because the two years are understood to be without missing a day, except for festival days" as one contract from 1761 stated. "For the five years must be the full five years" was said in another. The days of illnesses or absence are not counted "with respect for the fact that the term must be without interruption," read another contract.

The master himself was empowered to determine how many days the pupil still had left to serve. If the apprentice ran away, the days of absence had to be made up at the end of the contract. The tailor Francisco Sánchez told his new pupil Manuel that he would end the four years "a full-fledged tailor, discounting the days he missed [...] and giving his master the power to go and fetch him from the part and place where he has gone and bring him back to learn his trade." The gold wire maker, Doncella Margarita Tamayo de Loyola remarked to Juan Barrionuevo Ramírez in 1701 that his contract required him to be at home day and night.[29] Silversmith Ignacio de Ayala y Carrillo exaggerated yet further when

28 AGN Prot. L. 776 f.149; Prot. L. 1030 f.62.

29 AGN Prot. L. 67 f.199; Prot. L. 713 f.915; L. 821 f.651v.

he specified that if his pupil Alejo de la Cueva escaped he would keep him in his workshop for six more months.

It is likely that work discipline had also undergone a change by this time, as is suggested by the sacking of assistants for lack of application, or due to petty theft or crimes (*drogas* as they were called then). In any case, the rigour to be applied to apprentices at work remained linked to the traditionally paternalistic relationship still in force between the lord and his dependents.

Very sporadically it is found that at the end of the contract, the new tradesman received a set of tools of his trade. It is important to note that the tools he received would have been more useful as a "worker" than for becoming an independent master craftsman in his own right. Common formulas were to deliver "the necessary tools" or stipulate that the master "has to give him all the tools." The tailors' trade included the awarding of a set of scissors of different sizes. The watchmaker Juan de Salazar had to give the Indian apprentice Rafael Colqui Puma a set of tools consisting of a file, pincers, pliers, compass and lathe in 1738.[30]

The archaic labour relations of the artisan workshops of the 16th century were reproduced throughout the colonial period. Nevertheless, as colonialism progressed, strictly economic ties and monetary relations did become more important, although they never became exclusive. Even in the 18th century, there were wages, but they were not the wage relationships we know today. There were elements of free work contracts, but not actual free contracts. The supply and demand of labour, as well as the systems of remuneration, were not shaped by purely economic conditions.

Payment in money appears in contracts in artisan workshops and in manufacturing; for enslaved and free workers; and for white workers as well as other *castes*. However, that monetary payment might only be nominal, and serve as a measure of the debt existing between the producer to the worker.[31] However, only a very small number of contracts established payment exclusively in money. Even when the payment – or part of it – was stipulated in money, it often only served as a measure of value, to replace payment in goods or services and, in many contracts, this was explicitly stipulated. Payment in money was justified "so that he can dress himself with it." The silversmith José Vilela paid José Antonio Seminario a *real* each day, so that it be used for the assistant

30 AGN Prot. L. 565 f.712v; Prot. L. 37 f.404v; Prot. L. 293 f.115v; Prot. L. 126 f.956.

31 The payment of debts with work is reminiscent of better known situations from rural areas of the Andes. By way of example, we have the work carried out in 1736 by the free black carpenter Juan Bautista for five months for a debt owed to the Marquis of Torre Tagle (Archivo General de la Nación. Cabildo Causasciviles 1736 leg. 10 c. 135 fs.1–6).

to feed himself. This money increased to two *reales* a day when the first year of training in the shop was completed. His co-worker Juan Ventura González Paredes was more fortunate because he received food in addition to two *reales* per day for his expenses. In 1718, the hatter Luis Pérez gave Miguel Arellano, apart from a pair of shoes a month, 20 *eight-real pesos* the first year, 30 *pesos* the second and 50 *pesos* the third so that he could buy with them what he needed. In this way, the master freed himself of the obligation to provide other goods and services: "without the aforementioned Miguel Arellano being able to ask me for anything else". The same were conditions agreed in 1719 by his colleague Francisco Galeano. The two *reales* daily that the blacksmith Domingo de Sarria gave to the *zambo* Fermín Valladares were expressly for him to feed and clothe himself. The same amount was paid by the shoemaker Pedro Mateo to Juan de Guzmán, for the similar ends. Likewise, the 3 *reales* per day that the carpenter Pedro José Betanzos gave to Francisco de Céspedes.[32]

Also, in the 18th century money was paid when those who were really receiving it were the owners, relatives or guardians of the journeymen and apprentices. The carpenter Manuel Sánchez Blanco gave the master of the enslaved Francisco Javier de Sacramento two *reales* daily in addition to the training that Francisco received. In 1706 Manuel José de Paredes was enslaved to a religious order that made him learn to weave ribbons. His master promised to pay the order 4 *reales* for working days, "with respect to there not always being continuous work to do in the trade." A daily *peso* (that is, 8 *reales*) was given to the slave potter Juan Antonio de San Francisco. In practice, that money would be given directly to the convent of San Francisco. It was not only in the case of enslaved people that the payment went to another person. That was also the case when paying minors. José Galvis, uncle to Juan de Santana, received the two *reales* per day that Juan Manuel de Ojeda owed him for his work as an apprentice in the pottery shop in 1769.[33]

The timing of payment in money was very varied in the 18th century. An advance payment is found that could be interpreted as a mechanism of *enganche*, a hook to tie the worker to the workshop, or the result of a previous request that the worker cover an emergency. The opposite was payment in money only at the end of the contract. This final payment was made even in the case of contracts lasting two, three or more years. A very common formula was the payment "for work served," which was accompanied by another clarifying phrase "and asked for." That is, they were paid in unspecified instalments, with the worker himself

32 AGN Prot. L. 258 f.552; Prot. L. 963 f.276.
33 AGN Prot. L. 525 f.11.

having to remind his master of payment deadlines. Payment "by thirds" or "by half parts" was also common. The most frequent form was the former and consisted of paying the worker what he was entitled to, once every four months, for that third of the year. The latter, referring to payment each semester, was less common. Although contracts often assess payment by the day, that would be verified at the end of the week or the month.

The money paid was below minimum subsistence levels, which were between 4 and 8 *reales* per day per person. A salary of 8 *reales* or 1 *peso* per day was the dream of a free and single worker, but not many made their dreams come true, because although a journeyman's pay could exceed 6 *reales*, the amounts that appear in the documentation for payment in money are really meagre: between 20 and 50 *pesos* a year. Dividing these figures by the 220 or 240 working days per year, you get sums of between a quarter of a *real* and one and a half *reales* per day, which is equivalent to saying that a craftsman had to live 365 days a year off wages amounting to half of a *quartillo* to a *real* per day. When the payment was monthly, similar results are obtained, although somewhat more favourable. For example, the baker Nicolás de Segura paid José Zubieta 4 *eight-real pesos* a month and the cake maker Cipriano Fernández paid Francisco Cervantes 6 *eight-real pesos* a month. Counting 20 working days, these amounts correspond to one and a half and two *reales* per day, respectively, although they drop to one *real* and one and a half *reales* per day if you count all 30 days of the month.

To encourage productivity in the 18th century, some master craftsmen granted an additional payment to their dependents. This was the payment known as 'tobacco' or 'brandy' money, paid on Sundays. Thus, the 4 *reales* a week (a little more than three *quartillos* a day), that the mason Luis García gave to the free black Francisco de Paula from the second year of instruction, were only a tip. Masters gave their pupils two hours *hueco* (time off), in the afternoons of holidays, to have fun. Sometimes that *huelga* (idle time) could last until evensong. Many masters committed to pay a *real* or half *real* on Sundays as a tip expressly for eating and buying fruit. In practice, that money was served to buy *picante* and *aguardiente* or *chicha* (alcoholic *beverages* sold in the *picanterías* or taverns). More generous was the blacksmith Miguel Palomino who gave Antonio Cabrera 4 *reales* a day as he already had experience in the work. Gradually, Santos Chávez's pay would rise in the Bernabé Iglesias tailor shop in 1777. Chávez had to complete his instruction in two years, receiving, respectively, 3 and 4 *reales* a day throughout each year.[34]

---

34 AGN Prot. L. 731 f.423; Prot. L. 537 f.864; Prot. L. 749 fs.1v, 2v; Prot. L. 925 f.98.

Above all, from the second part of the 17th century, free contracts are made with payment according to production (payment by "tasks" or "piecework"). Often, once the daily mandatory tasks were completed, the worker could stay in the workshop to perform an additional half or full task for which he received better remuneration. For example, Adrián de Rojas was a Huaylino Indian who received 2 *reales* a day from the shoemaker Juan Pascual de Abregú and 4 *reales* for each additional task that he completed.[35]

Payment in money was not, however, the prevailing form of payment in the workshops of Lima, since it only occurred in times of good market conditions. In reality, improvements in pay were not always used to attract (or retain) labour. In industry, the use of enslaved people as "day labourers" was very common. Although only 102 slaves appear in the formal apprenticeship contracts of the 18th century, this is because the masters preferred to set their slaves free so that they themselves could find a job with which to pay their "wages." In effect, while owned and rented slaves were often used to complement the servile workforce in artisan workshops, in manufacturing it was more common that slaves were sent to earn a wage. Work in the large workshops or even in one's own home did not require great skill on the part of the worker and, when training was required, it was obtained thanks to some previous experience in artisan workshops, or it was learned on the job.

In the 18th century, the practice of settling slaves with producers for their training and thus obtaining a better return from their daily wages did occur, but on a much smaller scale. In 1756, for example, the accountant Francisco de Alarcón gave the master tailor Manuel Dávila his slave named Pedro José "in his iron arms so that he could hold him for the time referred to, as if he were his slave."[36]

A slave sent 'to earn' had to give his master a *real* for every 100 *pesos* of his purchase price every day. That is to say, the *jornal* (daily payment) was equal to 0.125 percent of the slave's cost. If a qualified slave cost 800 *eight-real pesos*, he had to pay 8 *reales* each working day to his rentier master. It is evident that in order to survive outside the master's house, the day labourer had to earn more and this may explain the concentration of 'rented' slaves and day labourers in bakeries, mills, butter shops, candle shops and hat stores where the work was not precisely distinguished by being qualified, but it guaranteed an effective payment with which to meet the demands of the master. Other jobs that regularly

35 AGN Prot. L. 928 f.155v.

36 AGN Prot. L. 484 f.375; Prot. L. 507 f.567v; Prot. L. 535 f.127; Prot. L. 1170 f.350; Prot. L. 401 f.980; Prot. L. 339 f.162.

provided money were cargo loading and water hauling services (*aguadores*) (Quiroz, 2016).

By way of a conclusion

The information shows that the artisan and manufacturing workshops of colonial Lima varied both in terms of their ownership and of their workforce. The master craftsmen and owners belonged to all of the city's existing castes, although the absolute figures may hide the reality as to who had the greatest number and the best workshops, there is no doubt that the Spanish prevailed in both criteria.

Something similar happens with workers. Although they belonged to all castes, the information shows that the treatment of Spanish apprentices and journeymen was better in terms of working conditions and their payment in goods, services and money. Living and working together generates bonds of friendship and companionship, but it also creates discord. Lima's caste-based society saw differing conditions in the workplace as something natural. In this sense, working together did not make people of different castes and social backgrounds equal.

As is evident, Lima in colonial times was very far from having a free labour market. Rather, different forms of servile and slave labour predominated, and this context significantly marked the elements of free labour that began to emerge in the city almost from the time of its Spanish foundation. This can be seen in the fact that the daily wage of *mitayos* and enslaved people served as the basis for determining the daily wage of formally free urban labourers.

Finally, it is clear that the system of guilds in colonial Lima was rooted in the existing regime of castes and social classes. The guild emerges and develops in response to the need to control an ethnically diverse society.

Sources

Archivo Histórico Municipal de Lima (HML). Libros de cédulas y provisiones de Lima. Libros de cabildos de Lima iii: 577, 491, 592, 595, 672; viii: 275–276, 587.
Archivo General de la Nación (AGN), Lima.
Cabildo Penal 1730 leg. 11 c. [8].
Cabildo Penal Provincias 1805 leg. 16 paquete [4].
Cabildo Causas criminales 1773 leg. 5 c. [4].
Cabildo Causas criminales 1777 leg. 39 c. 461.
Cabildo Causas criminales 1785 leg. 57 c. 665.

Cabildo Causas criminales 1786 leg. 58 c. 683.
Cabildo Causas criminales 1811 leg. 120 c. 1463.
Cabildo Causas civiles 1736 leg. 10 c. 135.

Sección Notarial Protocolos (Prot.) siglo XVI y Siglo XVIII

Libro 5		Libro 8	Libro 14	Libro 28	
Libro 37	Libro 42	Libro 44	Libro 53		
Libro 57	Libro 60	Libro 60	Libro 61	Libro 65	Libro 66
Libro 67	Libro 71	Libro 72	Libro 74	Libro 93	Libro 115
Libro 123	Libro 126	Libro 128	Libro 144	Libro 150	Libro 167
Libro 180	Libro 258	Libro 293	Libro 525	Libro 533	Libro 537
Libro 565	Libro 632	Libro 648	Libro 713	Libro 731	Libro 732
Libro 749	Libro 749	Libro 776	Libro 821	Libro 868	Libro 925
Libro 928	Libro 963	Libro 1030			

Libros de cabildos de Lima (LCL). Lima: Municipalidad Provincial, 1935.

References

Bowser, Frederick P. 1977. *El esclavo africano en el Perú colonial (1524–1650).* México: Siglo XXI.

Cárdenas Ayaipoma, Mario. 2014. *La población aborigen en Lima colonial.* Lima: Fondo Editorial del Congreso del Perú.

Cook, Noble David. 1968. *Padrón de los indios de Lima 1613.* Lima: Seminario de Historia Rural Andina, Universidad Nacional Mayor de San Marcos.

Cook, Noble David. 1985. *Numeración general de todas las personas de ambos sexos, edades y calidades que se ha hecho en esta ciudad de Lima, año de 1700.* Lima: COFIDE.

Fernández Villanova, David. 2017. "Identidad corporativa y religiosidad popular. Las cofradías del gremio de sastres españoles de Lima (siglos XVI–XVIII)." In *Cofradías en el Perú y otros ámbitos del mundo hispánico (siglos xvi–xix)*, edited by David Fernández Villanova, et al. Lima: Conferencia Episcopal Peruana, Comisión Episcopal de Liturgia del Perú.

Harth-Terré, Emilio. 1960. *El indígena peruano en las bellas artes virreinales.* Cuzco: Ed. Garcilaso.

Harth-Terré, Emilio. 1973. *Negros e indios. Un estamento social ignorado del Perú colonial.* Lima: Ed. Juan Mejía Baca.

Harth-Terré, Emilio and Alberto Márquez Abanto. 1962. "Perspectiva social y económica del artesanado virreynal en Lima." *Revista del Archivo Nacional del Perú* 26 (2): 353–446.

Lockhart, James. 1982. *El mundo hispanoperuano, 1532–1560.* Mexico: Fondo de Cultura Económica.

Pérez Cantó, María Pilar. 1985. *Lima en el siglo xviii. Estudio socioeconómico.* Madrid: Ediciones de la Universidad Autónoma de Madrid, Instituto de Cooperación Iberoamericana.

Quiroz Chueca, Francisco. 1995. *Gremios, razas y libertad de industria. Lima colonial.* Lima: Universidad Nacional Mayor de San Marcos.
Quiroz Chueca, Francisco. 2008. *Artesanos y manufactureros en Lima colonial.* Lima: Instituto de Estudios Peruanos, Banco Central de Reserva del Perú.
Quiroz Chueca, Francisco. 2016. "Historia de muchas ciudades: esclavitud urbana en las Américas." *RELEA, Revista Latino-Americana de Estudos Avançados* 1: 29–45.
Vergara Ormeño, Teresa. 2005. "La población indígena". In *Lima en el siglo XVI*, edited by Laura Gutiérrez Arbulú, 175–225. Lima: Instituto Riva Agüero, Pontificia Universidad Católica del Perú.

María Luisa Soux

Yanaconas, *colonos* and *arrenderos*: Contradictions between the law and practice in rural labour in 19th and 20th century Bolivia

Abstract: This chapter seeks to analyse the contradictions that existed between the law and practice at work on the Bolivian *haciendas* between 1825 and 1952. Although the regulations, through the 1832 Civil Code, established a labour system based on forms of leasehold paid through the work or service of the leaseholder or *colono*; in practice, until 1952, a system persisted in which labour was given in exchange for the usufruct of a plot on the estate, and that encompassed not only agricultural labour but also servile labour for the landowner, such as *pongueaje*. This contradiction led to several debates in the 1940s. Although the 1945 Indigenous Congress determined the end of *pongueaje*, it only really disappeared with the Land Reform of 1952.

Keywords: work systems; *yanaconas*; *colonos*; *arrendamiento*; *pongueaje*.

Introduction

Labour relations on the *haciendas* (large estates) of the highlands and valleys of Bolivia have not yet been studied in sufficient depth. Studies of rural and agrarian history have focused largely on the issue of property and land ownership. Those studies almost all repeat the key events in the creation of private property and the struggle for land. In this way, the issue of rural labour has been subsumed by the topic of land ownership, and the assumption that each system of tenure and ownership corresponds to a given form of labour relations. These gaps in the literature looking at forms of labour, as well as the political use that is sometimes made of the issue of land, have led to concepts becoming established, even in laws and decrees, that are not entirely correct. This has led to confusion, and has hindered accurate historical analysis. An example of this is the debate, still ongoing after many years, about the feudal character of the

Doctor in History at the Universidad Nacional de San Marcos. Academia Boliviana de la Historia, Universidad Mayor de San Andrés (UMSA) Contact: mlsoux@yahoo.es.

https://doi.org/10.1515/9783110759303-005

haciendas, which constituted one of the basic arguments for the Land Reform of 1953.[1]

This study aims to analyse the legal changes that took place, and the *de facto* persistence of the old systems of labour on the *haciendas* from the beginning of the republican system, in 1825, until the Land Reform of 1953. It looks at how the name and legal status of the colonial *yanaconas* gradually shifted towards the concept and legal status of *colono* or settler. However, labour relations did not undergo the same changes, which resulted in contradictory figures such as that of *pongueaje*[2]. It is therefore important to establish the relationship between three concepts: property, the leasing of land, and labour systems, because the contradiction stems largely from the practice of "payment for land through labour."

This chapter begins with an analysis of the laws regulating property and labour systems. We will then go on to analyse labour relations in daily practice, as well as the contradictions that allowed the regulations themselves to be gradually modified.

Land ownership laws in the early years of the republic

The property and land tenure systems established by the Republic went some way towards modifying traditional colonial forms. There was a tension between the recognition, or not, of forms of communal ownership, and the definitive introduction of individualised property ownership, based on the premise of liberalism.

Bolívar was one of the first to refer to land distribution, seeking to establish more secure forms of property especially for the *agregados* and *forasteros* (indigenous migrants), in the face of both the authorities and original indigenous com-

1 The debate about the feudal nature of the *hacienda* system has been fundamental in studies of agrarian history in Bolivia and Latin America. The positions in favour of understanding the *hacienda* system as feudal, focus specifically on the slave and servile labour systems which existed in the majority of cases. The contrary proposal maintains that, despite the fact that the system of labour in exchange for use of the land predominated, it cannot be considered feudal because it did not contemplate dominion, which was central in the concept of a feudal system. This chapter seeks to demonstrate that, although the laws of the nineteenth century did not recognise servitude, in practice it was maintained.

2 The custom by which the *colonos* had to serve in the urban house of the owner, and/or in the farmhouse, doing domestic tasks.

munities. To that end, he promoted the individualisation of property (Antezana, 1992). From then on, Bolivarian legislation was mainly directed at the issue of property in the indigenous communities, as the already private and individualised ownership of the *haciendas* was never called into question.

Based on the Bolivarian decrees, subsequent governments implemented agrarian policies that were often confused and ambivalent. For example, the government of Antonio José de Sucre sought to consolidate ownership of community lands in individual hands and establish a general tax on them. However, the single tax was rejected both by the Creole owners of the *haciendas* and by the indigenous communities. For the former, the payment of a single tax implied equating them with the indios, whom they had always considered to be inferior in status and belonging to their own republic. Meanwhile, for the indigenous peoples, the payment of the single property tax, instead of the tribute, required a prior cadastre, which would bring to light the internal arrangements that existed within the communities, between the original landowners and the *agregados* and *forasteros* who had usufruct of the land. From the point of view of the indigenous people, this was state interference in the internal affairs of the community (Soux, 2012). Faced with widespread refusal to comply, the decrees were suspended, and the tribute was maintained, and given the name "indigenous contribution" (Lofstrom, 2010).

According to Marta Irurozqui and Víctor Peralta (2000: 217), the tribute was central to the recognition of land ownership for indigenous people. The fiscal contribution guaranteed access to land in the sense that it generated an income for the State. However, for this to happen, land ownership had to be individualised. It is in this context that we see the Law of 28 September 1831, issued during the government of Andrés de Santa Cruz, which consolidated ownership "of the lands of the blood *caciques*, as well as of the indigenous taxpayers who had held possession of the land for more than 10 years." The Constituent Assembly of the same year confirmed the property rights of indigenous peoples, although it was done individually (Soux, 1997).

In 1838, the *Resolución Suprema* of 22 November, known as the "Indigenous Succession," confirmed indigenous ownership of the land, establishing a system of primogeniture for inheritance of the land, "giving preference to the oldest over the younger siblings and to the male over the female." Under this law, possession was also clear: only property could be given in inheritance, and primogeniture system avoided the division of land.

This new special law arose from the Civil Code, also promulgated during the government of Andrés de Santa Cruz in 1832. It was based largely on the Napoleonic Civil Code, which was inspired, in turn, by the property principles of Roman Law and the modern principles of legal equality. It was not rooted in colonial custom, which means that the code did not fully respond to the specific needs of the indigenous people. Thus, while for the general population it was feasible to divide the land, for the indigenous people it was necessary to establish a principle of primogeniture to avoid division.

During the first years of the Republic, based on liberal postulates, the State gradually slid towards a recognition of indigenous ownership of communal lands, although in an increasingly individualised fashion. The perfect title of the non-indigenous *hacienda* owners was also recognised and confirmed, although ties of primogeniture in land ownership were ignored, as these were privileges that the new system did not accept. At this point it is important to highlight that the principle that governed the republican legal systems was based on an apparent concept of citizens' equality, which necessarily implied the substitution of the privileges and exemptions that had existed in the hierarchical and caste-based society, to create a society in which all were equal before the law.

In 1842, emphyteusis was established for indigenous peoples on communal lands, by means of a circular. In the years that followed, through the Melgarejo land-auction laws (1868–1869), and the 1874 *Ley de Exvinculación*, the general tendency was to weaken community property either by recognising state ownership, auctioning off communal lands to private landowners or, finally, individualising ownership by declaring that the communities had disappeared. One way or another, the result was the consolidation of a system of *haciendas* characterised not by capitalist labour systems but by the persistence of the ancient indigenous occupants as *colonos*. This system was officially maintained until 1953.

Ways of acquiring property

Although in studies of the *haciendas* considered to be capitalist in form, land ownership is separated from labour systems, on the understanding that the relationship between the landowner and the labourers was based only on wages, the same is not the case when approaching an analysis of precapitalist *haciendas* in which non-salaried labour relations are related to forms of precarious tenure or tenancy.

Since the colonial period, various ways of acquiring ownership of the land had subsisted, for indigenous groups, but also for Spanish and creole landowners. We will not go in depth here into the debate that surrounds the *encomienda* (the system by which indigenous labourers were granted by the Crown to a conquistador), because by the 19th century, the impact of the *encomienda* was already negligible. Likewise, grants, which was the principal way for Spanish and creole settlers to obtain land in the 16th century. However, it is important to understand that the so-called "*composición de tierras.*" This took place from the end of the 16th century following the *Visita* (inspection) by the Bishop of Quito; throughout the 17th century (the inspections of Gerónimo Luis de Cabrera and others (Ballivián de Romero, 1987); and until the 18th century (the inspections of Juan Bravo del Rivero), and created the framework for the consolidation of property rights, both individually in *haciendas*, and collectively in communities. In both cases, not only possession but also title was guaranteed, although in the case of indigenous people and communities that title was held collectively (Mamani, 2012).

With the republican system, ways of acquiring and transferring land ownership took the following legal forms:

Immemorial possession

Although this form of acquiring rights was more important during the first years of the conquest, it subsisted in part as the guaranteeing of ancient property rights. This was the argument used by the indigenous populations, resorting to colonial norms which indicated that so-called "immemorial possession" dated back 100 years, that is, the maximum possible existence of a witness who could testify to ownership of the land. This argument was especially useful when there was no other written way to demonstrate ownership or to transform some non-perfect form of ownership into perfect title.

Inheritance or succession

This was one of the most common ways to transfer individual ownership of land to successors. Land inheritance systems contemplated both *intervivo* succession and inheritance after the death of the owner. Land inheritance systems were not exclusive to creole or *mestizo* landowners. The indigenous population could also pass on both their *huertas* or *sayañas*[3], and their rights to usufruct of *aynoqas.*[4] Depending on the location, succession contemplated deep-rooted customs in re-

3 Individual or family plot where the peasant house is located. *Sayañas* existed both on the *haciendas* and in the communities even before the Land Reform. In the first case, the peasant served a certain number of days working in exchange for the usufruct of his *sayaña.*

4 Community lands in which a dynamic of crop rotation is followed. They are of individual or family usufruct in the years of agricultural use (*liwakallpas*) and become common use land when they are resting, to be used as pasture for livestock.

lation to gender and age group, always with a greater emphasis on male succession, which guaranteed both community work and the payment of tributes (Soux, 1995).

Buying and selling

This was a common form of transfer of individual land ownership, especially among creole and *mestizo* groups. It was based on the right of perfect title that guaranteed the possibility to give up that property to another in exchange for a given amount of money. For this to be possible, it was essential that the seller demonstrate ownership of the land through specific documents, as well as the status of the property, to show that it was free of outstanding charges. The system of buying and selling could not be officially implemented in the indigenous communities, since various laws prevented those lands from being freely bought. Nevertheless, despite the prohibition, there was no shortage of cases of community *sayañas* being bought and sold. This legal figure was later permitted, following the *Ley de Exvinculación*, which opened the community lands up to the market by individualizing their ownership. (Soux, 2012)

For each of the forms of property transfer described above, a central point was that the land was transferred along with its "uses and customs," which implied that any labourers were transferred with it, marking a precapitalist characteristic of land ownership.

Leasing and work systems

Another characteristic of perfect title was the possibility of leasing the land, that is, of handing it over to another without transferring ownership, so that the tenant or lessor could work it in exchange for a fee. That rental fee could be paid in money, in produce, or in labour. It was the system of rent payments for land use in labour that had the most significant impact on labour relations in rural areas.

In the *haciendas* owned by creoles and *mestizos*, the land was not worked directly by the owners, so labour relations followed similar work modalities to the European manor system, with two variants: the *Gutsherrschaft* system, in which a significant part of the land was cultivated for the owner by *yanaconas*[5]

5 System whose origin dates back to pre-Hispanic times and referred to specialised servile work

(peasant-serfs) who served a given number of weekly workdays in exchange for the use of a plot of land for themselves; and the *Grundherrschaft* system, in which the owner divided up and gave all the lands to the peasants in exchange for the payment of rent in money or in kind (Barragán et al, 2015). These systems could be combined, resulting in the following forms of leasehold:

- A lease with the payment of rent in money, which occurred mainly between creole or *mestizo* owners and lessors. This type of contract did not establish any obligations beyond the payment of rent, and there was no dependant relationship.
- A lease with payment in labour was mainly established between a creole owner and an indigenous person. It was usually a verbal contract for a part of the property, and it generally did establish a dependent relationship.
- A lease within the indigenous community could be made by a indigenous person to an *agregado* and from the latter to a *yanapaco* or an *utawawa.*[6] This type of oral contract was later reproduced as a form of sublease between the lessor or *colono*[7] and the *yanapacos* or *utawawas.*
- A lease of rights to common lands such as *aynoqas* and *liwaqallpas*, used in the communities.

As seen above, in practice there were various forms of tenancy that distinguished a number of different relationships between groups that were themselves diverse. However, looking at the regulations, the Civil Code, promulgated in 1832 during the government of Andrés de Santa Cruz, established the lease as a legal act, typified as a contract related to property, participated in by civil persons who enjoy the same rights, leaving the aside differences of social class. Thus, the Civil Code established the following forms of leasing:

- A lease or rental can be one of two kinds: the renting of things and the renting of labour.
- Renting of things was a contract by which one of the parties is obliged to give the other a thing, in exchange for a given price, and for a given period of time (Art. 1129).

---

for the authorities. It was maintained during the colonial period and involved work for which the worker performed certain agricultural and service jobs for the usufruct of a piece of land.

6 Names given to individuals who lived in the communities and *haciendas* and who, in exchange for fulfilling certain obligations, received small plots for their usufruct by the community members or *yanaconas.* In some cases, they only received housing and food in exchange for their labour.

7 Result of lease contracts, usually verbal, of in which the *colono* or tenant paid for the use of his *sayaña* with labour. As will be seen, it also led to servile obligations.

– A labour contract, by which one of the parties is obliged to complete a service or task, for a price stipulated between the parties (Art. 1130).

As a share-cropper, cultivating land "*al partir,*" that is, giving a share of the produce or fruits of his or her labour to the landowner, could neither sublet nor cede use of the land, if the power to do so had not been expressly granted in the contract. In the event of a violation, the contract was terminated, and the tenant had to pay damages and interest. (Art. 1163). Tenants and *colonos* were liable for any damage caused by them, or by any of their sub-tenants or people who lived with them, (Art. 1145) and both parties were subject to the obligations of usufruct (Art. 1140).

The cited articles use the terms *arrendero, inquilino* or *colono* synonymously. They are also equated in certain articles with the concept of usufructuary. This represents an essential change to the old relationship between the owner of the land and the farmer who works it. The relationship based on servitude, and inheritance, as part of vassal relationships, was modified to become leasehold contracts between capable persons considered to be of a similar legal status. In a society that proclaims equality among all its inhabitants, even if it was only rhetoric, forms of servitude could no longer be sustained.

This new way of conceptualizing the relationship between the leasing of land and labour was endorsed by José María Dalence in 1851, whose work, *Bosquejo Estadístico de Bolivia*, stated:

> The renters are the settlers (*colonos*) on the *haciendas*; they have fields that the owners give them for a stipulated rate, that can be paid in part in money, and in part through the service that they must render to the owner for sowing, harvesting, etc. This contract is very useful, if it is not abused; the owner possesses the workforce he needs for cultivation, and the *colono* secures lands to sow for himself and his descendants; thus, it is very rare that a landowner dismisses a *colono* or that a *colono* leaves the farm where he and his grandparents were born. The number of tenants amounts to more than 80,000 heads of household. (Dalence, 1975 (1851): 211, cited in Froilán Mamani 2012)

This fundamental legal change in the relationship between landowners and labourers, which goes from being a hierarchical system in which indigenous workers are subject to a form of servitude to the existence of a contract between equals, necessarily implies the disappearance of the *yanacona* system. However, that is not what happened. This has led to a semantic confusion between the *yanacona* or *yanakuna* and the *colono* or *peón*.

In this sense, Ximena Medinaceli indicates that the terms *colono* and *yanacona* were used at different times and in different places, and that there are certain subtle differences between these two categories: "If the *yanacona* was in principle, an Indian dependent on a patron, the *colono* is one who, subject to his land, becomes dependent on a new owner" (Medinaceli, 1986: 171). For Medinaceli it is precisely this "subjection to the land" that is key to explaining the persistence of serfdom and *yanaconaje* at a stage in which it was no longer officially recognised but had been replaced with leases and with the *colonato* system.

The land auctions and the new *latifundistas*

Between 1866 and 1868, the government of Mariano Melgarejo decreed a series of measures, seeking to increase income to the national treasury. Through them, the collective property of the indigenous communities was no longer recognised, and the land became the property of the State. It was decreed that within a set period of time the communities had to consolidate their property by paying a fee, and if they failed to do so, their lands would be put up for auction. There were very few cases where the communities were able to pay the fee, so from 1867 on, through processes that were quite irregular, large parts of the highland and valley provinces were auctioned off or put out to tender.

These auctions above all benefited members of the Melgarejo government and their relatives, who took possession of the land. Under the same government, the Constitution of 1868 was promulgated, assuring that: "Equality is the basis of tax and public charges. Personal service cannot be demanded, except by virtue of the law" (Choque, 1994). In this context of contradictions, what happened to the relationship between the new *latifundistas* (large landowners) and the indigenous communities whose communal lands had been auctioned? The new owners took advantage of their influence in government and the fact that the old indigenous owners could not leave their lands immediately, to convert them into *colonos*, forced settler-tenants on their own lands, meaning they would have pay not only with agricultural labour but through fulfilling other obligations, just like on the *haciendas* of colonial times. In this way, not only had the indigenous people lost legal ownership of their community lands, but they began to pay with rural labour and domestic service to be able to use the lands that had previously belonged to them. The only difference, at least on paper, was that, since the old personal tribute had been transformed into a contribution based on property, the new *latifundistas* would have to pay the taxes to the State that corresponded to their tenant-settlers.

The deeply disgruntled indigenous movement supported the deposition of the Melgarejo government in January 1871, in the midst of a general indigenous uprising across the entire *Altiplano*. All of Melgarejo's measures relating to land auctions were repealed and there was a return to the previous circumstances.

In October of 1874, under the government of Tomás Frías, a new land-ownership Law was promulgated, that of *Exvinculación*, which declared all the indigenous communities extinct. The state, this time free of charge, would deliver the title of the lands to each of the indigenous people individually. Although these measures implied the recognition of the indigenous peoples' ownership of their lands, the failure to recognise the communities and communal property caused a series of tensions and conflicts. It distorted the existing forms of internal ownership and, therefore, also the systems of labour and working relationships within those communities.

It is well known that the *Ley de Exvinculación* of 1874, by establishing perfect and individual ownership of communal lands, led from 1880 (following an extensive re-inspection and subsequent cadastre of the lands) to many ex-community members selling their plots to neighbours in the village or to members of the elites from the cities. From the perspective of liberal principles, a step was taken towards capitalist forms of production, where workers, deprived of the ownership of their lands, would become wage labourers. However, traditional practice and the persistence of a hierarchical society led to the sale of the *sayañas* and even of entire communities, which meant not only the acquisition of the land, but also the 'customs and habits' associated with it, which, in other terms, meant that the indigenous person selling their land accepted 'as a grace' to remain on it, and pay for the usufruct of the land through labour. In other words, he unofficially became a tenant-settler of his own *sayaña*. In return, the new owner agreed to pay the land tax (a descendant of the tribute but which was supposed to be a tax on property, not on the person). At that time, tax was paid to the regional treasuries.[8] In addition, similar to the situation on the old colonial haciendas, the new '*colono*' would have to fulfil other servile obligations, such as *pongueaje* for men and *mitanaje* for women (Soux 1999).

Alongside these changes in the ex-communities, on the old colonial *haciendas*, which had traditionally worked with the system of *yanaconaje*, new republican laws such as the Civil Code failed to alter the labour systems in practice. Defining the *yanconas* as *colonos*, peons or tenants, was nothing more than semantics. The indigenous worker ceased to be called *yanacona*, but his daily reality did not change. The *haciendas* maintained non-agricultural obligations and personal service for their *colonos*, meaning labour relations were similar to a system of *yanaconaje* and servitude.

This contradiction, between laws that pushed towards a "modern" solution to agricultural labour relations, and practices that maintained the old regime,

8 *ALP. Fondo de la Prefectura. Registro de Tierras Comunales, 1880–1899.*

persisted until the middle of the 20th century, because of the principle of "customs and habits" that went with the land.

Labour systems and servitude on the *haciendas*

The payment of rent on the *hacienda* was specifically related to agricultural labour, according to the location and characteristics of each *hacienda*. It amounted to three or four days a week working the landlord's land or, failing that, a week for the boss and a week for the *sayaña*. This labour obligation, was not exclusive to the head of the household, and the work often had to be carried out by the whole family. Thus, for example, in the case of the Yungas, the specialised work of *quiche* (harvesting) was done by women, while weeding was done by men, which effectively doubled the number of days worked for the landowner.

Added to these obligations were extra jobs or services, which could be of different types; from the obligation to collect *cinchona*, as described by Eugenia Bridikhina in her work on the blacks of Yungas (Bridikhina, 1997),[9] to the *muleteer* and *apiri* (loader) work carried out by the men of the highland and valley *haciendas*, or the specialised work producing *muku* (a base product for the production of *chicha*) by the women of the Cochabamba *haciendas*. Of all these tasks, the one considered most abusive, due to its clearly servile nature, were those of *pongo* and *mitani*, which were a form of free domestic service in the *hacienda* house or in the urban dwelling of the owners.

These labour relations, involving personal service, were so normalised in Bolivian society that the new contractual relationship, between the landowner and the *colono* as tenant, was practically imperceptible. This can be confirmed by various types of actions, including legal ones, that demonstrate this relationship. So, for example, when a member of an indigenous community sold his *sayaña* to his neighbour or to the new landowner, in most cases it was noted in the corresponding registry that the seller agreed to stay on the land, fulfilling his obligations according to "uses and customs." Likewise, until well into the 20th century, it was common to find signs in the streets of La Paz, and notices in the newspapers, stating: "*Pongo* with *taquia* for rent," that is to say that La Paz's landowners who owned more than one *hacienda*, and therefore received more than one weekly *pongo*, had no problem renting their *pongos* out to do non-agricultural

9 The work carried out by the black population after the abolition of slavery in 1851, did not differ from that carried out by the other workers on the *haciendas*, that is, they came to be considered *colonos* and worked a few days a week in exchange for the usufruct of a *sayaña*.

jobs for others, with the addition that the *pongo* had to provide their own food and fuel (the *taquia*), which was the llama excrement used to heat the kitchens and prepare food. (Barragán et al, 1997).

The *pongueaje* debate

This relationship, which many of the landowners and society as a whole saw as normal and natural, began to be criticised by leftist groups at the beginning of the 20th century. Criticism grew in the 1920s and deepened with the Chaco War (Soliz, 2012). Many young people, including the children of the landowners themselves, stopped seeing the renting out of *pongos* and even the institution of *pongueaje* itself as 'normal'. The issue was also addressed in the context of the problem of municipal or ecclesiastical properties in Cochabamba, resulting in the measures taken during the government of David Toro (1936–1937) with the creation of the first agrarian unions and the recognition of leases (Soliz, 2012). It was dealt with in the debates of the National Convention of 1938, which finally ruled on the matter, stating in the Constitution of that year that "slavery does not exist in Bolivia. No type of servitude is recognised and no one could be forced to provide personal service without just compensation and without full consent" (Gotkowitz, 2012; Barragán, 2007). In this way, more than one hundred years after the promulgation of the Civil Code, not only the issue of land ownership, but also that of labour relations on the *haciendas* and the contradictions that existed between the law and what happened in practice, was called into question.

Despite the fact that serfdom had been specifically abolished, in practice, *pongueaje* and *mitanaje* continued. The problem was addressed again in the legislatures of 1940 and 1941. Under pressure from the *Partido de la Izquierda Revolucionaria* (left wing revolutionary party of Stalinist influence), Eduardo Arce Loureiro pushed for measures in favour of lease contracts "that would allow the peasants to free themselves of their condition as *colonos*", as a precondition for achieving access to land ownership (Soliz 2012). With these projects it was clear that, at that time, without taking into account the concepts laid down in the Civil Code of 1832 that was still in force, a difference was established between the figure of the lease (with rental payments in money) and that of *colonato*, which was based on the payment for use of the land through labour, and which also implied other personal services.

During the government of Enrique Peñaranda, Eguino Rodas presented a project to abolish *pongueaje*, but the project was rejected by Congressman Salmón based on an argument related to the civilised status of the Indian. Salmon indicated:

> The *pongo* is now the only tie that links us to the Indian. Once this has been removed, the last link will be cut and the Indian will be cut off. It must be borne in mind that the Indian who serves as a *pongo* in the city hears the radio, walks the streets, is interested in the news and is well fed. (cited in Carmen Soliz, 2012)

The first Indigenous Congress of 1945, convened by the government of Gualberto Villarroel, again took up the issue of abolishing *pongueaje* and other forms of personal service, which it had not been possible to approve under previous governments. We will not tackle the entire debate around these issues here, as it has already been considered in depth by a number of other historians (Gotkowitz, 2011; Soliz, 2012). Nevertheless, it is important to analyse the interview, cited by Carmen Soliz, which was conducted with one of the main Congress leaders. This gives us a glimpse in greater depth the perspective the Congress had on the subject:

When Francisco Chipana Ramos, president of the Congress, was asked his opinion on the decrees that had been signed during the Congress, his answer highlighted the following points: that their condition as slaves had disappeared and that the freedom lost with the conquest had been regained; that compulsory work on the haciendas had been limited to a maximum of four days a week; that, through the elaboration of an Agrarian Labour Code, better working conditions would be established, preventing "free work" and "work on other haciendas"; that "extra" jobs should be paid with wages, that is, as salaried workers; that the 'abuses' of the employer such as the forced handing over of animals and other products would be controlled and that schools would be established for the education of workers and their families. Finally, Chipana Ramos indicated as the most important decree, the death of *pongueaje*, that is, of working in the employer's house for free.

For the Ramos, and apparently for all those who participated in the Congress, it was clear that there were two totally different forms of labour relationship between landowners and workers: agricultural labour and "extra jobs" linked to domestic service or servitude. Regarding the first, Chipana Ramos himself stated: "We will gladly work for the *hacienda*, for, as the owners of our crops, we will be able to make use of them", while on the second he explained: "From now on our services will be paid as would any other trade or job."

Despite the Decree abolishing *pongueaje* coming into effect in 1945, cases of conflicts over the attempt to enforce personal services by the landowners continued for several more years, and it was not until after the Land Reform of 1953 that *pongueaje* and other personal services would disappear altogether, with the handing of the land to "those who work it," as stated in the postulate of Land Reform.

Conclusions

How can we explain the fact that, despite the republican Civil Code establishing a legal basis for the labour relationship between landowner and labourer, based on the existence of a contract between equals and focused on the leasing of land in exchange for work, for more than one hundred years this was normalised as a relationship of two types, on the one hand, the payment of rents through labour, "gladly working for the hacienda," as Ramos stated, and, on the other, a servile relationship of colonial origin? Why was the first type of relationship considered legitimate and the second an abuse by the landowner?

I believe that to explain this perception it is necessary to analyse the principles that underlay labour relationships in the colonial period, and the way in which liberalism and modernity tried to modify them. The regulations – fundamentally the Civil Code – were based on modern and liberal principles of equality, and on the need to regulate a relationship of equals through the execution of contracts, be that for the transfer of ownership, leasing or work. However, the principles of the old regime persisted with great force, including the principle of reciprocity. That principle could be seen as a perverse way of disguising unequal relationships and exploitation. Nevertheless, certain elements of the "pact," in this case between the *hacienda* owner and his labourers, which had its origins in the conquest and the ancient regime, were superimposed on the modern rules of contracts between equals. In this way, servile labour relations were interlinked with traditional forms that guaranteed access to land. This allowed those servile relationships not only to survive, but to be seen as natural in rural Bolivian labour relations, for more than 100 years, despite a legal framework based on liberal equality. Finally, servile forms of labour did not disappear with the transformation and modernisation of the *haciendas*, nor did they give rise to an agrarian wage system. That had to wait for an agrarian reform that directly handed over ownership of the land to those who worked it.

References

Antezana Salvatierra, Alejandro. 1992. *Estructura agraria en el siglo XIX: Legislación agraria y transformación de la realidad rural en Bolivia.* La Paz: CID.

Antezana Salvatierra, Alejandro. 1996. *Los liberales y el problema agrario de Bolivia.* La Paz: CID.

Ballivián de Romero, Florencia. 1987. "La visita de Gerónimo Luís de Cabrera a Larecaja y Omasuyos." *Historia y Cultura* 12: 39–48.

Barragán, Rossana. 2007. *Asambleas constituyentes. Ciudadanía y elecciones, convenciones y debates (1825–1971).* La Paz: Muela del Diablo.

Barragán, Rossana, Dora Cajías, and Seemin Qayum, eds. 1997. *El siglo XIX. Bolivia y América Latina.* La Paz: IFEA-Historias Coordinadora de Historia.

Barragán, Rossana, Seemin Qayum, and María Luisa Soux. 1997. *De terratenientes a amas de casa.* La Paz: Coordinadora de Historia, Secretaría Nacional de Asuntos étnicos, de género y generacionales.

Choque Canqui, Roberto. 1997. "La servidumbre indígena andina de Bolivia." In *El siglo XIX. Bolivia y América Latina*, edited by Barragán Rossana et al. La Paz: IFEA-Historias.

Dalence, José María. 1975 [1851]. *Bosquejo Estadístico de Bolivia.* La Paz: Universidad Mayor de San Andrés.

Gotkowitz, Laura. 2011. *La revolución antes de la Revolución: luchas indígenas por tierra y justicia en Bolivia. 1880–1952.* La Paz: Plural.

Klein, Herbert S. 1995. *Haciendas y ayllus en Bolivia: la región de La Paz, S. XVIII y XIX.* IEP. Lima.

Lofstrom, William Lee. 2010. *La presidencia de Sucre en Bolivia.* Instituto Internacional de Integración del Convenio Andrés Bello. La Paz.

Mamani Humérez, Froilán. 2012. "La práctica del arrendamiento durante el siglo XIX en la región de Santiago de Huata." In *El proceso histórico hacia la territorialización del poder*, edited by María Luisa Soux et al. La Paz: IEB-ASDI.

Mamani Siñani, Roger. 2012. "Tierra, litigio y títulos. La visita de tierras de Gerónimo Luis de Cabrera y don Juan Segura Ávalos de Ayala." In *El proceso histórico hacia la territorialización del poder.* María Luisa Soux et al. La Paz: IEB-ASDI.

Medinaceli, Ximena. 1986. Comunarios y yanaconas. Resistencia pacífica de los indios de Omasuyus. Siglo XIX. Tesis de licenciatura en Historia. UMSA-La Paz.

Platt, Tristan. 1982. *Estado boliviano y ayllu andino. Tierra y tributo en el norte de Potosí.* Lima: Instituto de Estudios Peruanos.

Rodríguez Ostria, Gustavo. 1986. *¿Expansión del latifundio o supervivencia de las comunidades indígenas? Cambios en la estructura agraria boliviana del siglo XIX.* Cochabamba: IESE.

Rivera Cusicanqui, Silvia. 1978. "La expansión del latifundio en el altiplano boliviano: elementos para la caracterización de una oligarquía regional." *Avances* 2: 95–118.

Rojas, Antonio. 1978. La tierra y el trabajo en la articulación de la economía campesina con la hacienda." *Avances* 2: 51–71.

Soliz, Carmen. 2012. "La modernidad esquiva: debates políticos e intelectuales sobre la reforma agraria en Bolivia (1935–1952)." *Revista Ciencia y Cultura* 29. www.scielo.org.bo/scielo.php?script=sci_arttext&pid=S2077-33232012000200003.

Soux, María Luisa. 1995. "Individuo, familia y comunidad. El derecho sucesorio entre los comunarios de La Paz. (1825 – 1850)." *Estudios Bolivianos* 2: 437 – 465.
Soux, María Luisa. 1997. "El problema de la propiedad en las comunidades indígenas. Patrimonio y herencia. (1825 – 1850)." In *El siglo XIX. Bolivia y América Latina*, edited by Barragán Rossana et al. La Paz: IFEA-Historias.
Soux, María Luisa. 1999. "Agricultura y estructura agraria. Del latifundio a la reforma agraria." *Historia y Cultura* 25: 105 – 128.
Soux, María Luisa. 2012. "Territorialización y construcción del Estado-Nación: El caso del gobierno de Antonio José de Sucre." In *El proceso histórico hacia la territorialización del poder*, edited by María Luisa Soux. La Paz: IEB-ASDI.

Cristiana Schettini, Diego Galeano

A credible history of the Princess of Bourbon: Labour, gender, and sexuality in South America, 1905 – 1919

Abstract: This essay explores elements of the career and migration of the person known as the Princess of Bourbon, Luis Fernández, Pedro Pérez, or Armando Ariatti. A range of possible intersections between labour, gender, and immigration can be seen in her journeys through Rio de Janeiro and Buenos Aires. Along with many migrants, the Princess of Bourbon looked for ways to survive that involved diverse strategies and job opportunities, criss-crossed by gender. These survival methods tend to be addressed separately by different areas of historiography (the history of crime, labour, and international migrations), but for the protagonists they were a range of survival tactics that could occur simultaneously. By addressing them together, this essay aims to reflect on the options for survival and work within the South American migration circuit in the years before the First World War, at the intersection of various frontiers: gender, sexual identity, paid and unpaid work, legality and illegality. The main documentation consulted is the commercial press from Argentina, Brazil, and Uruguay, records of expulsions, and correspondence between police authorities. The gendered actions of the Princess of Bourbon and her inclusion in the category known as "men dressed as women" reveals a set of activities considered feminine at the beginning of the 20th century: domestic work, prostitution, and artistic work. The essay is organised into two parts: first there is an analysis of contemporary perceptions of gender identities in relation to geographic mobility of individuals in contexts of migration, then, the itineraries of the Princess of Bourbon are ex-

Note: We are grateful to those who organised the "Congreso Trabajo y Trabajadores," and to the anonymous reviewers for their comments. Previous versions of this text were discussed in the "Crimen y Sociedad" group (Buenos Aires, 2017) and at the round table coordinated by William Acree at the symposium of the Southern Cone section of LASA (Montevideo, 2017). We are grateful for the careful reading and comments received on both occasions.

PhD in Social History from the State University of Campinas. National Council for Scientific and Technical Research (CONICET), National University of San Martin (UNSAM). Contact: crischettini@gmail.com / PhD from the Federal University of Rio de Janeiro. History Department, Pontifical Catholic University of Rio de Janeiro (PUC-Rio). Contact: dgaleano@puc-rio.br.

https://doi.org/10.1515/9783110759303-006

amined to shed light on the shifting meanings ascribed to the women recorded in historical documents as thieves, servants, prostitutes, and travellers.

Keywords: gender; sexuality; migration; labour; crime

Introduction

A character in police reports and entertainment magazines, the Princess of Bourbon achieved a certain notoriety on the Atlantic coast of South America in the early 20th century. Her life was marked by various transitions: between gender identities, between artistic experiences and criminal charges, and finally, between the cities in Brazil, Argentina, and Uruguay through which she circulated. The story of the Princess of Bourbon, Luis Fernández, Pedro Pérez, or Armando Ariatti, depending on the time in her life, the network of relationships in which she was involved, and the ways in which her existence was recorded by third parties, shed light on a series of questions relevant to historical scholarship with a gendered perspective. This essay takes the sparse records of her life as a starting point to confront the changing boundaries of contemporary notions of labour against the complex survival strategies of a "man-woman." In this approach, her gender identity, apart from being a point of interest in itself offers a window to analyse the contested meanings of feminised work in a labour market shaped by mass migration from Europe. Taking place at the start of the 20th century, her travels through South American cities shed light on a range of possible intersections between work, gender, and immigration, calling into question some axioms that are well established in academic literature.

Amid the constant flow of men and women disembarking at South American ports, on the fringes of the labour market and the entertainment market, there emerged a class of immigrants involved in theft, deception, and pretence. Their lives became linked to social anxieties about the consequences of mass migration from Europe and changes in gender relations stemming from the expansion of circuits for the consumption of culture. In cases where a transition between gender identities was also involved, the confusion was greater, and their bodies and actions became a battleground. That unease was expressed in the multiplicity of names they were given: "man-woman" (*hombre-mujer*), "transvestites" (*travestis*), "female impersonators" (*transformistas*), "inverts" (*invertidos*), "celebrity impersonators" (*imitadores de estrellas*), "thieves dressed as women" (*ladrones vestidos de mujer*).

A few decades ago, labour historians in South America focused their attention on unwaged forms of labour in the framework of complex dependent relationships. This intensified the debate on the advantages and risks of expanding the concept of "worker." Many social experiences previously relegated to other analytical fields became subjects of interest to labour historians: domestic, sexual, artistic, and slave labour came to be seen as vital to understanding narratives in which white, male, industrial, unionised workers were in the minority, or even non-existent. A myriad of social relations came to light, and they stand out for the intimate, close, emotional, and silent relationships, in which class identities and antagonisms are shaped.[1] We begin with a set of records that are full of confusion, sarcasm, and violence, recounting the many legends and deeds of the Princess of Bourbon in Buenos Aires, Montevideo, and Rio de Janeiro in the first two decades of the 20th century. The widespread perception of people like her as men that acted out feminine identities, be that on a theatre stage (as vocalists), or away from it (as servants, prostitutes, or thieves), brought to light changing relations between gender and labour in the cities of South America. Indeed, their bodies, their gestures, their looks, and their actions unveil implicit intersections between gender hierarchies and broader social relations, including labour relations. In this sense, as indicated by Anne McClintock with respect to certain practices of transvestitism in Victorian England, it is possible to read those identities in the light of broader disputes regarding female labour (and its invisibility in the context of the so-called "cult of domesticity"), and regarding the racialisation of gender hierarchies in an imperial context (McClintock, 2010: 201–170). Nonetheless, however suggestive these ideas may be, we will move away from their theoretical and psychoanalytical inspirations, to offer a response from the perspective of social history, anchored in contemporary disputes on the gendered meanings of domestic work, prostitution, and artistic work in South America.

If we are to historicise the notion of homosexuality, we cannot ignore the study by George Chauncey (1995) among migrant European communities, and Italians in particular, at the start of the 20th century. He showed that many "conventionally masculine" men had sexual relations with other males considered effeminate, without abandoning the category of "normal." Chauncey's work has stimulated innovative research that contextualised the primacy of media discourses on masculine sexuality vis-a-vis cultures of urban workers marked by

---

1 One example of this is the English historian Carolyn Steedman, who highlights the importance of studying domestic service as a means of understanding the formation of labour links and class antagonisms (Steedman, 1994: 117). For a defence of the utility of considering sex work, with its proximity to illegal activities, nomadism, and forms of autonomous work, in terms of labour history, see Voss (2012).

migration.[2] Taking these contributions as a starting point, we attempt to analyse contemporary perceptions of gender identities in relation to the geographic mobility of individuals in a context of mass migration from Europe to South America. We are also keen to highlight the fact that, along with a vast number of women, the Princess of Bourbon looked for ways to survive that involved diverse strategies and job opportunities. These tend to have been addressed separately by different branches of the historiography (history of crime, labour, and international migrations), but for the protagonists, the same – highly limited – range of survival tactics were involved. The journeys of the Princess of Bourbon reveal something of what was at stake for the women recorded in the historical documents as thieves, servants, prostitutes, and travellers.

Thieves dressed as women

> A gentleman asks for an evening newspaper and has barely opened it when, surprised, he exclaims to the person at his table:
> – Look! The Princess of Bourbon has died!
> – That thief that was recently here in Montevideo?
> – Yes, he was killed by an old man in Chile [...].[3]

On 7 May 1916, a newspaper in Rio de Janeiro announced the "tragic end" of the Princess of Bourbon with this fictional dialogue. There was no need to explain to readers that the deceased was not a member of the Spanish royal family. When Raúl Gómez (correspondent for *A Noite* in Uruguay) explains how he found out about the death, he provides some biographical details: The Princess of Bourbon, who appeared in police files under the name Luis Fernández, was a "thief known to all the police forces in South America, especially in Buenos Aires, Montevideo and Rio". According to this version, she was found dead in an abandoned car in the Chilean city of Quillota. The story suggested that a senile, jealous lover had stabbed her. At the time she was 26 years old, and she had left her birthplace, La Coruña, 10 years before, more in search of adventure than

---

2 For instance, in Pablo Ben's work (2007, 2009), the figure of the *marica* (a generally pejorative term for homosexuals) emerges from "plebeian sociability," constructed in the framework of specific demographic and labour characteristics. Ben establishes a critical dialogue with the classic study by Jorge Salessi (1995), who focused on the repressive dimensions. For the case of Rio de Janeiro, the key text is James Green (2000).

3 "Especial para A Noite. O fim trágico de uma vida de ousadas aventuras," *A Noite*, Rio de Janeiro, 7 May 1916:1.

out of necessity, as her parents were wealthy merchants and she had no siblings, so she was set to be the sole heir to this fortune. Although Luis Fernández is a very common name in Latin America, if this account is correct, she set sail for Argentina in 1905. Indeed, the records for migrant arrivals at the port of Buenos Aires show a Luis Fernández, single, 16 years of age, arriving on 27 March 1905 on the ship *Oruba*, coming from the port of La Coruña.[4] Five years after her arrival, she must have witnessed the fastuous celebrations for the centenary of the Republic of Argentina, attended by the Infanta Isabel of Bourbon herself, Princess of Asturias, representing the Spanish Crown. Given that the first references to the nickname, the Princess of Bourbon, date from 1912, it is likely that this could have been a parody of this high-profile visit.

The account of her tragic death, although it was later questioned, echoed concepts of moral decadence attributed to a life that was difficult to categorise in the eyes of her contemporaries. In mid-1912, the Princess of Bourbon appeared as a criminal in a report by the renowned Argentinian journalist, Juan José de Soiza Reilly, published in the illustrated magazine *Fray Mocho* under the title "*Ladrones vestidos de mujer*" (thieves dressed as women).[5] According to this account, the journalist had met an old friend from Montevideo in Buenos Aires, who had become a criminal, and who told him of the existence of a "fraternity of thieves dressing as women to steal." As in other reports, Soiza Reilly used his contacts with the criminal investigations department to verify the information from his informant, and received a bulging file with names, nicknames, and photographs that were later reproduced on the pages of the magazine. It all came from the compendiums of the Robbery and Theft department; according to the author, its secret agents knew the names of these "*Evas hombrunas*" (manly Eves) off by heart. Luis Fernández was not alone: Juan Soya, better known as "*La Tana*"; Hipólito Vázquez, alias "*La Madrileña*"; José Sanguinetti, "*La María Luisa*"; Eduardo Liester, "*La Inglesa*"; Juan Pumilla, "*La Insípida*"; Jesús Campos, "*La Reina de la Gracia*," and Julio Gimenez, "*La Brisa de la Primavera*," were among the cases recounted. Through Soiza Reilly, their portraits went from the police archives to the pages of a weekly society magazine.[6] Soiza Reilly and his readers identified these "*Evas hombrunas*" as part of the

4 From the database of CEMLA (Centre for Latin American Migratory Studies): http://cemla.com/buscador/.

5 Juan José de Soiza Reilly, "Buenos Aires tenebroso: ladrones vestidos de mujer," *Fray Mocho* 1, no. 6, Buenos Aires, (7 June 1912). Report later reproduced in Soiza Reilly, 1920: 88–94.

6 The same narrative procedure had been used in the previous report published in *Fray Mocho* (Juan José de Soiza Reilly, "Buenos Aires tenebroso: los apaches", *Fray Mocho* 1, no. 3, Buenos Aires, 17 May 1912: 20–24).

world of crime and opened up a repertoire of further associations. This comparison with the "*cuento del tío*" (confidence tricks) ran through Soiza Reilly's reporting. Like confidence tricksters (Galeano 2016a), the "thieves dressed as women" sought, it was said, to seduce their victims to get their money. The journalist thought that they shared the *modus operandi* and the local slang (*Lunfardo*) of the thieves of Buenos Aires. However, Soiza Reilly recorded a range of words that did not appear in the *Lunfardo* dictionaries of the time, such as "*plumiar*" (to go out looking for men to seduce), or "*chongos*," referring to workers. Thus, between references to rather "fine and cultivated" "professional criminals," and the use of a language shared with vast social groups, these "thieves dressed as women" took narrative form.

Another association inspired by Soiza Reilly's writings related to the world of domestic service: it was argued that one of the targets of these peculiar thieves was family homes. To gain access to these homes, they sometimes disguised themselves as maids. Culpiano Álvarez, alias "*La Bella Otero*" (taking the name of a famous Spanish dancer and courtesan) used to "be employed as a maid in rich houses," while another, known as "*Lucho*," was a servant for a "respected family" whose name Soiza Reilly preferred not to reveal. Thus, the journalism connected those mysterious characters to contemporary perceptions of the dangers of domestic service. Concerned with forms of "moral contagion," for years doctors and criminologists had been recording the practice of "*invertidos*" (queers) working as servants (Salessi, 1995: 293–297; Ben, 2007: 23). Soiza Reilly (1920) also addressed a more immediate situation: his writings were published at a time when there was an intense debate about a new municipal plan to regulate domestic service. The text resonated with widespread social fears about the safety and moral integrity of Argentine families, which habitually fed the debate about the regulation of the work of servants. Far from recognising labour rights, such debates focused on recording crime and moral contagion. In other words, the uncertain boundaries between thieves dressed as maids and men dressed as women invoked broader fears of moral contamination stemming from the arrival of strangers in the family environment, and the commodification of intimate relations (Allemandi, 2017: 183; Graham, 1992).

Another characteristic of these individuals, perhaps recognised by Soiza Reilly's readers, was their mobility. The wandering life of the Princess of Bourbon herself was played out between Buenos Aires, Montevideo, Rio de Janeiro, and other South American cities. Below one of the photos illustrating Soiza Reilly's writings, the caption said that "Fernández" had been "expelled various times from Buenos Aires," and that "he" ended up in Uruguay. In another photograph she wore the "ballerina's costume" in which she did her first performance at a live music café in Mercedes (in the province of Buenos Aires), and which she also wore at the Moulin Rouge theatre in Rio de Janeiro.[7] With the help of other records, it is possible to trace some of her journeys along the Atlantic coast of South America. A few months after this report mentions her time in Montevideo, the Princess of Bourbon erupted in the Rio de Janeiro daily press, in a minor scandal known as "*el caso del hombre-mujer*" (the case of the man-woman). Coverage in the Brazilian press makes it possible to follow her steps at a singular time: in the midst of a wave of expulsions of *apaches* (a new type of French criminal) and *cáftenes* (pimps) by the Buenos Aires police, towards the end of 1912, the police in Uruguay and Brazil were forced to take precautions to prepare for their possible arrival at their ports.[8] According to reports, the steamer *Pampa*, which carried various "pimps, *apaches* and thieves expelled from Buenos Aires and Montevideo", arrived in Rio de Janeiro on 22 December 1912. The police made sure that security agents kept watch on the "undesirables," to stop them disembarking, and to guarantee that they continued their forced journey to Europe. Among those kept under watch was the Princess of Bourbon, who had supposedly been expelled from Montevideo.

News in the Brazilian press did not name her as Luis Fernández, but rather as Pedro Pérez or Armando Ariatti, names she must have given to the police when she was arrested after a confused attempt to flee the ship. According to the first versions, she had arrived in Rio "dressed as a woman", and she managed to slip away in a small boat to the land, despite being watched by police officers, ironically named the "Rio Sherlocks" by the local press.[9] However, shortly after, a second version stated that she bribed a police officer called Ernesto Ribeiro Lopes to let her disembark from the *Pampa*. Agent Lopes was held accountable by the *2º Delegado Auxiliar* (police investigations authority) and was ultimately dismissed from the force.[10] Shortly after disembarking, and still being watched by police, the Princess of Bourbon checked into the Hotel Italia-Brasil, near the port and the central train station, where other recent arrivals also used

7 The *Moulin Rouge* was one of various live music cafés belonging to the Italian entrepreneur Paschoal Segreto, around the Plaza Tiradentes. The name referred to an attempt to create a centre for bohemian male socialising, with a stage for artistic performances, consumption of alcoholic drinks, and the introduction of the modern cinematograph, among other attractions. See: "A empresa Paschoal Segreto," *Gazeta de Notícias* (25 April 1910): 6 and Martins, 2007: 92.

8 A key figure in the French criminal underworld in the early 20th century, the *apaches* – described by the Parisian press as violent young men who exploited women – were studied by Perrot (1979) and Kalifa (2002).

9 "Em travesti. Um ladrão, fugindo de bordo, é preso quando procurava fugir à polícia, vestido de mulher," *Correio da Manhã*, Rio de Janeiro (24 December 1912): 5.

10 "O ladrão que desceu do bordo do Pampa subornou um agente de polícia," *Correio da Manhã*, Rio de Janeiro (25 December 1912): 3.

to settle. This hotel, which housed both anonymous immigrants and suspected pimps, featured with some frequency in the police pages of the daily press. It is significant that she ended up getting arrested while wandering in Lapa, the night-life neighbourhood of Rio that stretched from the Carioca Aqueduct towards the "Largo do Rocío" area (now the Plaza Tiradentes), a lively circuit of music-halls, cabarets, theatres and bars, alongside brothels, discreet houses for "in-and-out" rendezvous, homoerotic meeting places, and artists' lodgings (Schettini, 2006: 69–80; Green, 2000: 23–25).

Ariatti knew this circuit well and had previously been arrested there while dressed as a *demi-mondaine,* entering a house on the Travessa do Mosqueira, at the corner with the Calle Visconde de Maranguape, a street famous for its elegant brothels, known for their foreign prostitutes (Schettini, 2006: 69–74). Escorted by police officers and followed closely by a throng of curious onlookers, the Princess of Bourbon was driven to the central police department, where the *2º Delegado Auxiliar,* Dr. Ferreira de Almeida, was waiting for her. She suffered the same fate as other foreigners considered 'undesirable' by the authorities – after testifying, she was summarily expelled. Shortly after Christmas, and with no time to file a *habeas corpus* petition, she was forced aboard the steamer *Formosa, en route* to Montevideo.[11] The newspaper reports add details that give the story a comical tone. A supposed oath by Ariatti to the police authorities (that she would never again "change sex, except during carnival") sought to place the practice of transvestism in one of its accepted best-known settings, the carnival festivities. As it was customary for men to dress as women during those days (Cunha, 2001:217; Green, 2000: 329–343), the jocular record made the episode more intelligible for readers. In fact, illustrations with literary references to jesters from the 17th century, adorned the photos of Ariatti in the piece by Soiza Reilly published in Argentina. Nonetheless, the Rio de Janeiro press gives reason for interpreting the meaning of the actions of the Princess of Bourbon in a different way. By flatly refusing to be photographed by the police without her female clothing, Ariatti indicated that she was not playing by carnival rules: as someone who perceived herself as a woman, she wanted social recognition. This gesture was side-lined by the chroniclers, who insisted on using carnivalesque language to relate the events of her expulsion from Brazil: the image of the maritime police officers waiting impatiently for her while she carefully put away the pieces of her "costume" (dresses, boas, wigs, corsets, hats decorated with ribbons, feathers, and flowers), was repeated in pieces in the main Rio newspapers.

---

11 "No mar," *Jornal do Brasil*, Rio de Janeiro (27 December 1912): 6 and "Ladrão em travesti," *A Notícia*, Rio de Janeiro (27 December 1912): 2.

According to *A Época*, she confessed to one of the agents holding her in custody, Julio Bailly, that she would soon return to Brazil. When they informed her that they would not let her disembark again in Rio de Janeiro, she answered that it would be easy to evade the surveillance; all she had to do was change the colour of her hair, powder her face, and make her toilet with care "and then maybe I might end up getting off the ship hand in hand with the inspector."[12] The humorous intent of the account focused on two elements: the dangerous seductive abilities of Ariatti, and the weakness of the police inspector who was liable to fall prey to her charms. Before leaving, the Princess of Bourbon had time to tease Inspector Bailly again: she gave him a card that said "Armando Ariatti–Calle Rocha n. 2F–Montevideo." The account concludes with her winking and goes aboard. Another version of the same anecdote maintained that while she went up the ramp she turned around and said to Bailly: "I really got on well with you, shall we go to Santos together?"[13] Bailly was the highest authority in the maritime police, in charge of supervising the circulation of ships between the ports of the River Plate and the Brazilian coast.

Journalistic reports drew on narratives proven to be successful and well-known to their readers. The figure of the snubbed policeman encapsulated the potential risks faced by many men susceptible to being tricked by seductive performances in the big city. The way that inspector Bailly was ridiculed referred to other accounts of police officers defeated by the intelligence of modern tricksters. This was a potent metaphor for the storm facing police officers charged with policing port traffic: anarchists expelled from various countries, international tricksters, thieves, pimps, and other "travelling criminals" (Galeano, 2016b) created a devastating panorama for law enforcement officers. The story of the "thief dressed as a woman," who seduced and deceived the inspector, was one of many news stories about police officers who did not fare well in the overflowing ports.[14]As usually happens with winks, the one from the Princess of Bourbon could have had various meanings, invoking both the seduction of the *demi-mondaines* and the vulnerability of those who might be seduced. For many readers, the wink may have expressed the ironic triumph of the figure of the travelling thief, who sooner or later would keep their promise to return to Brazil, slipping through the gaps in porous police controls. For others, it may

---

12 "Homem-mulher. O conhecido gatuno embarcou ontem," *A Época*, Rio de Janeiro (26 December 1912): 2.

13 "Os casos curiosos. Partiu o homem-mulher," *A Noite*, Rio de Janeiro (26 December 1912): 4.

14 Indeed, stories of the police officer who was seduced and deceived by fake women appeared again, in a similar form, in articles in the Argentinian newspaper *Crítica* on 1, 6 and 17 August 1919.

have suggested the erotic attraction of the Princess of Bourbon in the nocturnal world that included the brothels of the Lapa district and meeting places for furtive sexual encounters such as the Plaza Tiradentes. So, this gesture could allude to the complexities of the urban space frequented by the Princess of Bourbon, where prostitutes of various nationalities lived alongside the clients and habitués of the gardens, theatres, musical cafés and rendezvous, including many police officers (Green, 2000; Schettini, 2006).

Over the following months, the daily press played up these ambiguities regarding the rumours about the imminent arrival of the Princess of Bourbon in Brazil, right in the middle of carnival in 1913.[15] The newspapers reproduced a letter, written in doubtful Spanish, that Ariatti is supposed to have sent to an inspector in the Maritime Police. The mix of words in Spanish and in Portuguese suggests an imaginative play on the part of the Brazilian journalists. The text read:

> Dear Captain Miranda, The further I get from this good and beautiful land [where] I was so well and warmly received, I feel the deepest longing and I think that I will return very soon to embrace you. I am investigating the way to disembark without being recognised. Thousands of hugs from your friend who loves you – Armando Ariatti.[16]

Whether or not it was the fruit of journalistic imagination, the threat of the Princess of Bourbon's return was taken seriously by the police. A reporter from the *Correio da Manhã* said that during the first months of 1913, various women were arrested because they "looked like men." In the Galería Cruzeiro alone there were three such arrests, and, in the Lapa district, a young woman called Martha was detained by a secret agent who confused her with Ariatti.[17] These police mistakes led to further ridicule of police officers. This time they were accused of not knowing the difference between an "ugly woman" and a "man dressed as a woman."

---

15 "Um escândalo policial," *A Época*, Rio de Janeiro (14 February 1913): 2 and "A audácia de um ladrão. A mulher homem," *A Noite*, Rio de Janeiro (17 March 1913): 2.

16 "O homem-mulher. A polícia marítima redobra a vigilância a bordo," *Correio da Manhã*, Rio de Janeiro (19 March 1913): 4. According to a version from the newspaper *O Imparcial*, this letter was shown by the sub-inspector Joaquim Miranda to a reporter who had it published in the Rio press, leading to the most "jocular comments." "Um ladrão audacioso," *O Imparcial*, Rio de Janeiro (16 May 1913): 4.

17 "Um homem-mulher. Armando Arriarte, o célebre ladrão argentino, já está nas malhas da polícia," *Correio da Manhã*, Rio de Janeiro (16 May 1913): 2. Other later cases of detention of women confused with Ariatti appear in: "É mulher ou homem?," *O Paiz*, Rio de Janeiro (3 June 1913): 3.

Although it was not known exactly when, or how she disembarked, in mid-May 1913, she was arrested again in Rio de Janeiro. An agent of the Maritime Police thought he had seen Ariatti in the form of an elegantly dressed woman who followed the same route as before: on a tram, going from the Plaza Tiradentes to Lapa. In this busy area of transit, it was common to see couples walking to and from the boarding houses that charged by the hour, while the *gouveias*, the stereotypical image of an old man looking for sex with a younger man, wandered about seeking the *meninos bonitos* (beautiful boys) who gathered around the statue of Pedro I on horseback, situated in the middle of the square.[18] Taking the same path as the *habitués* of that circuit, the agent took the tram and followed her to Lapa. Upon noticing he was looking at her, Ariatti – maybe not suspecting that it was a police officer – invited him to come over to talk, following the predictable steps for this type of relations. They made a date for later, and that evening, the agent returned with a civil guard officer who helped him to detain the Princess of Bourbon. She had changed clothes for the date: wearing a long aquamarine silk dress, with a line of mother of pearl buttons. She also carried a hat with feathers that covered half of her face. Playing in the swampy terrain of the interaction between the police and Ariatti, the journalist recreated a dialogue: when the Princess of Bourbon heard the arrest warrant, she asked the agent angrily: "And what about our *rendezvous?*" "Our *rendezvous* – he supposedly responded – is at the 13th precinct."[19]Among her belongings the police officers found Brazilian money, and two *pesos* in Argentinian currency, which suggests that this time she arrived from the port of Buenos Aires. In 1912, Soiza Reilly had mentioned that the Princess of Bourbon had "more than 20 entries with the Buenos Aires police." In fact, in the version that the Brazilian police officers gave to the press, Ariatti had supposedly confessed that she had disembarked the day before from the steamer *Avon*, coming from Buenos Aires. As the Brazilian police and press had feared, she had managed once again to elude the controls of the Maritime Police, spent a night in a hotel, and walked to the Largo de San Francisco, a few metres from the Plaza Tiradentes, where

18 Often the Rio police did raids, looking for what they considered to be "young pederasts" in the Plaza Tiradentes and neighbouring areas. See, for example, the arrest of ten young men between 16 and 25 years of age, accused of the "vice of passive pederasty" in October 1907: Archivo Nacional del Brasil, Fondo GIFI - Secretaría de Policía, Caja 6C223. On the *gouveias* and the *meninos bonitos*, see Green, 2000: 51–106.

19 "Os desbriados. Armando Ariatti, o célebre larapio que operava em travesti, mais uma vez foi preso ontem," *A Época*, Rio de Janeiro (16 May 1913): 2.

she supposedly took the tram to Lapa.[20] As a result, not long after her arrival in Rio de Janeiro she once again fell into police custody. It is clear that the Brazilian police did not lose her trail and, furthermore, despite the journalistic reports that continued to describe her as a "thief," nothing indicates that she had committed any theft.

Once more, she was deported on a steamer (*Oronsa*) to the River Plate, and once more, she swore to return. The Rio police, concerned about possible disembarkation where the ship stopped, sent telegrams to San Pablo asking for strict surveillance in the port of Santos.[21] Some newspapers such as *Jornal do Comércio*, critical of the police actions, were already making fun of the cyclical story: The reporter wrote that "Ariatti was taken from the 13th district to the Central Department, from where he would *again* be put on board [a boat], to be deported, so that later on the officer of the [Maritime] Police, Mr Julio Bailly could let him disembark again."[22] "Will he return?," wondered a journalist from *O Século*. "Certainly, within three months people will be laughing in the face of Belisario Távora's ineffable police force" (referring to the police chief).[23] Over the following months, false news stories spread about supposed trips to Brazil by the Princess of Bourbon, resulting in the mobilisation of Maritime Police agents for fruitless searches. In August, the arrival of the *Oronsa* at the port of Rio de Janeiro was surrounded by a "diabolical scandal" when police officers confused a Montevidean *divetti* with the by now famous Princess of Bourbon. The Uruguayan resisted having to 'demonstrate' that she was a woman. Days later, another rumour of the arrival of Ariatti in the steamer *Principessa Mafalda* was a hot topic around the port: the guards searched the boat from bow to stern, to no avail. The press took it upon itself to spread all kinds of versions of possible sightings of individuals that could be "the real Ariatti, Princess of Bourbon" walking the streets of Rio under other monikers, such as *Lulú* or *Manón*. The entire underworld of brothels and nightlife in the Brazilian capital seemed to be under suspicion.[24]

---

20 "Homem-mulher. Armando Ariatti novamente no Rio," *Jornal do Brasil*, Rio de Janeiro (16 May 1913): 9 and "Ladrão em travesti. Voltou ao Rio," *O Paiz*, Rio de Janeiro (16 May 1913): 6.
21 "O homem-mulher. A polícia marítima está seriamente preocupada com o grande pandego," *Correio da Manhã*, Rio de Janeiro (18 May 1913): 3.
22 "Disfarçado em mulher," *Jornal do Comércio*, Rio de Janeiro (16 May 1913): 5 (italics in the original).
23 "Armando Arriarte no Rio," *O Século*, Rio de Janeiro (16 May 1913): 3.
24 "Manon voltou ao Rio? A polícia teve denúncia de achar-se entre nós o conhecido ladrão Armando Ariarte," *Gazeta de Notícias*, Rio de Janeiro, 31 March 1913: 4. "Ainda Armando Arriarte. Barafunda a bordo," *O Século*, Rio de Janeiro (14 August 1913): 2 and "Ainda Armando Ariarte," *O Século*, Rio de Janeiro (9 September 1913): 2.

Itinerant artists

Part of the humour of the exploits and rumours surrounding the Princess of Bourbon stemmed from her power of seduction and the mockery she made of police incompetence. But it is necessary to stress that Ariatti's Atlantic journeys were not always motivated by her own decisions. They were, rather, a mix of survival strategies, in the face of restricted labour opportunities and police surveillance practices. At the start of the 20th century, the South American Police – particularly in Argentina and Brazil – had a set of tools at their disposal for the surveillance of suspicious and undesirable people travelling along the Atlantic routes. Laws for the expulsion of foreigners passed in Argentina (1902) and Brazil (1907) consolidated the instrument for the deportation of individuals born in other countries through a procedure that gave the police a broad margin for action and discretion. The entire initial stage of investigation and instruction was in the hands of police officers. Then, a minister (a justice minister in the case of Brazil, an interior minister in the case of Argentina), was to sign the decree of expulsion. Furthermore, police headquarters in Buenos Aires, Rio de Janeiro, Montevideo, and other cities in the region, were now exchanging information in order to establish a systematic surveillance of movements, and produce evidence for expulsion processes.[25] Along with "formal" expulsions, i. e. expulsions initiated with a police report and ending with the signature of a minister, there were more widespread "informal" proceedings, which also ended with the forced deportation of an undesirable foreigner. In fact, expulsions without decree, carried out summarily by senior police officers, had already existed since before receiving legal sanctioning in the first decade of the 20th century. Along with this resource, the police prevented the disembarkation of individuals who had been expelled from Europe and other South American countries, or simply travellers who had "bad records," according to information received from police headquarters. This appears to be what happened to the Princess of Bourbon during her brief sojourns in Rio de Janeiro in 1912 and 1913.

The embarkation of various undesirables expelled from Buenos Aires in December 1912, on board the steamer *Pampa*, on which the Princess of Bourbon was also travelling, was the subject of an intense exchange of telegrams between the police forces of Argentina and Brazil.[26] Exactly a year later, the police forces

25 Regarding the practice of expulsion of foreigners in Argentina and Brazil see Menezes, 1996; Schettini, 2012a; Galeano, 2016b; Galeano, 2016b; Albornoz and Galeano, 2017.

26 The telegrams to the police headquarters in Buenos Aires and Rio are found in: Archivo Nacional del Brasil, Fondo GIFI – Secretaría de Policía, Caja 6C392.

of Brazil were waiting for her, to prevent her disembarking in Santos and Rio de Janeiro, after receiving a telegram from Buenos Aires, which warned that Ariatti was being expelled aboard the steamer *Cap Verde*.[27] Official lists of foreigners expelled from Brazil during those two years show many names of pimps travelling to Europe and the River Plate, but nobody appears with the name Luis Fernández, nor Armando Ariatti, nor "Ariarte," as some newspapers called her.[28] This indicates that police action was limited to preventing disembarkation, or, when the Princess of Bourbon managed to evade port surveillance and vanish into the city, to summary arrest and expeditious expulsion, resolved at police headquarters.

Although in the specific case of Ariatti the legislation for expulsion of foreigners was not used, the enforcement of Brazilian expulsion law of 1907 covered guarding 'morality and decency'. In fact, two 'eastern lads' (Uruguayans), arrested in a bar in the centre while "dressed as women", faced a 'regular' trial that ended in expulsion. They were accused of "vagrancy," "practicing passive pederasty," and not having a "profession or honest livelihood," and ended up being expelled without objections. Rafael Manso and Héctor Oliveira were 21 years old. The police arrested them in April 1912 and, in the very office of the *Delegado Auxiliar* through which the Princess of Bourbon would pass some months later, subjected them to interrogations.[29] Rafael said that he had arrived in Brazil on 19 March of that year, on board the steamer *Cap Ancona*, from his hometown of Montevideo. A tailor by trade, he got a job at a dry cleaners, but he ended up leaving because he felt the wage was not enough to cover his costs. Héctor was also from Montevideo. He had arrived in Brazil before his friend, on 2 November 1911, and got a job in a commercial establishment. According to the "witnesses" (who, as was common in expulsion processes, were police employees), Rafael and Héctor had no fixed abode, and "spent the night in rented houses and low-class boarding houses." As well as "passive pederasty," they engaged in "theft of jewels and money, from victims who were depraved individuals that the accused invited to such immoral acts." To find their "victims," they hung around the Plaza Tiradentes, so well-known to the Princess, "an area frequented by degenerates and queers."[30] The absence of evidence to substantiate the criminal accusation did not prevent the press – as occurred with Ariatti and in so many other cases – from constructing an account based

27 "Armando Ariarte volta ao Rio? A polícia recebe um aviso," *A Imprensa*, Rio de Janeiro (2 December 1913): 2.
28 The official lists of expelled people appear in Relatório, 1912: 59 and Relatório, 1913: 61–62.
29 Archivo Nacional del Brasil, Fondo IJJ7 – Expulsión de Extranjeros, Caja 150.
30 *Ibid.*

on the idea of "thieves that dressed as women to steal." The same narrative that sustained the arrest and expulsion of Ariatti worked for Rafael and Héctor, who were put on the steamer *Vauban* after spending a month in prison.[31] Although in one case it was a formal expulsion, and in the other an even more summary deportation, the parallels between the young Uruguayans and the Princess of Bourbon are striking: trips back and forth on the same Atlantic routes (from the River Plate to Brazil), the same area of action in the night life of Rio de Janeiro, and the same rationale of police persecution (not allowing them to stay in the city for long). Otherwise, there was a vast difference between the little-known lives of Rafael and Héctor, and the famous Princess of Bourbon, whose South American exploits, according to the writings of Soiza Reilly, made her "the king of the thieves dressed as women." The Princess' fame outlived the immediate context. Two years after her expulsions, she became a character in the play *Los Invertidos*, by the playwright José González Castillo, which premièred in September 1914. In the second act, the Princess of Bourbon burst onto the stage, defined as an individual who dressed "like an elegant woman," spoke in the Lunfardo slang of Buenos Aires "with an exaggerated feminine voice," and danced "with exaggerated movements" (González Castillo, 2011: 58).[32]

This première was her zenith, but her fame was already consolidated before this. For Soiza Reilly, her "picaresque adventures" did not even need to be explained in 1912, because they were well known to the reading public. He just recalled that she was "a lad of singular beauty," tall, big black eyes, smart appearance, who attended dances. During her stays in Buenos Aires, she used to work at musical cafés, and "took the opportunity of the carnival to dress as a woman". If at this point it is already clear to us that the Princess of Bourbon not only dressed as a woman during carnival the possibility that it enabled her to get work in musical cafés should be explored further. In addition to the carnival rituals, the practice of *transformismo* (female impersonation) was often used and was recognised in the variety theatres which, in the early years of the 20th century, connected cities and small towns in South America with large European

---

31 "Os mocinhos argentinos", *Gazeta de Notícias*, Rio de Janeiro (5 April 1912): 3 and "Deportados," *Gazeta de Notícias*, Rio de Janeiro (23 May 1912): 7.

32 Much later, in the early 1930s, the characteristic elements of the art world, relating to prostitution, expulsion, and finally the practice of transvestism, were once more combined and associated with a Princess of Bourbon, who was a 'courtesan' frequenting the elegant Tabarís cabaret, on the calle Corrientes (Vincelle, 1933: 110 – 124) The fact that even in later years, Sebreli and other authors would take up the Princess and her stories again suggests the extent to which the name of the 'Princess of Bourbon' came to be associated with this social *milieu* of cross-dressing in Buenos Aires (Sebreli, 2011).

metropoles. The meanings and effects of the circulation of feminine images in this *milieu* also played a key role in the careers of transgender women like the Princess of Bourbon.

The variety theatre, with its constant flow of attractions that changed each week in cabarets and casino theatres, grew from an unprecedented organisation of entrepreneurs in the show business world. It also meant that the artists travelled more due to precarious working arrangements. In terms of cultural consumption, the artistic circuits commodified on-stage performances in a feminine style, in a process that one cultural critic called the "spectacularisation of the female body."[33]

For women, this commodifying process translated to very specific labour arrangements, involving international tours, poorly paid contracts, and constant moral suspicion, which in many cases, involved an intersection between artistic work and prostitution (Schettini, 2012b). Some of the nicknames chosen by Ariatti and her friends referred to this universe, often characterised by performances that toyed with pretend authenticity, mimicking traditional dances and musical styles, while adopting regional monikers such as *La Sevillanita* (the little Sevillian woman), *La Argentinita* (the little Argentinian woman), *La Cordobesita* (the little Woman from Cordoba), etc.[34] In this context, it was common for various artists to specialise in impersonating well known figures, and, in fact, to build their entire career on that ability. This was the case of *la Bella Otero*. Spanish by birth, she achieved unprecedented notoriety as a mixture of courtesan, dancer, and singer on the stages of Europe and South America. She inspired a chain of impersonators. These kinds of performances were among the most popular and best paid variety acts at the turn of the 20th century (Toll, 1976). Classified as *transformistas* (female impersonators), *imitadores* (impersonators) or *parodistas* (parodists), these artists filled rooms in the concert cafés of the main urban centres of Europe and the Americas.

In his writings, Soiza Reilly took note of the importance of artistic activities for the Princess of Bourbon's peers. José Rodríguez Gonzáles, alias *La Morosoni*, who had worked as an actress and chorus girl until she fled to Brazil. Francisco Torres, who used the name *La Venus*, performed numbers in the club La Socie-

---

33 Anastasio (2009), when referring to the popularity of Spanish *cuplé*, stressed the commodification of the circulation of images of women on postcards, photos in magazines, and of their voices on gramophone and phonograph records.

34 The challenge, according to a nostalgic chronicler in the mid-20th century, was to invent "something of your own and modern," in the midst of repetitions of "folk" material, and the endless imitation of "foreign fashions." Federico de Onis, "La Argentinita," *Revista Hispânica Moderna* 12 (1946): 180 – 184.

dad de los Pimpollos (calle Talcahuano 860). Ángel Cessani, *La Choricera*, had a dance studio in Puente Alsina. A decade earlier, in her autobiographical tale told to criminologist Francisco de Veyga, "*La Marica*" assumed the identity of *La Bella Otero* to an extreme, playing an intricate imitation game: "I was in Paris, where I danced in the concert cafés, making another woman jealous; she uses my name to pass herself off as me" (de Veyga, 1903).

Stage names like *La Bella Otero*, the Princess of Bourbon, and others, were far more than mere nicknames. On entering this genre of entertainment at the dawn of the 20th century, they were participating in a continuum of performances of identities and characters, in which there was a confluence between copies and originals, to produce various versions of glamorous and seductive femininity. Using those names, and the opportunity to act on a stage, threw into question scientific assumptions about "sexual inversion." This kind of artistic expression was also a way to earn a living. Monsieur Bertin, for example, was on the stage of Casino in 1912 as a "*transformista famoso*" (famous female impersonator), recently arrived after performing "with great success, on the stage in London." Bertin was a point of reference for impersonators who specialised in portraying "the most beautiful actresses and the most celebrated professional beauties."[35] Proving that "there was Bertin for many nights," the female impersonator showed the people of Buenos Aires that he "sings with a beautify treble timbre, and modulates with surprising ease, with actions, and characteristics that are sometimes suggestive, and sometimes beautifying for the audience."

These descriptions suggest the way in which performances by female impersonators may have been viewed at the time. Success did not just result from an effective wardrobe, but also from the accuracy of the feminine performance, including, sometimes, erotic undertones. So, the Princess of Bourbon was part of this continuum of artistic performances of a 'picaresque' femininity, in which dancers and singers participated, along with their impersonators, both male and female. Female impersonation in the variety theatre certainly offered Princess of Bourbon and her peers a repertoire of available and socially acceptable performances, delineating the versions of femininity that they also assumed off stage. In this context, the photos of the Princess of Bourbon repeatedly published in newspapers and magazines in South America make more sense.

Part of the fascination around female impersonators was the possibility of radicalising gender performance, as observed by Sharon Ullman (1995) in an article about similar performances in the United States during the same period. In

---

35 "Menudencias," *Caras y Caretas* 517, Buenos Aires (29 August 1908): 84 and "Casino – El debut del transformista Bertin," *Caras y Caretas* 706, Buenos Aires (13 April 1912): 6.

this sense, the artistic world may have been an outlet for people who managed to escape the police camera lenses.

Figure 1: Source: Soiza Reilly, 1912.

Figure 2: Source: Soiza Reilly, 1912.

Figure 3: Source: *O Malho*, Río de Janeiro, 4 January 1913.

Artistic performances involving impersonating femininities embodied intersections between new trends in cultural consumption, status, and nationality. In this light, the life of the Princess of Bourbon also suggests how such performances and the persistent images they produced, could give many other people the opportunity to construct their own gender identities, offering them an intelligible "symbolic vocabulary." In other words, imitation or reference to variety artists such as female impersonators, gave form to styles of femininities with various meanings, some of them undecipherable for contemporaries.

Final considerations

Behind the unequivocal accusation that they were "thieves dressed as women," the Princess of Bourbon and others took on multiple identities: servants, prostitutes, variety artists. Police officers implied that they were suspected of theft, and this notion was taken up by local newspapers. Even considering that theft may have been a strategy to get money in a social universe of limited opportunities for survival among *maricas*, it was certainly not their main activity, and certainly not an ideal prospect. In an era when many men dedicated to criminality started to see themselves as "professional thieves," none of the figures mentioned in this piece participated in this criminal world as their livelihood.

Strictly speaking, apart from *La Bella Otero*, who spoke to the criminologist Francisco de Veyga, who wrote her words down, and made them available to historians (Salessi, 1995; Ben, 2007), the career of other protagonists of gender transformations in the early 20th century, like the Princess of Bourbon, reach us only through newspaper and police reports. These narratives seek to create a key for reading their lives as deceitful, simulated, criminal existences, sometimes comical and amusing, others take a more threatening, pathological tone. Maybe it was Juan José de Soiza Reilly who, in a piece in 1912, best summed up this idea, in relation to the story of "thieves that dress as women," who "use their effeminate appearance" to deceive rich men and other *otarios* (patsies), unaware of the secrets of modern urban life, just like victims of confidence tricks. The record thus, predominantly oscillates between presenting them as "able thieves" and "mentally ill."

A thorough reading of the same accounts, from the writings of Soiza Reilly and the many unsigned newspapers stories, offers arguments against the hypothesis that they themselves support. Like the "eastern lads," the Uruguayans Rafael and Héctor, expelled from Brazil in 1912, in whose case the accusation that they were "thieves dressed as women" was not backed up by any evidence of crime, the entire story of the Princess of Bourbon does not offer any precise data regarding her status as a 'thief'. Neither Soiza Reilly's account, nor the numerous police reports in the press in Argentina and Brazil, offer details of any specific robbery. This vacuum was filled by curious and amusing anecdotes about the seduction of police officers and urban legends that said she had managed to walk the streets of Montevideo arm in arm with a police commissioner, or to present herself to the Argentinian parliament to ask for a pension as the widow of a soldier who died in the Paraguayan War, all mentioned in the writings of Soiza Reilly.

Maybe these anecdotes partly refer to actual adventures. However, reading for signs of criminal pretence, or of a member of the cast of tricksters and con artists that circulated along the Atlantic coast of South America looking for easy money, they seem rather to be a gesture to legitimate the violent police procedures. Another interpretation is possible, an examination of the methods of survival and the work available to people who assumed a feminine social identity at the crossroads of various frontiers: gendered and sexual identities; paid and unpaid activities; legality and illegality. The connection between the circuits of art, labour, and crime deserves to be dealt with in greater depth than as a note of colour or a brief observation on what was happening at the time. It should, rather, be researched as fragments of the experience of individuals who assumed feminine gender identities and built-up survival strategies based on what was available to them on the labour market as it was constructed at the time. Taken literally, the identity chosen by the person police forces and journalists insisted on calling Armando Ariatti or Luis Fernández, namely the Princess of Bourbon, is a call to consider her career outside the hermetic cage constructed by those telling her story, which always leads to the idea of a costume, pretence, and carnival revelry.

Her steps, on and off the stage, enable reflection on the possibilities and limits of an incipient entertainment market, in which social practices linked to intimacy and sexuality were given a price. Like many people who self-identify as women seeking refuge in domestic service, adopting a female stage name (intelligible to their contemporaries) as a figure in variety theatre, was a strategy for physical survival and building dignity. It was more than "resistance" to the inclemency's of an oppressive world: it meant inventing a space for existence, which was fragile and sometimes all too fleeting, on the boundaries of women's work. The accusation of that they were "thieves dressed as a woman" sought to close this field of possibilities, and restore the masculine identity at any cost.

The reference to domestic service is more complicated and ambiguous. Some historians have shown that, in South America, debates about regulation of this work brought up various fears regarding autonomy, the demand for women's rights, and fear of crime in homes (Allemandi, 2017; Fernandes de Souza, 2014; Graham, 1992). It is possible to imagine that the writings of Soiza Reilly, by associating the journalistic figure of "men dressed as women" with crime, may also have been read in connection with the social controversy about the regulation of domestic service. Thus, the two universes of meaning are combined: association with refining of pretence techniques, like that of tricksters, and those more specific fears of "moral contagion." Nothing better represented these fears than the world of domestic service, a working relationship in which intimacy strengthened fears of the other. The narrative strategy of finger-pointing, to characterise and explain the transvestism of these young women, took the classic criminological cliché of "deceit" to the field of gender identity. These individuals threatened to enter the most intimate areas of the family – as the police warned and journalists reaffirmed – and they were not what they "appeared to be," and did not appear to be what they "really were," thieves dressed as women.

This accusation disguised, but did not entirely hide, the integration of these women into the labour market, on the fringes of variety theatre and the world of entertainment: from hair stylists and make-up artists for actresses (Soiza Reilly said that ladies hairstylist, was the "trade in which they all said they worked when arrested") or variety artists, an activity which tended to be linked to their feminine name. For its part, the malleable boundary between the world of the theatre and the world of prostitution, both built amid intense transnational flows of women, ran through the lives and survival strategies of individuals like the Princess of Bourbon. Finally, the gender meaning of certain types of unpaid domestic work was certainly another constituent, if not glamorous, part of the experience of being a woman in that world. This dimension is striking in the memoirs, in the mid-20th century, of a famous scoundrel in Rio de Janeiro, known for transforming into Madame Satã. Sweeping floors and cleaning the police station, which police officers considered typical women's work, was the activity that the police assigned to the transvestites they arrested in the 1920s (Green, 2003: 213).

Despite rumours of her death in 1916, the Princess of Bourbon appeared again on the pages of the Argentinian newspaper *Crítica* in 1919, which claimed she was living in Montevideo in an artists' boarding house, looking for "a quiet life."[36] The Buenos Aires journalist recalled that "since childhood, she enjoyed women's clothes and feeling the emotions of the weaker sex", and that this gained her a place "in the gallant world." A few lines below, however, he returned to the now familiar line, when explained that "theft was the aim of all the passions provoked." Between recognition of a feminine identity and the idea of criminal pretence, one repeatedly found the same repertoire of categories used by others to define their life and make it credible; a life that spanned Spain, Argentina, Uruguay, Brazil, and perhaps Chile; a life that crossed national borders, and the boundaries between various labour spaces, and which, although precarious, allowed her to travel and find a way to exist in accordance with the identity that she claimed.

36 "La princesa está herida", *Crítica*, 6 August 1919.

Sources

Newspapers

A Noite, Rio de Janeiro, 1912, 1913, 1916.
Fray Mocho, 1912.
Gazeta de Notícias, 1910, 1912, 1913.
Correio da Manhã, Rio de Janeiro, 1912, 1913.
Jornal do Brasil, Rio de Janeiro, 1912, 1913.
A Notícia, Rio de Janeiro, 1912.
A Época, Rio de Janeiro, 1912, 1913.
Crítica, Buenos Aires, 1919.
O Imparcial, Rio de Janeiro, 1913.
O Paiz, Rio de Janeiro, 1913.
Jornal do Commercio, Rio de Janeiro, 1913.
O Século, Rio de Janeiro, 1913.
A Imprensa, Rio de Janeiro, 1913.
Caras y Caretas, Buenos Aires, 1908, 1912.

Manuscripts

The database of CEMLA (Centre for Latin American Migratory Studies): http://cemla.com/buscador/.
Archivo Nacional del Brasil, Fondo GIFI–Secretaría de Policía, Caja 6C223.
Archivo Nacional del Brasil, Fondo GIFI–Secretaría de Policía, Caja 6C392.
Archivo Nacional del Brasil, Fondo Ministerio de Justicia y Negocios Interiores–Expulsión de Extranjeros, IJJ7 – Caja 150.

References

Albornoz, Martín, and Diego Galeano. 2017. "El momento Beastly: la Policía de Buenos Aires y la expulsión de extranjeros, 1896–1904." *Astrolabio* magazine 17: 6–41.

Allemandi, Cecilia. 2017. *Sirvientes, criados y nodrizas. Una historia del servicio doméstico en la ciudad de Buenos Aires (fines del siglo XIX y principios del XX)*. Buenos Aires: Teseo/Udesa.

Anastasio, Pepa. 2009. "Pisa con Garbo: el cuplé como performance." *Trans Revista Transcultural de Música* 13: np.

Ben, Pablo. 2007. "Plebeian masculinity and sexual comedy in Buenos Aires, 1880–1930." *Journal of the History of Sexuality* 16 (3): 436–458.

Ben, Pablo. 2009. "Male sexuality, the popular classes and the state: Buenos Aires, 1880–1955." PhD Dissertation, University of Chicago.

Chauncey, George. 1995. *Gay New York. Gender, Urban Culture and the Making of Gay Male World, 1890–1940.* New York: Basic Books.

Cunha, María Clementina Pereira. 2001. *Ecos da folia: uma história social do carnaval carioca entre 1880 e 1920.* São Paulo: Companhia das Letras.

de Veyga, Francisco. 1903. "La inversión sexual adquirida. Tipo profesional: un invertido comerciante." *Archivos de Psiquiatría, Criminología y Ciencias Afines.* 2: 492–496.

Fernandes de Souza, Flavia. 2014. "A criadagem sob suspeita: as relações entre o poder público e os trabalhadores domésticos na cidade do Rio de Janeiro no entre séculos XIX–XX." *Anais do XVI Encontro Regional de História da Anpuh-Rio* 1: 1–16.

Galeano, Diego. 2016 (a). "Entre cuenteros y otarios: Historia transnacional de una estafa en América Latina, 1870–1930." *Historia* 49 (2):395–427.

Galeano, Diego. 2016 (b). *Criminosos viajantes: circulações transnacionais entre Rio de Janeiro e Buenos Aires, 1890–1930.* Rio de Janeiro: National Archive.

González Castillo, José. 2011. *Los invertidos y otras obras.* Buenos Aires: Ediciones R y R.

Graham, Sandra. 1992. *Proteção e obediência. Criados e seus patrões no Rio de Janeiro (1860–1910).* São Paulo: Companhia das Letras.

Green, James. 2000. *Além do carnaval. A homossexualidade masculina no Brasil do século XX.* São Paulo: UNESP.

Green, James. 2003. "O Pasquim e Madame Satã, a rainha negra da boemia brasileira." *Topoi* 4 (7): 201–221.

Kalifa, Dominique. 2002. "Archéologie de l'Apachisme. Les représentations des Peaux-Rouges dans la France du XIXe siècle." *Revue d'histoire de l'enfance « irrégulière »* 4: 19–37.

Martins, William. 2007. "Paschoal Segreto: Ministro das Diversões do Rio de Janeiro (1883–1920)." *Cidade Nova* 1: 83–96.

McClintock, Anne. 2010. *Couro imperial. Raça, gênero e sexualidade no embate colonial.* Campinas: Unicamp.

Menezes, Lená Medeiros de. 1996. *Os Indesejáveis–desclassificados da modernidade. Protesto, crime e expulsão na Capital Federal (1890–1930).* Rio de Janeiro: EdUERJ.

Perrot, Michelle. 1979. "Dans le Paris de la Belle Époque, les Apaches, premières bandes de jeunes." *Les marginaux et les exclus dans l'histoire.* Paris Union générale d'éditions.

Relatório. 1912. *Relatório do Ministro da Justiça e Negócios Interiores.* Rio de Janeiro: Imprensa Nacional.

Relatório. 1913. *Relatório do Ministro da Justiça e Negócios Interiores.* Rio de Janeiro: Imprensa Nacional.

Salessi, Jorge. 1995. *Médicos, maleantes y maricas: higiene, criminología y homosexualidad en la construcción de la nación argentina. Buenos Aires: 1871–1914.* Rosario: Beatriz Viterbo.

Schettini, Cristiana. 2006. *Que Tenhas Teu Corpo. Uma História social da prostituição no Rio de Janeiro das primeiras décadas republicanas.* Rio de Janeiro: National Archive.

Schettini, Cristiana. 2012 (a). "Exploração, gênero e circuitos sul-americanos nos processos de expulsão de estrangeiros (1907–1920)." *Tempo* 33: 51–73.

Schettini, Cristiana. 2012 (b). "South American Tours: work relations in the entertainment market in South America." *International Review of Social History* 57: 129–160.

Schettini, Cristiana. 2013. "Los transformistas en el varieté de comienzos del siglo XX." *Actas de las XIV Jornadas Interescuelas/Departamentos de Historia.* Mendoza: Universidad Nacional de Cuyo.

Sebreli, Juan José. 2011 [1964]. *Buenos Aires, Vida cotidiana y alienación: seguido de Buenos Aires, ciudad en crisis.* Buenos Aires: Sudamericana.

Soiza Reilly, Juan José de. 1920. *La escuela de los pillos.* Buenos Aires/Montevideo: Matera/de Angelis.

Steedman, Carolyn. 1994. "The Price of Experience: Women and the Making of the English Working Class." *Radical History Review* 59: 108–119.

Toll, Robert. 1976. *On with the show. The First Century of Show Business in America New York.* Oxford University Press.

Ullman, Sharon. 1995. "The Twentieth Century Way: Female Impersonation and Sexual Practice in Turn of the Century America." *Journal of the History of Sexuality* 5 (4): 573–600.

Voss, Lex Heerma van. 2012. "The worst class of workers: migration, labour relations and living strategies of prostitutes around 1900." In *Working on Labour*, edited by Marcel van der Linden, and L. Lucassen. Leiden: Brill.

Vincelle, Claudio. 1933. *El amor en la Argentina.* Buenos Aires: Editorial El Ombu.

Laura Caruso, Andrés Stagnaro

Towards a history of the ILO and Latin America: Perspectives, problems and collaborative work

Abstract: This essay reflects on the links between a key labour organisation of the interwar period, the International Labour Organisation (ILO), and experiences and labour policies in Latin America. This relationship has been neglected, if not ignored, by the literature on the institutional history of the ILO, which has focused primarily on other regions. An attempt has been made by Latin American academic researchers, to restore Latin America to its rightful place in the history of the development of the ILO. That work allows us to rethink some of the networks, actors and tensions in the regional and national spaces of the American continent, which saw in the ILO a new arena for dispute and legitimacy. The complex links between the ILO and Latin America form the focus of study for an interdisciplinary network that we set up some years ago, feeding into these reflections. The work of that network enables us to trace a tentative timeline for the different stages in that relationship. Finally, we address some challenges and propose an agenda for future research that considers the connection between the ILO and Latin America, and its role in defining, regulating and configuring the world of labour. In turn, these efforts will feed into the history of the international organisation itself.

Keywords: ILO; Latin America; networks; timeline; historiography

Introduction

The International Labour Organisation (ILO) celebrated its centenary in 2019. At this commemorative juncture, the institution proposed a number of initiatives to enhance and celebrate its history and identity. Its official website lists seven initiatives: social justice, the creation of a future that serves all of humanity – that is to say, an equative globalisation; the future of work; bringing an end to pov-

Doctor in History at the Universidad de Buenos Aires. Consejo Nacional de Investigaciones Científicas y Técnicas (CONICET), Instituto De Altos Estudios Sociales (IDAES), Universidad Nacional de San Martín (USAM) Contact: lauracaruso@gmail.com / Doctor in History at the Universidad Nacional de La Plata. Consejo Nacional de Investigaciones Científicas y Técnicas (CONICET). Contact: andres.stagnaro81@gmail.com.

https://doi.org/10.1515/9783110759303-007

erty, reviewing the place of women in the world of labour, the green initiative or the development of tools for a transition to a just and sustainable future; and finally, the strengthening of the tripartite consensus upon which the organisation was founded, together with a process of self-reflection on its rules and membership. Thus listed, with the exception of the issues relating to environmental damage and, to some extent, to the participation of women,[1] these statements were already listed in a similar way when the organisation was founded, a century ago.

The persistence of the same workplace issues that framed the emergence of the ILO demonstrates the endurance of those difficulties and inequalities on a global scale. It also alerts us to the importance of historicising the existence, policies, processes and dynamics of the ILO in Geneva, in order to rethink these problems and the conflicts that surround them.

For those of us from various disciplines within the social sciences who are interested in the historical and current configurations of the world of labour, the ILO has played a significant role in the reinterpretation of those configurations. The organisation acts as a legitimate and legitimizing voice for the policies, actors and complaints involved in industrial disputes, making it possible to visualise constructive tensions around the political significance of practices relating to the "problems of labour." Reflection is also needed on the absence of the ILO in certain contexts, demonstrating a need to divide the 20th century into different periods, according to the form and intensity of its connection, in this case, with the Latin American region.

When studying the initiatives of the international organisation, as well as its limitations, it is particularly important to consider the role played by Latin America in the configuration of the ILO, in the context of the diversity of social situations on our continent, the processes, people and developments they engage, and the mosaic of national and local realities. This work proposes a rethink of the history of the ILO from the perspective of our region, reviewing recent literature and academic developments that have created the space and impetus for that endeavour. The aim of this chapter is to focus on this Latin American perspective and relate it to the official narrative of the ILO itself, in order to offer a novel perspective and contrast that with the views that dominate the existing

1 Despite not being explicitly part of the 1919 agenda, the activities carried out, the links with other transnational networks, and the very presence of women in the different administrative spheres of the ILO, nevertheless make it possible to link this axis to the policies of the ILO since its inception. In relation to transnational networks, women's work and global governance with a gender perspective, see Eileen Boris, Dorothea Hoecker & Susan Zimmermann (Eds.), 2018, especially the works of Dorothy Sue Cobble, Susan Zimmermann and Paula Lucía Aguilar.

literature, centred as it is on the European arena and, for certain periods, specifically on networks of European social reformism (Van Daele, 2008). When it comes to considering other geographies, networks, periods of time and subjects that have shaped the history of the ILO, Latin America is not insignificant, and the first part of this chapter develops an overview of that perspective, entitled "The ILO through the Latin American prism."

The proposal to approach the history of the ILO from a Latin American perspective and from within Latin America, raises new questions and challenges. Who represented the countries of the Latin American continent at the ILO? How, and within what webs of tensions and national and regional agreements, were these delegations constructed? What representations did the nations of the region make to the world's delegates at the ILO? How was participation in the supranational entity in Geneva linked to the conflicts and processes taking place in national spaces? Did the problems of labour in Latin American permeate the ILO agenda, if so, how and in what context? How were the debates, concepts and regulations produced at the ILO used and appropriated by the various Latin American actors, be they states, employers or workers? What place and role did Latin American experiences have in defining the field and problems of labour, such as child labour, women's labour, indigenous labour or slave labour, among others? What role did the interaction of Latin American actors within the ILO have in the defence of labour rights and in the context of dictatorships in the region? Without being exhaustive or complete, this list demonstrates the types of questions that the Latin American perspective opens up for historical studies of the ILO.

The second part of this chapter is titled "A collaborative work: The ILO-Latin America interdisciplinary network, its work, methods and questions." In it, we review research conducted in recent years, within the framework of collaborative, regional and interdisciplinary studies centred around a new network of researchers from universities in various Latin American countries–Chile, Brazil, Argentina and Bolivia, among others. Finally, in the third and last section entitled "Recovering the ILO-Latin America connection in the configurations of the world of labour, its definition and regulation: a new agenda" we allow ourselves to briefly propose new questions and challenges for the future of this line of research, based on the experiences of the network and its recent publications.

By considering the ILO as an actor in labour relations in the context of experiences of labour on the American continent, we highlight the links and establish the various subjects within each space, in order to set the scene for an analysis of the links between the ILO and Latin America at a local, national, regional or global level. Ongoing debates about the meaning and definition of what should be considered work, and who the workers are (understood as subjects with certain rights and conditions), can and should be investigated in the relationship between the ILO and the different Latin American actors in the world of labour. Likewise, we must study the ways in which those definitions were constructed and the changes and transformations they have undergone in the light of different interests, demands, conjunctures and power relations in the various spaces involved. From the initial contact between the ILO and government, workers' and employers' representatives, and intellectuals and jurists, through the normative crusade of the ILO in relation to the definition of work – a product of its own myth of origin and its links with the International Association for the Legal Protection of Workers (AIPLT) (Kott, 2015) – the ILO sought to set parameters that were based on the standards of the most central countries. ILO policy took a decisive turn in the post-war period, when the focus of attention turned to the problem of decolonisation (Maul, 2017), and to what would later come to be called the countries of the *Third World* (Jensen and Lichtenstein, 2016), adding a North-South divide to the already existing East-West divide. However, the multiple realities around labour in Latin America presented a challenge for officials in Geneva. From their very first contact in the 1920s it created tensions for some of the institution's Eurocentric postulates, even leading to some changes to the institution in 1934 that aimed to address problems in non-European countries (Plata-Stenger, 2016). At the same time, Latin Americans looked to the ILO as a beacon that would allow them to measure their own levels of civilised development in the field of industrial relations, to the extent that the reality of working conditions in each of the countries were sometimes ignored. This is shown by various studies of the meaning and debates around the status and definition of indigenous labour in the Andean region, and how it was dealt with by the ILO (Barragán, 2017). It can also be seen in studies of the considerations that led to redefinitions of slave labour and forced labour in Brazil (Ferreras, 2017).

We are also committed to revisiting the conflicts that took place at different levels, in different spaces and with different subjects, in the arena of dispute that the ILO constituted for governments and employers' and workers' organisations alike. Local disputes were resignified by the participants linking local spaces with the ILOs supposedly international rules. Many international responses also encountered opposition in the course of domestic disputes which emerged at different times and in different countries (Caruso, 2017; Basualdo, 2017; Zorzoli, 2016; Yañez, 2017; Nunes, 2017), not only in Latin America (Cobble, 2016). By traversing borders, these disputes became a struggle of alliances that included not only the officials of the ILO itself, but also other actors with whom overlapping alliances and ties were forged.

Last, but by no means least, we aim to raise awareness of the active participation of actors of the region, which was neither linear nor uniform, and their role in the history of the ILO itself. We look at how the ILO did, on occasion, set the definition and limits in a specific labour field – for example in relation to child labour or unemployment – and whether that function was not simply imposed on or adopted by Latin American actors, but rather built with their participation. Highlighting the often-clear purpose of Latin American actors in their relationship with the ILO also highlights their impact and contribution to the history of the organisation, which often gets subsumed in the literature, stressing the imposition of an agenda from Geneva.

In recent decades, historical studies linked to international organisations like the ILO have shown increasing qualitative and quantitative interest in the impact of global historiography (Iriye, 2002; Maul, 2012, 2017; Kott and Droux, 2013; McPherson and Wehrli, 2015; Jensen and Lichtenstein, 2016). This is due, in the first instance, as Jasmine Van Daele (2008) has argued, to the end of the Cold War, and to a new wave in the process of globalisation. Nation states resumed their interest in coordinating international policies through multilateral structures; and this context revitalised the role of international organisations such as the ILO. This in turn has led to congresses, lectures, symposia and articles that show, in a fragmentary way, the need to unravel the transnational dimension of the regulation, definition and conception of labour and its roots in Latin America. Lifting our vision from nation states, this new line of analysis reframes the relevance of other actors and processes that arise from the intersection of the international and the local, in the form of workers' and business delegations, as well as delegations from colonial countries and countries in various situations of subjugation. These studies converge in postulating the centrality of the impact of international institutions and the links with the actors and dynamics involved in local processes. However, studies of Latin America are relatively scarce in this new repertoire of research, and a critical analysis of the relationship between Latin America and the ILO is perhaps one of the features still to be addressed. Until recently, the consideration and historicisation of the ILO from a Latin American perspective was not a priority for historians or social scientists. It was the ILO itself that created the search for greater understanding of the multiple realities and experiences of labour around the world, in order to set itself up as supranational entity that encompasses, understands and regulates them all. This relative scarcity of research is even more striking if one considers that Latin America was the first region to hold an ILO Regional Conference (in Santiago de Chile, in 1936), initiating an institutional form that only became standard for the institution in Asia in 1947, in Europe in 1954, and in Africa in 1960. Today we have various contributions, which follow the path opened up five years ago by the book compiled by Herrera and González (2013). Inspiration for that book stemmed from the conviction that the only real way to generate this type of knowledge is through dialogue and exchange between researchers and institutions, in a fraternal, collective and collaborative way.

The ILO through the Latin American prism

The end of the First World War led to the founding of an international body dedicated to promoting the regulation of labour within the framework of the European peace treaties. The course of the 20th century saw its exponential expansion into a number geographical areas, developing issues linked to labour around the world. Generally, the expansion of ILO activities is associated with the end of the Second World War as, under the leadership of the North American David Morse, from 1948, it was integrated into the nascent United Nations (UN). This is considered to be the period of the greatest expansion in the organisation's history, with the multiplication of its members and officials, the opening of local and regional offices, and the comprehensive implementation of regional programs related to employment. These years of feverish activity – which earned the organisation the Nobel Peace Prize – are also considered to be the period of most effective internationalisation, fundamentally due to the organisation's role in the processes of decolonisation and its work on the link between social rights and human rights (Maul, 2017). However, the focus on these issues – rather than on aspects of the debates about development – relegates Latin America to second place in a chronology based on the European space.

Viewed from Latin America, the process of the previous decades acquires greater relevance. In this expansion – which was central to the organisation's very survival in the early years – Latin America played a fundamental role. As Ferreras (2011) demonstrates, Albert Thomas, the first director of the ILO, sought in Latin American countries the support he did not find among Europeans in the interwar period. We must remember that Germany, Italy and Japan all abandoned the organisation between 1934 and 1935. Recognising this privileged link with Latin America during this initial period, helps to reconsider the chronology of the ILO itself, to the extent that in this decade, the most relevant feature in the historiography of the organisation is considered to be the entry of the United States in 1934 under President Roosevelt.[2]

2 The relationship between the United States and the ILO has occupied much of the literature on the entity, especially after the withdrawal of the US from the organisation in 1977 and its re-

When the ILO went beyond the European space with its proposals and regulatory initiatives, it aimed to configure a response to the mobilisation of labour through the internationalisation of the principles of labour legislation and other forms of intervention that sought to define a legal and legitimate shared field of action, disputes and demands. From its inception in 1919, the ILO set itself up as a relevant actor, and that was increasingly the case throughout the 20th century. As such, the intervention of nation states in the world of labour, and the definition of certain areas based on what was defined as work within it, relied on a set of meanings and assumptions that are worthy of analysis. The definition of these aspects of labour was shaped by a diversity of interests and tensions in the member states, between employers in different sectors, business interests of different sizes, and workers in various countries. The peculiar characteristic that even today sets the ILO apart among the world's organisations, is the inclusion of representatives from all three key socio-economic and political sectors (state, capital and labour), to create a tripartite structure that endowed it with legitimacy, uniqueness and potential in those early years, and that is still recognised today as a key element in the global political construction that takes place in Geneva. Tripartite participation also allowed the debates that took place within the organisation to continue in the member states, thus guaranteeing the role of the International Labour Office – the ILO's executive body – as a powerhouse of political thought, with the ability to influence labour policies around the world.

In the historical and negotiated construction of the various areas in which the world of labour was to be affected by policies, such as on maritime labour, child labour, women's work, work in non-metropolitan areas, indigenous labour, and forced labour, to name but a few. Demands were expressed, and the conflicting interests and positions of these three key actors – employers, nation states and workers' organisations – were debated. Their expectations and strategies were developed, and the hierarchies and tensions between the various countries of the world were played out. These were essential in the fields of work in the global south and maritime work. A fundamental consensus shaped and defined the fields of labour to be regulated. Conceiving activities as work implied endowing the workers with rights. In this way, in the inter-war period, in the face of the growing activity of the working class around the world, the notion of work that defined a field was directly linked, or at least was understood to be linked, to a set of workers' rights that were recognised in the new order promoted by the ILO

entry in 1980, which had a significant impact on the historiography, and with regard to the processes of decolonisation, in which the United States assumed a position diametrically opposed to the interests of European countries like France and Great Britain.

in the face of war and revolution. Social justice as an integrating and homogeneous project and policy was at least the intention of the Genevan proposals (Kott and Droux, 2013). Issues such as indigenous work since the 1960s, or forced labour, even today, constitute milestones on that projected path.

New reflections on this issue build a greater understanding of our continent. Take for example the work of Rossana Barragán, who invites us to think about the ILO's links to Latin America based on "a differential geography of rights" (Barragán, 2017). Barragán's contribution, in accordance with a long-standing Latin American tradition, calls for reflection on the tensions inherent in integrative processes like the ILO, in global terms, and in their local, national and supranational implications. In the case of Latin America, this requires recognition of the special condition derived both from its distance from the central countries (which had greater weight in decisions about the direction of the organisation, mainly from within the Office), and from its distance from other peripheral countries. This created truly 'special' situations which must be taken into account when considering the role of the various Latin American actors (Stagnaro and Caruso, 2017). However, while the ILO generated discourses in global "public opinion" (Maul, 2017), it also set certain standards for what constituted development, and established the scale against which Latin American were countries measured and compared, and upon which they built their aspirations.

At present, some concepts, such as the provincialisation of Europe, allow us to tackle complex processes, such as the expansion of an institution such as the ILO, without succumbing to antinomy between the central and peripheral countries. By thinking of Europe as just another case – albeit in many ways a determinant one – and not as a measure of normality or a benchmark, we obtain new analytical frameworks. These enable us to reinstate the connectivity in which the definitions of work are configured and deployed, without falling into national peculiarities as explanatory distinctions. Although this historiographical process is yet to be fully developed, it has great potential for studies from the Latin American perspective. It allows us to cease to think of these situations as divergences or exceptions, generally of the state authorities that participated in the organisation, but rather to consider them within the framework of the very configuration of what can be classified as work.

In this process, it is worth at least sketching out a tentative chronology of the relationship between the ILO and Latin America and attempting to make some initial generalisations. Without rejecting the chronology that the existing literature has established for the ILO (although that chronology is also itself in dispute) the aim here is to outline what we understand to be the key moments in the relationship between the ILO and Latin America. This does not mean that there are no national variations or exceptions. Venezuela went through a number of moments of extreme tension with the ILO, which even resulted in the country's withdrawal from the organisation in 1955. Nor does it mean that this chronology should be adopted autonomously as independent from those established for other regions. There is no doubt that certain problems, which had a strong impact on the ILO, did not arouse the interest of Latin American countries – for example, the decolonisation processes of the 1950s and 1960s – whereas other debates, for example on development or human rights, as well as the technical assistance missions, did have a strong impact on Latin American agendas. In this way, six stages are presented here that do not seek to offer a finished interpretation, but rather to propose an overall approach.

An initial phase, between 1919 and 1925, was characterised by great expectations, and a certain anxious distancing, largely the product of a distrust of the universal nature of the ILO. This was not the first time that an attempt was made to establish a body dedicated to or promoting labour legislation on a global scale, and its antecedents had failed to permanently transcend the limits imposed by European or North American industrial development.[3] With the exception of Cuba and Mexico, no Latin American country officially participated in those attempts, although in some cases unofficial contacts were established with second and third order agencies and officials related to the world of labour. These prior ties, weak as they were, were fundamental in terms of building expectations. Links with figures who were prominent in Latin American social reform guaranteed a strong dissemination of ILO activities in local settings and even favoured the incorporation of some workers' organisations into the debate.

The years from 1925 to 1936 witnessed attempts at institutionalisation that are the key to this new phase. Once the initial suspicions were overcome, Latin American countries began to forge permanent ties with the ILO, materialised in an increasingly large network of correspondents, publications, communication and the consolidation of already close academic and professional ties. Latin America became a fertile space for the ILO's preaching of peace and social justice, in the form of visits by the French director of the organisation, Albert Thomas, to different countries of the region in 1925. On his travels, Thomas welcomed the progress by Latin American countries in ratifying ILO conventions, and the growing body of labour legislation in the region. The positive response he encountered in Latin America made it possible to sustain the internationalist preaching of the ILO at a time when North American isolationism and scant ratification of its conventions by other members had left the organisation in crisis.

3 On the importance of the Europe in the ILO's background, see Kott, 2015.

From 1936, and until the mid-1950s, we see a new period, characterised by the relevance and autonomy of Latin American countries in the ILO, deploying their own agenda within the organisation and at times seemingly also outside it. In 1936, in Santiago de Chile, the Latin American Regional Labour Conference of the member states of the ILO was held. This was the first of its kind anywhere in the world, and, as we said, it marked an organisational innovation which is now a well-established institutional form.

From then on, regional conferences, have been held continuously to this day, even at a time when the ILO itself had to suspend its general conferences in the midst of the Second World War between 1939 and 1944. The Santiago de Chile Conference initiated the construction of an agenda for, and coming out of, the participating Latin American countries. This was an indication of the maturity of relations between the region and the ILO, in which primacy was given to the autonomy of Latin American countries from the headquarters in Geneva.

From the mid-1950s to the late 1960s, we see a relative loss of importance of Latin America in the ILO, coinciding with a decentralisation proposed by the organisation that focused on the decolonisation processes in Africa and parts of Asia (Maul, 2017). This period is marked by bilateral relations between member states and the Geneva body. It has been noted that there was some continuity of previously established links, while new mechanisms were also created that relate this chronology to the ILO's own official chronology. These mechanisms were the technical assistance missions, and in the particular case of Latin America, the Andean Programme, set up in 1953, which established a privileged link between the nations of Peru, Ecuador, Bolivia, Colombia, Argentina and Chile (although the latter two to a lesser extent), and the ILO. In addition, it opened a new role for the ILO in the region as a technical agency of the United Nations (UN), a role that it would play from then on. This programme was also linked to a whole series of discourses on development, in tune with the stance of the UN and the ILO itself during that period. Bilateralism can also be perceived in the disputes between Venezuela and the ILO that led to the withdrawal of the Marcos Pérez Jiménez dictatorship from the organisation in 1955, following years of complaints about union freedoms and freedom of association (Yañez Andrade, 2017). The development of the technical missions created a new map of relations between Geneva and Latin America. Thus, if in its early years these links had Buenos Aires as their axis, and from the mid-1920s that moved to Santiago de Chile, the importance of the Andean Program transferred that axis to the city of Lima, where from 1968 to the present, the ILO was to establish its regional headquarters.

At the height of the Cold War, this period was also marked by the enmities inspired in some sectors by an institution perceived as imperialist. This accusation has its own history for Latin America, which has been marked by an anti-imperialist cultural constitution at least since the 1920s and found support in the ILO's links with unions under the aegis of the North American Federation of Labor and Congress of Industrial Organisations. The global unions found the ILO to be closer to the institutional constructions of the free trade union movement. It even offered space in its union training to these ideological expressions (Scodeller, 2017; Correa, 2017).

The 1970s saw the rise of authoritarian regimes and military dictatorships, which once again created tensions in the relationship between the Geneva body and Latin America. This tension manifested itself around central points such as freedom of association or the persecution of union leaders, until at least the middle of the 1980s. The criticisms levelled against Venezuela since the late 1940s intensified at a regional level, and the growing links between discourses on development and human rights – in keeping with the UN agenda – marked the relationship between Latin America and the ILO. The ILO agenda at this time marks the beginning of a growing interest human rights directed towards the field of labour, generating an intense dynamic between labour rights and human rights. Thus, the issue of labour was given a new perspective in the relationship between the ILO and Latin America, and it became an important arena for complaints about the authoritarian character of the Latin American dictatorships.

In the 1980s, in the next phase of our hypothetical chronology, we begin a period marked by attempts to consolidate the emerging democracies on the continent. A central concern was the challenge of achieving the ILO's objectives in the face of recurrent and extreme economic crises. The widespread application of neoliberal reforms began a final stage, in which the organisation's concerns were reflected in the slogan or objective of 'decent work' at the precise moment when precarity and tertiarisation – known as the casualisation of labour – begins an escalation that is still on the rise throughout the continent (Basualdo and Morales, 2014).

The chronology presented here seeks to briefly reflect on relations between Latin America and the ILO, but fundamentally it seeks to express concern about the centrality of European events in the creation of the history of the ILO, in which periods are established based on internal changes within the organisation – fundamentally in its executive body and its bureaucratic structure, the International Labour Office – or through levels of European and North American interest in their relationship with the body. Without discarding these chronologies, what is presented here seeks to reaffirm the agenda of the Latin American states. That agenda was often secondary within the organisation, but nevertheless it was of fundamental importance for the Latin American actors involved.

A collaborative work: The ILO-Latin America Interdisciplinary Network, its work, methods and questions

The development of a Latin American perspective on the ILO and the world of labour requires dialogue and exchange across national borders, leading to a body of research founded on collaboration. That made it possible to think about the regulation of Latin American worlds of work and their links to the ILO, as well as the ILO's own history on the continent, how local policies were reconfigured, and the responses of different actors (unions, governments, professional associations, experts and others) to this new institution, which was both present in the field of labour, and constitutive of it at the same time. It was necessary to create a new, regional, interdisciplinary academic space, and that is how the ILO-Latin America Interdisciplinary Network was born. It emerged as interdisciplinary workshops held biannually at the National University of La Plata (2015) and at the Fluminense Federal University in the city of Niteroi (2017), with a further meeting in Lima (2019). A common body of work was presented in a thematic dossier (Stagnaro and Caruso, 2017) and published in a book (Caruso and Stagnaro, 2017), both of which were the product of discussions and research done on the networks' main lines of research. Today, the network brings together researchers from various countries in the region, including Chile, Brazil, Argentina and Bolivia, and has links with Paraguay, Uruguay and Ecuador.

A review of the literature produced by the network makes it possible to identify contributions on some of the questions posed in the introduction to this chapter in relation to the first half of the 20th century. For example, debates about categories, forms of work, and rights in relation to indigenous workers, which emerged both within the ILO and in dialogue with the broader Andean and colonial experiences (Barragán, 2017); the concepts and actors involved in discussions on forced labour and slave labour, as they were debated within the ILO, and variations on the same debates that took place in Brazil and Argentina (Ferreras, 2017); definitions of women's work and the problems they posed as they were discussed at international labour conferences, largely was centred on the wage gap between women and men performing similar tasks; and the impact of these debates on participating states and actors, for example in the case of Argentina (Queirolo, 2017). We see temporalities, subjects and categories of labour that emerged in Latin America and played a role in the historical configuration of these three key issues in the field of labour. The existence of these studies reveals powerful contradictions and the limitations of the ILO's own discourse, constructed as it was around the universality of rights and regulations, in full tension with the peculiarities of different places such as those cited above, and linked to existing inequalities and power dynamics.

A similar case is presented when we consider the regulation and configuration of leisure and holiday time, particularly in Brazil in the first half of the 20th century, where the first laws in the 1920s led to a more comprehensive law being passed in 1934. Both legal projects displayed varying degrees of connection to and incorporation of the proposals coming out of Geneva on this issue at the time (Nunes, 2017). Child labour is an area that also gave rise to debates at both of the Latin American Regional Labour Conferences, held in Chile (1936) and Cuba (1939). In these, the region can be seen to have had its own voice and not merely to have appropriated the Geneva accords and debates. In that voice, we find traces of the performative construction of model childhoods and youths – where children are seen as the agents of the future and the workers of tomorrow – as well as of the role of the family as a legitimate space in which work takes place, and the forms adopted in the construction of international regulations about boys, girls and young people at work. These were embodied in agreements as instruments of classification, and in debates and disputes around the ratification of those agreements in various Latin American countries.

Other fields, such as spaces for multidimensional state intervention, were established in dialogue with the ILO, and these were particularly influential in Geneva. For example, around labour law (Stagnaro, 2017) and the regulation of maritime labour (Caruso, 2017). In both cases it is evident that Latin American experts and intellectuals participated in the ILO and its agencies, and played a leading role, weaving an increasingly wide and dense network based on mutual interests and the needs of the ILO, in their construction and legitimacy. It is also possible here to see how the delegation and election of Latin American representatives to the ILO, and the representations made by union leaders, have caused tension and conflict (Stagnaro and Caruso, 2017). The particular case of the Mexican labour leader Vicente Lombardo Toledano and his links with Moisés Poblete as a member of the ILO, are an example of that mutual configuration and of how that relationship built labour institutions in Latin America. Specialised publications played a central role in the relationship between local actors and the ILO, and in the circulation of expertise and ideas; for example, the *Boletin Informativo de Leyes del Trabajo* towards the middle of the 20th century, which covered the key issues and actors in regional social policy and at the ILO. These served as local references and provided fundamental input for the discussion and legitimisation of such policies (Ramacciotti, 2017).

A set of works produced within the framework of the network has reflected on the particular dynamics and challenges that Latin America presented to the ILO. Our continent was marked by constant changes to exceptional, authoritarian regimes, mostly led by military forces and weak democratic governments, which greatly affected and conditioned the forms of work and the exercise of workers' rights as recognised by the ILO. In the case of mid-20th-century Venezuela, we have studied the way in which relations with the Latin American trade union movement intensified, in particular in the face of complaints of violations of the right to freedom of association during the military dictatorship of Carlos Delgado that began in 1948 (Yañez Andrade, 2017). On the other hand, and against the expectation that these regimes would be monolithic and closed to dialogue with the ILO, or totally reject the international organisation, other studies have shown both the significant place given to the ILO at critical moments by the last dictatorship in Argentina, as a space to gain legitimacy in the eyes of both the world and national actors, particularly as this international space allowed a reconfiguration of relations with the local trade union movement. At the same time, the ILO was a space for denouncing the Argentine military government for violations of the right to freedom of association (Basualdo, 2017; Zorzoli, 2017). At the peak of the military coups in the region, from the post-war period until the 1970s, the ILO implemented a strategy of labour education. This is shown by a study on trade union training programmes for developing countries, as an educational strategy deployed by the ILO to promote labour rights in Latin America, based on the Workers' Education Division's Workers' Education Programme. Regarding the institutional forms of the programme, the author looks into its content, looking for meaning and ideas about work, workers and rights, and the consolidation of those ideas in the links between local actors and Geneva, through which certain notions of work, workers and rights were reinforced (Scodeller, 2017).

Taken as a whole, the studies that make up a large part of the ILO-Latin America Network's production, reposition the region in the history of labour and of the ILO, by looking in a new way at the participation of Latin America in the constitution of policies that intervene in the world of labour throughout the last century, and to date. At the same time, they aim to build new and innovative knowledge around the multiple, complex links between the ILO, as an almost global body for the regulation of labour relations, and state actions, policies, debates and projects on matters of labour in the region. Knowledge of the various dimensions that linked the ILO with Latin America and its polyphonic, national and local realities, will in turn, allow us to give visibility to Latin

America's own place in the international regulatory arena. This perspective is absent in existing historical production and debates on these issues. It may even contribute to a revision of the ILO's own institutional history, with various contemporary investigations marking prosperous paths to follow.

These works and investigations are diverse in their geographical focus, themes and approaches, and they make up a common web of interests, scientific itineraries, collaborations and questions. They emphasise both labour policies and agencies, focussing on debates and draft legislation, and on the interaction between local and international labour institutions and the development of labour law, as well as the participating actors from and within the ILO, such as tripartite delegates, experts, and others. Together, they allow the articulation of a dialogue that forms the basis of the ILO-Latin America Interdisciplinary Network. It is a network for collaboration and the exchange of ideas, issues and resources that facilitates the creation of a common agenda of problems and questions, which, without dislodging the importance of case studies and specificities, guides efforts into the construction of a regional history of labour regulation in general, and of our region's link with the ILO in particular. The immediate objective of the network was to create dialogue between individual pieces of research that, in concert, would produce a qualitative leap in the questions, scale, resources, and documents, and the perspectives with which the history of the ILO is approached via its connections with the policies, actors and regulation of labour in Latin American countries. The network, is very diverse in its geographical approach and methodology, creating a common web of interests, scientific itineraries, collaborations and questions. We believe that collaborative and constructive work and dialogue between disciplines, institutions, projects and colleagues will allow the production of knowledge related to these issues, displaying their complexity and methodological challenges, as well as raising new questions.

Recovering the ILO-Latin America connection in the configurations of the world of labour, its definition and regulation: A new agenda

The experience developed at the meetings of the ILO-Latin America Interdisciplinary Network, and the various lines of inquiry that come together within the network, have opened up questions on a wide spectrum of topics and processes regarding the international organisation's relationship with Latin America. At the same time, it enhances the need for collaboration and exchanges with researchers from other continents, to compare and connect the processes, chronologies and forms of such links. What has been done to date, and the resources available, allows us to propose with a certain optimism, a common agenda that connects the region with the ILO, while being strongly situated in the world of labour in the various Latin American countries. The historical and present-day realities of these societies and their specificities form the prism through which we look at the ILO, making an effort to build a regional history of labour regulation and links with the ILO.

The need for a broader, global but not globalizing view is clear. We need to go beyond historiographic nationalism, without nullifying specificities and local processes. The impulse of research anchored in the local, illuminates the multiple linkages, networks, actors and reciprocal processes at different levels and on different scales.

It is worth a brief and positive reflection on the archive. Based on our own work, with its limitations and difficulties, the diversity and originality of sources and repositories of documentation, with which it is possible to approach the ILO from within the region, stands out. Reports, delegations, writings and books written by Latin American delegates and politicians; reporting by national or international correspondents and experts; specialised state, professional and expert publications on labour issues; various newspapers, trade publications, trades union and political party material; letters and correspondence between sectoral delegates; laws and parliamentary debates; minutes of conferences, many of which have been digitised; and the list goes on. The breadth and variety of this body of documentary evidence can and should be deepened through recourse to the archive of the ILO itself, which offers multiple search paths: by topics debated, by correspondents or officials, by conferences and sections. Thus, the archive of the Geneva-based institution, approached with questions anchored in the Latin American space, has enormous potential to develop future research.

Moving forward in this sense, we are aware of the enormous need that exists in our national historiographies to understand, for each period and in depth, the mechanisms, institutional logics and structural transformations (the organisational map) of the ILO, the dependencies linked to Latin America, and the forms of presence in our region (offices, correspondents, conferences). Better known than the rest, government delegates and experts or technicians at the International Labour Conferences still merit extensive analysis at various levels, looking at their selection processes, the degree of autonomy they had, their initiatives, positions, links with the ILO and their respective governments, and with the delegates of the trade unions and employers. These last two actors are perhaps the most neglected in the works developed on the subject to date.

This map of issues and questions, unfinished and incipient as it is, seeks to organise the state of the field of knowledge as a diagnostic tool. Although there are already some well-directed works on the subject, it reveals the need to further consider parallel regulatory spaces (whether in competition or collaboration with the ILO directives); Inter-American and Pan-American Conferences; the construction of a Latin American agenda, its meanings and policies and the local actors who built them. The challenges of such a research program, thus outlined, can only be faced and overcome by extensive collaborative work, across political, geographical and disciplinary boundaries, and the promotion of a fruitful dialogue to which this chapter is an invitation.

References

Barragán, Rossana. 2017. "La geografía diferencial de los derechos: Entre la regulación del trabajo forzado en los países coloniales y la disociación entre trabajadores e indígenas en los Andes (1920–1954)." In *Una historia regional de la OIT. Aportes sobre regulación y legislación del trabajo latinoamericano*, edited by L. Caruso, and A. Stagnaro. La Plata: FaHCE.

Basualdo, Victoria, and Diego Morales, eds. 2014. *La tercerización laboral. Orígenes, impacto y claves para su análisis en América Latina.* Buenos Aires: Editorial Siglo Veintiuno.

Basualdo, Victoria. 2017. "La OIT entre la dictadura y la democracia en la Argentina: aportes sobre el papel de organizaciones internacionales en la reconfiguración de las relaciones laborales en la primera mitad de los años 80." *Anuario Del Instituto De Historia Argentina* 17 (1). http://dx.doi.org/10.24215/2314257Xe038.

Boris, Eileen, et al., eds. 2018. *Women's ILO. Transnational Networks, Global labour Standards and Gender Equity, 1919 to present.* Leiden/Boston: Brill/ILO.

Caruso, Laura. 2017. "Legislando en aguas profundas. La OIT, nuevas reglas para el trabajo marítimo y su desarrollo en la Argentina de la primera posguerra." In *Una historia regional de la OIT. Aportes sobre regulación y legislación del trabajo latinoamericano*, edited by L. Caruso, and A. Stagnaro. La Plata: FaHCE.

Caruso, Laura, and Andrés Stagnaro, eds. 2017. *Una historia regional de la OIT: Aportes sobre regulación y legislación del trabajo latinoamericano.* La Plata: Universidad Nacional de La Plata. Facultad de Humanidades y Ciencias de la Educación. http://www.libros.fahce.unlp.edu.ar/index.php/libros/catalog/book/93.

Cobble, Dorothy Sue. 2016. "Japan and the 1919 ILO debates over Rights, representation and Global Labour Standards." In *The ILO from Geneva to the Pacific Rim. West meets East*, edited by Jill M. Jensen, and Nelson Lichtenstein. London: Palgrave Macmillan and International Labour Organisation,

Corrêa, Larissa Rosa. 2017. *Disseram que voltei Americanizado. Relaçôes sindicais Brasil-Estados Unidos na ditadura militar.* Campinas: Unicamp.

Ferreras, Norberto. 2011. "Entre a expansáo e a sobrevivencia: a viagem de Albert Thomas ao Cone Sul da América". *Antíteses* 4: 127–150.

Ferreras, Norberto. 2017. "Trabajo esclavo contemporáneo y trabajo forzado. Las políticas de la OIT y el Brasil en diálogo y conflicto, 1930–1990." In *Una historia regional de la OIT. Aportes sobre regulación y legislación del trabajo latinoamericano*, edted by L. Caruso, and A. Stagnaro. La Plata: FaHCE.

Herrera, León F., and González P. Herrera, eds. 2013. *América Latina y la Organización Internacional del Trabajo: redes, cooperación técnica e institucionalidad social, 1919–1950.* Mexico: UMSNH, UM, UFF.

Iriye Akira. 2002. *Global Community: The Role of International Organizations in the Making of the Contemporary World.* California: Berkeley.

Jensen, Jill M., and Nelson Lichtenstein, eds. 2016. *The ILO from Geneva to de Pacific Rim. West meets East.* London: Palgrave Macmillan and International Labour Organisation.

Kott, Sandrine. 2015. "From Transnational Reformist Network to an International Organization: The International Association for Labour Legislation and the International Labour Organization, 1900–1930s." In *Shaping the Transnational Sphere. Experts, networks and Issues from the 1840s to the 1930s*, edited by Davide Rodogno, Bernhard Struck, and Jacob Vogel. New York-Oxford: Berghan.

Kott Sandrine, and Joëlle Droux, eds. 2013. *Globalizing Social Right. The International Labour Organization and Beyond.* London: Palgrave-Macmillan.

Maul, Daniel. 2012. *Human Rights, Development and Decolonization. The International Labour Organization (ILO)1940–1970.* UK: Palgrave Macmillan.

Maul, Daniel. 2017. *Derechos Humanos, Desarrollo y Descolonización. La Organización Internacional del Trabajo entre 1940 y 1970.* Madrid: Plaza y Valdés Editores y Organización Internacional del Trabajo.

McPherson, Alan, and Yannick Wehrli, eds. 2015. *Beyond Geopolitics: New Histories of Latin America at the League of Nations.* Albuquerque: University of New Mexico Press.

Nunes, Guillherme. 2017. "Ócio e lazer na regulamentação das férias operárias: a OIT e o caso brasileiro na primeira metade do século XX." *Anuario del Instituto de Historia Argentina* 17 (1): https://doi.org/10.24215/2314257Xe033.

Pacheco dos Santos, José. 2017. "Pelos pequenos trabalhadores do Novo Mundo: OIT e trabalho infantojuvenil nas Américas (1936–1939)." *Anuario del Instituto de Historia Argentina* 17(1): 1–20. https://doi.org/10.24215/2314257Xe035.

Plata-Stenger, V. 2016. "Europe, the ILO and the wider world (1919–1954)." *EGO, European History Online.* http://ieg-ego.eu/en/threads/transnational-movements-and-organisations/international-organisations-and-congresses/veronique-plata-stenger-europe-the-ilo-and-the-wider-world-1919-1954.

Queirololo, Graciela. 2017. "'Igual salario por igual trabajo.' La Organziación Internacioanal del trabajo y el Estado argentino frente al trabajo femenino (1919–1951)." In *Una historia regional de la OIT. Aportes sobre regulación y legislación del trabajo latinoamericano*, edited by Laura Caruso, and Andrés Staganaro. La Plata: FAHCE.

Ramaciotti, Karina. 2017. "El Boletín informative de Leyes de Trabajo: circulación de ideas y actores latinoamericanos sobre políticas sociales (1942–1951)." In *Una historia regional de la OIT. Aportes sobre regulación y legislación del trabajo latinoamericano*, edited by Laura Caruso, and Andrés Staganaro. La Plata: FAHCE.

Scodeller, Gabriela. 2017. "Educar en derechos laborales: políticas y acciones desplegadas por la OIT en América Latina durante los años 1950–1970." In *Una historia regional de*

la OIT. Aportes sobre regulación y legislación del trabajo latinoamericano, edited by Laura Caruso, and Andrés Staganaro. La Plata: FAHCE.
Stagnaro, Andrés. 2017. "La delegación argentina en Washington (1919): entre el prestigio internacional y la acción local." In *Una historia regional de la OIT. Aportes sobre regulación y legislación del trabajo latinoamericano*, edited by Laura Caruso, and Andrés Staganaro. La Plata: FAHCE.
Stagnaro, Andrés, and Caruso, Laura. 2017. "Representantes y representaciones de Argentina en la Organización Internacional del Trabajo en la década de 1920." *Anuario del Instituto de Historia Argentina* 17 (1): 1–17.
Van Daele, J. 2008. "The International Labour Organization (ILO) in Past and Present Research." *International Review of Social History* 53: 485–511.
Yañez, Juan Carlos. 2017. "La Organización Internacional del Trabajo y la libertad sindical en América Latina: el caso de Venezuela en 1949". *Anuario del Instituto de Historia Argentina* 17 (1): 1–14.
Zorzoli, María Luciana. 2016. "Operativo Ginebra. La dirigencia sindical ante la instalación internacional de la dictadura militar (1976)." *Archivos de Historia del Movimiento Obrero y la Izquierda* 8: 13–32.
Zorzoli, María Luciana. 2017. "La OIT y las dictaduras latinoamericanas: una aproximación al Caso 842 contra Argentina." *Anuario del Instituto de Historia Argentina.* 17(1): 1–21.

Norberto O. Ferreras

Discussions on forced labour: Brazil and Argentina in dialogue with the ILO

Abstract: In this essay we analyse the definition of the category of forced labour in international organisations in the first half of the 20th century, and how that was received in Latin America. At the same time, we look into the behaviour of two major countries in South America, Argentina and Brazil, in order to understand how the regulations developed in Geneva were received, and the nature of the relationship between the parties.

Keywords: forced labour; Brazil; Argentina; ILO

Introduction

A little-analysed question in the social history of labour in Latin America, even though it runs throughout the whole continent, is the making of labour markets in each country. Labour markets are generally analysed by looking at the leading sectors.[1] For some countries, the starting point is the configuration of an urban labour market and for others, a rural one. The interesting thing about these analyses is that they take a small part and consider it to be representative of the whole. In doing so they the cease to consider the evolution of the whole (if we take the nation, with its links to different regions, to be the principal whole). In this essay we specifically seek to advance a regional and global analysis, emphasising the cases of Brazil and Argentina, and placing them in dialogue with existing international debates, based on the link that these countries had with the International Labour Organisation (ILO). We focus on these two South American countries because they had the largest workforce in the period in question. This allows us to develop an understanding of what was happening and how they behaved when faced with the complaints about forced labour presented to them.

1 The study by Charles Bergquist (1988) presents the creation of the Latin American proletariat from the point of view of each leading national sector.

Associate Professor at the Universidade Federal Fluminense (Brazil). Doctor in social history at the Universidad Estadual de Campinas. Universidad Federal Fluminense (UFF). Contact: norbertoferreras@id.uff.br.

https://doi.org/10.1515/9783110759303-008

The creation of a free labour market in the region began in the 19th century and is closely related to forms of captive labour. Free workers, generally individuals who had mastered a specific technique or who were skilled in the use of certain tools, found themselves in a context in which extra-economic coercion prevailed. The structuring of the labour market in Latin America coincides with the final years of the organisation of the workforce through slavery or other coercive forms of control.

The end of slavery did not immediately mean the adoption of the sale of labour power and free negotiation between labour and capital. Rather, the workforce tended to be controlled by other means. At the same time as free workers began to negotiate with employers in certain sectors, and later to organise, workers were also subjected to pressures that went beyond the sphere of economics. This phenomenon was not peculiar to Latin America. The process of proletarianisation occurred mostly in the primary export sector, following different patterns including the importation of labour and mechanisms to force the existing population to join the production processes as workers for an employer. In regions with a significant indigenous population, the mechanisms created to force their proletarianisation went back to colonial times. In regions with small indigenous populations, living alongside *mestizos*, migrants and immigrants, it was necessary to create other ways to contain the workforce.

In the two countries analysed, Brazil and Argentina, workers' mobility was restricted in the 19th century, with the introduction of certificates linking a worker to a rural landowner, that bestowed control over the workforce in addition to ownership of the land. Argentina's *conchabo ballots*, and the *passports* issued in various Brazilian territories to free rural workers, were intended to stem the circulation of workers in order restrict the autonomy of individuals who had many opportunities to fend for themselves in an open and rural region that was very difficult to control. In this way, the landlord guaranteed himself a workforce by restricting the movements of his subordinates. At the same time, those workers were forced to form local militias to defend the landowners' land against the "Indians," against other landowners or against the State (Secreto, 2011).

This is an example of why it was difficult to abandon coercive forms of work in the 19th century. In the cases of Brazil and Argentina, free labour relationships began to emerge in the cities, although not all urban workers had contractual relationships with their employers. Also, in the urban sector we find workers, mainly women, in the domestic service sector, involved in paternalistic and, in the case of women, also patriarchal relationships, that included control over their freedom and their bodies. Working in this sector meant it was impossible to have rest time, as workers remained in service beyond ordinary working hours. Scheduled rest times were not respected if the needs of the employer required it. This type of work was carried out by people who were included in the family nucleus as the daily help. This category can be divided into three large groups: workers who performed extraordinary services and who, once those services were completed, left the house; workers who provided daily services but did not reside with the family; and finally, those who lived in as part of the family nucleus. The latter were not seen as workers, but as domestic servants who were able to coordinate occasional or daily workers, but who were also in a relationship of direct dependence on the family nucleus. Some would remain with the family until the end of their lives, others were temporary employees. Control of their time and activities was dependent on the needs of the household and as a result, these workers did not control their own time, workload or the pace of their work.[2]

The existence of working conditions in which the exploitation of the workforce and the control of some attributes of individual freedom were normalised within the family nucleus, serves to help us understand the dynamics of forced or slave labour in the two main countries of the Southern Cone. The historiography of labour establishes a dichotomy between dependence and freedom, without analysing that these are not two poles that correspond to clearly defined and different periods of time. There is no moment of rupture or point of no return.[3] We must see them as two poles in constant tension and that tension is not resolved at any given moment. This is the great trap of teleological analyses that normalise class divisions as a dispute between two organised social classes, in which both enjoy and value freedom. Captivity is part of the class struggle and of the correlation of forces.

In recent years, the mass media have provided us with a wealth of information about cases of so-called "contemporary slave labour." The use of this terminology grew primarily as a form of critique or complaint rather than as an analytical category. Marcel van der Linden (2013: 75–92) shows us that freedom is not an irreversible good nor is capitalism its exclusive custodian. The return of this category that was thought to be banished shows that "captivity" and "freedom" remain constant, antagonistic poles in the organisation of labour. In this article we briefly analyse the way in which forced labour formed part of the debates relating to labour issues in some Latin American countries in the first decades of the 20th century. The way in which forced labour was tackled in the re-

2 Despite being under-studied, this is a growing field, particularly among Brazilian historians. For Argentina, see Allemandi, 2017; for Brazil, see Da Silva Telles, 2011 and Roncador, 2014.
3 As posited in the pioneering study by Hobart Spalding Jr. (1977).

gion led to the establishment of consensus, and tension between these countries and the ILO.

The dense and extensive debate surrounding the issue of forced labour has been on the agenda of various international institutions since their creation. Throughout the 19th century and until the constitution of the Geneva system, pressure grew against captivity at work. From the founding of the *Anti-slavery International* in 1839, this pressure was expressed as the expansion of European forms organising labour, on the understanding that captive labour impeded the development of a free workforce. At the end of the 19th century, the great anti-slavery conferences of Berlin (1885) and Brussels (1890), which resulted in the division of Africa between the colonising powers, established free labour to be a central element in the process of civilisation (Drescher, 2009: 398; Miers, 2003: 20–21). At that time, American countries were not a concern because they were able to present credentials to the say that they had already abolished slavery, some around the same time as those treaties, such as Cuba (1886) and Brazil (1888).

However, the 20th century revealed a new reality that had been brewing since the end of the previous century. With the expansion of cycles of consumption of cheap raw materials sent to Europe from the production centres on the periphery, the need for labour increased, mainly in production centres far from the large urban nuclei. The beginnings of the 20th century revealed the great efforts to eliminate slavery to have been smoke and mirrors. The same actors who had decried slavery and forced labour became the ones who transgressed the new norms. In 1904, the terrible conditions facing rubber workers in the Congo Free State, personal property of King Leopold of Belgium, were exposed. King Leopold had sponsored the international conferences of 1885 and 1900, yet 20 years later he was denounced for his own appetite for cheap labour. British diplomat Roger Casement exposed the enslavement of the population of the Congolese territory for rubber extraction, generating a wave of concern that would spread to the Americas (Hochschild, 2017, 365–395; Miers, 2003: 51–53).

A series of complaints revealed that various Latin American countries also deployed forms of captive labour, even if the workers were not considered property. When Casement presented his complaints about the Congo, one of the most important reports of the time on working conditions in Latin America, the "Bialet Massé Report" (Bialet Massé, 2010), was being prepared. Juan Bialet Massé, a Spanish doctor based in Argentina, was hired by the government of Julio Argentino Roca to conduct a study of the situation facing workers in Argentina. The result was *the Informe sobre el estado de las clases obreras Argentina,* presented to the government in 1904. This study presented the situation facing various categories of workers in the interior of Argentina and demonstrated the existence of forced labour and people being reduced to servitude in certain areas, mainly in the production of sugar cane, yerba mate and timber. In the same year as Casement's complaint and the Bialet Massé Report, the writer, geographer and military officer Euclides da Cunha travelled the Amazonian border of Brazil and wrote about the production of rubber in the Amazon. The text was published posthumously in 1909 under the title of *Nas margens* (1999) and although it did not have a great impact, it was a wake-up call.

Not long after, journalists, union activists, travellers and social researchers corroborated these studies with their own observations, revealing the different forms of servitude or forced labour that were present in the region. Spanish journalist Rafael Barret compared the gathering of yerba mate in Paraguay to slavery in the Congo. His newspaper articles were published in 1909 as *Lo que son los yerbales paraguayos* (2008) describing the situation of the *mensús*, the name given to day labourers in that country. Barret's investigation had a strong impact in Buenos Aires, which partly relied on yerba production from Paraguay. The descriptions of the American journalist John Kenneth Turner (2014), collected in the book *México bárbaro*, published in 1908, showed the use of prisoners, Yaqui and Maya peoples, *coolies*, Chinese immigrants and indebted workers in the collection of *henequén* in Mexico's Yucatan and Quintana Roo regions.

New research by Roger Casement (2011), published in 1910, proved decisive for the region. Casement was sent by the British government to investigate the conditions facing the Barbadian workers, British subjects, hired to work in rubber extraction in the Peruvian Amazon. However, what caused the most impact in London was his accounts of the situation of the indigenous peoples in the Amazon. The company responsible for the Putumayo indigenous peoples' slave conditions was Casa Arana, the main rubber producer in the region. This company was based in London and its board of directors was made up of important members of the Royal family and the City of London. It was the first time that complaints about indigenous slavery gained international significance, and it would not be forgotten quickly (Taussig, 1984). Other complaints and investigations would show that the end of slavery had not achieved an end to extreme forms of exploitation. Instead, new and intricate mechanisms emerged and were superimposed over the old strategies used to keep workers in the workplace.

The misalignment between European concerns, American complaints and the absence of a legal framework in Latin America is related, in part, to regional economic history and the institutional and legal developments that could have led to the creation of a legislative framework that contemplated these situations. Until that moment, free labour had not seemed sufficient to meet the growing need for cheap labour, and contracts for indentured service or traditional forms of servitude such as *yanaconazgo*, were not sufficient either. No legal sanction existed to oppose the forms of coercive labour being denounced. Those workers were in a legislative limbo, as the conditions they faced did not actually contravene the few existing codes, and although the practices were not fully accepted, they were not an object of legal concern. Concerns relating to workers' rights focused on urban workers or on more well-known production sites and premises closer to the large urban centres.

The terminology of slave labour or forced labour was ignored in Latin America. Brazil is a paradigmatic case: after abolition, the term "slavery" was erased from the Penal Code and the Civil Code. Legally, slavery did not exist, just as there was no legal figure to deal with debt bondage or any other form of captivity linked to work. The Penal Code did not reincorporate the term "slavery" until 1942. Slavery needed to be redefined following the creation of a complex of international institutions constituted after the end of the First World War, but responses were limited, late and did not define slavery or forced labour clearly enough.

International institutions were created after the First World War to regulate relations between countries and to establish standards for communications, health, culture, transportation, work, etc. As mentioned above, these international institutions gave new life to reflections on slavery and forced labour. We will see here how these debates impacted on Latin America, especially Brazil and Argentina, accompanying the existence of the truck system, international debates about slavery and forced labour, and the way these categories were received in Brazil and Argentina.

The international situation

In order to understand the way in which a field of debate on the question of forced labour was constituted, we are going to present, briefly, the journey of slavery, and its twin, forced labour, through the international organisations.

In 1919 the Treaty of Versailles, the name given to the First World War peace treaty, was signed between the warring parties. The Treaty sought to resolve some issues by way of agreements between governments, for which an administrative institution was required: the League of Nations. The ILO was created simultaneously as a complementary agency whose role was to improve conditions for workers. Although the two institutions had their own activities, some issues were dealt with in parallel and there were lines of communication, for example on the issue of slavery and forced labour.

Along with the Peace Treaty, other conventions were approved, such as the Treaty of Saint-Germain-en-Laye of 1919 (Great Britain, 1919: 108) which deals with slavery in Article 11, reviewing agreements reached at the Conferences of Berlin (1885) and Brussels (1890), which laid the foundations of the modern fight against slavery and trafficking, but which had also served as the basis for the division of Colonial Africa. The actions of the League of Nations represented an important shift in the fight against slavery, compared to the previous period, because, through them, the anti-slavers directly confronted those who were accused of practising slavery and also because the system required consensus rather than the imposition of a majority.

To address this issue, the League decided that the territories that had been colonies of the defeated countries would be governed through a system of mandates. This meant that the colonisers would have, among other rights and responsibilities, certain powers to end slavery (Macmillan, 2002: 100). This policy gave Western civilisation responsibility over the customs of countries considered "barbaric." Europe thus gave itself responsibility for the civilizing feat. The administration of Africa by European countries was to guarantee the overthrow of atavistic and backward customs such as slavery. To the extent that the League of Nations understood that these measures would not be sufficient, other instruments were developed that called for research to assist in reaching consensus among the member states.

In 1922 and 1923, the League of Nations ran consultations on slavery and indigenous labour in member countries. Indigenous work emerged as a common source of the more serious labour problems, linked to the absence of labour markets in colonial regions. The lack of response, or the ambiguity of the responses of the member states led to the creation of a commission, which included a member of the ILO, to consider legal measures to eliminate slavery. The powers of this commission, known as the Temporary Slave Commission, were limited, as its role was simply to gather information. Even so, the commission managed to place the issue of slavery on the institutional agenda. However, slavery was differentiated from what was known as forced or compulsory labour, as the latter forms did not imply the permanent deprivation of freedom for the worker, and because they largely applied to workers outside of Africa or the colonial centres, which were the main focus of the drive against slave labour (Miers, 2003: 100–121).

In 1926 it was possible to table a Convention at the League of Nations on the subject. This Convention, which forms part of the framework of international law, remains in force to this day, with only a few alterations. The 1926 Slavery Convention consists of a few articles that define slavery as the ownership of a person. In this way the League, and its heir, the United Nations (UN), which ratified the Convention, defined the loss of freedom and ownership of the person, as the main elements that establish the difference between freedom and slavery. Article 5 of the Convention recognises the existence of forms of forced or compulsory labour but does not assimilate them into the definition of slave labour (League of Nations, 1926). The Convention does, however, mention that forced labour should not create "forms analogous to slavery," which allowed for interpretations of the relationship between slavery and forced labour (Allain, 2008).

For the ILO, slavery meant an extreme form of the suppression of labour rights, however it was not the only such form. In the debates on the ILO Convention on forced labour, which took place in 1930, the word "slave" was not used as a specific category. While the League of Nations dealt with loss of freedom and ownership over the person, the ILO analysed compulsory forms that tied workers to the workplace.[4] No regulations were developed until 1926 because other topics, linked to already-established labour markets, and ongoing disputes in the metropoles, were given priority.

Recognition of the issue allowed Albert Thomas, then Secretary General of the ILO, to represent the institution on the League of Nations' Temporary Slave Commission in 1926. His role and the eventual approval of the Slavery Convention gave the ILO the opportunity to intensify its work on the issue and to ratify its own legislation, taking into account those aspects that had been set aside by the League. Although the 1926 Convention dealt only with ownership of people, the ILO analysed situations considered analogous to slavery, in the form of forced labour. The role of the ILO, as complementary to the League of Nations, and its focus on labour issues, prompted studies that would enable an approach to this issue based on the use of coercive forms to control the workers and the appropriation of labour, and propose solutions (ILO, 1924: 737).

Social research and data received by the ILO showed that physical or economic coercion did not equate to the definitive restriction of liberty. They were considered to be transient forms of control over the workforce. The focus was on colonial labour, mainly in Africa and Asia, although outside the colonies, the use of debt as a form of control was mentioned. This took various forms and was given a number of different names such as *acasillamiento*, *aviamento*, *habilitación* or *enganche*, all Latin American terms analogous to the practice we know as peonage. These forms of debt servitude or payment in kind were brought together in a category known as the *truck system*. In Latin America, it is also important to consider the ways in which indigenous people were mobilised to work using the colonial practice of obligatory community service. This situation would later create a new category: indigenous labour (Turner, 2014).

4 In the Recommendations, Conventions and Resolutions of the ILO, the term used is "forced labour."

It is important to clarify the terminology and how the truck system relates to what is known as debt peonage (sometimes called simply peonage) in Latin America. Some authors compare peonage to slavery for a number of reasons, either because there was no separate legal category to define it, or in order to make an impact among their readers. An example of the latter is John Kenneth Turner's book *México Bárbaro*. His position is that of an investigative journalist decrying the practice of forced labour. The first chapter of the book is titled "Slavery in Yucatan" and the fourth "Slaves hired in the National Valley." Two forms of captivity – debt peonage and indentured service – were thus assimilated into the definition of slavery. Debt peonage referred to loans of money or goods, such as food or clothing, which generated a debt that the worker was forced to pay through labour. Indentured service referred to workers recruited from another region or country to work exclusively for an employer, for a predetermined wage, that was generally paid in advance. They are different situations, however by using the term "slavery," Turner highlights the resulting subjugation rather than the origin or form of captivity.

The truck system is a category used in International Labour Law, while *Debt Peonage* corresponds to a descriptive category from the world of labour that refers to a set of working modalities that emerged in different parts of the world in the so-called "global transition from slave labour to free labour." This discussion had, and has, a greater impact in those regions where slave labour lasted the longest and coincided with the introduction of legalised free labour. The use of the term truck system refers to the subjugation of the worker in the context of the expansion of a free labour market and is intended to repress individuals and restrict access to free labour. (Hilton, 1960: 2)

At the 1926 International Labour Conference, the ILO proposed research on forced labour among indigenous people in Africa and America, organised by the *Native Labour Committee*, through which it was intended to demonstrate the close relationship between the two themes. Reactions were regionalised, and representatives mainly adopted positions according to their country of origin. While workers' and government from India clashed over the existence of forced labour, the Latin American delegates rejected the possibility that this initiative could be useful in their region, because they denied the existence of forced labour or because they felt that the issue could not be geographically isolated in that way. Both this research and the resulting recommendations would only be approved once the mention of "Africa and America" was eliminated from the title, keeping only the word "indigenous." For delegates from Argentina, Brazil, Chile, Cuba, Uruguay and Venezuela, slavery and forced labour were a feature of colonial societies, and, as such, did not affect the independent American countries that had abolished slavery in the 19th century (ILO, 1926: 263–264).

These countries deliberately confused "slavery" with "forced labour" to show that abolition had marked the end point of compulsory labour, denying any continuation of the forced appropriation of labour by other means.

Following this attempt, the debate on forced labour at the ILO became separated from discussions on "indigenous" labour, which was understood to refer to non-Europeanised or "native" workers in the European colonies in Africa, Asia and Oceania. Although these concerns focussed on colonial countries, the descriptions affected Latin American countries, which refused to be included in these categories. That led the ILO to refine its definitions. The ILO's interest in slavery and forced labour was the result of studies and research carried out by the *Temporary Committee* already mentioned above (ILO, 1922: 737).

Despite this opposition, in 1929 the ILO discussed the possibility of carrying out an investigation that would inform a Convention on forced labour. The Latin American members of the ILO did not participate in the commission and rejected this measure because they understood that in their countries indigenous labour was either protected, or simply did not exist as a separate kind of compulsory labour (which was the equivalent of saying that the only forced labour that could be considered to be the kind of forced labour proposed by the ILO, was indigenous labour). In this way, they reduced forced labour to indigenous labour, in order to avoid having to answer for situations where compulsory exploitation took the form of imposing compulsory labour on native communities. For European countries, the focus was their own responsibility for "civilising" Africa and Asia. Forced labour was not considered to be a matter of concern for their own region. The countries most called into question were Japan and the independent regions of India. At that Conference, as at the Conference the following year which approved Convention 29, it was demonstrated that the focus of concern was specifically European colonies employing a native workforce (ILO, 1929: 35–62 and 953–964; ILO, 1930: 267–363).

In 1930, following debates that began in the League of Nations and continued in the ILO, Convention No. 29, "on forced or compulsory labour," was approved. Article 2 of this Convention, defined forced labour as "all work or service which is exacted from any person under the menace of any penalty and for which the said person has not offered himself voluntarily." Despite the fact that this legislation was intended to be universal, and applicable to any case or situation, and that it only allowed for compulsion in states of emergency, it was clear that the focus was very much on non-Western peoples. The Convention mentioned the existence of chiefdoms or leaders who acted as mediators for native workers with foreign authorities, clearly referring to situations not contemplated by European institutions (ILO, 1929). The first ratifications of this Convention also showed the interest certain countries had in controlling slavery and trafficking, beyond the bounds of the Convention. In 1931 the Convention was adopted by Great Britain, Ireland, Liberia and Sweden; and a year later Australia, Bulgaria, Denmark, Spain, Japan and Norway did the same.

The international refusal of Latin American countries to recognise the issue of forced labour did not mean that there were no such cases in Latin America. As we mentioned at the beginning of this article, the existence of forced labour was well known. Initially, governments preferred not to discuss these situations, reducing them to isolated cases or relegating them to a specific moment in time. Latin American countries tried to distance themselves from the discourse on forced and indigenous labour. Speeches from the region's representatives presented a Europeanised Latin America, adapted to industrialised rhythms of work, with an active labour movement and workers' rights. There were two big problems with this self-image. On the one hand, the information in circulation did not support it. In an economic crisis, unemployment in the world economy grew rapidly; states protected local businessmen and this hindered workers' organisations; there was an obvious difference between immigrant and local workers, the latter being mostly indigenous people; legislation was sparse and was mostly geared to ensuring workers fulfilled their work obligations rather than defending social rights.

The other issue was the poor representation of Latin American workers at the ILO. That left the working group at a disadvantage in terms of national representation. More often than not, only state representatives attended the International Labour Conferences. The next most represented sector was the business community, which could afford the costs of travelling to international events, unlike the workers representatives. Thus, the information presented by governments was incomplete. It lacked sectoral representation, and that was hugely detrimental to understanding the Latin American phenomenon.

During the 1920s, the countries of Latin America presented peculiarities and problems, and they could not claim that work had been homogeneously Europeanised. At the first International Labour Conference, in 1919, Argentina faced criticism for not appointing a representative of the country's largest union as the workers' delegate, instead appointing someone closer to the government of the time (ILO, 1919: 107). Even sending a full complement of representatives did not necessarily mean there was democratic representation. At the assemblies that followed, Argentina chose to send only limited representations or not to send workers' representatives at all.

The Argentine case is not an isolated one. It was repeated in other countries in the region. Mexico was only admitted to the ILO in 1933; Brazil faced crises with Geneva, and only sent state representatives who happened to be in Europe at the time, at either the Swiss or French embassies; Uruguay, Chile and Cuba maintained greater continuity in representation. As a result, the ILO did not have a great impact on the region in the 1920s. However, that changed in the following decade.

The lack of workers' representation distorted debates in Geneva on the Latin American situation, leaving the region on the margins of discussions during that first decade of international associationism. In reality, there were no specifically Latin American issues raised in this period. However, that does not mean that forced labour was totally ignored in Latin American countries.

While forced labour was increasingly understood to be a problem in parallel with slavery throughout the 1920s, the same did not occur in Latin American countries. Nevertheless, the situation was not completely ignored. Argentina and Brazil behaved differently in their responses to forced labour, and we could say that they formed two poles around which regional positions on this issue were organised.

The Latin American perspective: the case of Brazil

After abolition in 1888, Brazil annulled slavery and those analogous institutions such as forced labour or servitude from its legal language. However, that did not mean that all forms of captive labour by other means had ended, as we can see in from the references in Euclides da Cunha's *Nas Margens*. Slavery was to be erased from the official memory of Brazil. In 1891 Ruy Barbosa ordered existing records relating to the origin, arrival and trade of slaves in Brazil to be burned. Barbosa, who had been one of the most important abolitionists, was at that time Minister for the Economy.[5]

For a long time, no one wanted to know about slavery. It was considered a sordid matter that should remain buried in the past. The abolition of slavery in 1888 had divided the groups that controlled Brazilian politics and economics. After abolition, the Empire collapsed and a year later the Republic was declared. The consequences of abolition were so profound that it ended up being one of the triggers for the liberal distrust of Emperor Pedro II, his subsequent deposition and the setting up of the Republic in 1889. Abolitionists and slaveholders

5 Ruy Barbosa's intentions have been interpreted in various ways, one of which is that he sought to frustrate slave owners wishing to request monetary compensation for the liberation of their slaves (Assis Barbosa, 1988: 11).

alike became suspicious of the Emperor's ability to lead the country. Among the Republicans were the leading abolitionists, including Ruy Barbosa.

Until 1930 slavery was not officially contemplated. In that year Getúlio Vargas led the revolution that deposed the so-called *Republica Velha*, and members of that movement received complaints about "slavery" in Brazil. Certainly, political use was made of the word in order to delegitimise members of the previous government. "Slavery" was used in newspapers in the context of complaints about people being held in captivity or forced into prostitution. With this same objective, a complaint was presented to the government focussing on the treatment of workers gathering yerba mate in the state of Mato Grosso, which was under control of a group opposed to Vargas. That complaint was made by the *interventor* of Mato Grosso, Antonio Mena Gonçalves, who presented accounts and photographs showing what he defined as slavery.[6]

These complaints were published in the newspapers of the capital, Rio de Janeiro, so that the government could not claim to be unaware of the abuses. The government preferred not to take action, beyond the liberation of the workers involved, which was arranged by Mena Gonçalves. Shortly afterwards, Mena Gonçalves was replaced, and as soon as the conflict between the local elites had been resolved, organisation of the workforce reverted to the traditional ways. Central government also had to face complaints sent to the ILO by the *Trabalhista do Brasil Party.*[7] While the letter did not cause any real problems for Brazil, it did demonstrate the importance of the issue for Brazilian politics. Throughout the decade, further complaints were presented, with no measures being taken in response.

Brazil's international presentations on the issue of forced labour or indigenous slavery were predicated on denials of the possibility of its existence, because recognition would bring them back to a situation that it was believed had been resolved. In this way, Brazil kept the issue of forced labour at bay until 1942, when the Penal Code, drawn up a year after the Republic was proclaimed, was updated. Slavery and forced labour were ignored in the first republican Penal Code. In the second it was mentioned but only in passing. The 1942 Penal Code, drafted 54 years after abolition, dealt with the issue of slavery as follows: "Reduction to a condition analogous to that of a slave. Art. 149. Reducing

6 On 19 January 1931 the first note appeared in the daily newspaper *O Globo* in Río de Janeiro under the title: "*Libertos em fim do cativeiro e do martírio*". In February articles appeared more frequently, reporting on the the situation in Mato Grosso, and referring directly to the actions of the state's *interventor.* For example, "*Prosegue o combate ao escravagismo*" (18 February 1931) and "*A escravidão em Matto Grosso*" (25 February 1931).

7 Letter from Silva Relle to M. Staal dated 26 February 1931, Archive of the ILO, Geneva.

someone to a condition analogous to that of a slave: Penalty, two to eight years in prison."[8] It is important to clarify that slavery was included under the title of "crimes against individual freedom," which means it was treated as a matter of restriction of individual freedoms, rather than an issue relating to the world of labour. As we see the definition is tautological, it does not define slavery except by mentioning the condition of the slave, no other situations are described.

When the Penal Code was published, the Minister for Justice Francisco de Campos, in charge of drafting it, justified the incorporation of Article 149 as follows:

> On Article 149, a criminal entity ignored by the current Code is foreseen: the fact of reducing someone, by any means, to a condition analogous to that of a slave, that is, suppressing, de facto, his status *libertatis*, and subjecting him to full and discretionary power. It's the crime the ancients called *plagium*. Its practice is not unknown among us, principally in certain remote parts of our hinterland. (Fields, 1969: 142)

According to the Ley Fabia, *Plagium* is defined as "the alienation of free people and holding them against their will" (Betancourt, 2007: 434), it was therefore difficult to link this to forced labour.

In 1943, the *Consolidación de las Leyes del Trabajo* (CLT) was enacted. This was an instrument that brought together all previous legislation on labour relations into a single law. Neither forced labour nor any of the possible categories related to it were incorporated. Although the CLT determined that salaries should be paid in national currency (Art. 463), it also left open the possibility that part of that salary could be paid in kind, according to local customs (Art. 458). In this way, a dangerous correlation was established with ways of fixing the worker to the workplace through the provision of goods, a situation that could lead to peonage.[9]

We therefore see that, although the issue of forced labour was not unheard of in Brazil, it remained unregulated. The government focused on the main categories of urban labour, leaving the possibility of forced labour aside. This was as close as Brazilian legislation got to dealing with forced labour or slavery in the first half of the 20th century.

---

8 Brasil *Decreto-Lei Nº 2.848, DE 7 de dezembro DE 1940. Código Penal,* available at: http://www2.camara.leg.br/legin/fed/declei/1940-1949/decreto-lei-2848-7-dezembro-1940-412868-publicacaooriginal-1-pe.html, consulted on 1 October 2017.

9 Brasil *Decreto-Lei nº 5.452, de 1º de maio de 1943. Consolidação das Leis do Trabalho,* available at: http://www2.camara.leg.br/legin/fed/declei/1940-1949/decreto-lei-5452-1-maio-1943-415500-publicacaooriginal-1-pe.html, consulted on 1/10/2017.

The labour market in Brazil was created during the slave period, so both types of workers (free and slave) faced similar conditions and high degrees of exploitation. Slaveholders did not want to lose the capital they had invested in their slaves and understood that they belonged to them, however, nor did they want to lose their freely availability of workforce. At the same time, a shortage of free labour, mainly in rural sectors, led to working conditions for free workers being similar to those of the slaves, as work relationships were created that sought to tie the worker to the workplace (Eisemberg, 1989). The need to trap workers in the workplace was decisive for the presentation of the free labour market in Brazil, in contrast to international attempts to "monetarise" labour.

The Latin American perspective: Argentina

The case of Argentina is somewhat different. Slavery in Argentina was definitively abolished with the Constitution of 1853. Article 15 established that the few remaining slaves should be freed from the very moment the Constitution was signed (Argentina, 2010: 33). However, that did not mean other forms of compulsory labour were not implemented to compensate for the resulting shortage of workers, particularly in rural areas. Accumulated social reporting from the beginning of the century, reveals a situation that, while not comparable to the period of slavery, nevertheless showed a tendency to trap workers in forms of servitude. Those situations were not necessarily permanent, and indeed, they were often temporary, particularly in those places where work was seasonal. Two closely interconnected mechanisms were common: the use of the debt and payment in kind. When a worker was no longer needed, the debt could be cancelled.

The above-mentioned Bialet Massé Report presented an overview of what was happening in some corners of Argentina and, taken together with other reports, it is possible to construct more details about how the labour market functioned in Argentina. The *Departamento Nacional del Trabajo* (DNT), created in 1907, conducted research that permitted deputies and senators to denounce conditions in the so-called *obrajes*, the name given to the rural establishments, isolated in the jungle across the north of Argentina. From 1913, reports from the DNT clearly showed what was happening on yerba mate, *quebracho* and sugar cane plantations. On several occasions, prosecutors, especially José Niklíson, had also exposed the role of debt bondage and its devious mechanisms in those production centres.

The exploitation of workers in the *obrajes* received increased visibility with the murder of hundreds of workers in the so-called Forestal Massacre, the culmination of a series of strikes that took place between 1919 and 1921. Although without great victories, those strikes did encourage workers' organisation and raised awareness of the forms of exploitation that existed in these territories, far from Buenos Aires and the other big cities. The final strike ended with the massacre of an indeterminate number of strikers, estimated by the socialist newspaper *La Vanguardia* at between 500 and 600 dead (Jasinski, 2013). The scale of the repression revealed a situation that could no longer be ignored. Further awareness was fostered by the reports of the DNT which reinforced awareness of the high degree of exploitation in the *obrajes* in the north of Argentina. Something similar happened in the south of the country as, almost simultaneously, workers' strikes exposed rural exploitation in Patagonia. The strikes ended with a massacre of rural and urban workers known as *Patagonia Trágica* or *Patagonia Rebelde*.

Argentina opted to deal with forced labour in an indirect way. The reasoning was as follows: if there was a possibility for employers to exploit workers, it was because the workers received their wages in kind or in vouchers. The modality Argentinian legislators adopted to inhibit this practice was therefore the obligatory payment of wages in paper currency. This formed the basis for the fight against forced labour. Payment in kind was classified as a part of the truck system, relying on a specific and well-known category from international legislation that would not create shock among the business community.

In 1925, Law 11,728 was passed, known as the "Law of payment in national currency." Debates over this law lasted across several legislative periods, starting in 1920, following the strikes in *La Forestal*. The aim was to control and limit the exploitation of workers in some production areas, mainly in extractive activities and the production of yerba mate or *quebracho*, but also in labour-intensive activities, such as the production of sugar cane. The law faced enormous difficulties. On the one hand, the debates were long and drawn out to delay its approval, and when it was finally approved it was vetoed by the executive branch.

The legislators promoting the law only got it approved following a series of negotiations that concluded with significant amendments, including for example, the provision that payment in checks was permitted for those receiving salaries greater than $300, on the basis that it was difficult to transport money through remote regions. In that way, it was enshrined in law that some workers would receive their pay through the companies' own financial systems. By this rule, companies or local merchants would benefit from workers deducting the checks corresponding to their salary for less than nominal values. This restarted the wheel of indebtedness in the workplace.[10]

10 The debates and the text of the law can be seen in Argentina, 1927: 808 and 813.

This was an important starting point for the consolidation of legislation to control forced labour. The debates revolved around debt bondage, although the terminology used referred to the truck system. This adoption of a restrictive definition of forced labour based on one of its aspects, the most well known in Latin America, is important because it is the starting point upon which later arguments against compulsory labour were to rest.

Latin America and the ILO: From forced labour to the truck system

As we can see, both Argentina and Brazil faced the issue of forced labour, at different times. The different approaches of the two countries stem from their own national histories, which caused them to adopt different responses when faced with complaints about forced labour. As we saw at the beginning of the chapter, during the 1920s, neither Argentina nor Brazil, nor any other country in Latin America, was open to a discussion on forced labour or slavery. When the topic was broached at International Labour Conferences, the reaction was to defend the region as one voice, ruling out any possibility of the subject being restricted to a discussion of Asia and America. This does not mean that forced exploitation of labour did not exist. On the contrary, we see that in both Argentina and Brazil practices existed that were analogous to forced labour. Complaints related to forms of exploitation in rural work show that workers suffered extra-economic forms of workforce coercion.

The relationship between the ILO and Latin American countries zigzagged somewhat. American countries didn't pay much attention to Geneva because they expected a closer relationship; Geneva, expected Latin American to follow the rules, adapt to their demands, and pay their membership fees. Neither side got what they wanted (Ferreras, 2009). In an attempt to resolve that situation, ILO Secretary General Albert Thomas and other officials visited some South American countries with the hope of overcoming some of the misunderstandings, however, those visits were ineffective (Ferreras, 2011). The second attempt to bring the parties closer together was to hold a Conference that would allow the American countries to present their concerns, without the most influential countries of the ILO conditioning the debate (Ferreras, 2015). This conference, known as the Conference of American Countries members of the ILO, took place in Santiago de Chile in 1936, and at it, the issue of forced labour was put on the agenda.

To get to that conference, which was to alter some of the ILO's practices, it was necessary to overcome certain resistance. At the 19th International Labour Conference in 1935, Latin American delegates returned to the question of forced labour. Convention 29 had been approved in 1930, however it was ignored by representatives from Latin America who did not seek to apply it because they felt that it was not suited to the regional situation. The Latin Americans referred to the truck system, however they did so in such a way that it was presented as though it were a totally different practice to forced labour.

The Brazilian workers' representative, Chrisosthomo Antônio de Oliveira, was in charge of presenting the truck system as one of the priority issues for the workers' representatives of Latin America. The truck system was described as a way to compel the agricultural worker to repay loans for merchandise received in advance, and it was understood that this form of exploitation made labour reforms unfeasible in Latin American countries as it created a double standard. He also questioned the colonial powers, because the extent to which this practice was used as a form payment and control of labour in the colonies gave them a competitive advantage over the countries of Latin America (ILO, 1935: 368–369).

The Argentinian government representative, Enrique Ruiz Guiñazú, approached the issue from a technical point of view, stressing the role of Argentina, going back to the first International Conference and to the implementation of Law 11,728 in 1925. According to Ruíz Guiñazú, rural wages were depressed and the truck system helped to depress them even more. The defence of payment in paper currency was linked to the need for wages to correspond to standards of living for workers. The draft resolution should give way to a convention on the issue that accompanied existing legislation in other countries in Europe and America. A convention would allow for more homogeneous and predictable wages for workers without extra exploitation in the sphere of consumption. Ruíz Guiñazú's position was supported by Brazilian government representatives, Affonso Bandeira de Mello, and the Venezuelan, César Zumeta. The latter understood payment in kind or bonds to be a cause of unfair competition on the international markets. The resolution was unanimously approved, although we must remember that the approval had no real consequences, it simply meant research into the impact of the truck system on workers' wages would continue (ILO, 1935a: 479, 480 and 484).[11]

We understand that, for the Latin American representatives, the truck system was not considered to be an extraordinary form of exploitation. We could say

11 The complete resolution was published on page 744.

that it was understood to be a crime committed against work, but not against the humanity of the worker. That is why the discourse sought to prioritise the fight against the truck system, as that terminology allowed it to be seen in a very differently than if it were called forced labour. The Latin American analysis of the issue made very few advances at that time, but the topic remained a lively issue and was raised a few months later at the International Conference of the American Member Countries of the ILO which took place in January 1936 in Santiago de Chile. Several European countries encouraged the holding of an American summit where American issues could be resolved by the Americans themselves.

The First International Conference of the American Member Countries of the ILO

When the ILO agreed to the First International Conference of American Member Countries taking place, it was a recognition that some issues that were important to these countries needed to be treated in a more specific way than was possible at the International Conferences taking place in Geneva. The meeting, which took place in Santiago de Chile between December 1935 and January 1936, was joined by all the American countries, including Canada, which until then had not participated in any Pan American Conference. However, Argentina, despite its proximity and the interest expressed in the event being organised, only sent government representation, due to a strike paralysing the city of Buenos Aires at the time.

The content of the conference was highly political, as the idea of creating an American Labour Organisation was subtly being discussed, and debates were marked by this possibility. Among the topics discussed were women's work, indigenous work, popular nutrition and a minimum wage. The truck system also figured on the agenda. Two groups were committed to this issue, the workers, and the representatives of the Argentinian government, with Enrique Forn the sole representative of that country as spokesperson. The workers' group placed the truck system alongside other issues of social legislation that needed to be addressed and were being neglected by national governments.

The Argentine delegate, on the other hand, discussed technical issues linked to the exploitation of workers in areas far from urban centres. Forn brought 20 years of Argentinian debates on the issue to the table, linking the truck system to practices typical in rural labour, specifically those establishments dedicated to the harvesting of yerba mate or timber, and the labour-intensive sugar refineries and *obrajes*. The second characteristic of the truck system for Enrique Forn was the role of the company stores in these production centres. Concern was focussed on the exploitation of the consumer rather than on the link between the company hiring labour and its privileged position as a supplier of consumer goods to its workers. The way debt was created became an extra-economic constraint on workers. Forn's proposal was to continue the ILO's research on the issue, and that was approved without debate. He also called for further research and requested any data available in Geneva that would enable the approval of a future convention (ILO, 1936: 145, 158 and 291–298).[12] This was an attempt to involve the international community so that the Americas did not become the only place to legislate on the issue, while expanding the available information about regional cases.

Later positions on the truck system

The debates of the ILC in 1935 and the International Conference of the American countries in 1936, were based on impressions or on data contributed by a small number of countries, such as the laws passed in Argentina and Paraguay. These were not sufficient to feed into discussions about universal legislation. In 1936, the ILO began a wider investigation into the truck system, sending a questionnaire to all member countries. The responses to that questionnaire were to form the basis for a future convention. Despite the effort made, the responses were few and frustrating. The countries that responded to the consultation were: Argentina, Bolivia, Brazil, Chile, the United States, Liberia, Mexico, Peru, and the Soviet Union. The countries of Latin America provided some data along with their respective legislation. The others sent general comments without providing specific information. It appeared the question was confined to Latin America alone (ILO, 1935 b).

The Latin American representatives returned to the question of the truck system at the ILC in 1937. The Venezuelan workers' representative, Luis Alfonso Parra, denounced the continuity of the truck system and the payment of rural workers and oil workers in company vouchers. The Indian workers' representative, Satis Sen, presented the situation of workers in his country, framing the truck system in the debates around forced labour and indigenous labour. It was understood that systems of exploitation through debt, advanced payment

12 As a result of this, Paraguay presented a national Law, 1218 of 6 August 1931, which made it obligatory for companies operating in the Alto Paraná region to pay their workers in country and in hard currency as a way of combatting the truck system.

in consumer goods and/or the obligation to use company suppliers, were among the ways of trapping and exploiting workers which persisted throughout the British colonial system and were responsible for food crises and generalised malnutrition among indigenous peoples. Certainly, the criticism was much more serious and had a greater impact than the positions taken by Latin America had been. That led to a review of the previously approved conventions. For the first time, the truck system was clearly linked to forced labour and one of the main European countries, Great Britain, was at the centre of the debate. Britain was also the main promoter of measures against slavery or forced labour. In this way, the truck system was linked to the picture of hunger and poverty in India, as it was seen by the western world, and placed the coloniser at the centre of the story. The truck system and other forms of extra-economic control of the workforce, such as the obligation to grow your own food, emerged as another way to circumvent the limits placed on exploitation by the existing conventions. Once again, the proposal for a resolution called for ILO studies of the truck system and other forms of exploitation to be expanded (ILO, 1937: 263, 460 and 461–562).[13]

At the Second Conference of American countries that took place in Santiago de Cuba in November 1939, the matter remained on the agenda. At that meeting, a brief summary of what had been done on the issue was presented. It did not amount to much, simply stating that the ILO had collected some more data. The novelty was that the debates on the truck system had introduced peonage into the dialogue, albeit as a brief mention that did not give rise to further reflection.

No further progress was possible on the issue while the world powers were preparing to go to war. The overwhelming interest was in maintaining and expanding labour capacity, and all the international legal scaffolding was abandoned in the face of the demands of the approaching war. In fact, the truck system was discussed again at the American Conference after the war in 1946. The peculiarity there was that the approach clearly intended to treat the issue as unique to indigenous communities. As such, it no longer referred to the workers as a whole, but to a specific category: the indigenous workers of Latin America (ILO, 1939: 22–23; ILO, 1946: 46 and 47).

Evidently, the truck system corresponded to a very wide range of forms of control and payment of wages and operated under different names. While this

---

13 In 1938, the Swedish workers' representative, Gunnar Andersson, raised this issue in a marginal context, when he requested a resolution on workers in the timber industry that included a presentation on the use of the truck system there (ILO, 1938: 482).

was a fringe issue for urban workers, the *milieu* from which most workers' representatives came, the situation facing agricultural labourers could not be ignored, and showed the most serious face of the exploitation of workers in the region. It is necessary to remember that rural life was a characteristic of Latin American countries, as the majority of the population lived and worked in rural areas.

Conclusions

In this chapter we have sought to present the creation of international legislation on forced labour in which the ILO had a decisive influence. However, we have also seen how Latin America received those initiatives with mistrust and sought to take them another way, for example, by focussing on the truck system. In this way, Latin America struck a discordant note with attempts to impose a universal, international understanding of forced labour. In fact, only three countries in the region adopted Convention 29 in the first half of the 20th century: Chile, in 1933, and Mexico and Nicaragua, in 1934. The other countries opted to contest the existence of the Convention, and prioritised discussion of the truck system. Although that approach included forms of extra-economic control of labour, it restricted understanding of the practice to a technical category focused on the workforce rather than on the producer, and effectively reversed the logic of exploitation – the worker worked to pay his debts rather than debt being created to force the worker to work. Latin American state representatives focused on the debt and not the labour, which needed to be cheap and abundant. Debt was the excuse for exploitation rather than the centre of the system.

In any case, the discourse on the truck system (payment in kind) and forced labour due to debt, was incorporated by the workers representatives, mainly at the American Labour Conferences. In this case, it was the workers themselves who linked this discourse and their resulting struggles, to a vindication of their rights before the authorities. The logic was to expand representation and social rights, which led to a policy of the universality of rights and the consolidation of those rights into law.

It is important to mention that there is a significant body of theoretical literature that analyses the limitations of free labour and the emergence of forced or compulsory labour. The discussions revolved, to a large extent, around the relationship between slavery and capitalism and the compatibility of both in an openly capitalist society. This led to notions that capitalism could not only be compatible with slavery, but that it created other possible forms of exploitation that linked work to money in a different way to that proclaimed by liberalism and the free sale of one's "labour" in exchange for a wage. We are faced with the relationship established in the Brazilian and Argentinian hinterlands which operated in reverse: money was offered by the capitalists and later had to be paid for in labour by the worker. This not only reversed the logic but also ensured that there was never enough of the commodity "labour" to satisfy the initial loan. In this way, capitalism subjugated the worker. Orlando Paterson, one of the most recognised theorists on slavery, understood that there were two forms of debt bondage: slavery and peonage. The first was permanent, a product of poverty and inequality, and the second transitory, a product of poor harvests (Patterson, 1982: 124). The Latin American case seems to be a bit more complex. Although in Yucatán the two varieties of slavery and peonage seemed to exist, that does not seem to be the case in Argentina or Brazil, where debt was created following the dispossession of lands. The labourer was forced into debt to be able to exercise his trade: the purchase of an axe or the tools for the harvest of latex, to which he had to add food and clothing to be able to raise a family and thus replenish the work force. In other words, it was caused by an alteration of the regional productive cycle due to the privatisation of a space that had hitherto been common land. That is why the truck system brings us to the legal rather than the social and economic aspects of debt peonage in the region, which is what we study here.

The linking of regional and universal aspects of the law in Brazil and Argentina, their practices and reflections, and the solutions that each country adopted in their attempts to deal with forced labour, allows us to see a complex reality, traversed by the history of local labour and the forms of exploitation that were consecrated and accepted in each society. The way in which Brazil avoided the existence of forced labour, even when there were existing complaints and attempts by civil society to frame these forms of compulsory, or even criminal, labour as slavery, is related to the longevity of an institution that had been abolished throughout the rest of the continent. This prevented a correct understanding of what was happening in rural areas, as it was treated in terms of an extinct institution rather than as an existing culture of exploitation. The way to process this ambiguity was through local legislation and an international commitment to the fight against the truck system.

In the case of Argentina, we have a different situation, despite the fact that the two countries arrived at the common point of tackling the truck system. Argentina sought to present its production relations as modern, consisting of a free relationship between capital and labour. This freedom, in reality, was defined by a subscription to the ideas of classical liberalism that inhibited any form of association between workers, but not between owners, as evidenced by the creation and actions of various business associations in defence of liberalism at work.[14] It was held that there could be no forced labour in a society that advocated "freedom" as the basis of its political and social organisation. What social researchers might find were abuses of power and domination. Owners exercised an extraordinary function by creating a monopoly and taking advantage of their privilege in the situation, restricting the worker-consumer's free access to goods. The problem was centred on the sphere of consumption and not production. However, the truck system showed that debt was used to trap the worker and was closer to debt peonage and forced labour than the abuse of a dominant position in the consumer market.

Both countries, along with the rest of Latin America, agreed that the reflections on forced labour in Convention 29 were not appropriate for the region and that they should be restricted to the colonial environment. All the debates went in this direction, despite the fact that the available evidence indicated the contrary.

References

Allain, Jean. 2008. *The Slavery Conventions: The Travaux Préparatoires of the 1926 League of Nations Convention and the 1956 United Nations Convention* Leiden: Martinus Nijhoff.

Allemandi, Cecilia. 2017. *Sirvientes, criados y nodrizas: una historia del servicio domestico en la ciudad de Buenos Aires: fines del siglo XIX y principios del XX.* Buenos Aires: Teseo.

Argentina. 2010. *Constitución de la Nación Argentina: publicación del Bicentenario (Facsimil).* Buenos Aires: Corte Suprema de Justicia de la Nación – Biblioteca del Congreso de la Nación – Biblioteca Nacional.

Argentina, Congreso Nacional. 1927. *Diario de Sesiones de la Cámara de Diputados de la Nación. Año 1926. Tomo IV. Sesiones ordinarias. Agosto 12-Septiembre 1.* Buenos Aires: Imprenta y encuadernación de la Cámara de Diputados.

Assis Barbosa, Francisco. 1988. "Apresentação." In *Rui Barbosa e a Queima dos Arquivos,* edited by Américo Jacobina Lacombe, et al. Brasília: Ministério da Justiça – Fundação Casa de Rui Barbosa, Rio de Janeiro.

Barret, Rafael. 2008. "Lo que son los yerbales paraguayos." In *El dolor paraguayo*, edited by Rafael Barret. Caracas: Biblioteca Ayacucho.

Bergquist, Charles. 1988. *Los trabajadores en la historia latinoamericana: estudios comparativos de Chile, Argentina, Venezuela y Colombia.* México: Siglo XXI.

Betancourt, Fernando. 2007. *Derecho Romano Clásico.* Sevilla: Universidad de Sevilla.

Bialet Massé, Juan. 2010. *Informe sobre el estado de las clases obreras argentinas.* La Plata: Ministerio de Trabajo de la Provincia de Buenos Aires.

---

14 The most well-known of these being the *Asociación del Trabajo*, created in 1918 (Rapalo, 2012).

Brasil, Senado Federal. Subsecretaria de Informações. 1890. *Decreto N. 847–de 11 de outubro de 1890. Código Penal.* http://www2.camara.leg.br/legin/fed/decret/1824-1899/decreto-847-11-outubro-1890-503086-publicacaooriginal-1-pe.html. Accessed 1/10/2017.

Brasil, Senado Federal. Subsecretaria de Informações. 1940. *Decreto-Lei 2.848, de 7/12/1940. Código Penal.* http://www6.senado.gov.br/legislacao/ListaPublicacoes.action?id=102343.

Brasil, Senado Federal. Subsecretaria de Informações. 1943. *Decreto-Lei Nº 5.452, de1º de Maio de MAIO1943. Consolidação das Leis do Trabalho.* http://www2.camara.leg.br/legin/fed/declei/1940-1949/decreto-lei-5452-1-maio-1943-415500-publicacaooriginal-1-pe.html. Accessed 1/10/2017.

Campos, Francisco de. 1969. "Exposição de motivos do Código Penal de 1940". *Revista de Informação Legislativa 6. 24.* Brasília: Senado Federal – Diretoria de Informação Legislativa.

Casement, Roger. 2011. *El Libro Azul. Informes de Roger Casement y otras cartas sobre las atrocidades en el Putumayo.* Lima: Centro Amazónico de Antropología y Aplicación Práctica.

Da Cunha, Euclides. 1999. *À Margem Da História.* São Paulo: Martins Fontes.

Da Silva Telles, Lorena Féres. 2011. Libertas entre sobrados: Contratos de trabalho Doméstico em São Paulo na derrocada da Escravidão. São Paulo, Tese de Doutorado–USP.

Drescher, Seymour. 2009. *Abolition. A History of Slavery and Antislavery.* New York: Cambridge University Press.

Eisenberg, Peter. 1989. *Homens esquecidos: escravos e trabalhadores no Brasil–séc. XVII e XIX.* Campinas: Editora da Unicamp.

Ferreras, Norberto. 2009. "O Prêmio Nobel e o burocrata: a conformação de um campo intelectual no Direito do Trabalho na Argentina da década de 1930." *Anos 90* 16 (29): 213–236.

Ferreras, Norberto. 2011. "Entre a expansão e a sobrevivência: a viagem de Albert Thomas ao Cone Sul da América." *Antíteses* 4 (7): 127–150.

Ferreras, Norberto. 2012. "La modernité intégrée par les peuples indigènes. L'Organisation internationale du travail et l'Amérique latine, la question des peuples indigènes et tribaux." In *Modernités Nationales, Modernités Importées entre Ancien et Nouveau Monde XIXe–XXIe siècle*, edited by Daniel Aarão Reis, and Rolland Denis. Paris: L'Harmattan.

Ferreras, Norberto. 2015. "Europa-Geneva-America: The First International Conference of American States Members of the International Labour Organization." In *Beyond Geopolitics. New Histories of Latin American at the League of Nations*, edited by Alan Mcpherson, and Yannick Wehrli. Albuquerque: University of New Mexico Press

Ferreras, Norberto, and María Verónica Secreto. 2013. "Trabalho decente, trabalho escravo, trabalho degradante, trabalho análogo à escravidão e outras categorias do Mundo do Trabalho Contemporâneo." In *Os pobres e a política. História e Movimentos Sociais na América Latina*, edited by Norberto Ferreras, and María Verónica Secreto. Río de Janeiro: Mauad Ed.

Gotkowitz, Laura. 2007. *A Revolution for Our Rights: Indigenous Struggles for Land and Justice in Bolivia (1880–1952).* Durham: Duke University Press.

Great Britain. Parliament. 1919. *Convention Revising the General Act of Berlin, February 26, 1885, and the General Act and Declaration of Brussels, July 2, 1890, Signed at Saint-Germain-en-Laye, September 10, 1919.* London: H.M. Stationery Office.

Hilton, George W. 1960. *The Truck System Including a History of the British Truck Acts, 1465–1960.* Cambridge: W. Heffer.
Hochschild, Adam. 2017. *El fantasma del Rey Leopoldo. Una historia de codicia, terror y heroísmo en el África Colonial.* Barcelona: Malpaso.
Jasinski, Alejandro. 2013. *Revuelta obrera y masacre en La Forestal: sindicalización y violencia empresaria en tiempos de Yrigoyen.* Buenos Aires: Biblos.
Linden, Marcel van der. 2013. *Trabalhadores do Mundo. Ensaios para uma História Global do trabalho.* Campinas: Edunicamp.
Macmillan, Margaret. 2002. *Paris 1919. Six months that changed the world.* New York: Random House.
Miers, Suzanne. 2003. *Slavery in the Twentieth Century. The Evolution of a Global Problem.* Walnut Creek: AltaMira Press.
Organización Internacional del Trabajo. 1919. *International Labour Conference. Fourth annual meeting. Geneva, 1919* Washington: Government Printing Office.
Organización Internacional del Trabajo. 1922. *International Labour Conference. Fourth annual meeting. Geneva, 1922.* Geneva: International Labour Organisation.
Organización Internacional del Trabajo. 1924. *International Labour Conference. Sixth annual meeting. Geneva, 1924.* Geneva: International Labour Organisation.
Organización Internacional del Trabajo. 1926. *International Labour Conference. Eighth annual meeting. Geneva, 1926. Vol. 1* Geneva: International Labour Organisation.
Organización Internacional del Trabajo. 1929. *International Labour Conference. Twelfth annual meeting. Geneva, 1929. Vol. 1.* Ginebra: Organización Internacional del Trabajo.
Organización Internacional del Trabajo. 1930. *Convenção N°29. Sobre o Trabalho Forçado ou Obrigatório.* http://www.ilo.org/ilolex/portug/docs/C29.htm.
Organización Internacional del Trabajo. 1930b. *International Labour Conference. Fourteenth annual meeting. Geneva, 1930. Vol. 1.* Geneva: International Labour Organisation.
Organización Internacional del Trabajo. 1935a. *International Labour Conference. Nineteenth Session. Records of Proceedings.* Geneva: International Labour Organisation.
Organización Internacional del Trabajo. 1935b. "Dossier N 102/6. Study on the "Truck system" (payment of wages). State of Resolution, 19th Session". ILO Archive.
Organización Internacional del Trabajo. 1936. *Conferencia del Trabajo de los Estados de América Miembros de la Organización Internacional del Trabajo. Actas de las Sesiones. Santiago de Chile. 2 al 14 de Enero de 1936.* Geneva: International Labour Organisation.
Organización Internacional del Trabajo. 1937. *International Labour Conference. Twenty-third Session. Records of Proceedings.* Geneva: International Labour Organisation.
Organización Internacional del Trabajo. 1938. *International Labour Conference. Twenty-fourth Session. Records of Proceedings.* Geneva: International Labour Organisation.
Organización Internacional del Trabajo. 1939. *Segunda Conferencia del Trabajo de los Estados de América Miembros de la Organización Internacional del Trabajo. Informe de la Oficina Internacional del Trabajo acerca de las medidas tomadas para dar cumplimiento a las resoluciones adoptadas por la Conferencia de Santiago de Chile* Geneva: International Labour Organisation.
Organización Internacional del Trabajo. 1946. *Tercera Conferencia del Trabajo de los estados de América miembros de la Organización Internacional del Trabajo. Acta de las Sesiones, México, Abril de 1946.* Montreal: International Labour Organisation.

Patterson, Orlando. 1982. *Slavery and Social Death: A Comparative Study.* Cambridge: Cambridge University Press.
Rapalo, María Ester. 2012. *Patrones y obreros. La ofensiva de la clase propietaria, 1918–1930.* Buenos Aires: Siglo XXI.
Roncador, Sônia. 2014. *Domestic Servants in Literature and Testimony in Brazil, 1889–1999.* New York: Palgrave McMillan.
Secreto, María Verónica. 2011. *Fronteiras em movimento. História comparada–Argentina e Brasil no século XIX.* Niterói: Eduff.
Sociedad de Naciones. 1926. *Convención Sobre la Esclavitud.* http://www.acnur.org/t3/fileadmin/scripts/doc.php?file=biblioteca/pdf/2448.
Spalding Jr., Hobart A. 1977. *Organized Labor in Latin America. Historical cases of Urban Workers in Dependent Societies.* New York: Harper Torchbooks.
Taussig, Michael. 1984. "Culture of Terror – Space of Death. Roger Casement's Putumayo Report and the Explanation of Torture." *Comparative Studies in Society and History* 26 (3): 473–478.
Turner, John Kenneth. 2014. "México Bárbaro" In *México Bárbaro / México Insurgente*, edited by John Reed, and John Kenneth Turner. México DF: Grupo Editorial Tomo.

Renán Vega Cantor, Luz Ángela Núñez Espinel

Oil workers in the enclave of the Tropical Oil Company: Composition, culture and resistance (1920–1948)

Abstract: This essay reconstructs the history of the oil workers of the Tropical Oil Company (Troco) in the Magdalena Medio area (Colombia), during the period 1920 to 1948. We start by examining the characteristics of the enclave set up in Barrancabermeja by the oil company, highlighting the spatial and socio-economic segregation that occurred in the region, between the American city and the Colombian town. These characteristics are fundamental when it comes to explaining the workers' struggles and resistance. We go on to consider the historical composition of the working population, showing their diverse geographical and cultural origins, to explain how the social and cultural particularities of this first generation of oil workers went on to shape their struggles throughout the 20th century. We study the creation of cosmopolitan working communities, which forms the backdrop to the social radicalism of the oil workers, and the particular forms taken by the ideology of workers' protest. Finally, these three aspects are related to the struggles of oil workers in the period under consideration, highlighting processes of resistance to proletarianisation, and the strikes that took place, culminating in the experience of the Popular Commune of 1948 in Barrancabermeja.

Keywords: enclaves; labour movement; oil workers; unions; Colombia

Introduction

> Colombian Obrerismo, robbed and murdered by the masters of Wall Street, already knows full well what the law is, as the persecution of our companions is already beginning, they are reduced to prisoners, sent to jail for having miraculously survived the Praetorian bullet of the mercenaries in the pay of the Tropical Oil Company.
> *Declaration of the Labour Union of Barrancabermeja, on the occasion of the repression of the oil strike of January 1927,* 24 January 1927.

Doctor at the University of Paris VIII. Universidad Pedagógica Nacional (UPN). Contact: colombia_carajo@hotmail.com / Doctor in Historia at the Universidad de los Andes. Professor at the Universidad Colegio Mayor de Cundinamarca (UCMC). Contact: lanunez@unicolmayor.edu.co

https://doi.org/10.1515/9783110759303-009

Oil workers formed the backbone of the Colombian labour movement in the 20th century due to their levels of organisation, radicalism and leadership. Their importance has given rise to a significant volume of literature on this topic. However, many studies are limited to specific aspects and lack a comprehensive analysis that would allow us to understand both the complexity of the processes and the dynamics of how they changed over time. With that in mind, this chapter reconstructs the history of the oil workers of the Tropical Oil Company (Troco) in the Magdalena Medio area of Colombia, in the period between 1920 and 1948. The text is structured in four parts: the first part examines the characteristics of the enclave, which are fundamental when it comes to explaining the types of workers' struggles and resistance that emerged; the second part considers the composition of the working population, showing their diverse geographical and cultural origins; the third part looks at the creation of cosmopolitan working class communities, which provides a background to the social radicalism of the oil workers, and the particular forms taken by the ideology of workers' protest. Finally, these three aspects are related to the oil-workers' struggles, culminating in the experience of the Popular Commune of 1948 in Barrancabermeja.

The enclaves and oil exploitation

From the end of the 19th century, the global expansion of industrial capitalism became a form of imperialism, which aimed to dominate and control foreign territories based on economic criteria. Control of reserves of raw materials for the development of the main lines of capitalist activity (rubber, minerals, wood and oil, among others) was a priority. Zones of geopolitical and economic influence were established for the export of capital in the form of direct investments or financial loans. Abundant reserves of cheap labour were sought to reduce costs in the production of commodities that were strategic for global capitalist competition. In peripheral areas, the consumption of merchandise produced in the capitalist centres was imposed, under conditions that favoured those in power, in order to increase profits from industrial production.

These characteristics of imperialist domination are embodied in a particular type of relationship between large companies based in the dominant countries worldwide (principally the United States, France and England) and the dependent and peripheral countries. The nature of this relationship is clearly expressed in the imposition of enclaves, whereby a foreign company, linked to one of the major world powers, would implant itself in a strip of territory in a peripheral country with the sole purpose of appropriating a natural resource, exploiting it and transferring it to the company's country of origin, without this activity having any real, lasting, positive impact on the country where the enclave had been established.

The enclaves are often described as 'states within the State', an appropriate metaphor that reflects how a foreign company controls a vast territory in another country, through the legal mechanism of concessions. The local state cedes both territory and sovereignty, so that the company can carry out its activity without participating in the development of the national market. The enclave has an "extractive infrastructure," that is, it connects the resource-rich area to the rivers, seas and ports that allow the product to be transported and exported to the world market. For dependent countries, the enclaves have negative consequences, due to environmental deterioration, the destruction of ecosystems, pollution, and the intensive exploitation of local workers, as well as repression and discrimination by foreign companies. Some of the most infamous enclaves in Latin American history developed between 1870 and 1945, around banana plantations, oil wells, and tin, copper, and saltpetre mines.

Oil exploitation in Colombia began a century ago and, from the very beginning, transnational capital's control over hydrocarbons was evident, although figureheads born in Colombia were used to facilitate the legal process, for example in the cases of the two most important concessions in the country in the first half of the 20th century: the De Mares Concession, located in the Magdalena Medio region, and the Barco Concession, located in El Catatumbo, on the border with Venezuela. In the first case, the beneficiary was Rockefeller's Standard Oil Company, although it was introduced under the name of the Tropical Oil Company. In the second case, the Barco Concession was controlled by South American Gulf Oil (Sagot) and the Colombian Petroleum Company (Colpet), in which the billionaire Andrew Mellon had interests.

When oil extraction began, those companies established two separate enclaves, the characteristics of which determined the configuration of the oil industry in the country. Due to its size and social importance, we will focus here on the case of Barrancabermeja, as an example of an enclave economy.

Spatial and demographic features

Before the enclave was set up, Barrancabermeja was a small hamlet located on the banks of the Magdalena River, inhabited by fishermen, peasant farmers and wood cutters. It was a way point, through which small quantities of wood, ivory nut, rubber and medicinal bark circulated in small boats. Over land, the village was reached via bridleways, designed according to the slow but steady rhythm of the mule trains.

The tiny port had 415 inhabitants in 1907, by 1919 that had grown to 1,450 and in 1927 some 5,000 local workers and 200 Americans lived in the town, as part of a total of 12,000 inhabitants (Galvis, 1997: 69 and 93; Galán, 1945: 560 – 561). In the late 1920s, Barrancabermeja had the highest concentration of workers anywhere in Colombia. Having emerged and grown as a municipality around the oil enclave, there were demographic imbalances, as recorded by the 1938 Census: 15,400 people lived there, 9,300 of them in the municipal area; most of the population (61 percent) were men; there were very few children or people over 60; around 45 percent of the total population was made up of young men over 15 years of age, and there were very few married women (Galvis, 1997; Galán, 1945). This strange demographic panorama was a result of the characteristics of the enclave, where the company employed young, single men of working age. Oil exploitation created spatial divisions in the work, between the extraction phase and the processing phase, which created social segmentation and a sexual division by territories. In El Centro, in Infantas, and in the camps around the oil wells, the population was single and male. The women lived in Barrancabermeja.

The social, economic and cultural life of the enclave revolved around the extraction, processing and transportation of oil. The space was designed and structured around these activities: the largest urban centre was Barrancabermeja, with smaller centres around the oil extraction sites (the wells) and the sites for the collection and transformation of oil (the refinery). Troco employees worked in both places, which were about 30 kilometres apart. This spatial organisation gave rise to "a daily, to-and-fro, movement of labour" between the extraction sites of Infantas and El Centro, and the processing sites (Aprille-Gniset, 1997: 147 – 148).

Prostitution and enclave society

At the end of the 1910s, a discriminatory policy was created in the enclave with regards to family: workers were confined in isolated camps, where "the attendance of women and the use of alcohol were prohibited" (AGN, MME, TOC, CM., 1919: 240 – 241), whereas the Americans arrived with their families, and could travel to their country whenever they wanted. This situation reached the extreme where the wives of company officials were taken to their country of origin when they were going to have a child, so that the birth could take place there, and a few months later they would return to their luxurious Californian-style houses, built alongside the poor and miserable neighbourhoods of Barrancabermeja (Álvarez, 1983: 181).

Women came to the port from various regions of the country, and even from other parts of the world, attracted by the legend of "black gold." They carried out many jobs fundamental to the operation of the enclave, such as laundresses, cooks or street-food sellers, however, their work was not recognised and they were all stigmatised and labelled "prostitutes" from the start. In fact, prostitution was an important economic activity in Barrancabermeja, upon which the double standards of society rested, pointing the finger at single women (regardless of their occupation) whilst accepting without question the economic returns they produced. In this regard, it is enough to point out that the operation of hotels, bars and brothels generated tax revenues that were as important for the municipality as those generated by the oil industry. For example, in 1926 the income produced by prostitution was equivalent to 50 percent of oil income (Álvarez, 1983: 220 – 221; Valbuena, 1947: 289).

Prostitution had social and cultural implications. It was a space for the workers to let off steam when they arrived on Saturday evening, after six days working in the camps without the company of their families. As long as the workers' amorous nights did not generate problems for the health of the workforce, Troco did not concern itself with the matter. If the revelry helped keep the workers away from the unions and political struggle, so much the better. However, when syphilis and venereal diseases appeared, the company was alarmed by the healthcare costs it was incurring and the consequences that this could have for the workforce.

Prostitution generated very specific customs among the workers, which over time became characteristics of the oil port. On Saturday nights Barrancabermeja was transformed by the arrival of the "hairy ones," money began to circulate and the nightlife of the town ground into action. A leisure industry was created so that the workers would spend most of their wages in the 24 hours they were in town, from Saturday to Sunday. The workers were the clients of the prostitution business, which create paradoxical attitudes. Prostitution was the expression of moral degradation, sin and bad habits, but it was also an essential source of economic life for the town. Hence the workers were awaited on Saturdays with contradictory feelings of anticipation and fear. Someone once described Barrancabermeja was "a brothel with a mayor and a priest," which was particularly true as the Church was located in the middle of the red-light district (Aprille-Gniset, 1997: 216).

Socio-spatial segregation

At the dizzying pace of capital, with the acceleration of time and contraction of space that it brings, the lives of men, women and the natural landscape were transformed. Jungle was cleared, trails opened and trees cut down to build camps and houses; wells were drilled, roads and railway lines built, telegraph and telephone lines spliced, fences erected, and oil pipelines installed. This was unusual for the time, and very different from the agricultural and precapitalist space that had previously prevailed. Whatever served no function for that noisy capitalism, be that human beings or natural space, had to disappear.

Repression occupied a central and singular position in the use of space. In the 1920s there were three police barracks (national, departmental and local) as well as a military barracks. The police force ensured the proper functioning of the enclave, and the population was kept at bay and subjected to new social and economic impositions through the use of military force. Indeed, the police force was so important for the company, that it provided accommodation to house the first contingents of officers and offered a space to serve as the telegraph headquarters.[1]

In spatial terms, two antagonistic urban habitats were created. On the one hand, the Troco city, with houses built in a style typical of some parts of the United States, with spacious and airy buildings, and adequate hospitals and public services. This was the so-called *Staff* neighbourhood, where foreign technicians and administrators lived. On the other side of the wire, the neighbourhoods and camps where the workers lived were characterised by poor architectural, hygienic and sanitary conditions.

The spatial segregation between the "American Barranca" and the "Colombian Barranca" was physically maintained by means of a wire fence. A forceful element, both materially and symbolically, the fence prevented the passage of Colombians to the Troco side of the wire. The two were not only different cities. Between them, by way of protection and segregation, there lay a buffer zone of security installations, made up of company guards and the National Police, whose mission was to protect the company and control access to Troco facilities. For the locals, the wire fence was a 'border' that separated Colombia from *Yankeeland* (Buenahora, 1997: 30), offering foreign residents security, and acting as a mechanism for control and confinement for the Colombians.

This spatial separation between US Americans and Colombians is evidence of the social segregation that characterised the enclave, and it cannot be consid-

1 Archivo General de la Nación, hereafter AGN, FMG, S.1, T. 989: 340.

ered in isolation. It was a logic that permeated all activities. One of the starkest examples of this was the Troco railway, where a special wagon – with all the comforts – was arranged for the Americans; another for clerks, foremen and their families; a third for married workers; and, the last, for single workers who travelled "fourth class," in rickety wagons without seats, stuffed in with construction materials.

The oil workers

The first workers were of peasant origin, they had been rural workers, smallholders or fishermen before joining the company. Afro-peasant influences from the Savannas of Bolívar, Sucre and Córdoba made up the largest ethnic groups, however workers also came from the impoverished Antioquia mountains, the surrounding areas of Santander and other parts of the interior of the country. In terms of their family trajectories, they were the first generation of workers, but their situation was representative of the country at large, since salaried work in industrial activities was just beginning to take off in Colombia.

Skilled workers of Caribbean origin, known as *yumecas*, arrived from abroad, having demonstrated their abilities in other agro-industrial enclaves in the Caribbean, and the Panama Canal. This workforce had the added advantage of speaking English, affording them a privileged place in the workplace. The *yumecas* were considered by Colombian workers to be part of the company elite, as they were incorporated as permanent staff and 'housed' in facilities far superior to the squalid and dilapidated camps where the Colombian workers resided. Consequently, there was no integration between these two working populations either in leisure time or at work. On the contrary, their uneasy coexistence tended to reinforce segregation and conflict.

The nascent oil proletariat was engaged in a varied range of activities, beginning with those related to the extraction and processing of crude oil (the sounding and drilling of wells) initially carried out by qualified workers from the United States or by some *yumecas,* and later by national workers. However, there was also forest clearance, the construction of roads, railway lines, company facilities, camps and the laying of an oil pipeline over more than 500 kilometres to the Atlantic Coast. Many of those activities were carried out by the first workers. Along with these, complementary tasks emerged (such as cooking, washing, and cleaning the company's camps and rooms), leading to the creation of a heterogeneous group of salaried workers, made up of men linked to the company. At the same time, in the municipal centre, women, at their own risk and expense, cooked, tended the street food stalls and cleaned the hotels.

The foundation of the *Sociedad Unión Obrera*

In response to the dire living and working conditions in the enclave, workers' protests were not long in coming. At first, they were spontaneous, individual and disorganised. There were complaints about the terrible state of the camps, the constant threat of illnesses, the lack of a hospital, the poor quality of the food and the mistreatment to which Colombian workers were subjected by foremen, the vast majority of whom were fellow countrymen. In this context, in 1923, *La Unión Obrera* – the original name given to the *Unión Sindical Obrera* (USO) – began to organise underground. This was the main union in the oil industry, and it survives to this day.

Its creation is explained by the convergence of objective and subjective conditions at that time. Among the former were the terrible material living and working conditions that the workers endured. At the same time, subjective factors created an embryonic class consciousness, which was consolidated through experiences of struggle against exploitation and oppression, as explained below.

In 1918, Colombia experienced a high point of mobilisation and labour struggles, unprecedented in the history of the country. Expressions of protest took a political turn with the founding of the Socialist Party in Bogotá that same year. Although the Party did not have sufficient electoral weight to threaten the historic bipartisan dominion, it did gain strength on the banks of the Magdalena River, where voices began to be heard, preaching on social issues, and speaking of an end to the conservative hegemony.

In the early years, Troco and the local authorities opted for the repression and persecution of any attempted protest in the region. Police forces were used to expel protesters who were marked as unhealthy and undesirable subjects. Thus, in August 1922, police commissioner Martiniano Valbuena exiled José Calixto Mesa for attempting to organise a strike against Troco, "determining the penalty to be expulsion for a term of six months from the Santander territory adjacent to the banks of the Magdalena River, over which this Police Station has jurisdiction."[2]

In 1922, a significant change occurred in the conditions for organisation and struggle among the oil workers, with the arrival in the region of the labour leader Raúl Eduardo Mahecha, who brought his experiences of organising in various parts of the country, especially in the ports of the Magdalena River. In September of that year, Mahecha settled as just another tenant in one of the crowded houses in the town, offering his services as a lawyer. He immediately began to organise

2 *AGN, FMG*, S. 4, T. 156: 493.

the peasants and workers, founding a store (similar to a consumer cooperative) where basic necessities were sold at low cost. Peasants became affiliates of an organisation that Mahecha called *Sociedad Unión Obrera*. These activities were conducted in secret, however Troco discovered them and had the recently arrived police commissioner Martiniano Valbuena, seize the food from the store (Valbuena, 1947: 176).

On 10 February 1923, the first board of directors of the *Unión Obrera* met in hiding, on the banks of the Quebrada River. To enable it to operate, a fee of 10 cents per member was approved, and it was paid by a significant number of workers, despite the fact that it represented a large percentage of their salary. In 1923, the union already had more than 400 peasant settlers and 1,500 affiliated members, and a year later membership had already reached 3,000 (*The viewer*, 1924). This organisation led workers' struggles in the period, including the strikes of 1924, 1927, 1935 and 1938. It played prominent role in the shaping of a radical working-class culture in the valley of Magdalena Medio.

Cosmopolitan working-class communities

The enclaves were kept isolated from the nation's economic centres, where the traditional institutions of social control were located. That isolation would prove key for the creation of bonds of solidarity between oil workers, because by sharing work and leisure routines in remote territories, they created workers' communities with strong levels of social cohesion. Working communities are structured groups based on the companionship generated through sharing work and daily activities: similar working conditions, housing, food, life habits, entertainment, material deprivation, social aspirations and sexual behaviour. Broadly speaking, these were communities "in the objective sense that they were composed of people who shared the common experience of selling their labour power to capitalists who were not part of that community" (Rule, 1990: 227–244).

In addition to the sale of their labour power, political oppression and misery, the oil workers shared other elements that reinforced their community identity. This identity was the product of an acquired awareness of the collective experience of subordination and exploitation, and of cultural practices generated by the material circumstances. This fostered shared social aspirations, which, by being against the interests of other social classes, contributed to reinforcing community cohesion and the awareness of belonging to a different social class.

The isolation in which these workers lived in the jungle areas was relative. Although they were forced to spend long periods in the oil fields, they mixed with people of many different origins who converged there and in the surrounding areas. Under these conditions, cosmopolitan workers' communities were formed in the oil fields. We understand cosmopolitanism to refer to a kind of open mindedness, generated by the interaction of multiple social actors with a diversity of cultural identities grouped in the same place, where social heterogeneity enables cultural enrichment, the reception of new ideas, and the reproduction of a variety of patterns of behaviour. This cosmopolitanism gave workers a deeper and broader understanding of the world, which was reflected in the breakdown of mentalities that had previously been confined by village or parochial localism. From a political perspective, the influence of cosmopolitanism was to give workers a more complex vision of social relations, since it afforded them a better understanding of power, and helped them to design novel ways to confront it.

Because of their seniority and greater numbers, the workers of the De Mares Concession had more accumulated social and political experience in the mid-1940s. The working-class community there was the most cohesive, and the best organised. It offered examples to follow for its peers in other companies. This helps to explain the political leadership exercised by the *Unión Sindical Obrera* (USO) among other grassroots organisations. The actions of Troco also became a model to follow for the other oil companies in their dealings with the State and the workers.

As oil workers emigrated from their hometowns and met people from other regions, they had the opportunity to acquire a broader understanding of what it meant to be Colombian, that is, about the idea of the nation. This did not mean that the confluence of groups with different regional identities did not result in cultural clashes. The events of the strike of 1938, when supposed differences between workers from the coastal regions and those from Santander were instrumentalised to weaken the movement, showed that regionalism could be used to divide the working class. Nevertheless, the existence of these regionalist expressions implied a recognition among workers of the existence of people with cultural identities different from their own. This in itself lent itself to acquiring a broader view of the country, for it was only by seeing the parts that made up the nation that they could develop a better idea of the whole. For people who, for the most part, had not gone to school, and did not have facilities to move from one place to another in the country, such coexistence could be decisive in the process of acquiring an expanded notion of what it meant to be Colombian. The characteristics of the oil industry favoured a national identity that prevailed over regional identity among workers.

The companies were owned by foreign capital and the bosses were foreign. That had consequences for reinforcing national identity. The distance between a worker and his employer acquired political traits in these enclave areas, since it was easy for any worker to identify imperialism as that blond boss, who not only had different customs, but also spoke in another language.

Workers' communities and patriarchy

Before the end of the 1940s, oil workers had formed an identity not only as a community, but also as a class, as a result of the life they shared in the oil fields. The highest concentration of workers was in the middle of the Magdalena River valley, in the three largest, fully active oil concessions. In order of size and age these were: the De Mares Concession administered by Troco since 1916, the Barco Concession managed by Colpet since 1931, and the Yondó Concession controlled by the Shell Group as of 1938. What set the oil enclaves and the population of Barrancabermeja apart was the role of community ties woven by the workers in the oil fields. Workers' solidarity was forged there, and brought to the city, creating extremely cohesive and radical working-class communities.

In the mid-1940s the number of oil workers hovered around 8,000 and the company's total staff was close to 15,000. In 1947 the largest number of personnel was registered, with 17,857, of which 8,442 were oil workers. That same year, the First Trade Union Census took place, recording 7,878 unionised workers in the oil industry, representing a unionisation rate of over 90 percent. This percentage is surprising, because in 1947 the unionisation rate across the entire country barely reached 5 percent (Archila, 1991: 359). In other words, workers in the oil industry showed very high levels of organisation that contrasted starkly with the rest of the country. This was due to high levels of class consciousness and community cohesion among these workers by that time, which was evidenced, to give just one example, in the language used, as the worker who did not join the union "or was de-unionised, was called *esquirol* (strikebreaker)" (Interview Aranda, 1982).

The high rate of unionisation among oil workers was probably due to the political maturity of their community. The idea of unionising was so widespread that there were even small unions such as the El Centro Domestic Service Workers' Union, which had 61 members, all female (Contraloría General de la República, 1947: 66).

One might think that the lack of visibility of female work in this industrial sector was a consequence of the small number of women workers, but it seems that this is less significant than the levels of machismo that prevailed among the oil workers. Over and above the macho characteristics of Colombian culture itself, oil-worker machismo was reinforced by the harsh conditions they were subject to in the oil fields, where all-male work crews lived in crowded conditions, isolated from the rest of society. This gave rise to behavioural guidelines governed by rules where it was not enough to simply be a man, you had to constantly demonstrate your manhood. One consequence of this machismo among oil workers was to politically marginalise women within the union movement, already in the minority due to the low number of women workers hired by the companies.

Cultural circulation in working communities

In addition to the various collective experiences that oil workers shared in their work and daily lives, which gradually formed their community and class identities, they also benefited from the ideological background and political experience acquired through conflicts against their bosses and the government. A third element that defined the political identity of these workers was cultural contact with intellectuals who linked up with the oil workers as part of their political activism.

That is not to say that class consciousness was brought to the oil workers from outside, but rather that, by virtue of the relationships they established with intellectuals who identified, ideologically, with their struggles, they broadened their political and cultural perspectives. This can be seen in the interest that the workers showed in having the Mexican union leader Vicente Lombardo Toledano come to visit them in Barrancabermeja in 1943, or in the reception given to the Cuban poet, Nicolás Guillén, during his visit to the city and at the recitals he gave at the Shell and El Centro enclaves (Guillén, 1997: 282).

During the first part of the 20th century, union leaders, politicians and left-wing intellectuals all came into contact with the oil workers. Some passed through the region offering lectures or talks, others accompanied the workers on longer trajectories, participating in strikes and events that generated cultural and political exchanges (such as publishing newspapers or making speeches in public squares).

Intellectuals close to the oil workers had the opportunity to learn from them. Proof of this can be seen in the ideological trajectory of Gonzalo Buenahora. If he had not been linked to the struggles of the workers of the USO, it would have been very difficult for him to write, as he did, about the workers of Barrancabermeja, much less assume the radical perspectives contained in his social interpretations. These workers, facing down the oil companies, exerted a special attraction for the intellectuals who were motivated to spread their ideas among the inhabitants of Barrancabermeja, because “this articulation between the world of 'scientific' knowledge embodied by the intellectuals, and the world of popular "empirical" knowledge, constitutes an excellent example of cultural circulation" (Archila, 1991: 156).

Cultural circulation is a notion that allows us to understand the exchange of ideas between workers and intellectuals, or between the culture of the subaltern classes and the culture of the dominant classes. In the dichotomy between popular culture and elite culture, there is no passive adaptation on the part of the popular sectors in the sense in which we might understand acculturation. There tends to be reciprocal influences and convergences of ideas, which might better be termed cultural circulation (Ginzburg, 1986: 20 – 21). In the relationship between workers and intellectuals, who were bearers of an elite culture, cultural circulation was more fluid, because of the political identification of these intellectuals with the struggles of the workers.

Between comedy and tragedy

The iniquities experienced in the concession zones generated unease among the workers, which helped to strengthen their community ties and their class consciousness. These identities were not mutually exclusive, but rather worked to reinforce each other. The work crews generated informal groups of friends whose daily expression was in the form of camaraderie, teasing, sharing jokes, and giving each other nicknames. This integration, produced within the friendship groups formed in the field, was important for the maturity of the working community, the development of a proletarian consciousness, and the conflicts that emerged with the companies over working conditions.

It is difficult to imagine the happiness that these workers must have felt at the end of six long days of hard work out in the oil fields. For those who were married there was the possibility of seeing their family. For the single workers they could meet their lady friends in the bar, or sit down for a drink with workmates from other oil wells far from their own. The work, in isolated camps under the hot sun in 37-degree heat, was recompensed by the lowered inhibitions and revelry of Saturday night. While the rest of the country slept, Barrancabermeja awoke, as it did every Saturday, with the arrival of the workers, and life erupted in the tropical port. Barrancabermeja was agitated and lustful. Any fisherman who went out on Saturday night would hear the boundless cries of flirtatious prostitutes carrying across the river as they danced with lit candles. With envy in their eyes, the policemen went out on patrol, while the merchants and pimps sought ways to take the workers' wages from them. Even those who had wives looked for ways to escape to bars with their workmates. Everyone laughed, got drunk, fought, listened to music, sang and danced.

However, although the revelry that began on Saturday night in Barrancabermeja could be seen as a simple outpouring of joy, the party hid a profound tragedy. These first generations of workers experienced the breakdown of the traditional peasant family, as the bond with the village or hamlet they came from was broken. If they had a wife and children nearby, it was only possible to see them at weekends. If anything, the situation facing workers without a family was worse: they left the camps and entered the void, because apart from the working girls in the bars, they had nobody waiting for them.

This situation eventually created the new working family. But, before the emergence of that working family, oil workers must have suffered a deterioration in their affective relationships, because their working conditions seriously limited the possibilities for expressing filial love. Everyday language become more abrupt, macho and profane. Thus, small-village courtship rituals were replaced by a brutalised sexuality, in which love at first sight had no place, because affection had to be paid for, to a woman who was so poor that she was selling her body (Interview, Morón, 1982).

Working-class romanticism, tragic and corny as it was, was a dramatic expression of this exacerbated pain, a product of the breakdown of family affection and the disappearance of traditional, sentimental relationships. Facing death for asking a woman to dance should not only be understood as competition for virility, in a world made up mostly of men subjected to harsh ways of life and work. It also expressed a search for affection so desperate that it did not measure consequences, despite the fleetingness of a caress that, in any case, had to be paid for in cash.

These workers immersed themselves in a commodified life, a routine in which time became money. The profit motive and utilitarian values imposed new norms of conduct, accentuating individualism and competition for more money. Although the work was not well paid and there was grief for the life that had been lost, the incentive was to earn more money than before or, at least, to have the security of knowing a salary would be paid on a certain date. Many returned home to their villages because they could not bear the harsh conditions of the work, but most waited, hoping to save enough to leave one day and buy a plot of land in their parents' village. Salaries were insufficient and the mentality for saving was rare (much of what was earned got spent at the weekend parties) so most of the workers ended up settling in the towns near the oil fields. Some formed families with the prostitutes, others brought their sweethearts, wives and children from the villages they had left behind.

Experiences of struggle

Experience is a mediating factor between the social existence and class consciousness, because the lived experiences of the workers exert a pressure that alters their consciousness, tracing new problems and providing "much of the raw material for more elaborate intellectual exercises" (Thompson, 1981: 20). Lived experiences do not occur without thought or, to say it another way, as rational beings, every individual thinks and develops an interpretation of his or her experiences, based on the position he or she occupies in society. In short, experiences produce knowledge, which means that no matter how limited a worker's intellectual education may be, the experiences he or she has in the material world enable him or her to perceive social realities. This direct way of accessing an understanding of reality, allows a basic sense of belonging to a community and a social class to develop. In this way, experience plays a mediating role between a social existence, and class consciousness. The experiences afforded by conflict with other social groups or, rather, the experiences of political practice during struggles with other social classes, are therefore crucial to the process of maturing class consciousness.

The community identity that was generated was stimulated by, and, at the same time, helped foster, that class consciousness which was in the process of forming and maturing. The same experiences that created community ties also fostered a class identity among the workers. The daily lived experiences at work, and during recreation, favoured the rapid emergence of community cohesion. One might even speak of a workers' brotherhood. However, the process of developing class consciousness was not so immediate. For class consciousness to mature required the experiences of political practices generated during social conflict. Nevertheless, the derived ideology of the ordinary oil worker contained a mix of ideas, which, while they were not indicative of a defined political consciousness, did reveal anti-capitalist traits that could favour the formation of a radical class consciousness.

Ideology and culture in workers' protests

The spontaneous way in which the urban area of Barrancabermeja emerged and grew, the resulting migration and cultural mixing of people from various regions of the country, and the arrival of foreigners, combined to create cultural elements that conflicted with the dominant parameters of the rest of Colombian society. This manifested as an implicit criticism of the religious values of submission, resignation, conformity, hypocrisy and prudishness, that were dominant during the Conservative Hegemony (the period from 1886–1930 in which the Conservative Party held power). Although the conservatives, through priests and the police, tried to defend elements of conventional Catholicism, their efforts were unsuccessful. The most bitter criticisms directed at Barrancabermeja and its population described her as the embodiment of the "four Ps": pennies, port, petroleum and prostitutes (Barreto and Giraldo, 1998: 136). These cultural elements became established at the end of the 1910s and were manifested throughout the ideology of workers' protests, whose most significant features were an anti-imperialist stance, a focus on nationalism, and the dignity of the worker.

Anti-imperialism and nationalism were intimately linked, and they became a central aspect of the mental horizon of workers struggle and popular protest. The immediate issues raised by the arrival and installation of Troco were linked to the anti-American sentiment that began to emerge among different sectors of the Colombian population at the beginning of the 20th century as a result of the events surrounding the loss of Panama in 1903.

Workers' struggles acquired an anti-imperialist and nationalist tinge, because the alliance between Troco and the Colombian authorities was evident in Barrancabermeja. Although the workers were not always able to grasp the strategic significance of this alliance, they did understand that it formed the basis for the exploitation and injustice that they experienced first-hand. In Barrancabermeja, being a worker was not just a question of labour, it acquired political dimensions, since it represented a defence of the best of Colombian nationality. The dignity of the worker and his work was expressed in the constant outcry against the humiliations that workers were subjected to by Troco, the Colombian and foreign foremen, and the police. Throughout the fight against discrimination, the workers defended the dignity of the worker, which included the right to rebel. It was argued that striking was not only a form of struggle, but an action in itself aimed at vindicating the Colombian worker and his dignity in the face of a foreign company.

Some of the workers' slogans of the 1920s expressed this process of dignifying work as a generator of wealth:

> "DON'T TELL ME THAT YOU SUFFER FROM HUNGER AND SLAVERY, TELL ME WHAT YOU DO TO EMANCIPATE YOURSELF"
> WORKERS: he who does not protest against his executioner does not deserve to live in a free republic like ours.
> Freedoms are not asked for, they are taken
> Justice is not bought or begged for like charity: justice is done
> ALL the freedoms we enjoy today have been won by men who loved universal freedom more than their own well-being
> (*Vanguardia Obrera*, 1926; *Germinal*, 1926, capital letters in the original).

It is notable that demands for workers' dignity included the right to read and study. The petitions of 1924 and 1938 called on Troco to allow national newspapers to be read at its facilities. In the midst of the strict order of the enclave, governed by the capitalist logic that controlled time and extracted the maximum possible value from it, it was significant that the workers defended their right to read the papers, especially as illiteracy was widespread among the Colombian population. Reading was understood to be a collective activity – a page, a flyer, a manifesto, or a small newspaper could circulate widely, passing from hand to hand and reach many workers by being read aloud. Access to newspapers meant appropriating knowledge to understand the reasons why people lived like this and outlining forms of resistance based on understanding those problems.

Oil workers' struggles

Since the sinking of the first oil wells, the oilmen resorted to various mechanisms of struggle, both 'passive' and active. Among the former, the resistance to proletarianisation stands out, with the avoidance of work and a decrease in the working rhythm. Among the latter were a number of strikes and one particularly special political event: the Popular Commune of 1948. In this last section we will analyse each of these aspects.

Resistance to proletarianisation

A principal aspect of the oilmen's identity stemmed from the cultural alteration they experienced by being forced to assume new working rhythms. Coming from peasant stock, the workers who joined the oil companies had to endure the breakdown of their rural traditions. This was not an absolute rupture, but a process of uneven transition which affected the first generations of workers from the 1920s, and was evidenced, among other ways, in their resistance to proletarianisation.

The most visible form of this resistance was the occupation, by some workers, of land on oil company property. In response to the low wages and job instability suffered up until the signing of labour conventions in the mid-1940s, some workers occupied farms to grow their own crops. Workers and landless peasants who came to the concession territories participated in these land occupations, fleeing poverty in their places of origin. One of the main motivations for creating their own plots was the illusion of obtaining additional income, although they also had expectations, from their peasant past, of being able to control their own time and maintain an independence that would allow them to determine their own rhythms of work and leisure, and maintain the irregular rhythms of the agrarian world.

This search for a link with the land was a double-edged sword for the political culture of the oil worker. On the one hand, it maintained the peasant dream of having his own land, which could generate a somewhat individualistic mentality, similar to that of the smallholder peasant, which in certain circumstances was not favourable to the development of ties of workers' solidarity. Ironically, on the other hand, the bond with the land could foster nostalgia for traditional peasant customs, with a marked anti-capitalist tone, making workers more open to ideas of collectivist political utopias. These customs kept the resistance to proletarianisation alive, although that does not mean that the peasantry enjoyed an idyllic existence. After all, those who came to work for the oil companies, came in the hope of improving their quality of life.

The peasant culture of those who later became workers, involved irregular working hours in the fields, more subject to climatic cycles than to clocks. The needs of the worker could be accommodated, with time for both farming and recreation. Whenever he wanted, he could see his family, or lie in a hammock and smoke tobacco, without having to differentiate between the workplace and the recreational area, since both were on the farm. He could stop attending Catholic worship and dedicate that valuable time to the next town festival, where around a bottle of rum, he would talk for hours and hours with his comrades. In many cases, contact with the boss was direct, and face to face, disguised as that tricky paternalism that allowed the rich rural elites to baptise the son of one of their peasants. This direct, non-horizontal relationship was not possible in the oil fields, where the boss was invisible, but omnipresent, controlling the intensity of the work and the hours for clocking on and clocking off in the company.

In the work of the enclave, the supervisors and the company's strident siren heralded the start and end of the working day, marking when it was time to eat, or when and for how long you could rest. It was strict time, measured in money. An observer described the new discipline experienced by the workers of El Catatumbo, by explaining that "when the exact, 'North American' time to start work arrives, those who have not had breakfast have to work without breakfast, and there is no appeal" (Bautista, 1939: 12). Obviously, this change in the patterns of work and recreation implied a significant cultural alteration for the customs of these workers.

When compared with their previous existence, these circumstances could inspire workers to hate the work rhythms of capitalism. The resistance to proletarianisation was eventually defeated, and in the 1940s the majority accepted that they were workers. However, the nostalgia that some felt for their old life could lead them to create a mentality of contempt for capitalism, which was an easy bridge to revolutionary ideas. That nostalgia was expressed by one worker who stated: "The era of the fishermen is in my soul, it sleeps in my heart" (*Vínculo*, 1950: 11).

The temperament of popular culture from these coastal regions is reflected in anti-aristocratic attitudes and anti-capitalist tendencies, which were typical of the amphibious tri-ethnic mix that occurred in the Colombian Caribbean. The cultural attitudes of these tri-ethnic populations are expressed in the informal and careless behaviour of people, in predominantly horizontal relationships, where a sense of humour was important and non-compliance was not a crime.

Apart from this cultural temperament, nostalgia for the positive elements of the peasant family economy led the first generations of workers to perceive capitalist exploitation as an attack on their customs. The conscious awareness that personal independence was being given up, along with all the things that previously made life pleasant, led to a perception of being exploited. As this was a shared condition, it generated the sense of belonging to a community; and this community feeling was nurtured by everyday situations that were experienced collectively, largely conditioned by the forms of exploitation to which everyone was subjected.

Thus, nonconformity, and the lifestyle and habits created by exploitation, favoured the rapid emergence of a community identity, however, that did not necessarily imply the emergence of a class identity. The common malaise over exploitation could be expressed as a rejection of capitalism, which took many forms and did not have a defined political coherence: getting drunk to the point of being penniless, arriving at work drunk, going slow in carrying out assigned tasks, planting crops on company land, or even "coming to blows" with one of the company supervisors. Although these attitudes did not have an explicit political aim, they expressed a certain unruliness, which could open the doors to the acquisition of class consciousness.

Strikes

By 1948, there had been six oil-worker strikes, in 1924, 1927, 1935, 1938, 1946 and 1948. The first two occurred within the framework of the Conservative Hegemony, when the nascent USO was not yet legally recognised, and labour disputes were treated as a matter of public order. In those first two strikes, demands were aimed at solving the workers' most pressing problems: adequate food, hospitals, wage increases, double pay on holidays and the recognition of overtime for night work, improving the accommodation camps, the removal of officials who mistreated the workers, and permission to read newspapers.

As the oil workers were the epicentre of life in Barrancabermeja, from the time of these first strikes there was a confluence of interests between the Troco workers and the rest of the inhabitants of the port (peasants and settlers, merchants, shopkeepers, landlords and prostitutes), which gave the workers' protests a civic character, and was a source of material support for the strikers.

These first two strikes were brutally repressed. In 1924 some 1,500 workers were expelled from the region and the principal leaders were imprisoned. In 1927, the strike resulted in the deaths of several workers. As part of the repression, the leaders of the movement were arrested and tortured. One of them, who was confined to the city of Tunja, claimed that Troco law, supported by the Colombian government and its armed forces, could be summarised by a laconic motto: "Killing Colombians was just like killing monkeys in the jungle" (Almario, 1984: 82).

The next two strikes occurred during the Liberal Republic (1930–1946), when the USO was recognised as representing the oil workers and some legal measures were implemented that favoured union organisation, although there continued to be restrictions on strikes in the "public services," an elastic concept that included many activities, including the extraction of crude oil.

The *Unión Obrera*, which had been destroyed in 1927 after the second strike, went underground to evade Troco control, and was rebuilt. It received legal recognition in 1934 and by 1935 had 1,500 members. That year, a third strike was organised, with demands similar to those of the 1920s. The strike was declared illegal and there was massive participation among the inhabitants of the port. The '*barrio* girls' supported the strike with financial contributions and a campaign to collect money for the workers (Rivera, 1984; Morón, 1982; Foronda, 1984). The strike committee issued passports, licenses and permits, and in practice acted as a legislative body, emitting decrees, such as those prohibiting alcohol, or controlling prices for the sale of food, maintaining order and surveillance, and the storage and distribution of supplies for the rationing system. The *Vanguardia Liberal* correspondent solemnly and concisely commented that, "in this port there is a government within a government" (*Liberal Vanguard,* 1935). In the end, the strike came to a bitter end, as the demands were not met and Troco expelled the strike leaders.

In 1938 the fourth strike took place, calling for better wages, better treatment of workers, the creation of a collective bargaining agreement, permission to read newspapers and, in a new turn, it also included the demands of the domestic service workers of El Centro and Barrancabermeja. This strike ended in bloodshed and a wave of repression that left an unknown number of dead and wounded. The USO was seriously weakened and, again, would have to rebuild in hiding in the years that followed.

In 1946, in a new political era, following the victory of the Conservative Party in the presidential elections of that year, another strike broke out, with the peculiarity that it was not exclusively against Troco, but rather part of a general strike against all the country's oil companies. The principal demand was for a new labour law to regulate relations between foreign companies and Colombian workers. To this end, the *Federación de Trabajadores del Petróleo* (Fedepetrol) was created to represent oil workers, in which the USO played an important role. This strike, which ended in victory for the oil workers' trade union movement, put the nationalisation of hydrocarbons on the negotiating table and showed the workers to be the clearest spokespersons for a nationalism that had been building over several decades. An editorial in *El Tiempo* stated:

> We have the impression that the oil strike is being diverted, in a dangerous and irrefutable way, towards political interests, which will seriously undermine the economic and social interests that should dominate its aims. [...] Among the new demands presented by the workers is the nationalisation of the oil industry, which is a specifically political issue. Of course, the country must be prepared, when the opportunity arises, to take on the exploitation of its own natural resources. But that policy cannot be adopted overnight, nor be improvised under the revolutionary pressure of a strike. (*El Tiempo*, 1946)

In 1948, one of the most transcendental strikes took place not only in the history of the USO, but in the history of Colombia in the 20th century. This was the strike that defeated Troco, and laid the foundations for the reversal of the De Mares Concession, as well as the creation of the state-owned *Empresa Colombiana de Petróleos* (Ecopetrol) in 1951. The public uproar generated by this last strike impacted on broad sectors of society that began to demonstrate in favour of the reversal of the Concession and the prompt nationalisation of oil. As a result, the government was forced to pass Law 165 of 27 December 1948, which authorised the founding of a Colombian oil company. Although this did not include the workers' proposal for nationalisation in its entirety, it did have the courage to subject any subsequent measures to state tender. This was what eventually happened, although in the years that followed, persecution and official violence limited the participation of the workers in their alternative vision of a complete nationalisation of the De Mares concession.

The Commune of Barrancabermeja (April 1948)

At the entrance to the Nueva Granada Anti-aircraft Battalion in Barrancabermeja, a rustic steel artillery cannon rested for decades. This cannon, along with eight others, was made by Troco and Shell workers to defend the alternative government that emerged in Barrancabermeja after the assassination of liberal leader Jorge Eliécer Gaitán, on 9 April 1948. With brigades and workers' militias, the oil workers set up a Revolutionary Junta that led the Barrancabermeja Commune for ten days. This experience of popular power was unique in the country and can only be understood if the radical identity that the oil workers had forged during the first part of the 20th century, in their struggles against the oil companies and the country's ruling classes, is taken into account (Ortiz, 1978: 192–195; Alape, 1981, Díaz Callejas, 1989). As in other cities and towns, in Barrancabermeja people took to the streets after the assassination of Gaitán, under the slogan of social justice, and attacked the conservatives, calling for the fall of the regime.

The workers' militias were one of the pillars of the Revolutionary Junta. With numerical superiority and the organisational experiences of the USO, Troco workers stood out from the crowd, but those who worked for Shell in Casabe, on the other side of the river, and workers from nearby stations along the Andean pipeline, were also present. These militias controlled the means of transportation and communication relied on by the companies. Outboard motorboats, motor vehicles, the railroad, ships and barges, were seized and made available to the new government, along with radio telephone, telegraph, postal and telephone services. Gasoline and other fuels were commandeered to ensure supplies for the revolutionary government and the population of Barrancabermeja. The company commissariats were placed under surveillance and controlled to ensure supplies for the rebels.

The revolutionary government was based on three pillars: the mayor's office, under the leadership of Rafael Rangel, a Revolutionary Junta that carried out functions similar to that of a municipal assembly, and the workers' militias. These three institutions achieved such a coordination of forces that, at the municipal level, they managed to displace the traditional forms of the Colombian two-party system of government, embodying the counter-hegemonic aspirations of both the radical sectors of Barrancabermeja and the oil workers.

This government created a de facto form of direct, self-managed and participatory democracy. This was influenced by the political experiences of the oil workers who already held assemblies and organised work committees as part of their union organising. Just as the Revolutionary Junta was elected by popular vote, justice was administered with the participation of the residents themselves, through the mediation of community associations or existing union organisations. Minor conflicts that could not be dealt with by the Revolutionary Junta were resolved by the inhabitants themselves, who discussed the problems and acted together. Crimes, like robbery and theft, were punished and there was even an "office for stolen objects" set up, to return items that had been looted from shops before the new power took over.

The popular and workers' assemblies administered public services, such as aqueducts, energy, and communications; health services were free and the radio was made available to the revolutionary government. The old-fashioned community kitchens which had been used during the oil strikes, were extended to be used by all residents, including conservatives and top company employees. The ingredients used in the kitchens were mostly seized by workers from the food stores and commissariats of their respective companies, although agricultural products were also purchased from the peasants of the region, through a supply committee created for this purpose. The money used to buy these products came from a tax collection system that was implemented to tax those with the highest income: landowners, shops and other establishments.

The new government stimulated the active participation of the people, achieving, for the first time in the history of the country, a form of localised state capable of regulating the needs of the common people, through self-management, mutual aid and the collection of taxes from the wealthiest citizens. It was a redistributive municipal regime, which sought to put the oil companies at the service of Colombians. The companies were controlled by the workers, so the export of crude oil was suspended, and fuel stores were used to defend and supply the local government and the population in general. With the confiscation of explosive charges from the company workshops and with the weapons seized from the official repressive forces, military power passed into the hands of the people.

After a week, the power of central government began to be re-established in Bogotá and other cities and towns where popular uprisings had taken place. However, in Barrancabermeja, thanks to levels of internal organisation, revolutionary power persisted, making it the last bastion of resistance in the entire country. The *Barranqueños* were politically isolated and military forces threatened to invade the oil port with blood and fire if the revolutionary government did not surrender. To break the resistance, the military dropped flyers from planes which announced that they would be taking the port by force. But "the army could not enter, because the workers threatened to place dynamite. I don't know how it was known that a plane with soldiers was coming, but they placed gasoline and dynamite at the airport" (Bolaño, 1984).

Eight days after the Revolutionary Junta surrendered, the army entered and imprisoned the most high-profile members of the popular uprising. The luckiest ones were tried at an oral hearing of a council of war. Many others were imprisoned without any trial, and a significant number were killed by the police who arrived in the region killing reds (communists) and *cachiporros* (liberals). Faced with this scenario, some fled and took refuge in the mountains and formed a guerrilla group, led by Rafael Rangel, to do battle with the conservative regime for several years in the lands of Santander.

The Ninth of April cannon was captured and kept by a military battalion, because of the danger that a popular memorial to resistance would represent to the ruling classes. Memories of experiences of struggle might lead to the creation of a popular counterculture that delegitimises the consensus imposed by the ruling classes to sustain their hegemony. It is difficult to imagine another object that could better symbolise the class identity achieved by the oil workers than that haunting steel cannon – used to defend the popular power that displaced the ruling classes for a few days, but which today rests in a state battalion, like a piece of collective memory stolen from the working class.

Final Words

This essay traces the actions of anonymous men who, with the strength of their own two arms transformed the landscape of mountainous jungle into work camps and made it possible to extract crude oil and ship it to the world market. The first generations of oil workers endured harsh living and working conditions, and hundreds of them gave their lives, without us ever knowing their names, because the human beings born in this nation had no value for the Tropical Oil Company, except as producers of material wealth.

From the establishment of the enclave in Magdalena Medio a despotic system ruled ver Colombian workers who travelled there in the hope of improving their living conditions. They encountered a harsh reality, in which they endured a humiliating regime of unhealthy working conditions, disease, shortages and repression. This continued throughout the 20th century, everywhere that the oil companies were established.

These material conditions formed the foundations upon which workers' struggles were built, as they learned from their experiences and assimilated socialist and radical ideas from a variety of ideological influences. Through their resistance and the struggles in the enclaves against the foreign companies, they forged an identity. A social conscience and nationalist sentiment emerged which led to struggles that called for the reversal of the various concessions.

This nationalist sentiment was fed by the experience of imperialist exploitation and the looting of the country's natural resources.

Colombia has since returned to the time of concessions and enclaves. Entire areas, such as El Centro in Barrancabermeja or Tibú in El Catatumbo, have once again been ceded to US multinationals and facilities, such as the refineries, have been sold to foreign companies at very low cost.

The oil companies enjoy the protection of the State and their own private, para-state armies, and a policy of terror reigns in the oil fields and surrounding areas, put in place to remove any obstacle to the free extraction of crude oil. This means that, just as in the times of the enclaves, disagreements and social protest are contained by blood and fire, in order to ensure that oil flows without interruption to the global centres of consumption.

Unions are seen as obstacles that have no reason to exist, unless they are a bureaucratic façade for endorsing the dominance of the multinationals. As a consequence, some of the workers' achievements have been eliminated, starting with job stability (replaced with the widespread use of third-party contractors), the rights to organise and protest, and achievements in education, health, recreation and culture that the workers had won.

Simply and laconically put, this represents a return to the fighting conditions of the 1920s, when union organising was not allowed, when you had to meet clandestinely in the jungles and mountains around the oil fields, facing off against powerful foreign companies that, in turn, enjoyed the support of the Colombian state, while workers were subjected to the worst forms of labour exploitation. Back then this took place in an environment of strong national identity (which today has been lost or blurred), that identity was built up over several decades, because it was clear that they were preparing to face a foreign power. That has not changed, but it has been camouflaged – which makes it more difficult to identify the adversary – under the guise of companies that are ostensible run by national officials, and whose actions benefit the country, or at least that is what is claimed by those who hand the country's oil, land, minerals and biodiversity over to imperialism.

To conclude, the story of the oil workers and their main organisation, the USO, teaches us that, in the project of linking present, past and future: "They were good times, those that we lost, in which we saw the beauty of the human being reaffirming his dignity and defending his rights. *It has been a long life, but perhaps the best is yet to come, even now, in the worst of times.*" (Petras, 2000: 13, emphasis by authors).

Sources

Archival documents

Informe de Rafael Antonio Ariza, Prefecto Provincial de Zapatota al Secretario de Gobierno, al Secretario de Gobierno de Santander, 1919. Archivo General de la Nación, Ministerio de Minas y Energía. Serie Minas, Transferencia 2, Tropical Oil Company. Concesión de Mares, Tomo 211. (AGN, MME, TOC, CM), 1919.

Archivo General de la Nación, Fondo Ministerio de Gobierno, Sección 1, Tomos 932 y 989. (AGN, FMG, S. 1).

Archivo General de la Nación, Fondo Ministerio de Gobierno, Sección 4, Tomo 156 (AGN, FMG, S. 4, T. 156).

Newspapers

Vanguardia Obrera. Barrancabermeja, 1926.
Germinal, Barrancabermeja, 1926.
El Espectador, Bogotá, 1924.
Vanguardia Liberal, 1935.
El Tiempo, 1946.

Interviews

Aranda, Marco Lino. 1982 (January).
Morón, Julio. 1982 (June).
Rivera, Félix. 1984 (March).
Foronda, Antonio. 1984 (May).
Bolaño, Ángel. 1984 (March).

References

Alape, Arturo. 1981. "Los días de abril del 48 en Barranca." *Magazín Dominical* (5 June): 6 – 8.

Almario, Gustavo. 1984. *Historia de los trabajadores petroleros*. Bogotá: Cedetrabajo.

Álvarez Gutiérrez, Jaime. 1983. *Las putas también van al cielo*. Mexico: Costa-Amic.

Aprile-Gniset, Jacques. 1997. *Génesis de Barrancabermeja*. Barrancabermeja: Instituto Universitario de la Paz.

Archila, Mauricio. 1991. *Cultura e identidad obrera. Colombia 1910 – 1945*. Bogotá: Cinep.

Barreto, Juanita, and Luz Giraldo. 1998. "Yo digo que ellos son un león de papel y que hay un tigre dormido. Barrancabermeja: palabras, imágenes y relaciones de género." *Mujeres, hombres y cambio social*. Bogotá: Universidad Nacional.

Bautista, Ramón. 1939. "Petróleo. Grandezas y miserias de una explotación minera en la selva del Catatumbo." *El Liberal* (21 May).
Buenahora, Gonzalo. 1997. *Sangre y petróleo.* Barrancabermeja: Alcaldía.
Contraloría General de la República. 1997. *Primer Censo Sindical de Colombia.* Bogotá: Publicaciones Contraloría.
Díaz Callejas, Apolinar. 1989. *Diez días de poder popular.* Bogotá: El labrador.
Galán Gómez, Mario. 1945. *Geografía Económica de Colombia*, Tomo VIII, Santander. Bogotá: Contraloría General de la Nación.
"El sindicalismo revolucionario, estimulo de la reacción" *El Tiempo* (12 November).
Galvis, Simón. 1997. *Monografía de Barrancabermeja.* Barrancabermeja: Alcaldía.
Ginzburg, Carlo. 1986. *El queso y los gusanos.* Barcelona: Muchnik.
Guillén, Nicolás. 1997. "Nicolás Guillén en Colombia." In *Viajeros extranjeros por Colombia*, edited by José Luis Díaz Granados. Bogotá: Presidencia de la República.
Guillén, Nicolás. 1935. "Los huelguistas piden apoyo monetario o en víveres a los comerciantes de Barranca" *Vanguardia Liberal* (12 January).
Ortiz Márquez, Julio. 1950. "Personal Shell: Cosme Ortiz Escobar." *Vinculo* 23/24 (April-May): 11.
Ortiz Márquez, Julio. 1978. *El hombre que fue un pueblo.* Bogotá: Carlos Valencia.
Petras, James. 2000. *Escribiendo historias.* Tafalla: Txalaparta.
Rule, John. 1990. *Clase obrera e industrialización. Historia social de la revolución industrial británica, 1750–1850.* Barcelona: Crítica.
Thompson, Edward. 1981. *Miseria de la teoría.* Barcelona: Crítica.
Valbuena, Martiniano. 1947. *Memorias de Barrancabermeja* Bucaramanga: El Frente.

Victoria Basualdo

Dictatorships, workers and trade-unions in the second half of the 20th century: Dialogue and connections among the cases of Argentina, Brazil, Chile, Paraguay and Uruguay

Abstract: This chapter aims to propose possible future lines of research for studies of workers and trade-unions in the dictatorships of five South American countries. Starting from a central focus in the last Argentinian dictatorship (1976–1983), it seeks to open lines of dialogue with recent academic contributions on the dictatorships of Brazil, Chile, Paraguay and Uruguay in the second half of the 20th century, and particularly during the Cold War period, which presented specific features in Latin America (Pettinà, 2018). These countries were selected for their historical and geographic proximity, the links between their historical processes, and also because of the growing contact between researchers and academic institutions that has enabled these exchanges. Recognising that, until very recently, studies of dictatorships, workers and unions have been relatively marginal in the overall consideration of the different phases of the dictatorships, three main issues will be addressed here. First, we will review some of the existing research on the impact of dictatorial policies on workers and trade-unions, looking at repression, but not limited to that. Second, we will look at analyses of what is commonly referred to as "resistance" to the dictatorships among workers and unions. This covers a wide range of action and forms of organisation within different sectors of the working class and the trade union movement during the dictatorships. Third, we will analyse some recent perspectives that seek to address "social consensus" or "consent" to the dic-

Note: This chapter has been possible thanks to the funding from the Agencia Nacional de Promoción de la Investigación, el Desarrollo Tecnológico y la Innovación, Argentina, through project PICT No. 2019–02354, entitled "Participación empresarial en la represión a trabajadores/as y sindicalistas durante procesos dictatoriales en América Latina en la segunda mitad del siglo XX: contribuciones desde el caso de Argentina (1976–1983)."

PhD in History from Columbia University. Researcher at the Consejo Nacional de Investigaciones Científicas y Técnicas (CONICET) and the Area of Economics and Technology of FLACSO Argentina. Contact: basuvic@yahoo.com.ar.

https://doi.org/10.1515/9783110759303-010

tatorship. Finally, we will make some proposals for future research in these fields, with the aim of consolidating a possible research agenda on the subject in South America.

Key words: Cold-war dictatorships; workers; unions; South America; dictatorial policies; workers' and union resistance

Introduction

Academic contributions on workers and dictatorships around the world has diversified in recent years, however, an overview of the cycle of dictatorships in South America during the second half of the 20th century remains a pending issue. Studies on the impacts of the dictatorships on economic and social structures, labour relations, and living and working conditions for workers, require deeper and more systematic approaches. We have established some areas that require further research, and, in line with that, this chapter seeks to contribute to the construction of transnational perspectives based on national case studies, from an interdisciplinary perspective that links the fields of economic, political, social and cultural history.

If we are to account for the transformations that occurred in productive systems, socio-economic structures and labour relations, it is essential to go beyond individual analyses focused on a single nation. It is important to identify transnational and/or regional dynamics and points of contact, because they indicate processes that transcend specific experiences. With this in mind, we have conducted a review of recent literature on workers and the dictatorship in Argentina, putting that into dialogue with new contributions on dictatorships during the Cold War in Brazil, Chile, Paraguay and Uruguay. These countries were selected for their historical and geographic proximity, the links between their historical processes and also because there is growing contact between researchers and academic institutions working on these themes. We are not aiming to conduct an exhaustive historiographical review of all the national case studies, nor at a comparison in the strictest sense of the term. Rather, we aim to establish key points of contact based on recent research contributions. The modest proposal of this text is simply to highlight points of contact and dialogue between some recent national case studies, as a possible, tentative starting point for the creation of new, more comprehensive lines of research that could shed light on regional dimensions that have, until now, been very difficult to approach.

This chapter analyses the impact of dictatorial policies on workers and trade-unions, with a particular emphasis on repressive policies. A preliminary review of the literature suggests that, beyond the peculiarities and specifics of the national cases, there are significant points of contact that demonstrate the importance of looking at dictatorships from the point of view of the history of the working class. In doing so we take into account structural transformations and their impact on distribution, as well as changes in labour relations and workers' rights, although significant difficulties remain when incorporating this perspective into global overviews. We also reconsider various analyses focused on "resistance," a concept often used to approach the wide range of forms of action and organisation deployed by different sectors of the working class and the trade union movement during the dictatorships. Thirdly, we address recent perspectives that explore and reflect on ideas of "consent" or "social consensus" in the context of dictatorships. Finally, we make some proposals for future research with the aim of consolidating a research agenda on this issue in South America and beyond.

The dictatorships and regional dynamics in figures

Putting the dictatorial processes of the five countries into dialogue with each other raises a series of challenges, not least of which is the chronological framework. While the dictatorship of Argentina, self-denominated as the "National Reorganisation Process," lasted from 1976 to 1983 (and previous dictatorial processes, 1955 to 58 and 1966 to 1973, must also be taken into account also); the Chilean dictatorship was in power from 1973 to 1990; the Uruguayan dictatorship lasted from 1973 to 1985 (according to the most accepted chronology); the Brazilian dictatorship is considered to have lasted from 1964 to 1985 (with debates about whether the period should be extended to 1988); and finally the Paraguayan dictatorship lasted from 1954 to 1989. With the exceptions of the dictatorships of Augusto Pinochet in Chile and Alfredo Stroessner in Paraguay, these countries saw changes to the top military leadership during their dictatorships. Although it is not possible to develop the subject in all its complexity here, we consider it important to frame these processes within the context of the Cold War (from the late 1940s to the late 1980s), the process of radicalisation of political, social and labour organisations after the Cuban revolution, and the links with the processes of decolonisation of the "Third World." There are also historical and judicial precedents for considering regional repressive dynamics, particularly those related to "Operation Condor" that are of great relevance for this analysis (Slatman, 2012).

The impact of the repressive policies of these dictatorships are enormously difficult to measure and conceptualise, not only because it is difficult to accessing key sources (due to the very nature of repression), but also because in each of these different countries, victims are defined and counted in very different ways. In its final report, the National Truth Commission of Brazil (CNV by its initials in Portuguese) set the number of killed or disappeared at 434, however no confirmed figures exist for other types of victims such as numbers of people imprisoned, tortured, kidnapped and released, or exiled, among other possible forms of repression. These difficulties grow when we look at events in rural areas, which, based on preliminary evidence, affected thousands of victims. Argentina has paid particular attention to the numbers of disappeared, estimated at 30,000, considering not only the statistics established by the National Commission on the Disappearance of Persons (CONADEP by its Spanish initials), but also data from the armed forces themselves, which estimated the number of victims disappeared by 1978 at 22,000 (with high levels of under-reporting and/or under-recording). However, the same emphasis has not been placed on counting the numbers of people murdered, imprisoned or tortured, or quantifying processes of exile, for which published figures vary widely. In the case of Chile, according to the reports of the Truth and Reconciliation Commission (the Rettig Report) and the National Commission on Political Prisons and Torture (the Valech Report), the number of direct victims of human rights violations is considered to be at least 35,000, of whom around 28,000 were tortured, 3,197 killed (counting 2,095 extrajudicial executions and 1,102 disappeared). Furthermore, some 200,000 people suffered exile, and an unknown number (estimated in the hundreds of thousands by some sources) passed through clandestine and illegal detention centres. In Paraguay, during the 35 years of dictatorship, serious and extensive human rights violations were perpetrated, which included the arbitrary or illegal detention of at least 19,862 people, the torture of 18,772, the extrajudicial execution of 58, the forced disappearance of 337 and the exile of 3,470 (Truth and Justice Commission, 2008). Finally, in the case of Uruguay, a 2011 government report recognises 465 victims of the last dictatorship (1973–1985), but it only counts those who were murdered and/or disappeared. Recent academic estimates place the number of people forced into exile by the Uruguayan dictatorship (1973–1985) at around 380,000 people, which is almost 14 percent of the population.

For various reasons, including differing criteria and methodology applied, it is difficult to compare these figures concerning human rights violations, all of which are provisional, despite the time that has elapsed, as new sources and information continue to modify our understanding of a process that was purposely covered up. Furthermore, numbers for victims who were workers and/or trade unionists are even more difficult to establish. Several attempts have been made in the case of Argentina, however, the results are still incomplete and do not fully account for the whole. Understanding repressive policies, the forms they took and their impact in each of the countries, is therefore a major challenge. It is also vital to develop an understanding of ways of life, forms of organisation, salaries and the presence of male and female workers in the workplace in the different countries, as well as union structures, their institutional dynamics, membership, scope and presence in the workplace. These aspects then need to be analysed in the context of economic and social structure, and of the economic policy transformations implemented by the dictatorships in their various stages and sub-stages. What we propose here is to open a dialogue between existing analyses of national cases, in order to identify possible points of convergence or counterpoint that may suggest regional trends. We will start by reconsidering the existing historical literature for the five countries, the analytical and conceptual frameworks deployed, and their contributions and limitations, with a view to consolidating a possible agenda for future collaborative work.

Dictatorships, trade-unions and workers

There is a growing recognition of the value of analysing recent history from the perspective of trade union and labour activism, which makes the authoritarian and disciplinary character of dictatorships a central feature of the regimes. Very significant contributions have been on this issue, making a comparative analysis possible, as can be seen in the work of Paul Drake (1996), which focuses mainly on the Southern Cone, particularly Argentina, Chile and Uruguay, although it also includes also, brief references to cases as Brazil and Southern Europe (Portugal, Spain and Greece). Coming from the field of political science, Drake's work attempts an initial systematic comparison, reaching the conclusion that although there were important variations, overall, the dictatorships shared a commitment to anti-union and anti-labour policies. The author argues that it is necessary to recognise the central role of workers and unions, as confrontation with these sectors was key to the history of these dictatorships (*ibid.*).

In recent years, a group of researchers from five countries, especially from Brazil and Argentina, and joined by specialists from Chile, Uruguay and Paraguay, have sought to promote a greater articulation of academic production on the subject in South America. This process took the form of meetings and publications, and the creation, in 2018, of a network to study "Repressive processes, business, workers and trade-unions in Latin America." The work of that network has been central to making the reflections discussed here possible (Winn, 2018;

Basualdo, 2018; Corrêa and Fontes, 2018; Vergara, 2018; Estevez, Sales, Corrêa and Fontes, 2018). The findings of most of these authors were that studies of workers, unions and dictatorships had long been marginalised, in the face of the predominance of approaches focussed on political history, with a strong emphasis on the role of the armed forces and of political and military organisations.

The case of Argentina is revealing in this regard. We can find some very relevant contributions on the anti-union and anti-worker character of the dictatorship (even from the time), and evidence of the persecution of workers and unionists is held in the archives of state investigations such as the CONADEP, and the judicialisation process of the 1980s. Nevertheless, the prevailing view, in the 1980s and 1990s, prioritised analysis of the political dimensions of the regime. To illustrate the difficulty of incorporating the wealth of studies of dictatorship, workers, and unions, into the historiography, it is worth considering an historiographical review conducted 40 years after the coup d'état (Canelo, 2016b), in which there are practically no references to this line of research, despite it having a trajectory of several decades of development. Surprisingly, another text published that same year, judges that attempts to consider economic and social transformations are essentially "economistic" and calls for historians to "reclaim the autonomy of politics from the economy as a fundamental interpretive key," or even more forcefully "to propose a political interpretation of the dictatorship" (Canelo, 2016a: 11–12).

In the case of Brazil, recent historiographical reviews highlight the difficulty of including workers and their organisations in the history of the dictatorship. In a very useful review, Corrêa and Fontes (2016) argue that despite the fact that workers were "one of the most notorious and expressive social sectors in the political situation prior to the coup," they have been marginalised in most recent analyses of the post-coup period. The authors state that in the events commemorating the 50th anniversary of the coup, the absence of reference to workers was "notable." Also noteworthy is the focus by historians on memoirs of the regime, centred above all on the testimonies of left-wing militants from the student movement, and from intellectuals and groups of artists, as well as studies of the armed struggle, the press, economic policy and the repressive apparatus. Workers and union leaders remained invisible for too long in all senses, including in the records of victims of the regime (Corrêa and Fontes, 2016: 130–131; Chaves Nagasava, 2018). This diagnosis is shared by other authors who also highlighted the importance of initiatives such as the National Truth Commission, even with its limitations, to promote research as part of a policy of social memory (Estevez and Assumpçao, 2013).

In the case of Chile, not only do political viewpoints dominate the literature, but existing studies on economic change also frequently highlight the positive achievements of the "economic miracle" attributed to the Pinochet dictatorship. In Ángela Vergara's view, however, despite the undeniable impact of the dictatorship on intellectual production, a rich and interesting historiography on labour and workers can be found, which over the decades, has included contributions from the field of the sociology of work, studies of urban working communities, and gender studies that offer a feminist perspective (Vergara, 2018). A number of these studies highlight the social costs and the extremely regressive impact that profound changes in labour policies and regulations had on workers and their organisations. An important book in this regard, which combined overviews and case studies (addressing the textile, metalwork, and copper industries as well as agriculture, fisheries, forestry and other sectors), questions the focus on the supposed "Chilean economic miracle," emphasizing the loss of labour and social rights under the dictatorship, and presenting approaches that combine a class perspective with very interesting ethnic and gender dimensions that open new paths for historical research (Winn, 2004). Recently, another collective book has offered crucial insight into the economic, social and labour transformations that took place during the dictatorship: including studies of the economic policies applied; the role of media and the relationship between the military and business organisations; privatisation of the pension system; changes in labour law, policies and practices; and the role of companies and business leaders in human rights violations, among many other related topics (Bohoslavsky, Fernández and Smart, eds., 2021).

In the case of Uruguay, recent contributions offering an overview of the impact of the dictatorship on workers and their union organisations, have indicated something similar. A recent work by Rodolfo Porrini (2018) is central to providing a review of the historiographic panorama, noting that initial exploratory studies have focused on the actions of clandestine unions and social movements, and on the recomposition that took place in the 1980s. Porrini also points out that social and historical studies of changes to working and living conditions and cultural processes of "hegemony and consensus" among the working class have received little attention, and that there is still limited knowledge about the working classes and their forms of expression during the dictatorship. In this regard he highlights clandestine groups and organisations, cooperatives, sports clubs, and social and cultural bodies, as well as the need to look at geographic location, comparing cities, neighbourhoods and towns in the interior of the country, as well as in rural areas (*ibid.*).

In the case of Paraguay, recent literature has contributed to analysis not only of the political features of the Stroessner dictatorship, but also the structural, socio-economic transformations it entailed, particularly the role of trade union organisations in the extended dictatorship period from 1954 and 1989, as well as their relations with the State (González Bozzolasco, 2014). These studies have led historians to the concept of corporatism a useful term to characterise the policies deployed by the dictatorship towards the trade union movement. Usually this means "that the State creates some form of labour organisation, usually with official financing, mandatory membership and the setting of strict limits regarding which sectors can organise" (*ibid.*: 68–69). According to these perspectives, this form of union control "leads sectors opposed to the authoritarian regime within unionism, to take one of two paths: use official spaces and engage in internal dispute in sectors friendly to the regime, or organise completely outside those spaces" (*ibid.*: 69).

Although it may occupy a secondary place among the predominant viewpoints and interpretations of these regimes, there is, in all these cases, a rich body of literature (more or less diverse, depending on the country), relating to the three issues of interest: state policies against workers and unions, with a strong focus on repression; contributions on workers' "resistance" and organisation against the dictatorships; more recent approaches looking at the so-called "social consensus" regarding the dictatorships. We will analyse those contributions in more detail below.

Dictatorial policies aimed at workers and unions

Recent studies illuminate not only the various impacts of the repressive policies of dictatorships on labour and union organisation, and their living, working and organising conditions, but also important issues such as the heterogeneity of different currents within the labour union movement; the varied impacts, in the different cases, of economic and labour policies on distinct groups; and the existence of different types of relationship between union leaders and the armed forces in each of the countries.

In case of Argentina, a number of studies analyse dictatorial policies affecting workers and trades unions. All coincide in suggesting that there were unprecedented levels of repression, major transformations in labour relations and the structure of workers' rights, and a massive decline in living and working conditions, along with significant changes to the trade union movement (Abós, 1984; Fernández, 1985; Pozzi, 1988 a and b; Gallitelli and Thompson, 1990; Basualdo, 2010a, among others). Several approaches refer to a series of contributions from the field of economics and economic history, although there are differences in methodology, theoretical, conceptual and analytical frameworks, and sources. Despite their differences, a significant number of the studies coincided in linking the establishment of the dictatorship with decisive transformations in industrialisation, and with the substitution of imports that had developed in previous decades. Many of these interpretations coincide in highlighting an economic turnaround of great importance in the mid-1970s, consolidated through changes in economic policy under the leadership of José Alfredo Martínez de Hoz. This includes the implementation of policies such as the Financial Reform of 1977, which, in conjunction with tariffs and increased external debt derived from the *apertura* (the opening up of the economy) in 1979, promoted a regressive restructuring of the industrial sector. Overall, this amounted to a deindustrialisation (that is to say, the role of the industrial sector in GDP decreased), with varying effects on the different branches of industry. This was combined with a process of economic concentration within the framework of an exponential increase in foreign debt, increasingly linked to the process of financialisaton (Basualdo, 2006). These changes to patterns of capital accumulation are considered by much of the academic literature to be key to any analysis of the transformations experienced by workers and their organisations during the military dictatorship, including changes in labour relations and the effects of repression. There is broad agreement as to the regressive character of those changes, both in distributive and organisational terms, although emphasis and nuances may differ.

Many of these studies demonstrate that the effects of the repression extended both to those most directly affected, such as trade union leaders, grass-roots delegates and labour activists who saw crackdowns on their personal freedom and even their lives, but also to all of the workers who remained in the factories and workplaces. There are numerous testimonies, documents and studies that reflect, in the context of an increasing concentration of economic and political power among the bosses and elites, and the increasing application of physical and psychological violence in the workplace, a severe reduction in communication and social interaction that dramatically affected basic social ties at a time when surveillance and social controls were increasing (Basualdo, 2010 among others). Added to this we have what some authors have called "a complex system of prevention": worker recruitment became provisional, and it was only after receiving an intelligence report from the armed forces that workers were granted relative stability in their jobs (Delich, 1982: 140). The repression aimed to eliminate the most active workers' representatives, "beheading" the rank and file in order to make brutally clear what the consequences of political and union militancy, as well solidarity at an international level and between relevant sectors, would be (Basualdo, 2010 a and c; AEyT de FLACSO, PVJ, SDH and CELS, 2015; Basualdo and Jasinski, 2016).

In addition to these forms of repression, the regime also intervened in a large number of unions and workers' federations, which began with appointing military officials to the *Confederación General del Trabajo* (CGT). Likewise, the military dictatorship passed a set of regulations aimed at legalising repressive activity and state intervention in the workplace. From the very beginning of the dictatorship, a freeze was placed on all types of trade-union activity, as well as a prohibition on all forms of workplace organisation and protest. Legislation was closely related to these measures, so, as workers found or created non-prohibited ways to organise or demonstrate, these were incorporated into further regulations to prohibit them (Pozzi, 1988a and b, Basualdo, 2010b).

In the case of Brazil, contributions such as those of Marco Aurelio Santana (2008 and 2014) provide useful syntheses of the accumulated evidence regarding the impact of the dictatorship on workers and unions in Brazil. Santana highlights that the 1950s mark an extremely important period for Brazilian workers, as the union movement, led by the alliance of militant communist and workers' activists, achieved great advances in mobilisation and organisation, resulting in the mass participation of workers at the heart of national political life. At the same time, he highlights how "following more than a decade of this intense growth and activity, the entire organisational structure was severely impacted by the 1964 civil-military coup, one of the central justifications for which was precisely to prevent the installation of a 'syndicalist republic' in the country" (Santana, 2008: 279–280). Activities were derailed by the imprisonment of leaders, persecution of militants, and disruption of the work of unions in factories. It would take a long time to recover. In terms of the labour movement, what was left, as is often the case in periods like these, was the small and silent work that went on in the workplace. It was necessary to rebuild forces in order to confront the dictatorship (Santana, 2008: 279–280).

In terms of the specific impacts of the dictatorship on workers, unions, and labour relations, Santana highlights how, after the military coup, interventions perpetrated by Castelo Branco (1964–1967) had a significant impact, in various ways, on the life of the unions, affecting the more progressive sectors most severely. He argues that in addition to a direct attack on trade union organisation, which aimed at immediate discipline, the dictatorship also sought to enact legislation that would implement long-term changes (Santana, 2008: 281). He analyses the dictatorship's approval of a series of measures to reinforce control over the trade union movement. Taking up elements already included in the *Consolidación de la Ley del Trabajo* (Labour Law), strict rules were set for the occupation of roles within the unions, with candidates subject to the approval of the Ministry of Labour and the political police. The use of and access to state welfare resources was drastically limited through their centralisation in the *Instituto Nacional de Previsión Social*, whose management would no longer be carried out with the participation of the workers, as the old pensions institute had been, being subject instead to direct management by the government. Regarding the mobilisations, Santana highlights how measures claiming to regulate the right to strike actually resulted in the prohibition of political and secondary striking, limiting the right to strike to demands for the payment of unpaid wages. In this first phase, the military dictatorship introduced the *Fondo de Garantía por Tiempo de Servicio*, which put an end to job security, encouraging bosses to deploy a high turnover of labour, which made more combative union activity in the workplace more difficult (Santana 2008, 281–283).

This analysis was enriched and expanded in a later book specifically focused on the Ministry of Labour during the Castelo Branco years of the dictatorship. Based on extensive archival materials and a wide range of other sources, this book showed that while there were different views about how best to deal with workers and their organisations, the main aim was to dramatically reconfigure labour and social rights, and to challenge the increasing role of labour struggles in economic, social and political spheres (Chaves Nagasava, 2018). Another quite significant recent book analysed the participation of workers and trade-unions in Sao Paulo's labour courts before the 1964 military coup, arguing that the "rights issue," imbedded in public institutions, was at the heart of the 1964 coup, and considering the coup a reaction to the advances of rights and the broader participation of diverse social actors within a democratic institutional framework. The analysis, based on an incredibly rich and complex empirical basis, illuminates very clearly the importance of labour issues in understanding the aims of the dictatorship (Teixeira da Silva, 2019).

In the case of Chile, the Pinochet dictatorship suspended the constitution and with it, all civil liberties and political rights (Winn, 2004). The parties that had supported Allende were banned, a measure that was later extended even to the parties that had previously been his opponents. Electoral processes were suspended, even in social organisations such as youth clubs, and especially in the unions. Military personnel were put in charge of schools and universities, whose teaching and library staff were fiercely purged. The public burning of 'subversive' books became a visible symbol of the new lack of freedom in Chile, inviting comparisons with Nazi Germany (*ibid.*).

These studies highlight how within its first few weeks in power, the Pinochet dictatorship had demonstrated itself to be a serial violator of human rights. Many of the victims were trade unionists, activists and/or workers, whom Pinochet considered primary targets of his 'internal war' between 1973 and 1978, based on the high degree of power, organisation, and the important political role they played as the social base of the left. They were considered dangerous enemies that had to be neutralised during the coup, making them key targets for repression. On the same day of the coup, the headquarters of the *Central Unica de Trabajadores* (CUT) was one of the first buildings taken by the armed forces. During the three days and nights of siege that followed the coup, military operations with tanks, helicopters and machine guns were deployed against the country's main industrial areas. The CUT was banned, its property confiscated, and its representatives publicly labelled as "subversives" with warrants issued for their capture (*ibid.*)

At the same time, Santana stresses that the presence of the armed forces grew in many workplaces and factories. Military intelligence interrogated workers one by one, pressuring them to report on militants and activists, particularly union leaders. Many were captured and disappeared, some were tortured, or forced into exile. Others were displaced within the country, with many then participating in the underground resistance elsewhere. The repression continued until 1978, based on Decree Law number 198 which allowed the government to remove union leaders at will, and the Pinochet regime promoted the ascent of more conservative sectors in lieu of union democracy. In a context where collective bargaining, strikes and union elections were all prohibited, military decrees banned many of the unions outright, decimating the CUT and the ranks of workers that could be mobilised. In connection with these repressive policies to govern labour, the dictatorship re-established the primacy of the free market, a freedom that did not apply in any way to labour rights or demands over wages. Under government control, real wages fell sharply between 1973 and 1975, and workers and their organisations lost significant power during this period (*ibid.*).

In the case of Paraguay, researchers have analysed the policies of the dictatorship towards the union movement according to their relative predominance at each stage. They consider the first years of the dictatorship, between 1954 and 1958, to have seen a predominance of repression in which all kinds of policies were deployed to limit and contain union activity. This was followed by a long period, between 1958 and 1985, dominated by policies of co-option. A significant part of "the vestiges of trade unionism that had survived the great repression, re-articulated their relationship with the government, the *Partido Colorado* and the state apparatus" (González Bozzolasco, 2014: 68). Finally, they highlight a period of 'resistance' against these policies, in the last years of Stronism between 1985 and 1989, during which "the model of co-option promulgated and consolidated by the regime begins to crack, together with the apparatus that promoted and sustained it" (*ibid:* 68).

Finally, in the case of Uruguay, Rodolfo Porrini makes a very valuable contribution stating that, following the coup d'état of 1973, there was an ambitious attempt to dominate and destroy the trade union movement, while at the same time seeking to co-opt their social bases, the broad, mobilised and mostly urban poor and working classes. He also notes that the dictatorial regime sought, at different times, to promote or build a trade unionism allied to its own ideas and purposes. Meanwhile it sought social control through various forms of repression of the political and social opposition. This was combined with specific policies aimed at the world of labour, guilds and unions that were expressions of the dictatorship's new form of domination, and the new framework of social relations it imposed (Porrini, 2018).

As with Argentina, Porrini argues that a significant concentration of income occurred in Uruguay during the dictatorship. If wages and pensions represented 45.8 percent of national income from 1968 to 1971, by 1978 they represented just 33.1 percent. Wage earners throughout the country saw their real income drop between 8 and 20 percent (Notaro, 1984: 77–78 cited in Porrini, 2018). An alternate expression of this phenomenon is the overall reduction in real wages. Taking wages in 1957 as a benchmark, real wages were down to 68.4 percent by 1974 and had fallen to just 35.2 percent by 1984 (Nahum et al., 2011: 84 cited in Porrini, 2018). Another aspect to consider, according to Porrini, is the practice of repressing political and social opponents, along with wider attempts to control other areas of Uruguayan society. The activities of the "traditional" *Colorado* and *Nacional* parties were suspended, as was the Christian Democratic Party. Other political parties and organisations were outlawed, and in October 1973, the executive power intervened in the *Universidad de la República* and banned the *Convención Nacional de Trabajadores* (CNT).

According to Porrini, during the early days of the dictatorship, three main policy axes were applied to the world of labour and unions. In the first place, an attempt was made to silence conflict, and to this end there was a policy of intense repression with workers being sacked, imprisoned or transferred, and public officials dismissed. In August 1973, the CNT reported almost 1,500 dismissals, and the AEBU (the Uruguayan Association of Bankers) reported the dismissal of 42 workers in its own sector and the punishment of around 1,400 workers across the board. The regime also attempted to reformulate labour relations based on a series of decrees intended to apply to all workers, restricting and setting limits on union activity. Finally, the dictatorship set out to create a new organisation in accordance with its own vision of what union activity should be. The interpretations state, therefore, that the dictatorship implemented a combination of "prohibition and permissiveness," alternating its line according to the moment, and also to the responses coming from both the trade union *milieu* and from business (Porrini, 2018).

Workers' and trade union's "resistance" to dictatorships

In all five cases, the concept of workers' "resistance" is used to describe forms of workers' action and organisation during the dictatorship. In the case of Argentina, the explicit or implicit debate on 'resistance' marked the development of research in this field from very early on. The evaluation and analysis of the reactions of the working class to dictatorial policies and processes of structural change has led to debates among historians. Francisco Delich was one of the first authors to refer to the immobility of the working class, a question that was much disputed by later historians. Pablo Pozzi critiqued this view in a book and an article published in the late 1980s (1988 a and b), in which he argued that, on the contrary, there was a wide range of resistance and oppositional activity. Pozzi not only questioned Delich's views on the absence of "classic," frontal conflict from the unions (in terms of historical forms of Argentinian workers' struggle), particularly citing the general strike of 1979, but he also emphasised the importance of "underground" acts of resistance, to which we will refer in more detail below. Pozzi's work has the merit of drawing attention to the existence of 'underground' practices at a plant level, which had been underestimated or simply omitted by most previous work on the subject. These covert forms of protest, conducted by groups of workers with reduced coordination and impact, included *trabajo a tristeza*, and *trabajo a desgano* (go-slow protests involving reductions in the pace of work), partial stoppages, sabotage, and a multiplicity of initiatives favouring workers' organisation to the detriment of the employer. Pozzi considers that these forms emerged from previous experiences, developed in the context of "resistance" to previous dictatorships since 1955 (Pozzi, 1988a). In summary, Pozzi demonstrates that there were numerous instances of workers' protest from the very first days of the dictatorship, and that they increased at the junctures where the greatest success was possible. Although repression and economic and employment policies had a profoundly negative impact on the working class, important sectors of that class developed forms of organisation and protest. Those forms varied and changed throughout the period according to the existing scope for action at the time. Recent studies have emphasised the importance of carrying out a complex analysis, both in the workplace and in the public sphere, using different methods and measures, and including a diversity of regions of the country. Forms of international resistance were also analysed, both in supranational organisations such as the International Labour Organisation (ILO), and through international campaigns involving the participation of trade union confederations from other countries and global trade union organisations (Basualdo 2006b, 2010c, 2013).

In the case of Brazil, it is necessary, according to Larissa Rosa Corrêa and Paulo Fontes (2016), to distinguish between different stages in which very different perspectives prevailed with respect to workers, unions and the dictatorship. They underline that, in an initial stage, "the idea of non-reaction, paralysis and/or passivity of the workers during the coup, severely limited studies of the workers." While President Joao Goulart had sought to associate himself with the workers until 1964, after the coup "Jango's decision not to resist the advance of the military troops and his silent flight to Uruguay, was taken as representative of what happened with the workers. They were imprisoned by interpretations that sought to scrutinise their supposed absence (absence of class organisation, of political conscience, of collective spirit, etc.)" (*ibid:* 134). They point out that a large part of the energy of academic production was devoted, at this stage, to trying to answer the question of why the workers had not reacted to the dictatorship. In general terms, initial lines of inquiry looked for the causes of this supposed "lack of resistance" in the history of unionism before the coup, and in the supposedly subordinate role of the left, particularly the Communist Party, in the defeat of 1964. In this context, theories of populism gained ground, arguing that corporatism acted as a populist net to capture workers in the fabric of state domination. From a different theoretical perspective, but also looking for answers in the Varguista period, the term "regulated citizenship" was coined, focussing on the top echelons of the State, generally reinforcing an idea of the absence, inaction and subordination of workers and their organisations, who were subjected to a logic alien to their own (Corrêa and Fontes, 2016).

These authors highlight that the memorialistic literature that emerged with force at the end of the 1970s, as politics opened up, reinforced the invisibility of workers in the resistance to the military dictatorship, particularly between 1964 and 1978. The 1968 strikes of metalworkers were presented, in this interpretative framework, as exceptions that proved the rule. The impact of activist memoires of the armed struggle helped to consolidate a vision of the workers as the bearers of political disinterest, acquiescence, and sometimes support for the regime. Some lines of interpretation pointed to a growing heterogeneity of the working class as a key factor to understanding the supposedly timid role of workers in the fight against the dictatorship (*ibid.*).

Within this framework, a change of vision took shape, from an emphasis on inaction it shifted to a growing recognition of the agency of workers and their organisations. The great strikes that began in São Paulo's ABC industrial districts in 1978, a movement that would later spread to different regions of the country, also became a symbol of changes to perceptions of the role of the working class and its relationship with the authoritarian regime. These massive and rebellious acts, and the leading role of the workers in them, were interpreted by some as a 'watershed' or turning point that implied both a break with the 'populist' past of 1964, and also with what was seen as the more recent subordination and immobility of workers during the dictatorship (*ibid.*).

As a result, this period was understood as "novel," an idea that prevailed in academic and political literature which spoke of the creation of a "new unionism," and "new" social movements that replaced the traditional, populist subordination to the State, mobilizing en masse in workplaces and neighbourhoods, and acting independently and autonomously. Corrêa and Fontes emphasise that the enthusiasm and effervescence of the climate of re-democratisation and activism means that the change is often understood to have been abrupt and absolute, however that was later revised by research that sought the origins of those changes in earlier periods and found prior progressive transformations that challenge that premise of the passivity of the working class. An increasingly rich field of studies was established, looking not only at a wide range of industrial activities and urban centres such as Baixada Fluminense, Niterói, Sao Paulo's ABC and Rio de Janeiro, but also looking at rural workers from different areas of the country, at Brazilian trade unionism's international relations, and other fields relating to labour law (Pessanha, 2014; Welch, 2014; Corrêa, 2014 and 2017; Gouveia de Oliveira Rovai, 2014; Montenegro, 2014, Nagasava, 2015, Pessanha and Medeiros, 2015, among many others). Despite these and many other valuable contributions, there is a need for greater geographical diversity in these studies, and to deepen the analysis of the forms of police and military repression used against workers both inside and outside the factories, as well as an analysis of transformations in living and working conditions during each of the sub-periods of the dictatorship.

Objective data also needs to be gathered on changes in workers' rights as well as the views and opinions of the workers about the dictatorship, including those who supported it in some way, for example, appreciating the 'economic miracle' and some of the beneficial consequences it had for some of them (Corrêa and Fontes, 2016). Cross referencing recent rich contributions on the world of labour, with those from the field of the economic history, looking at companies, entrepreneurs and the economic transformations that took place (Campos, 2014 among others), seems to be another enormously relevant task.

In the case of Uruguay, it has also been emphasised that "various forms of responses and resistance developed" to confront the dictatorship. Porrini highlights, in particular, attempts by the regime to organise meetings with trade unionists, for example, after a strike on 25 July 1973. That attempt ended in failure when it was denounced by the workers as a 'pantomime' that only sought to whitewash the dismissals and persecutions that took place (Porrini, 2018). Another example is the union response to moves made to regulate union activity. In August 1973, the government issued a decree proposing "union re-affiliation" that implied a regulation of union life, creating obstacles to, and limitations on, the right to strike. The clandestine command of the CNT held a Trade Union Plenary and promoted the re-affiliation of workers to their own unions. In a very short time, they had received a massive response from the country's wage earners in support of the unions that had previously been part of the dissolved CNT, which, in effect, made the initiative a failure for the regime (Porrini, 2018).

Other attempts also stand out, such as the creation in 1974 of an office in charge of controlling work within the companies: the *Oficina de Asuntos Laborales del Estado Mayor Conjunto* (Office of Labour Affairs of the Joint Chiefs of Staff). It was led by the military and acted fundamentally as a repressive organisation in charge of controlling workers. The Office coordinated with state intelligence agencies whose files have not been found, although some of their activities were recorded in the files of the *Dirección Nacional de Investigación e Inteligencia policial* (National Police Investigation and Intelligence Directorate) (Rico, 2009: 241 cited by Porrini, 2018).

Finally, Porrini highlights that following a very difficult period in a context where political room for manoeuvre was very limited, after the defeated Plebiscite of 1980, it once again became possible to create space for the reorganisation and reactivation of the trade unions and social movements. In a context of a revitalisation of society, an increase in collective action and the emergence of new cultural and union-type associations, the *Plenario Intersindical de Trabajadores* (PIT) (Inter-Union Plenary of Workers) was founded in May 1983. From 1983 onwards there was intense participation and mobilisations that resulted in demonstrations against the dictatorship, that brought together workers, university and high school students, cooperative members, human rights activists and activists from the opposition parties, especially from the left and from the more oppositional factions of the "traditional" parties, all of which marked the transition to democracy (Porrini, 2018).

In the case of Chile, recent contributions by Rodrigo Araya Gómez (2015) consider the union movement to have lived through a first stage of survival, marked by strong repression, the prohibition of the CUT, and the persecution of left-wing union leaders, favouring a weakening and splitting of the union movement into union groups that adopted different strategies to confront the dictatorship. He highlights that, in July 1974, the *Comité Exterior* of the CUT was formed, better known as Cexcut, which reported on the difficult situation facing union activity in the country subject to the power of a "fascist military junta," and called for international solidarity to sustain the struggles of Chilean workers and the trade union movement during the most complex times of the dictatorship. The task carried out by Cexcut was important because it maintained an active international presence in coordination with the large international centres. Union groups received financial support and some international leaders travelled to Chile to report on the unfavourable conditions facing union activists, enabling the International Labour Organisation (ILO) to observe and critique the Chilean government's labour policy (*ibid.*).

From these perspectives, it is considered that the most critical stage was 1973 to 1974, when survival was the only objective. After that, there followed a period of reactivation of the union movement with some protest actions such as strikes and *viandazos* that were harshly repressed by the regime, resulting in mass dismissals, arrests and demotions.[1] The 1979 "*Plan Laboral*" is seen as another turning point in the trajectory of Chilean trade unionism. It consolidated the privatisation of labour relations by regulating collective bargaining and eliminating the employment tribunals and their provisions on matters of lay-offs, working hours, severance pay for years of service, and union finances (*ibid.*). Nevertheless, the regulation itself, which in principle was contrary to the interests of the unions, was sometimes overwhelmed by the actions of the workers themselves (one specific example is the strike at *El Teniente* mining company), which reflected the potential of united action to confront the dictatorship and its business allies (*ibid.*).

In the context of the institutionalisation of the dictatorship, the plebiscite on the 1980 constitution, and the consolidation of the neo-liberal model expressed in the workplace as the implementation of the Labour Plan, union groups attempted an institutional consolidation that enabled them to be more critical of the regime. They proposed unity of action and the development of a common platform of protest on urgent issues facing workers, especially those of an economic nature, which had increased with the onset of the economic crisis in the early 1980s, and the end of the so-called "economic miracle" (*ibid.*). The trade union movement called the first national protest, which brought together various social sectors, and encouraged political parties to challenge the dictatorship. Various union groups were united in a coordinating body, the *Comando Nacional de Trabajadores* (CNT), initiating a new era for unionism and wider social movements. This so-called cycle of protests lasted from 11 May 1983, the date of the first protest, until the attack against General Pinochet in September 1986. The

1 The *viandazos* were a form of labour protest in which workers refused to eat at the company's canteen, and brought their own lunch, called *vianda*. The first *viandazo* took place in the El Teniente mining company in 1977.

failure of that attack marked the collapse of the strategy of social mobilisation to end the dictatorship (*ibid.*).

The attack against Pinochet led to the imposition of a state of siege, and a period of withdrawal for the opposition. However, in the context of the campaign for the re-election of the dictator in the 1988 succession plebiscite, new steps were taken towards organisation and unity. The call to reconstitute the CUT of the *Coordinadora Nacional Sindical* was well received by the vast majority of trade union organisations, and as a result a new central coordination began to function in May 1988. The CUT established a true political program that aspired to transform the neo-liberal model and to replace the authoritarian regime with a democratic system that was "just, based on solidarity, participatory, and deeply humanist," taking up proposals previously raised by the CNS and the CNT (*ibid.*).

In the case of Paraguay, as mentioned above, the issue of "resistance" has also been addressed with a strong emphasis on the final stage of the dictatorship. The founding of the *Movimiento Intersindical de Trabajadores del Paraguay* (MIT-P) on 1 May 1985, is considered to be a turning point. It is said that one of the first and main tasks of this organisation was to seek international backing that would guarantee some support against the dictatorship. This included the *Organizacion Regional Interamericana de Trabajadore*s (ORIT) and the *Central Latinoamericana de Trabajadores* (CLAT). However, even in a context of growing democratic openness at a regional level, and with international support and finance, repressive policies persisted.

On the occasion of the celebration of the first anniversary of the MIT-P, the regime unleashed a brutal wave of repression that had repercussions at a national and international level (González Bozzolasco, 2014). Even in this context of very strong repression, the MIT-P proposed to advance towards the promotion of a new central body, to strengthen union actions from the grassroots and, from all these positions, promote the return to a democratic system as an indispensable basis for union action. The overthrow of Stroessner and the beginning of the democratic transition, in February 1989 (in an international context that was increasingly averse to the dictatorship, with economic sanctions in place since 1987), were central to the constitution of a new independent labour union for Paraguay (*ibid.*).

From an analysis of "resistance" to a focus on social "consent" and "consensus"

In recent years, in critical dialogue with perspectives that emphasise "resistance," another line of analysis developed that, on the one hand, questioned whether it was correct to assume that any initiative for action and organisation by the workers constituted an act of conscious resistance to the dictatorship; and on the other, highlighted the importance of analysing what they considered to be widespread social support for the dictatorships, framing it as a form of "social consensus" or of "consent."

One example of this is Daniel Dicósimo's (2007) research into the history of the workers of two companies in Tandil (Metalúrgica Tandil and the Loma Negra Villa Cacique cement company, both in the Province of Buenos Aires), during the last military dictatorship in Argentina. His research, focused as it was on two specific cases, differs from other previous approaches that sought to account for major trends and conflicts at a national level. This study enables the author to state that, although these cases saw different protests and demands, and took place during the dictatorship, it is not possible to detect a unanimous and clear position within them against the dictatorship itself. On the contrary, the axis of the conflicts was predominantly economic and there was no political content of any magnitude. From his perspective, "the behaviour of the workers better supports an interpretation of a defence of economic class interests than one of political opposition to the National Reorganisation Process" (*ibid.*). Dicósimo tends to separate economic demands from politics, even within a context of extreme repression that included the prohibition and criminalisation of disputes and political agitating, that resulted in disappearances, torture and death. Although he recognises the presence of a policy of repression on the part of the State, and discipline on the part of employers, how those policies intersected is not fully explored in his work, and they appear only in the background:

> Although there were clear signs of what the cost of opposition would be, with the arrest in the previous days of six company union delegates, threats and even brief kidnappings [...] the consensus towards the *coup d'etat* seems to have been voluntary in nature: witnesses recall that the plant was fully operational that morning [...] and the comment was "we will be better off now, the mess will end, we will be able to work." (*ibid:* 98)

The reference to a "voluntary consensus" seems to suggest the existence of a freedom of choice and expression that in principle seems contrary to the social dynamics of a terrorist state, with military intervention in all areas, and the existence of disappearances, arrests, torture and concentration camps. This perspective is rooted in a broader historiographical current, which includes a very influential book that called for an historical revision of the dictatorship (Vezzetti, 2002), arguing that the last Argentinian military dictatorship "put its leaderships, the State and its institutions to the test, and in general, brought out the worst in society". From this perspective, this "acute episode of political barbarism and the degeneration of the State would not have been possible without the commitment, adherence, and conformity of the many". He proposes, therefore, that the central task for studies of this period should be to analyse "society's responsibilities" (*ibid:* 12–13). In any case, Dicósimo's case studies contains a warning of the pitfalls of automatically associating the existence of conflict with a position of conscious political opposition to the dictatorship. At the same time, they issue an alert concerning possibly simplified interpretations of a "social consensus" towards the dictatorship.

Recent research explicitly confronts perspectives centred on this supposed 'social consensus' that attributes blame very broadly. Instead, a number of studies emphasise that the role of specific subjects be analysed within a framework of strongly asymmetric power relations, paying particular attention to the role of business and business leaders, some of whom had been denounced since the beginning of the process of "Memory, Truth and Justice" in Argentina (Basualdo, 2006, 2010a, 2010b, 2010c; Verbitsky and Bohoslavsky, 2013).

A research project, carried out between 2014 and 2015, made it possible to develop a more complex view than those focused principally or exclusively on the role of the armed forces and the State in the repressive policies of the last Argentinian dictatorship. It analysed the responsibility of a sector of the national and foreign business community in the human rights violations that were committed at the time (AEyT-FLACSO, PVJ, SDH and CELS, 2015). The project focused on case studies of 25 companies located throughout the country, looking at the repressive process unleashed on workers in the workplace, and analysing the different forms of participation by high ranking business officials and owners.[2]

---

2 The companies analysed are: Ledesma, Minera El Aguilar, La Veloz del Norte, Grafanor and La Fronterita and Concepción sugar mills in the Northwestern region of Argentina (NOA); Alpargatas, Molinos Río de la Plata, Swift, Propulsora Siderúrgica, Astilleros Río Santiago and Petroquímica Sudamericana, are linked to the industrial area to the south of Buenos Aires that includes the southern area of the city and the suburban areas of La Plata, Berisso and Ensenada; Grafa, Ford, Mercedes Benz, Lozadur and Cattaneo, Astilleros Astarsa and Mestrina, Dálmine-Siderca and Acindar. The transnational company of Italian origin FIAT is used to approach a key territory in the country's labour history, the province of Córdoba, while the analysis of the company Las Marías provides preliminary evidence relating to the Northeast region of Argentina (NEA). The cases of Loma Negra and La Nueva Provincia, allow an approach to areas of the interior of the province of Buenos Aires.

When analysing the repertoire of repressive business practices, the study found a pattern of direct involvement in repression against workers and labour leaders and detailed a number of specific contributions made by business officials, board members, shareholders or even company owners, who were often in contact with the military. The specific contributions to repressive practices they detected include the provision of infrastructure and resources, including personal information about victims, funding and vehicles used in repression, the presence and/or participation of top business officials in kidnappings and even torture in a few cases and in 5 of the 25 cases, the existence of clandestine detention centres within the plants that were the private property of the firms.

A recent book connected evidence from several countries, making significant progress towards a regional analysis of the role of big business in Cold War dictatorships in Latin America. Providing national overviews and case studies for several countries (including Argentina, Brazil, Chile, Uruguay, Peru, Colombia and the region of Central America), the book simultaneously puts forward a dialogue incorporating studies of businesses and government in Nazi Germany. Conceived from an interdisciplinary approach, the book shows the need to consider the role of companies and business organisations in the development of dictatorships during the Cold War in Latin America, connecting contributions from many fields, including economic and business history, labour history and human rights analysis as well as the studies on transitional justice (Basualdo, Berghoff and Bucheli, 2021).

The need to address, in broad terms, attitudes towards dictatorships, and to examine the different forms of support they received as well as the strong impact on labour relations, emerges in different ways from the recent literature in all of the national cases. In the case of Brazil, Fontes and Corrêa, while clearly emphasizing the negative overall impact of the dictatorship on labour in terms of increasing repression, labour discipline and loss of rights, at the same time underline the importance of not forgetting those who "looked upon the dictatorial regime with sympathy," stating that sectors of the workers benefited from the so-called "economic miracle" that created jobs in a context of economic development. Even when economic policy was based on the increasing exploitation of a part of the workforce, with falling wages and a loss of rights, there were other sectors, particularly migrants from rural areas, who benefited from developments in civil engineering, construction and services, so some sectors of the working class shared the vision of sectors of the middle classes at this time of the "Brazil of the future" (Corrêa and Fontes, 2015). At the same time, other studies emphasise the importance of analysing the interactions and links not only between the armed forces and businessmen, but also the relationships both of these had with sectors of the union leadership, known as *pelegos*, who supported and developed policies that worked against the interests of sectors of the working class (Conselho Projeto Memória da CPM-SP, 2014).

In the case of Chile, the triumph of neoliberalism and its hegemony is taken as a starting point. It could be promoted not only due to the fierce repression already analysed above, but also through the discrediting of "statist" and "protectionist" policies. The core of this "consensus" was maintained throughout the transition to democracy and beyond, and lies behind the attempts to shed light on the cost paid by workers and their organisations (Winn, 2004).

In the case of Paraguay, some recent studies have considered the 'co-option' of the sectors of the unions that survived the repression of the early years, by the dictatorship and the governing *Colorado* party (González Bozzolasco, 2014). In the case of Uruguay, there is also a recognised need to explore a wide range of social behaviours "that ranged from net opposition to consensus and acceptance of the regime" (Porrini, 2018). There are also references to broader studies of 'social consensus' in Uruguay (Marchesi, 2009).

It can be said, therefore, that the drive to shed light on a diversity of positions and the extent to which the dictatorships achieved social legitimacy is present in all the national case studies. However, the case of Argentina serves as a useful example demonstrating the need for caution when deploying conceptual frameworks that are centred on dynamics of "consensus" in the context of a dictatorship.

Towards a research agenda from a regional perspective

This brief review offers a concise summary of approaches to the issue of dictatorships, workers and unions in five Latin American countries, and shows that, even now, after decades of development in the social sciences, the integration of economic, social, political and cultural aspects still constitutes an enormous challenge. Nevertheless, it also has enormous potential. It is difficult, given the predominantly political focus of existing research, to adequately take into account the role of workers and trade unions in this story, and to recognise and integrate that dimension into national histories. However, in all cases, recent contributions to the field can be found that provide a starting point for a broader regional view.

The analysis of the evidence on the five dictatorial processes selected, although still at an initial and summary stage, shows the existence of very significant points of contact in the two major fields studied. In the first place, with regard to the analysis of the policies of the dictatorships towards workers and their organisations, in all cases there are three main areas of analysis: economic policy, labour, and repression. Furthermore, in all cases the combination of these three aspects led to an overall retreat of the working class and the trade union movement. Although there are significant differences, not only between the different national cases, but also within them, with various currents and sectors undergoing different structural, and economic evolution in terms of organisation, strategy and understanding of the processes. At the same time, several of these contributions emphasise that repression was a central feature at different stages of the dictatorships, and still requires much more in-depth analysis to allow a more complex understanding of both the repressors and the repressed. They also highlight that repression was far from being the only policy deployed by the dictatorships with respect to the workers and their organisations. On the contrary, much remains to be understood about the operation of various institutions whose objective was the reconfiguration of labour relations, such as the Ministry of Labour, and a large number of additional agencies, that have received little attention to date.

Secondly, in terms of the forms of organisation and action deployed by workers and unions, there are also significant points in common. The concept of "resistance" is frequently used in studies of all the national cases and may be defined as the "action and effect of resisting," the "capacity to resist," the "people who, generally clandestinely, opposed the invaders of a territory or a dictatorship in different ways" or a "force that opposes the action of another force." This concept has the indubitable merit of having shed light on the actions of workers that had hitherto been invisible or underestimated in the histories of the period. However, although very useful to allude to the existence of workers' movements and challenge the images of passivity, absence or silence on the part of the working class, it may also run the risk of homogenizing and unifying a diverse range of actions by workers and unions, as well as the diversity of motives that underpinned them. The bibliographic review makes clear that there is a need not only to distinguish between the activities of the working class and union movement as specific subjects, but also to be able to analyse with sufficient openness and complexity, the different sectors within them, including those that may have supported the dictatorship as a matter of convenience, conviction, or under duress. In this sense, an analysis of the five national cases reveals the need to take into account different responses (including a possible lack of response) with the greatest breadth and diversity possible, making an effort to understand their logic and dynamics. Preconceived labels and tags, rather than offering accurate characterisations, tend to reinforce previously conceived classifications. It is therefore necessary to deepen the analysis of other key dimensions such as gender, ethnicity, or generational differences, among others. This perspective is not only essential to an understanding of the periods of dictatorship in all their complexity, but would also enable a better understanding of transformations in labour relations, the evolution of indicators of the working class, the uneven evolution of different sectors of the working class, and of different currents within the union movement, some of which consolidated their positions during the transformations of this period, precisely because they served a function in the processes of re-founding the union movement.

Thirdly, a brief review of some emergent studies seems to show a shift from a paradigm emphasising "resistance" to one emphasising "consensus" or "consent," and highlights the need to reconsider the ways in which these concepts are used. The concept of consensus, which can be defined as "agreement produced by consent between all the members of a group or between several groups" seems very difficult to apply, not only due to the asymmetrical nature of power relations between capital and labour, but also due to deepening restrictions on the possibility for free choice and the implementation of intensely repressive regimes. In this context, it also seems to be much more productive to adopt an analysis aimed at examining the ways the dictatorships legitimated themselves, the different components and subjects in that process, and the points at which they were able to gain support or a lack of adverse reaction from certain social sectors. It is important to define behaviour, in order to be able to empirically support the characterisations of these social attitudes. At the same time, even when explicit or implicit support for the dictatorship can be proven, it seems methodologically questionable to present it in a way that underestimates or displaces the social asymmetries and power imbalances that condition it.

In sum, this review seems to indicate that the issue of dictatorship, workers and unions, requires more profound study, not only locally and nationally, but also from a regional Latin American and an international perspective. This would account for crucial transformations at an international level, and common dimensions that could illuminate central issues in this story. To achieve this, an extension of the chronological framework would be useful to foster a perspective more anchored in major international trends, adequately historicizing the dictatorships within the framework of these cycles. The Argentinian dictatorship of 1976 to 1983 should, from this perspective, be analysed in connection to the other two dictatorships in that country during the Cold War period. That would allow for a much better dialogue with cases such as Paraguay (1954–1989), but also with that of Brazil with which a forced comparison is often established that ignores the different time frames. Avoiding a fragmented perspective allows us, for example, to reassess the classic contrast between the "industrialist" dictatorship and the "economic miracle" in Brazil on the one hand, and Argentina's deindustrialising dictatorship, 1976 to 1983 (a process that implied a profound reconfiguration of the industrial sector and processes of economic concentration and centralisation) on the other. That contrast can be enriched and nuanced by an understanding that the 1966 to 1973 dictatorship in Argentina also coexisted with a process of deepening of industrialisation, and the development of dynamic industries such as the automotive, metallurgical, steel and chemical industries, during the second *Industrialización por Sustitución de Importaciones* (ISI). Similarly, it is possible to distinguish economic slowdowns and other changes in the later stages of the dictatorship in Brazil. This is a clear example of how an overview that takes into account a longer period of time makes it possible to avoid comparisons or dialogues between factual processes that were marked by different stages and major international trends, thus promoting greater contextualsation and subtlety in our analysis.

References

Abós, Alvaro. 1984. *Las organizaciones sindicales y el poder militar.* Buenos Aires: CEAL.

Araya Gómez, Rodrigo. 2015. *Movimiento sindical en dictadura militar. Fuentes para la historia sindical en chile (1973–1990).* Santiago de Chile: Ediciones Universidad Alberto Hurtado.

AE&T de FLACSO, PVJ, SDH and CELS: Área de Economía y Tecnología de la Facultad Latinoamericana de Ciencias Sociales (FLACSO based in Argentina), Programa Verdad y Justicia y Secretaría de Derechos Humanos (Min. De Justicia y Derechos Humanos de la Nación) and Centro de Estudios Legales y Sociales (CELS). 2015. *Responsabilidad empresarial en delitos de lesa humanidad: represión a trabajadores en el Terrorismo de Estado*, Infojus. http://www.infojus.gob.ar/responsabilidad-empresarial-delitos-lesa-humanidad-tomo-represion-trabajadores-durante-terrorismo-estado-ministerio-justicia-derechos-humanos-nacion-lb000183-2015-11/123456789-0abc-defg-g38-1000blsorbil.

Azpiazu, Daniel, Eduardo Basualdo, and Miguel Khavisse. 1986. *El nuevo poder económico en la Argentina de los ochenta.* Buenos Aires: Editorial Legasa.

Basualdo, Eduardo. 2006. *Estudios de historia económica Argentina. Desde mediados del siglo XX a la actualidad.* Buenos Aires: Siglo XXI.

Basualdo, Victoria. 2006a. "Complicidad patronal-militar en la última dictadura argentina. Los casos de Acindar, Astarsa, Dálmine Siderca, Ford, Ledesma y Mercedes Benz." Special supplement. *Engranajes.* FETIA-CTA.

Basualdo, Victoria. 2006b. "La participación de trabajadores y sindicalistas en la campaña internacional contra la última dictadura militar argentina." *Revista Sociedad 25.* Buenos Aires: Facultad de Ciencias Sociales de la Universidad de Buenos Aires.

Basualdo, Victoria. 2010a. "Labour and structural change: shop-floor organization and militancy in Argentine industrial factories (1943–1983)."Doctoral thesis, Columbia University.

Basualdo, Victoria. 2010b. "La clase trabajadora durante la última dictadura militar argentina (1976–1983). Apuntes para una discusión de la 'resistencia' obrera." Dossier. Comisión Provincial por la Memoria, La Plata.
Basualdo, Victoria. 2010c. "The ILO and the Argentine dictatorship, 1976–1983." In *ILO Histories. Essays on the International Labour Organization and Its Impact on the World During the Twentieth Century*, edited by Jasmien Van Daele, et al. Berlin and New York: Peter Lang.
Basualdo, Victoria. 2011. *La clase trabajadora argentina en el siglo XX: experiencias de lucha y organización*. Buenos Aires: Cara o Ceca.
Basualdo, Victoria. 2013. "El movimiento sindical argentino y sus relaciones internacionales: una contribución sobre la presencia de la CIOSL y la ORIT en la Argentina desde fines de los '40 hasta comienzos de los '80." *Revista Mundos do Trabalho* 5 (10): 199–219.
Basualdo, Victoria. 2018. "The Argentine Dictatorship and Labor (1976–1983): A Historiographical Essay." *International Labor and Working-Class History* 93: 8–26.
Basualdo, Victoria, and Alejandro Jasinski. 2016. "La represión a los trabajadores y el movimiento sindical." In *Represión estatal y violencia paraestatal en la historia reciente argentina: nuevos abordajes a 40 años del golpe de estado*, edited by Gabriela Águila, et al. La Plata: FAHCE-UNLP.
Basualdo, Victoria, Hartmut Berghoff, and Marcelo Bucheli. 2021. *Big Business and Dictatorships in Latin America. A Transnational History of Profits and Repression*. New York: Palgrave Macmillan.
Bohoslavsky, Juan Pablo, ed. 2016. *El negocio del terrorismo de Estado. Los cómplices económicos de la dictadura uruguaya*. Montevideo: Penguin Random House.
Bohoslavsky, Juan Pablo, Karinna Fernández, and Sebastián Smart, eds. 2021. *Pinochet's Economic Accomplices: An Unequal Country by Force*. Maryland: Lexington books.
Canelo, Paula. 2016a. *La política secreta de la última dictadura argentina (1976–1983)*. Buenos Aires: Edhasa.
Canelo, Paula. 2016b. "¿Qué estudiamos sobre la última dictadura argentina? Tres ciclos de investigaciones entre 1983 y 2015." In *De militares y empresarios a políticos y CEOS. Reflexiones a 40 años del golpe*, edited by G. Levy. Buenos Aires: Editorial Gorla-UBA Sociales.
Calveiro, Pilar 1998. *Poder y desaparición. Los campos de concentración en la Argentina*. Buenos Aires: Colihue.
Campos, Pedro Henrique. 2014. *Estranhas catedrais: as empreiteiras brasileiras e a ditadura civil-militar, 1964–1988*, Rio de Janeiro: Editora da Universidade Federal Fluminense.
Canitrot, Adolfo. 1980. "La disciplina como objetivo de la política económica. Un ensayo sobre el programa del gobierno argentino desde 1976." *Desarrollo Económico* 19 (76): 453–475.
Castellani, Ana. 2009. *Estado, empresas y empresarios. La construcción de ámbitos privilegiados de acumulación 1966–1989*. Buenos Aires: Prometeo Libros.
Centro de Estudios Legales y Sociales (CELS). 2011. *Hacer Justicia. Nuevos debates sobre el juzgamiento de crímenes de lesa humanidad en la Argentina*. Buenos Aires: Editorial Siglo Veintiuno.
Chaves Nagasava, Heliene. 2018. *O sindicato que a ditadura quería. O Ministerio do Trabalho no Governo Castelo Branco (1964–1967)*. Rio de Janeiro: Paco Editorial.

Comisión Verdad y Justicia Paraguay. 2008. *Tierras Mal Habidas. Informe Final, Anive haguâ oiko.* Asunción: Comisión Verdad y Justicia Paraguay–CVJ.

Conselho Projeto Memória da Oposição Sindical Metalúrgica – Sao Paulo. 2014. Investigação operária: empresários, militares e pelegos contra os trabalhadores, São Paulo: IIEP (Intercâmbio, Informações, Estudos e Pesquisas)- OSM-SP (Oposição Sindical Metalúrgica–São Paulo)–Projeto Memória.

Corrêa, Larissa. 2014. "Os 'inimigos da pátria': repressão e luta dos trabalhadores do Sindicato dos Químicos de São Paulo (1964 – 1979)." *Revista Brasileira de Historia* 34 (67): 13 – 37. Corrêa, Larissa. 2017. *Disseram que voltei americanizado: relações sindicais Brasil-Estados Unidos na ditadura militar.* Campinas: Editora UNICAMP.

Corrêa, Larissa, and Paulo Fontes. 2016. "'As falas de Jerônimo': Trabalhadores, sindicatos e a historiografia da ditadura militar brasileira en Años Noventa." *Revista do Programa de Pós-Graduação em História da Universidade Federal do Rio Grande do Sul* 23 (43): 129 – 151.

Corrêa, Larissa, and Paulo Fontes. 2018. "Labor and dictatorship in Brazil: A Historiographical Review." *International Labor and Working Class History* 93: 27 – 51.

Damill, Mario. 2005. "La economía y la política económica: del viejo al nuevo endeudamiento." In *Nueva Historia Argentina. Dictadura y Democracia (1976 – 2001)*, edited by Juan Suriano. Buenos Aires: Sudamericana.

Delich, Francisco. 1982. "Después del diluvio, la clase obrera." In *Argentina, hoy*, edited by Alain Rouquié. Mexico: Siglo XIX.

Delich, Francisco. 1983. "Desmovilización social, reestructuración obrera y cambio sindical." In *El Poder militar en la Argentina, 1976 – 1981*, edited by Peter Waldmann, and Ernesto Garzón Valdés. Buenos Aires: Editorial Galerna.

Drake, Paul W. 1996. *Labour Movements and Dictatorships. The Southern Cone in Comparative Perspective.* Baltimore: Johns Hopkins University Press.

Duhalde, Eduardo Luis. 1983. *El Estado terrorista argentino.* Buenos Aires: El Caballito.

Dicósimo, Daniel. 2006. "Dirigentes sindicales, racionalización y conflictos durante la última dictadura militar." *Revista Entrepasados* 15 (29): 87 – 105.

Dicósimo, Daniel. 2007. "Disciplina y conflicto en la Historia durante el Proceso de Reorganización Nacional (1976 – 1983)." Doctoral thesis, Universidad Nacional del Centro.

Dicósimo, Daniel. 2016. *Los trabajadores argentinos y la última dictadura. Oposición, desobediencia y consentimiento.* Tandil: Universidad Nacional del Centro de la Provincia de Buenos Aires.

Estevez, Alejandra, et al. 2018. *Mundos do Trabalho e Ditaduras no Cone Sul (1964 – 1990).* Rio de Janeiro: Multifoco.

Estevez, Alejandra, and San Romanelli Assumpçao. 2013. "Ditadura E Repressao Contra a Classe Trabalhadora." *Revista Anistia. Política e Justiça de Transiçao* 10: 432 – 471.

Fernández, Arturo. 1985. *Las prácticas sociales del sindicalismo argentino, 1976 – 1982.* Buenos Aires: CEAL.

Gallitelli, Bernardo, and Andrés Thompson. 1990. "La política laboral en la Argentina del 'Proceso.'" In *Sindicatos bajo regímenes militares. Argentina, Brasil, Chile*, edited by Manuel Barrera, and Gonzalo Fallabella. Santiago de Chile: CES-Naciones Unidas.

González Bozzolasco, Ignacio. 2013. *El Nuevo Despertar. Breve historia del Movimiento Intersindical de Trabajadores del Paraguay (1985–1989)*. Asunción: Germinal-Revista Paraguaya de Estudios Políticos Contemporáneos.
González Bozzolasco, Ignacio. 2014. "Represión, cooptación y resistencia. El movimiento sindical paraguayo." In *Stronismo asediado*, edited by Rocco Carbone, and Lorena Soler. Asunción: Germinal – Centro de Estudios y Educación Popular. http://conteudo.pucrs.br/wp-content/uploads/sites/30/2016/03/Represion-cooptacion-y-resistencia-2013.pdf.
Gouveia de Oliveira Rovai, Marta. 2014. "A memória na luta contra o trauma: significados sobre a Greve de Osasco em 1968 nas narrativas de trabalhadores." *Revista Mundos do Trabalho* 6 (11): 41–56.
Ladosky, Mario Henrique, and Roberto Véras de Oliveira. 2014. "O 'novo sindicalismo' pela ótica dos estudos do trabalho." *Revista Mundos do Trabalho* 6 (11): 147–170.
Marchesi, Aldo. 2009. "Una parte del pueblo uruguayo, feliz, contento, alegre. Los caminos culturales del consenso autoritario durante la dictadura." In *La dictadura cívico-militar 1973–1985*, edited by Carlos Demasi et al. Montevideo: CEIU/EBO.
Montenegro, Antonio Torres. 2014. "Direitos trabalhistas e assassinato em tempos de regime civil-militar (1972–1973): o indiciamento dos irmãos Barreto." *Revista Mundos do Trabalho* 6 (11): 91–106.
Munck, Gerardo L. 1998. *Authoritarianism and Democratization: Soldiers and Workers in Argentina, 1976–1983*. Pennsylvania: Pennsylvania State University Press.
Nagasava, Heliene. 2015. "O sindicato que a ditadura queria": o Ministério do Trabalho no governo Castelo Branco (1964–1967). Dissertação (mestrado) – Centro de Pesquisa e Documentação de História Contemporânea do Brasil, Programa de Pós-Graduação em História, Política e Bens Culturais da FGV, Rio de Janeiro.
Novaro, Marcos and Vicente Palermo. 2003. *La dictadura militar, 1976–1983. Del golpe de estado a la restauración democrática*. Buenos Aires: Paidós.
Pessanha, Elina Gonçalves da Fonte. 2014. "Os operários navais do Rio de Janeiro sob a ditadura do pós-1964: repressão e resistencia." *Revista Mundos do Trabalho* 6 (11): 11–23.
Pessanha, Elina Gonçalves da Fonte, and Leonilde Servolo de Medeiros, eds. 2015. *Resistência dos Trabalhadores na Cidade e no Campo*. Coleção: Comunicações do 3º Seminário Internacional o Mundo dos Trabalhadores e seus Arquivos, São Paulo y Rio de Janeiro: Arquivo Nacional e Central Única dos Trabalhadores.
Pettinà, Vanni. 2018. *Historia mínima de la Guerra Fría en América Latina*. México: El Colegio de México.
Porrini, Rodolfo. 2018. "Trabajadores y sindicatos uruguayos durante la dictadura (1973–1985) Consensos y resistencias." In *Mundos do Trabalho e Ditaduras no Cone Sul (1964–1990)*, edited by Alejandra Esteves, et al. Rio de Janeiro: Multifoco.
Pozzi, Pablo. 1988a. *Oposición obrera a la dictadura, 1976–1982*. Buenos Aires: Contrapunto.
Pozzi, Pablo. 1988b. "Argentina 1976–1982: Labour Leadership and Military Government." *Journal of Latin American Studies* 20 (1): 111–138.
Santana, Marco Aurelio. 2014. "Um Sujeito Ocultado: trabalhadores e regime militar no Brasil." *Revista Em Pauta* 12: 85–98.
Santana, Marco Aurelio. 2008. "Ditadura militar e resistencia operaria: O movimiento sindical brasileiro do golpe a trasicao democrática." *Política & Sociedade* 13: 279–309.

Schvarzer, Jorge. 1987. *La política económica de Martínez de Hoz*. Buenos Aires: Hyspamérica.
Verbitsky, Horacio, and Juan Pablo Bohoslavsky, eds. 2013. *Cuentas pendientes: los cómplices económicos de la dictadura*. Buenos Aires: Siglo XXI.
Slatman, Marisa. 2012. "Archivos de la represión y ciclos de producción de conocimiento social sobre las coordinaciones represivas en el Cono Sur." *Revista de Sociedad, Cultura y Política en América Latina* 1 (1): 47–66.
Teixeira da Silva, Fernando. 2019. *Workers before the Court. Conflicts and the Labor Courts in the Context of the 1964 Coup in Brazil*. Berlin: Walter De Gruyter.
Vergara, Ángela. 2018. "Writing about Workers, Reflecting on Dictatorship and Neoliberalism: Chilean Labor History and the Pinochet Dictatorship." *International Labor and Working-Class History* 93: 52–73.
Vezzetti, Hugo. 2002. *Pasado y Presente. Guerra, dictadura y sociedad en la Argentina*. Buenos Aires: Siglo XXI.
Welch, Clifford Andrew. 2014. "Camponeses, a Verdade e a História da Ditadura em São Paulo". *Revista Mundos do Trabalho* 6 (11): 57–78.
Winn, Peter. 2004. *Victims of the Chilean Miracle. Workers and Neoliberalism in the Pinochet Era, 1973–2002*. Durham: Duke University Press.
Winn, Peter. 2018. "Dictatorships and the Worlds of Work in the Southern Cone: Argentina, Brazil and Chile." *International Labor and Working-Class History* 93: 1–4.
Yaffé, Jaime. 2012. "La dictadura uruguaya, 1973–1985: nuevas perspectivas de investigación e interpretación historiográfica." *Estudios Ibero-americanos* 38 (1):13–26.

Dasten Julián-Vejar

Precarious society in Chile. The 'tragedy' of the 33 miners

Abstract: The discussion around precarity and labour has become a global debate. In Latin America, this debate intersects with a highly segmented labour market dominated by racism, a colonial legacy, and patriarchal structures. It is accompanied by significant divisions between rural and urban spaces, and by cities that are highly differentiated due to processes of expulsion, informal structures, flexible wage earning, and a countryside undergoing a process of frank deagrarianisation, with the presence of a significant indigenous population and the expansion of extractive models. In this text we seek to analyse the reality of precarious societies, looking at the case of the 33 miners who became trapped in a collapsed mine in Chile in August 2010. We consider the conditions, implications and consequences revealed by this case study in relation to precarity at work.

Keywords: precarity; work; extractivism; mining; Chile

Note: This chapter has been possible thanks to the funding from the Agencia Nacional de Investigación y Desarrollo and its financing line Fondecyt Regular, through project No.1200990, entitled "Precariedades del trabajo en la Macrozona sur de Chile: Intersecciones, territorios y resistencias en las regiones del Maule, Ñuble, Biobío y La Araucanía (2020 – 2023)."

Doctor in Sociology at the Friedrich Schiller University in Jena (Germany). Academic and researcher at the Instituto de Historia y Ciencias Sociales. Universidad Austral de Chile. Research Assistant at the Society, Work & Politics Institute (SWOP). Witwatersrand University, South África. and the GT CLACSO: Trabajo, heterogeneidades sociopolíticas y actores. Researcher on the the FONDECYT Regular Project N° 1200990 "Precariedades del trabajo en la Macrozona sur de Chile: Intersecciones, territorios y resistencias en las regiones del Maule, Ñuble, Biobío y La Araucanía (2020 – 2023)" Agencia Nacional de Investigación y Desarrollo, Chile. DAAD Project Researcher: "Cambio transnacional, desigualdad social, intercambio cultural y manifestaciones estéticas: el ejemplo de la Patagonia" (2015 – 2021). Co-Researcher of the FONDECYT Regular Project No. 1210105 "Los límites de los posible para el capital en los nuevos espacios rurales del sur de Chile, en la era global (1980 – 2020)." (2020 – 2024). Agencia Nacional de Investigación y Desarrollo, Chile.

https://doi.org/10.1515/9783110759303-011

Introduction

The neoliberalisation of society has reached a point of maturity in Chile (Gaudichaud, 2015), in terms of the depth to which neoliberalism as a social order has penetrated various dimensions of life. Its rhizomatic way of spreading, through the commodification of common goods and the monetarisation of social welfare; the extension of the market into health, education, pensions, etc., has configured diverse spaces for profitability and competition, which have not only "streamlined" social relations, but have also configured subjects and subjectivities, as a result of the dependency and vulnerability it creates.

This "public" space is where the fiercest and most open disputes occur on today's political stage. Public outcry against the creation of differentiated insurance and welfare models, segregation based on money as a mechanism for integration, or the use of money to play a determining role in access, etc., has mobilised many actors to call for the reform of this selective system of social protectionism.

Neoliberalism remains a historical and spatial expression of capitalism. Capital relies on the colonisation of these spaces to extend its frontiers of accumulation, dynamically mobilising its interests, deactivating and redefining the political limits and consensus, and the structures of (common) sense. It increases investment and economic concentration in order to end "rrational competition for prices."

The maturation of this system, and its geographical expansion to other countries in the region, show the historical hallmarks of neoliberalism in the production of society and its special relationship with the historically dominant blocs. There is significant literature on the consequences and impacts of neoliberal policies and their particular model of power and domination, especially in terms of income inequality, poverty, labour deregulation, crime, privatisation, etc. (Harvey, 2007; Therborn, 2008).

Furthermore, taking into account the antecedents, we believe that the maturation of these policies, which have sunk their roots into the foundations of social organisation, may have shaped a particular type of precarious society. In this essay I will focus on the case of the 33 miners who, in the middle of a working day in 2010, became trapped in the San José Mine. We look into the causes, examining the precarious conditions in which they worked, as well as the institutional frameworks and agencies that shaped what came to be considered a "tragedy."

We believe that this example illustrates the extent of the spread of 'precarity' as a wider social dimension, as a subjective strategy for managing risk, and as a set of conditions induced by capital to coerce workers. Finally, we draw some conclusions and pose further questions for the study of precarity in social relationships, based on our experience of studies of labour in Chile.

"Chilean Neoliberalism": A paradigm of the capitalist periphery

Neoliberalism can be understood as a regeneration of the strategies of the ruling class. It is a new form and expression of a regime of plunder on a global scale (Silver, 2005; Harvey, 2007; Mezzadra and Neilson, 2016), which integrates the dynamics and historical marks of precarity, racism, vulnerability and violence, that were normalised by earlier regimes (Harvey, 2014). The central aim is the expansion of the "limits of capital" (Harvey, 2007; Altvater, 2011) and the creation of societies, social relations, and subjectivities based on the reproduction of strategies of commodification and the realisation of capitalism.

In this process, the emergence of precarity and the casualisation of labour, is understood as a global strategy to transform and readjust the conditions for the production of life and society. The ideas of precarity and the casualisation of labour (Julián, 2017) engage a series of debates about the ways in which working conditions, processes, relationships and workers have been remodelled, instituting new regimes.

In summary, there are three main approaches to an analysis of the phenomenon of job insecurity:

- *the institutionalist and regulationist approach,* focused on mechanisms and institutions for protection and social security, together with a definition of precarity as a product of decomposition of the State, an erosion of working conditions and the decline in policies for social welfare (Castel, 2010);
- *the neo-Marxist approach* that relates precarity to global processes and changes in patterns of capital accumulation, especially through the financialisation, dispossession and overexploitation of work (Dörre, 2009);
- *the poststructuralist approach,* which conceives precarity to be part of a strategy and regime of governance that controls social relations through the domination and subordination of specific populations. (Butler, 2004; Lorey, 2015)

In studies of work, precarity is intrinsically associated with uncertainty, insecurity and vulnerability. These are all aspects of casualised labour, which seems to have become an international trend in the reordering of workplaces and the restructuring of production since the 1980s (Castel, 1997; Auer and Cazes, 2000; Antunes, 2003; Castel and Dörre, 2009; Marín, 2013).

On the other hand, the incorporation of precarity into the new reality of employment exhibits: a) an apparent permeability to, and internalisation of, the debates in the science and study of work that surround changes to the socio-productive matrix (Kalleberg, 2003; Paugam and Zhou, 2007; van der Linden, 2014); b) a new scenario of flexibilisation of employment relations (Esping-Andersen and Regini, 2000; Thompson and Van der Broek, 2010), as well as c) a special connotation given to the constitutive processes of resistance, collectives and social mobilisation (Frege and Kelly, 2004; Ross, 2008; Barattini, 2009; De la Garza, 2011).

In this sense, precarity has become an extensive phenomenon in social relations that goes beyond work (De la Garza, 2005). Hence, we understand that, due to the centrality of work in the reproduction of social relations, precarity at work has shaped precarious societies, which, in turn, become both cause and effect in a complex web of power relations at a global and local level.

We understand a "precarious society"' to mean a society where social reproduction is affected by structural deficiencies that impact on the ability to meet basic needs, as well as the insufficient (or non-existent), consecration and exercise of social rights, where money has colonised the mechanisms of social regulation. A precarious society incorporates social vulnerability as a mechanism of normalisation and power that aims to ensure its government. To do this, it incorporates exploitation, racism, patriarchy, etc., as practices of social reproduction.

As a precarious society, Chilean neoliberalism is presented internationally as a "successful icon" of the application of the policies of the Washington Consensus, and the total deregulation of the market (Salazar, 2015). It was modelled in the totalitarian context of a military dictatorship (1973 – 1990) and state terror, in collaboration with of a group of Chilean economists who had studied under Milton Friedman at the University of Chicago, promoting a policy of United States' imperialism for the control of Latin America. Its consolidation was and has been the result of the work of a democratic post-dictatorial democratic regime that sought to improve, legitimise and extend those policies of social commodification (Garretón, 2012; Gaudichaud, 2015).

This creation of the means of social predation resulted in strong deregulation of the central axes of social security and protection. They constitute the modelling of individualised relationships, centred on the privatisation of many areas of life. This was instituted by the military dictatorship, through the spread of fear, horror, violence and poverty, as disciplinary strategies (Salazar, 2015).

In this context, neoliberalism is imposed through a series of "modernising" measures (Hoehn, 2005, pp. 10 – 14), such as: a) the 1981 Labour Code: José Piñera Echeñique's Labour Plan stands out as a transcendental reform of the Labour Code (in force since 1924 and the product of five decades of union struggle), which progressively eliminated all the gains of the labour movement in terms of labour law and union rights, deregulating the labour market, and implementing repressive policies against the union movement; b) the Pension System: a system of private pension fund administrators (AFP)[1] was created; c) Health Reform: this had two main objectives, first, to reduce state contributions to the maintenance of the system (mainly through the municipalisation of healthcare), and second, to open a new source of accumulation for entrepreneurs with the creation of the Social Security Institutions (ISAPRE); d) Educational Reform: this was expressed in the municipalisation of schools, in the dismembering of the Universidad de Chile, and in the privatisation of technical-professional training and higher education; e) Agrarian Counter-reform: this basically focussed on the liberalisation of the sector, opening it up to external markets, and incorporating neoliberal policies into an area hitherto characterised by protectionism; f) Political and Judicial Reform: The Constitution of 1980, contains a series of constitutional restrictions that seek to prevent the exercise of popular sovereignty, such as the "Laws of Qualified Quorum" (requiring two-thirds approval in parliament), appointed senators and senators for life, the immobility of the Commanders in Chief, and the Armed Forces as the guarantors of the State, the binomial electoral system, and the make-up of the Constitutional Court and the National Security Council (COSENA); and g) Reform in regional distribution: the military dictatorship had adopted a discourse of decentralisation (in itself a contradiction), as part of an economic strategy, this leads new businessmen involved in the export of natural resources to also assume the discourse of decentralisation as their own.

These pillars of the Chilean neoliberal regime remain in place to this day,[2] as mechanisms that create precarity in social relationships, projecting a logic of vulnerability and lack of insurance, and consolidating helplessness as a form of social discipline (Hoehn, 2005). The exercise of this power involves transferring public social insurance to the private sphere of investment and monetarisation, which in turn subsidises capital accumulation (Gaudichaud, 2015), making

1 The *Reforma Previsional* (another initiative of Minister Piñera), proposed to deliver workers' pension funds to large conglomerates of companies for financialisation and speculation. The results of that, to date, are that they have put 'contributors' on alert, in the face of uncertainty and insufficient pensions.

2 Appointed and life senators (suppressed in 2004) could be excluded from this list, as could the immobility of the Commanders in Chief (in 2005 with a constitutional reform), and the binominal electoral system (suppressed in 2015).

the State an active participant in the gestation and "perfecting" of neoliberal governmentality.

Thus, the model of social deregulation promoted by neoliberal capitalism is consolidated with the withdrawal of the State as the guarantor of protection against abuse of the asymmetry of power between the actors (Garretón, 2012: 21–38). In this 'retreat', the autonomous power of private interests is strengthened and deregulated. Ultimately, the State does not actually withdraw, but instead implicitly and tacitly endorses the repertoires of capital through the use of its influence and capital, which are transferred to the private sphere. Spaces for negotiation and action become dependent on money, as a mechanism for coordination and exchange, and on prescriptive ethical and individual norms, rather than on state bodies and institutional regulations created to protect against vulnerability.

Faced with this dependence on money, and on the predatory and irrational logic of capital accumulation, reflections on "risk" (Rosanvallon, 2006; Beck, 2006) become key to understanding the deterrent, coercive and disciplinay functions of precarity and social vulnerability. Modelling *risk* introduces the idea of a state of insecurity (Kessler, 2015; Lorey, 2015), and dependence, where subjects are coerced into positions and forms of work that offer no protection for their physical integrity, their health or their psychosocial well-being.

Neoliberalism seeks to dismantle the instruments of social security, transferring them to the area of "private insurance" (life insurance, health insurance, fire insurance, etc.), which are private and individual by nature (Castel, 2010). This exercise projects self-responsibility, the individual is responsible for his or her own work and circumstances, even where those may threaten his or her own existence, and in which, contradictorily, that transfer of risk seems to be the only way to earn a living for him or herself and his or her family.

In this identification of risk, another element enters the analysis: the historicity of risk as an induced possibility and reality in Latin America. The hierarchy established by the dynamics of the actors that shape the world system, now supports the creation of "suitable" populations that can be made "precarious" through risk. This has a historical, racial and global character that needs to be introduced into an understanding of precarious societies in order to be able to interpret data on the power relations that prefigure the reality of work in the present day.

In this case, we will consider mining as a sector that has historically involved the over exploitation of its workers, where accidents, death and psychological consequences intermingle in precarious, impoverished populations, deprived of their territory and their way of life (Sassen, 2010). Mining is also part of the backbone of the dependent economy in Latin America and continues to exhibit its strategic importance for transnational investment, and to be a model of ecological dispossession and predation at a global level (Harvey, 2004).

Mining, extractivism and precarity: A historical pattern

It is possible to trace the expansion and convergence of precarity through the symptoms of the articulation and reproduction of precarious societies, particularly in employment situations where risk to life is a constitutive element of the job. These events are considered to be social aberrations and "tragedies" that result from the synthesis of social relations, social insecurity and situations that pose a risk to life. They reveal the systemic confluence of mechanisms of impoverishment, how they are normalised and the consequences they have in terms of creating defencelessness and structural vulnerability for subjects marked for precarity (Butler, 2004). This is the case in the emblematic story of the 33 miners who were trapped in the San José Mine for almost 70 days at a depth of more than 700 metres. In the following section we will analyse this case as an example of our thesis.

By way of context, we can say that mining, as a branch of production, has a long history in Chile (Julián, 2013). A "company" can only engage in mining by means of a eurocentric (Amin, 1989), colonial, imperialist and classist logic. This results in the normalisation of precarity, overexploitation, slavery, forced labour, etc. (Bengoa, 2015), based on annihilation and dispossession, and the justification of the depredation of nature.[3] These three elements will become an historical condition for the reproduction of precarious societies on the peripheries of the world-system, which move between the colonisation of power, racism and economic-political dependence (Wallerstein, 1988; Escobar, 2014).

The peripheral location of Chile, spatially and historically, introduces a new question with regard to the creation of precarious societies; as a historical condition that defines their genesis, reproduction and expansion within the dialectic of the limits of capital (Harvey, 2007). In this context, mining is a strategic element of the extractivist "development model" (Salazar and Pinto, 2002), and as an expression of the model of dependent peripheral accumulation in Latin America. This model also leads to the creation of a specific form of state (Salazar,

3 Using an indigenous workforce, through overexploitation and slavery, the Spanish soon exhausted both the metal reserves and the Mapuche and Inca indigenous populations from the centre of what is now known as Chile (Bengoa, 2015).

2015: 244), with a racialised and hierarchical demarcation of the power in the population, and a specific relationship with nature.

In the neoliberal cycle, the promotion of an extractivist mining model was reinforced and took on a new expression in the Latin American democracies of the 1990s, with Chile as its pioneering case:

> [A]fter the military dictatorship, the successive governments of the *Concertación por la Democracia* maintained the basic architecture of the mining sector, encouraging its expansion through private enterprise, and attempts at productive diversification have not been very successful. (Gudynas, 2011: 79)

The main geographical location for mining activities is in the north of the country. It is an area marked by a "high territorial vulnerability" (Fuenzalida and Quiroz, 2012: 9–10), which is characterised by

> manifest environmental injustice, where an unequal or disproportionate participation of the most disadvantaged, and therefore more vulnerable population groups, can be observed in the negative impacts resulting from mining, industrial activities and infrastructure projects.

Large-scale mining in Chile was not exempted from plans for restructuring and modernising production, as part of a new logic of international competition. As a result, models of precarity and the casualisation of labour have opened a new breach at the heart of the historic "aristocratic core" of the working class in the copper-mining sector (Leiva, 2009). The constant erosion of their living conditions (social benefits, salaries, contracts, job security, etc.), have been made subject to the introduction of labour outsourcing (Leiva, 2009; 2012) and a worsening of working conditions, and mental and physical health of workers (Carrasco and Vega, 2011).

On the other hand, the nature of work in the mines varies according to the size of the company. In the larger copper mining ventures, where there is a greater involvement of foreign capital, we find a sector of workers that earns salaries above the average in Chile (Rivera and Aroca, 2014). At the same time, those jobs entail a high risk of accident[4], exposure to toxic materials and high temperatures, and considerable levels of sacrifice, in terms of long shifts and working hours (ILO, 2015: 21), exposure to high altitude, miserable living conditions in

4 As indicated in the ILO report (2015: 20), the majority of those surveyed (86.4 percent) considered that the jobs they performed were "risky," either because they could cause occupational accidents (86.4 percent), physical illnesses (57.6 percent) or mental illness (34.5 percent).

camps (Carrasco and Vega, 2011), as well as migration for work, and being subject to constant, intense isolation and homosociality (Pavez and Hernández, 2014).

Outsourcing in mining appears as the final synthesis of a mechanism for discipline and impoverishment, a final, technological reengineering of work by business (Muñoz, 2011; Pérez, 2016). Subcontracting creates its own symptoms, weakening the foundations of welfare, health and safety and corporate cooperation at the heart of the division of labour (Leiva, 2009). Subcontracted workers are deeply precarious and are set up as an alternative workforce with less protection and security (Muñoz, 2011; Leiva, 2013). The accelerated manner in which outsourcing has become established at all levels of large, medium and small-scale mining endeavours has increased the division and defencelessness of mine workers (Leiva, 2009), in terms of working conditions, creating competition between service providers that drives the casualisation of labour and increases job insecurity.

In this competitive regime, precarious social relations coincide with the vulnerability created by a neoliberal institutionalisation of precarity as a way of life. The consequences of this dynamic illustrate the symbiotic relationship that occurs between extractivism and the precarity of labour (Alister and Julián, 2018), expressed in bodies, subjectivities and practices that synthesise a set of power relations.

We intend to analyse the case of the miners of the San José copper mine, who became world famous when rescue attempts became an international spectacle, after they were trapped by the collapse of the mine in the North of Chile. We will see how precarity and the casualisation of labour became central components in the concept of tragedy, and in understanding how precarious social relationships institute forms of risk, suffering and exploitation in peripheral societies.

The 33 miners and the tragedy of the San José Mine

On 5 August 2010, the San José mine, located approximately 810 kilometres north of Santiago de Chile, suffered a landslide in which 33 miners became trapped for 69 days, 700 metres below ground. The disaster caught the world's attention, through the media, social networks, embassies and international news agencies. Media coverage characterised the collapse as an 'accident', a fortuitous event, in which the causes were less relevant than the ability of the miners to withstand the conditions of confinement and the arbitrariness of their situation, with a focus on the 'personality profiles' of each of them.

Going beyond the sensationalism and the spectacle of a news story abused by the government of Sebastián Piñera (2010–2014), the San José mine represents an historical icon of vulnerability and precarity in Chile. The mine which has been in operation almost 170 years, is part of the San Esteban Mining Company, founded in 1957 by Jorge Kemeny Letay, a wealthy Hungarian emigrant who came to Chile after the Communist Party came to power in his country. The mine was nationalised by the Popular Unity government in 1971 (with the nationalisation of copper), and then reprivatised by the military dictatorship as a series of state-owned enterprises in the 1980s. It went through a modernisation process in the 1990s, with a deep deregulation of labour and a new mining model based on overexploitation. The mine changed hands, passing to Marcelo Kemeny Fuller[5] and Alejandro Bohn Berenguer, and went from being a "small business" to a "medium-sized mining company."

The mine is part of the dependent extractive export model of neoliberal Chile, founded on the predation of nature, overexploitation of casualised labour and commodity generation for the global market (Gago and Mezzadra, 2015). By 2009, mining accounted for 15.5 percent of Chilean GDP, and by the first half of 2010, companies in the sector recorded profits of about US $4,656 million. That year (2010), mining would account for 20 percent of GDP, increasing dependence on the sector and strengthening the cycle of high copper prices (Muñoz, 2011), where medium-sized mines accounted for 4.5 percent of total copper production in 2009, 5.1 percent in 2010 and 5.8 percent in 2011 (Soname, 2014).

The collapse of the mine emerges as a phenomenon symptomatic of the profitability of the sector, its expansion and increases in production. The material basis for the collapse was a combination of these elements: inadequate safety infrastructure in an overexploited mine; casualised workers willing to take risks for "high" wages;[6] a boom in demand for commodities at a global level; in-

5 Marcelo Kemeny Füller was a member of the *Consejo General de la Sociedad Nacional de Minería*. On the eve of the collapse, his company had a list of 28 unpaid contracts, some more than two years overdue, amounting to $85.5 million, while he had individually defaulted 17 times, amounting to a total of $45.5 million. Among these debts was a debt of $1,300 million to almost 300 workers of the San Esteban Mine (*El Mostrador*, 18 October 2010).

6 As the newspaper *El Mercurio* (9 August 2010) pointed out, because it was a dangerous mine, it could only "seduce" the workers by offering "high salaries". This is how some workers received $700 thousand (US $1,000 approx), the average being $550 thousand (US $790).

substantial regulatory bodies (work, mines, etc.), and a capitalist class that is insatiable when it comes to the accumulation of capital.[7]

Workers at the San Jose mine worked under conditions of constant risk. They received high wages compared to those offered in the region's other productive sectors and worked as part of an outsourcing regime that meant serious job instability, long working hours (over the 45-hour legal maximum). Compliance with labour regulations was poor, and enforcement by labour institutions was almost entirely absent (The Clinic, 29 October 2010).

The predatory nature and economic exploitation of the Chilean capitalist class, and the commercial culture that objectivised human beings, were clear. A series of devices accentuated the vulnerability of the workers and lead them to assume the risk of death as part of their daily lives. Why take the risk? Helplessness and vulnerability encourage precariousness life strategies. The sale of their labour takes place in a framework of casualisation and precarity. The absence of social security forces workers to seek forms of integration or subordination in the private sphere, mediated by wages and/or other income from their work,[8] often regardless of the conditions of sale, or the risk-of-death versus the risk-of-staying-alive.

The case of Mario Gómez is iconic in illustrating the everyday tension that constitutes precarity. Diagnosed with silicosis at the age of 63, referred to a local health facility where he would not find a cure, and working an unstable, badly-paid job as a driver of a collective taxi, Mario Gómez "accepted the risk" of returning to work in the mine after learning that two of his daughters were pregnant.

As Robert Castel (2003: 35) points out, social risk can be defined as an "event that undermines the individual's capacity to ensure their own social independence. Without protection against those events, one lives in a state of insecurity." In the case of Mario Gómez, risk marked and defined the limits of social reproduction in his own life and that of his family. Surrounded by various needs (health, food and well-being), Mario is forced back into mining work by a

---

7 For Vincenot Tobar, former safety superintendent of the San José mine, the problem was that the methods of extraction prescribed by the company itself and endorsed by the Servicio Nacional de Geología y Minería (Sernageomin) were not respected. This was due to "the ambition to bring more ore to the plant," which meant that "mistakes were made" (The Clinic. 20 August 2010).

8 The report of the Senate Investigative Commission (2011: 11) indicates that "the trapped miners acknowledged knowing about the insecurity of the seam, but they worked it anyway, because wages were above market rates with no requirement for previous experience. For doing so, they were called *kamikaze* by miners from other companies."

"care crisis" (Lorey, 2015), because insufficient, casualised wages do not allow him solve that crisis.

Upon his return to mining work, he was not given a medical examination. Instead, and despite two amputated fingers on his right hand, he is assigned to drive the truck that collects workers from the depths of the mine. His insertion into work is precarious and involves a consent to normalise this precarity: it is the social risk that expresses itself in the struggle to stay alive. The higher wages paid in the mines represent a way of negotiating health and safety and risks at work, as well as the risk of chronic disease and job instability.

But this thesis, of precarity as a form of consent to risk, contains, at its heart, a supposition that stems, in part, from the logic of capital: risk is the responsibility of the individual who accepts precarity. This idea is typical of the subjectivity of classic liberalism, and it fails to recognise the problem of the social context that generates precarious conditions. It does not consider the asymmetrical relations between capital and labour or the subordination of workers in everyday life. Instead, it is understood as a relationship between equals, unaffected by social risk (Castel, 2003).

This is manifested in Luis Larraín's appeal (Cooperativa, 25 October 2010), to the employees' responsibility for his own health and safety in the San José mine. Larraín, director of the think-tank *Fundación Libertad y Desarrollo*, which is a self-confessedly neoliberal institution in Chile, linked to the *Unión Demócrata Independiente* (UDI) party, stated that he believes "the responsibility for life at work falls firstly to the worker, and there is a failing there."

For neoliberalism and its ideology, the collapse of the mine is not the central issue. The event itself is denied, instead giving centrality to the "individual decisions" of those who, with less power in the employment relationship, "freely" exposed themselves to that tragic event. According to Larraín, "there is a failure of a worker who agrees to go to work under conditions that do not protect his life." This transfer of the problem and the crime to the issue of "accepting precarity," with the concurrent "risk" and "increased danger," as Beck (1998) would say, has a catastrophic character beyond the will of the subject.

Larraín knows that a precarious society has promoted an unequal distribution of the risk-of-death and that this is present in life decisions, and he claims that individuals ought to be held responsible for themselves. This failure allows you to become trapped in a collapsed mine: not taking care of yourself, despite the options for security offered by the market (in this case, alternative employment).

Discretion in the face of "work" and "exploitation" is the responsibility of the workers themselves, they are felt to have cognitive sovereignty when it comes to accepting risk (Beck, 1998). The subordinate relationship takes the forms it is given by capital and by the workers, thus emptying state institutions of their regulatory function. In this discursive process of emptying public "regulations" of practical political content, the relationship between capital and workers is made subject to the influences of private actors with greater power and information in the social sphere.

This emptying of content is not only ideological but is also material. As the *Comisión Investigadora de la Cámara* (2011) pointed out, supervisory bodies do not have the funding or personnel to carry out a real inspection, since they lack the counterweight of a robust legal and political framework to ensure social rights are enforced. For his part, Alejandro Vio, who was fired by the President Sebastián Piñera from his position as director of the *Servicio Nacional de Geología y Minería* (Sernagoemin), pointed out to Diario U Chile (08 November 2010) that the service had only 16 inspectors nationwide, and only two in the entire Atacama region.

The fines imposed on companies that failed to comply with the rules, added to the system of business discretion. With fines only amounting to around 30 UTM[9] (US $ 2,118), companies prefer to simply pay the fines rather than invest in infrastructure for safe and adequate production processes. All these elements serve to actively legitimise precarity as a constitutive form of social relations that induce (through risk) tragedy as a symptom of the governmentality of precarious societies.

The "precarious societies" model is replicated in: a) the negligence of institutional (de)regulation of working conditions in the San José mine; b) the company's record on regulatory breaches and accidents at work;[10] c) the precarious dynamics in which the reproduction of the productive cycle was a part of the abusive power relations in the micro-physical space of the workplace;[11] d) the

---

9 *Unidad Tributaria Mensual*; this is an index expressed in *pesos* and determined by law, which is constantly updated according to the Consumer Price Index (CPI) and is used as a tax measure.
10 The report of the Senate Investigative Committee stated that "on January 5, 2007 Mr. Manuel Villagrán Díaz (28 years old), geological technician, was killed by a rock fall at the intersection of the ramp with the access to level 135 of the mine." In March of the same year, the company was forced to stop operations until the causes of the event were established.
11 As Héctor Tobar points out in the first chapter of his book (2015: 31–41), the discretion of the project managers served to dissuade those who had noticed failures and warning signs of the collapse of the mine. He appealed to "masculinity," "dismissive attitudes", status, etc., all associated with the homosocial nature of the sector (Pavez and Hernández, 2014). In the same vein we haves the statement by Estanislao Morales (CIPER, 16 July 2011) who points out that "I myself had been a witness to and target of teasing for making complaints. They immediately belittled you, implying that you were not man enough. In other words, they called you a fag. And of

permissiveness of the institutions and the irregularities that led to the reopening of the mine in 2008, without sufficient safety conditions in place.

After the collapse of the mine, an investigation was undertaken by a number of public bodies, led mainly by the Atacama Prosecutor's Office. The Prosecutor's Office tried to gather the necessary information to charge Alejandro Bohn and Marcelo Kemeny. After two years of investigation, the *Ministerio Público* closed the investigation after determining that "there was no precedent that would allow charges to be brought and it was not possible to establish the existence of a crime,"[12] while the *Comisión de Minería y Energía* of the Chilean *Cámara de Diputados del Congreso* had determined, in January 2011, that the principal responsibility was the owners of the company for non-compliance with the work of the regulatory bodies in the collapse (Cámara del Congreso, 2011: 195–199).

This reveals the helplessness of the miners when it came to "access to justice," subject as it was to the same logic that had led them to suffer in the mines. Their social position was not changed by the collapse, instead it was reaffirmed, preserved and transferred to another sphere of the precarious society: law and rights. In this instance, the same vulnerability and lack of social protection for the workers will ultimately exonerate the owners of the mine, interpreting the collapse as an unpredictable event.

Thus, the conflict between understanding the collapse as an "accident" or as a "human act" problematised the confrontation of the lawyers and prosecutors in the case. While Luis Urzúa, one of the miners, said on CNN Chile (8 January 2013) that "this was not an accident, nor was it an act of nature, but rather it was a human act," the company's defence lawyers pointed out in another interview for the same channel, that we were dealing with "an unfortunate accident" (CNN Chile, 08 January 2013).

The tension between these two interpretations of the collapse involves two equidistant positions on risk, expert knowledge and the cognitive subordination of risk (Beck, 1998). On the one hand, there is a fatalistic condition of the predictability of the collapse that normalises and naturalises the precarity of operating conditions in the mine, by stressing the unpredictable and unexpected process

course, the next time you want to complain, you keep quiet and convince yourself that nothing is going to happen."

12 As the newspaper La Tercera pointed out (08/01/2015), Alejandro Bohn lodged "a complaint for insults and slander against Vicenot Tobar, former safety superintendent of the San José mine, and the former regional head of Servicio Nacional de Geología y Minería, Anton Hraste, who made statements that they the company slipped out of their responsibility in the mining accident. Both had to back down and point out in court that their words had no basis."

of "risk detection." On the other, there is a perspective that focused on the technological capacity to "anticipate risk," based on knowledge of the morphological conditions of the mine, permanent safety measures in mining, and the inspections should have taken place.

In order to avoid treating this issue as a 'theoretical' debate, we must consider the systematic record of non-compliance with the requests for safety measures that the *Asociación Chilena de Seguridad* (ACHS), *Servicio Nacional de Geologia y Mineria* and the *Dirección del Trabajo* had made to the administrators of the San José mine. For example, in October 2006, the ACHS requested the provision of emergency exits, ventilation projects and a geo-mechanical study. At the time of the collapse, not one of these projects had taken place. Days before the collapse, the ACHS had insisted on the development of processes to reinforce the mine to prevent rockfalls. This request came as a result of the "accident" suffered by Gino Cortés on 3 July 2010, where the worker lost a leg.

Despite this record, the judicial system, through the *Juzgado de Garantía* in the city of Caldera, dismissed a case accusing the former owners of the San José Mine, Marcelo Kemeny Fuller and Alejandro Bohn Berenguer of the crimes of "minor injuries, prevarication, bribery and homicide" (*El Mercurio*, 21 November 2015). This occurred because "the application presented by the defence was accepted, as the statute of limitations for criminal action had expired on a case begun with the filing of complaints by family members in 2010" (*ibid.*).

This demonstrates the recursive nature of precarity. The arguments referring to the precarious governance of the mine, which had been ratified by various public inspection bodies, were attributed to unpredictable causes, an unforeseen event, an "accident," rather than a self-inflicted situation created by the company's breach of mining regulations and a lack of technical understanding of the geological morphology of the place.

The final redoubt of the helplessness of the miners was expressed in the narration of the "epic" story of their "accident." The idea of an accident in the interpretation and telling of the events in the mine, placed individual heroism in the face of tragedy at the forefront of the visual documentation of the story. Precarity appears once again as the background to a story centred on values such as effort and the struggle for survival, which hide the relationships of domination, exploitation and the absence of any corporate responsibility.

This proposal to visualise it as "tragedy" was embodied in the film "Los 33," directed by Mexican director Patricia Riggen, with the participation of Antonio Banderas and Martin Sheen, among others, and with a budget of US $26 million (mostly financed by Carlos Eugenio Lavin).[13] This film exhibits three dimensions of the expansion of precarity and tragedy into "the intangible": 1) the discursive phagocytation of the interpretation and narrative of tragedy, through a metonymic exercise to silence "the outcry" and replace it with individual heroism; 2) political and narrative appropriation in the service of political propaganda; and 3) the continued *vulnerability* of the miners "outside the mine," deprived of the possibility of intervening in representations "made by others."

This was also accompanied by a cultural industry and an apparatus of lawyers that appropriated "individual heroism" as the hegemonic narrative in "facing precarity" and the appropriation and copyrighting of the image of the miners. This culminated in the presentation of a lawsuit by nine of the miners in 2015 against their former lawyers for "fraud, misappropriation and simulated contract" (CNN Chile, 2 November 2015).[14] The *Cuarto Juzgado de Garantía* in Santiago refused to process it, alleging incompetence.

The summons was issued first by the Court in Caldera, in May 2016, and the preliminary statements were made in August 2016. The miners had to once again depend on the "advice" and mediation of a new lawyer, Alejandro Peña, who had previously been a government prosecutor in the persecution of "terrorist groups."

The legal process over promised royalties from the film would be the culmination of the miner's defencelessness. With the operation of different facets of governability in precarious societies, through the tortuous, cumbersome, slow and uneven process of the "search for justice," a new aspect of the institutionalisation and normalisation of precarity was written.

The "historical depth" of this normalisation is that, faced with their defencelessness, the miners had succeeded in articulating a figure of "protection" and

---

13 Together with his partner Carlos Alberto Délano, they were the founders of the holding Empresas Penta, based on business conducted in the 1980s in the field of life insurance. Later they acquired AFP Cuprum (1991), Isapre Vida Tres SA (1991) and Banco de Chile (1999), sold in 2000 to the Luksic Group. Currently the group's investments are concentrated in the companies Penta Vida, Penta Security, Banco Penta and Banmédica, among others. In 2014 it was indicted by the Internal Revenue Service and was charged in 2015 for fraud against the Treasury. Lavín used an irregular financing system for political campaigns that exempted him from paying taxes to the *fisco de carga tributaria* (the General Treasury of the Republic).

14 The workers accused the lawyers Remberto Rodrigo, Valdés Hueche and Fernando Darío García O'Nell (the latter linked to the Carey study) of "having engaged in a series of fraudulent and deceptive manoeuvres to mislead "*Los 33*," making them believe that they would have a company managed by them, in order, ultimately, to harm them and appropriate money that belonged to them" (EMOL, 4 November 2015). The lawyers denied this pointing out that at the time of the lawsuit they still represented 24 of the 33 miners.

collective defence, in the form of a (not-for-profit) foundation, which, with the help of compensation and solidarity mechanisms, channelled donations and financial aid to the miners. Despite being a body created by the workers themselves, the relationships between the unprotected (the victims threatened by a constant anxiety (for justice), lack of protection and precarity) were disrupted by the "barbarisation of social relationships" (Fernández, 2013). That was to have repercussions for their fragile bonds of solidarity, with the exercise of individualism and money as driving forces which accelerated the decomposition of the individual and collective identities created through the shared experiences of precarity, and especially through the experience of being trapped together underground.

The refusals to find the business community and supervisory institutions accountable; followed by the dominant narrative and material plunder of the film; mutual accusations between the miners, over misuse of funds; the complaint made by two miners to the *Subsecretaría de Justicia* requesting they investigate the use of funds received by the Los 33 Foundation; the dismissal of the Foundation's board of directors; and a demand from the *Consejo de Defensa del Estado* for the organisation to be disbanded – all served to turn the epilogue to the collapse of the mine into a tragedy of even greater historical depth.

Conclusions

In 2010, the death toll in the mining sector was 45 workers. No one was ever held responsible for what happened in the San José Mine. Three hundred workers at the San Esteban mine were made unemployed, and in 2011 they were still waiting for their severance payments. The mine was sold and the miners began a tortuous journey back from public spectacle to the precarity of everyday life.

After the "tragedy," the power structures of precarious societies persisted in their constant and "automatic" "creation of disposable and excluded individuals" (Zizek, 2013: 25). The end result of this long process has been the social stigmatisation of the affected miners, the creation of a "precarious brand" (Butler), which is manifested in the attitude of potential employers, who refuse to hire them or consider them for any work in the mines.

As José Ojeda pointed out in 2014 (*La Nación*, 2 November 2014), "We were public figures, no company would risk hiring us." The 33 miners had become a sort of blacklist. They were classified as "crazy" and "abnormal" (consequences of the confinement and trauma) and "conflictive" (because they had made statements denouncing unsafe practices and had sued the owners of the San José Mine).

It is interesting that the popular, public sanctification of the 33 miners, the miracle of their resurrection (having been presumed dead) and their salvation (when rescued), contrasts so starkly with their demonisation by the businesses mining in northern Chile, and ultimately in their exclusion. Because if the systemic violence of precarity at work was contained by the conversion of the miners into victims of fortune, an "unfortunate accident," to later return them as heroes, that violence returned within a year of the collapse in the form of social exclusion, making it impossible for them to reintegrate, and thus deepening their defencelessness.

It is in this return to the condition of helplessness, that work in the mine, despite being so symbolically charged and despite the psychological trauma the work could create for each of the 33 miners, once again becomes "an option" they would have to consider. By 2014, many had already returned to jobs in mining, and while some had begun independent ventures (in construction and transportation), others remained unemployed, facing psychological problems and alcoholism.

The governance of precarity deploys any means necessary to make its symptoms invisible to the public gaze. Having been exposed and idolised, used as political objects, and tools of emotional manipulation, the miners become a nuisance, a hindrance. It is "the hindrance" of persistently reminding public opinion that "if there had been greater security, this would never have happened" (Jimmy Sánchez, on the programme "Contacto," 24 August 2011), and that "there was no prison sentence, because none of us were left dead" (Mario Sepúlveda, Contacto, 24 August 2011).

What we want to highlight is how precarious society organised, modelled, and found closure around the tragedy that revealed its own symptoms. It involved a narrative process, a symbolic appropriation and the construction of an "image of the miner." That same "image" evoked at other moments in history by the ruling class to refer to the working and proletarian class (Salazar, 2015: 452–474). That class fulfils a sacrificial role ("for the fatherland"), experiencing redemption through a life of exclusion, barbarism and precarity.

However, it was not all "imaginary". The institutions supervising mining activities, the courts of justice, the economic power of the sector, political capital and the culture industry, all joined in a synchronous way to bury the miners. Precarious society shaped by neoliberalism will constantly see its symptoms emerging in cases such as: 1) the San Miguel jail fire, which left 81 dead (Tijoux, 2011). That event was modelled by the laws on incarceration and imprisonment (Salinero, 2012) that have seen Chilean prisons expanding and being opened up to private bidding, with a prison population living with severe overcrowding and violations of human rights (NHRI, 2014); 2) the hunger strike of the 34 members of the Mapuche community in 2010; 3) the 1,383 children killed in the *Servicio Nacional de Menores* by the failures of that body’s neoliberal management logic, in this case, to respond to the crisis of private care services for children in Chile (Cappella and Gutiérrez, 2014); 4) Tragedies associated with the natural disasters such as earthquakes, tsunamis, floods, eruptions, etc., that constantly shake Chilean social geography.

The experience of the Global South makes these contradictions more visible. They cannot be reduced to a single “discipline” of study, but rather require an enhancement of the emergent nature of research and a transformation of projects aimed at clarifying the scope of the institutionalised logic of commercialisation of the neo-colonial and neoliberal state, as well as the fragility of life and the social fabric in the contexts of racism, discrimination, poverty, sexism, classism and social vulnerability, that are found in Latin America. In this context, precarious societies introduce us to a “sociology of tragedy,” as the social risks assumed in the absence of social insurance or protection, and increased social vulnerability emerge as symptoms of the (re)production of capitalism and the perseverance of colonial structures of domination.

Sources

Press

ABC Internacional. 2015. “Cinco años después solo algunos de los 33 mineros han podido ver la luz.” (6 August). https://www.abc.es/internacional/20150805/abci-rescate-mineros-chile-201508051103.html. Accessed 13 August 2017.

Canal 13. 2011. “Los 33: Con los pies en la tierra.” La vida después del rescate.” (24 August). http://www.t13.cl/videos/contacto/contacto-los-33-con-los-pies-en-la-tierra-parte-1Programa Contacto. Accessed 23 August 2017.

Centro de investigación Periodística (CIPER). 2011. “Se salvan 33, mueren 45: siniestro balance de los accidentes de la minería chilena en 2010.” (17 July 2011). http://ciperchile.cl/2011/07/16/se-salvan-33-mueren-41-el-siniestro-balance-de-los-accidentes-de-la-mineria-chilena-en-2010/. Accessed 16 July 2011.

CNN Chile. 2015. “Quedan muchos de los 33 que no entienden lo que está pasando.” (2 November 2011). https://www.cnnchile.com/pais/luis-urzua-quedan-muchos-de-los-33-que-no-entienden-lo-que-esta-pasando_20151102/. Accessed 11 August 2018.

CNN Chile. 2013a. “Esta decisión no es antojadiza.” www.cnnchile.com. Accessed: 9 August 2017.

CNN Chile. 2013b. “Mineros tildaron de ‘rara’ la investigación tras el derrumbe en la mina San José.” (1 August 2013). https://www.cnnchile.com/pais/mineros-tildaron-de-rara-la-investigacion-tras-el-derrumbe-en-la-mina-san-jose_20130801/ Accessed 11 August 2017.

Cooperativa. 2010. “Director LyD y seguridad laboral: La responsabilidad es primero del trabajador.” (25 October 2010). https://www.cooperativa.cl/noticias/pais/trabajo/direc tor-lyd-y-seguridad-laboral-la-responsabilidad-es-primero-del/2010-10-25/121647.html. Accessed 9 August 2017.

Diario Ude Chile. 2010. “Mineros: Inseguridad bajo tierra.” Column by Sohad Houssein and Loreto Soto. (11 August 2010). https://radio.uchile.cl/2010/08/11/mineros- inseguridad-bajo-tierra/. Accessed 25 August 2017.

El Mostrador. 2010a. “Qué aprendimos de la mina San José.” Column by María Ester Feres. (3 September 2010). https://www.elmostrador.cl/noticias/opinion/2010/09/03/que-aprendimos-de-la-tragedia-de-la-mina-san-jose/. Accessed: 15 August 2017.

El Mostrador. 2010b. “El drama de los mineros que quedaron fuera: Bohn y Kemeny les deben $1.300 millones.” (18 October 2010). https://www.elmostrador.cl/noticias/pais/2010/10/18/el-drama-de-los-mineros-que-quedaron-fuera-bohn-y-kemeny-les-deben-1-300-millones/. Accessed 20 August 2017.

El Mercurio (Online). 2015. “Tribunal se declara incompetente para conocer querella de mineros de Atacama contra ex abogados.” (4 November 2015). https://www.emol.com/noticias/Nacional/2015/11/04/757656/Tribunal-se-declara-incompetente-para-conocer-querella-de-mineros-de-Atacama-contra-ex-abogados.html. Accessed 28 August 2017.

El Mercurio (Online). 2010. “Minera ofrecía altos sueldos para atraer a trabajadores a un yacimiento complejo”. 9 August 2010. Taken from: http://buscador.emol.com/vermas/El%20Mercurio/Nacional/2010-08-09/5332f379-6e40-4bcc-bc5e-bd34fb76291e/Minera_ofrec%C3%ADa_altos_sueldos_para_atraer_a_trabajadores_a_un_yacimiento_complejo/. Accessed: 12 August 2017.

Emol National. Source: Emol.com: https://www.emol.com/noticias/Nacional/2015/11/04/757656/Tribunal-se-declara-incompetente-para-conocer-querella-de-mineros-de-Atacama-contra-ex-abogados.html.

La Nación. 2014. “La vida luego del rescate: los 33 de Atacama, entre las divisiones, el éxito y el olvido.” (2 November 2014). https://www.lanacion.com.ar/el-mundo/la-vida-luego-del-rescate-los-33-de-atacama-entre-las-divisiones-el-exito-y-el-olvido-nid1740673. Accessed 20 August 2017.

La Tercera. 2015a. “Mina San José: dueños encargan últimos informes para vender yacimiento.” (1 August 2015). https://www.latercera.com/noticia/mina-san-jose-duenos-encargan-ultimos-informes-para-vender-yacimiento/. Accessed 9 August 2017.

La Tercera. 2015b. “Sobreseen causa en contra de los dueños de la mina San José.” (20 November 2015). https://www.latercera.com/noticia/sobreseen-de-manera-definitiva-a-duenos-de-mina-san-jose/. Accessed 12 August 2017.

The Clinic. 2010a. “Wall Street Journal: El capitalismo salvó a los mineros.” www.theclinic.cl. (14 October 2010). Accessed 31 August 2017.

The Clinic. 2010b. “El prontuario laboral de la san José. La mina maldita.” (29 October 2010). https://www.theclinic.cl/2010/08/29/el-prontuario-laboral-de-la-san-jose-la-mina-maldi ta/. Accessed 29 August 2017.

References

Alister, Cristian, and Dasten Julián-Vejar. 2018. Precariedad(es) laboral(es) en territorios extractivos de la Araucanía." In *¿Fin de la bonanza?: entradas, salidas y encrucijadas del extractivismo*, edited by M. Ramírez, and S. Schmalz, 175–194. Ciudad Autónoma de Buenos Aires: Biblos.

Altvater, Elmar. 2011. *Los límites del capitalismo. Acumulación, crecimiento y huella ecológica.* Buenos Aires: Mardulce.

Amin, Samir. 1989. *El eurocentrismo. Crítica de una ideología.* Mexico D.F.: Siglo XXI.

Antunes, Ricardo. 2003. *¿Adiós al Trabajo? Ensayo sobre metamorfosis del trabajo y el rol central del trabajo.* Argentina: Herramienta.

Auer, P. and Cazes, S. 2000. "The resilence of long-term employment relationship: Evidence in the industrialized countries." *International Labour Review* 139 (4): 379–407.

Barattini, M. 2009. "El trabajo precario en la era de la globalización ¿Es posible la organización?" *Polis Revista de la Universidad Boliviana* 8 (24): 17–37.

Beck, Ulrich. 1998. *La sociedad del riesgo: Hacia una nueva modernidad.* Barcelona, Paidos.

Beck, Ulrich. 2006. *La sociedad del riesgo global*, Madrid: Siglo XXI.

Bengoa, José. 2015. *Historia Rural de Chile central. Tomo I–II.* Santiago: LOM ediciones.

Butler, Judith. 2004. *Precarious Life: The Powers of Mourning and Violence.* London-New York:Verso.

Butler, Judith. 2010. *Frames of War.* London-New York: Verso.

Capella, Claudia, and Carolina Gutiérrez. 2014. "Psicoterapia con niños/as y adolescentes que han sido víctimas de agresiones sexuales: Sobre la reparación, la resignificación y la superación." *Psicoperspectivas*, 13 (3): 93–105.

Carrasco, Celina, and Patricia Vega. 2011. *Una aproximación a las condiciones de trabajo en la gran minería de altura.* Cuaderno de Investigación No. 40. Santiago: Dirección del Trabajo.

Castel, Robert. 1997. *La metamorfosis de la cuestión social. Una crónica del salariado.* Paidós Ibérica, España.

Castel, Robert. 2003. *La inseguridad social. ¿Qué es estar protegido?* Buenos Aires: Ediciones Manantial.

Castel, Robert. 2010. *El ascenso de las incertidumbres: trabajo, protecciones, estatuto del individuo.* Buenos Aires: Fondo de Cultura Económica.

De la Garza, Enrique. 2005. "Del concepto ampliado de trabajo al de sujeto laboral ampliado." In *Sindicatos y nuevos movimientos sociales en América Latina*, edited by De la Garza, E, 9–17. CLACSO.

De la Garza, Enrique. 2011. *Trabajo no clásico, organización y acción colectiva*, 2 vols, edited by Plaza and Valdés. México: Universidad Autónoma Metropolita–Unidad Iztapalapa,

Do Sousa, Boanaventura. 2009. *Epistemologías del Sur.* Mexico D.F.: Siglo XXI/CLACSO.

Donovan, Patrick, et al. 2008. "Niñez y Juventud en Situación de Riesgo: La Gestión Social del Riesgo. Una revisión bibliográfica." *Última década*, 16 (28): 51–78.

Dörre, Klaus. 2009. "La Precariedad ¿Centro cuestión social del siglo XXI?" *Revista Actuel Marx Intervenciones.* 8: 79–108.

Escobar, Antonio. 2014. "Instituciones y Trabajo Indígena en la América española." *Revista Mondos do Trabalho* 6 (12): 27–53.

Esping-Andersen, G., and M. Regini. 2000. *Why deregulate labour markets?* Oxford: Oxford University Press.
Fevre, R. 2007. "Employment insecurity and social theory: The power of nightmares." *Work, Employment & Society* 21 (3): 517 – 535.
Frege, C., and J. Kelly, eds. 2004. *Varieties of unionism: strategies for union revitalization in a globalizing economy.* Oxford/New York: Oxford University Press.
Fuenzalida, Manuel, and Rodolfo Quiroz. 2012. "La dimensión espacial de los conflictos ambientales en Chile." *Polis* 11 (31): 157 – 168.
Gago, Verónica, and Sandro Mezzadra. 2015. "Para una crítica de las operaciones extractivas del capital. Patrón de acumulación y luchas sociales en el tiempo de la financiarización." *Revista Nueva Sociedad* 255: 38 – 52.
Garretón, Manuel Antonio. 2012. *Neoliberalismo corregido y progresismo limitado: los gobiernos de la Concertación en Chile 1990 – 2010.* Santiago: Editorial ARCIS; CLACSO.
Gaudichaud, Franck. 2015. *Las fisuras del Neoliberalismo chileno. Trabajo, crisis de la democracia tutelada y conflicto de clases.* Santiago: Quimantú. Tiempo Robado Editoras.
Gudynas, Eduardo. 2011. "El nuevo extractivismo progresista en america del sur tesis sobre un viejo problema bajo nuevas expresiones." In *Colonialismos del Siglo XXI. Negocios Extractivos y defensas del territorio en América Latina*, edited by Alberto Acosta et al., 75 – 92. Barcelona: Icaria Editorial.
Harvey, David. 2004.
"The 'New' Imperialism: Accumulation by Dispossession." *Actuel Marx* 35: 71 – 90.
Harvey, David. 2007.
Espacios del Capital. Hacia una Geografía Crítica. Madrid; Akal.
Harvey, David. 2014. *Diecisiete contradicciones y el fin del capitalismo.* Madrid: Traficantes de Sueños.
Hoehn, Marek. 2005. "Neoliberalismo, vulnerabilidad y disciplinamiento." *Castalia, Revista de Psicología de la Academia* 9: 32 – 42.
INDH. 2014. *Estudio de las condiciones carcelarias en Chile: diagnóstico del cumplimiento de los estándares internacionales de derechos humanos.* Santiago: Instituto Nacional de Derechos Humanos.
Julián-Vejar, Dasten. 2013. "Precariedad laboral y neocolonialismo en Chile. Un acercamiento a la minería del cobre." *Revista CES contexto* 5: 28 – 43.
Julián-Vejar, Dasten. 2017. "Precariedad laboral y del trabajo en América Latina. Un modelo para armar." *Revista Colombiana de Sociología* 40 (2): 27 – 46.
Kalleberg, Arne. 2011. *Good jobs, bad jobs: the rise of polarized and precarious employment systems in the United States, 1970s to 2000s.* New York, Russell Sage Foundation.
Kessler, Gabriel. 2015. *Sentimiento de inseguridad. Sociología del delito.* Buenos Aires: Siglo XXI.
Leiva, Sandra. 2009. "La subcontratación en la minería en Chile: elementos teóricos para su análisis." *Polis* 24: 111 – 131.
Leiva, Sandra. 2013. "Movimiento social de trabajadores subcontratados en la minería privada del cobre en Chile." *Psicoperspectivas* 12 (2): 51 – 61.
Linden, Marcel van der. 2014. "Santo Precario: A new inspiration for Labor Historians." *Labor. Studies in Working-Class History of the Americas* 11 (1): 9 – 21.
Lorey, Isabel. 2015. *State of Insecurity.* London: Verso.

Marin, E. 2013. "Precarious Work: An International problem." *International Journal of labour Research* 5 (1): 153–168.
Mezzadra, Sandro, and Brett Neilson. 2016. *La frontera como método.* Buenos Aires: Tinta Limón ediciones.
Muñoz, Mauricio. 2011. *La minería del cobre en Chile.* Santiago: Instituto de Ciencias Alejandro Lipzchurt.
OIT. 2015. *Informe y análisis de la encuesta Vida de mineros: Condiciones de trabajo y salud sexual de mineros chilenos en la región de Tarapacá.* Santiago: Organización Internacional del Trabajo.
Paugam, S. and Y. Zhou. 2007. "Job Insecurity." In *Employment Regimes and the Quality of Work*, edited by D. Gallie. Oxford: Oxford University Press.
Pávez, Jorge, and Hernández, Gerardo. 2014. "Regímenes de Trabajo, relaciones laborales y masculinidades en la gran minería del cobre (norte de Chile)." In *Trabajos y familias en el neoliberalismo Hombres y mujeres en faenas de la uva, el salmón y el cobre*, edited by S. Ximena Valdés et al., 167–264. Santiago, LOM Ediciones.
Pérez, S. 2016. "Trabajo y política en el Chile contemporáneo. Contribución a una lectura crítica del régimen de subcontratación." *Revista Actuel Marx* 20: 231–256.
Rivera, Nathaly, and Patricio Aroca. 2014. "Escalas de producción en economías mineras: El caso de Chile en su dimensión regional." *EURE (Santiago)* 40 (121): 247–270.
Rosanvallon, Pierre. 2006. *El capitalismo utópico.* Buenos Aires: Nueva Visión.
Ross, Andrew. 2008. "The new Geography of Work: Power to the Precarious?" *Theory, Culture & Society* 25 (7/8): 31–49.
Salazar, Gabriel, and Julio Pinto. 2002. *Historia Contemporánea de Chile, Tomo III.* Santiago, Chile: LOM Ediciones.
Salazar, Gabriel. 2015. *La enervante levedad de la clase política civil. (Chile 1900–1973).* Santiago, Chile: Debate.
Salinero, Sebastián. 2012. "¿Por qué aumenta la población penal en chile?: Un estudio criminológico longitudinal." *Ius et Praxis* 18 (1): 113–150.
Sassen, Saskia. 2010. *Territorio, autoridad y derechos. De los ensamblajes medievales a los ensamblajes globales.* Buenos Aires: Katz Editores.
Silver, Beverly. 2005. *Fuerzas de Trabajo. Los movimientos obreros y la globalización desde 1870.* Madrid: AKAL.
SONAMI. 2014. "Caracterización de la pequeña y mediana minería en Chile," www.sonami.cl Sociedad Nacional de Minería. Gerencia de Investigación y Desarrollo. Accessed: 22 August 2017.
Therborn, Göran. 2008. *What does the ruling class do when it rules? State apparatuses and state power under feudalism, capitalism and socialism.* London; New York: Verso.
Thompson, P., and D. van den Broek. 2010. "Managerial control and workplace regimes: an introduction." *Work, Employment & Society* 24 (3): 1–12.
Tijoux, María Emilia. 2011. "El infierno en la torre 5. Reflexiones sobre la cárcel en Chile." *Revista Latinoamericana sobre Cuerpos, Emociones y Sociedad* 3 (5) (April/June): 39–49.
Wallerstein, Immanuel. 1988. *El capitalismo histórico.* México D.F.: Siglo XXI.
Zizek, Slavoj. 2013. *Sobre la violencia.* Madrid: Austral.

Printed in the USA
CPSIA information can be obtained
at www.ICGtesting.com
JSHW022008290224
58358JS00002B/2